The Institute of Chartered Accountants in England and Wales

ACCOUNTING

Professional Stage Knowledge Level

For exams in 2012

Study Manual

www.icaew.com

Accounting
The Institute of Chartered Accountants in England and Wales Professional Stage

ISBN: 978-08576-0218-3
First edition 2007
Second edition 2008
Third edition 2009
Fourth edition 2010
Fifth edition 2011

British Library Cataloguing-in-Publication Data
A catalogue record for this book has been applied for from the British Library

Printed in Great Britain

Your learning materials are printed on paper sourced from sustainable,
managed forests.

Welcome to ICAEW

ICAEW is much more than just the accountancy body that awards you your ACA or Certificate in Finance, Accounting, and Business (CFAB) qualification.

As a world-leading professional accountancy body, we provide leadership and practical support to over 150,000 members and students in more than 160 countries. We work with governments, regulators and industry to ensure the highest professional standards are maintained, and the skills of our members are constantly developed, recognised and valued. In addition to the ACA and CFAB qualifications, ICAEW offers a suite of qualifications and development programmes designed to support you throughout your career.

If you are a CFAB student, you may decide to continue on to the ACA when you complete your studies. CFAB can be used as a stepping stone to the ACA qualification, as it consists of the first six modules that make up the first stage of the ACA.

As a CFAB or ACA student, you can take advantage of the following support and services throughout your studies:

Dedicated student website
The dedicated student area of the website will give you access to support and services, including exam resources such as sample exams and information on e-assessments, and key information regarding training and work experience. Visit icaew.com/students to access these resources.

Online student community
Meet and share ideas with other ACA and CFAB students around the world on the online community. Access resources such as recorded webinars, and share exam hints and tips and find out about events in your area. Ask an Expert sessions also take place throughout the year on the community, and cover areas such as ethical dilemmas and skills development. You can access the community at icaew.com/studentcommunity

Student support helpline
The student support helpline is on hand to assist you with any questions you may have throughout your studies and training. You can contact the helpline on +44 (0)1908 248 040 between the hours of 08.30 and 17.30 GMT Monday – Friday.

Faculties and special interest groups (SIGs)
The ICAEW faculties, which include the Financial Reporting faculty, provide additional specialised support to their members in key areas and invaluable networking opportunities. The ICAEW special interest groups further extend the building of sector-specific knowledge within the profession. ACA and CFAB students can register for provisional faculty membership of one of the seven technical faculties free of charge. ACA students can also register for free membership of a SIG. You can find out more on page xiii.

In addition, **CFAB Ambition** is now available to current CFAB students and holders. **CFAB Ambition** provides you with the resources you need to prepare for an interview, make career choices, develop your professional skills and update your technical knowledge. To subscribe or for more information visit icaew.com/cfabambition

You can, of course, find more information about all of the above at icaew.com

We wish you the very best of luck with your studies; if you have any questions remember that the student support helpline is here to help.

Michael Izza
Chief Executive
ICAEW

Contents

1 Introduction

1.1 What is Accounting and how does it fit within the ACA Professional Stage?

Structure

The ACA syllabus has been designed to develop core technical, commercial, and ethical skills and knowledge in a structured and rigorous manner.

The diagram below shows the twelve modules at the ACA Professional Stage, where the focus is on the acquisition and application of technical skills and knowledge, and the ACA Advanced Stage which comprises two technical integration modules and the Case Study.

If you are studying for CFAB, you will only complete the first six knowledge modules. However, you may decide to progress to the ACA after you have completed the CFAB qualification.

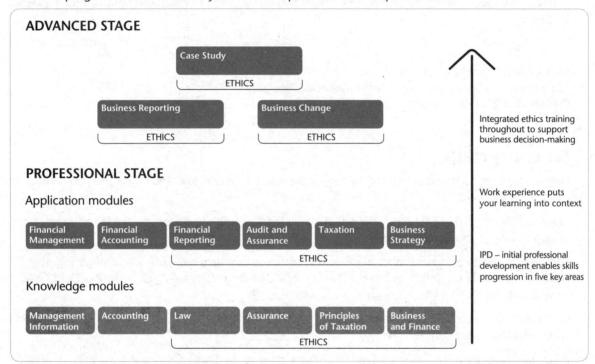

The knowledge level

The aim of the Accounting module is to ensure that students have a sound understanding of the techniques of double entry accounting and can apply its principles in recording transactions, adjusting financial records and preparing non-complex financial statements.

Progression to ACA application level

The knowledge base that is put into place here will be taken further in two application stage modules. In the Financial Accounting module the aim is to prepare a complete set of financial statements for single entities and for groups in conformity with International Financial Reporting Standards (IFRS). In the Financial Reporting module the aim is to prepare and present extracts from financial statements, including accounting policies, for entities undertaking a wide range of accounting transactions, and to conduct financial analysis.

Progression to ACA Advanced Stage

The Advanced Stage papers – Business Reporting (BR) and Business Change (BC) – then take things further again. The aims of BR are that students can apply analysis techniques, technical knowledge and professional skills to resolve real-life compliance issues faced by businesses. In the BC paper the aim is to ensure that students can provide technical advice in respect of issues arising in business transformations eg mergers and acquisitions.

The above illustrates how the knowledge base of accounting gives a platform from which a progression of skills and technical expertise is developed.

2 Accounting

2.1 Module aim

To ensure that students have a sound understanding of the techniques of double entry accounting and can apply its principles in recording transactions, adjusting financial records and preparing non-complex financial statements.

2.2 Specification grid

This grid shows the relative weightings of subjects within this module and should guide the relative study time spent on each. Over time the marks available in the assessment will equate to the weightings below, while slight variations may occur in individual assessments to enable suitably rigorous questions to be set.

	Weighting (%)
Maintaining financial records	30
Adjustments to accounting records and financial statements	35
Preparing financial statements	35
	100

3 Getting help

Firstly, if you are receiving structured tuition, make sure you know how and when you can contact your tutors for extra help.

Identify a work colleague who is qualified, or has at least passed the paper you are studying for, who is willing to help if you have questions.

Form a group with a small number of other students. You can help each other and study together, providing informal support. You can meet and share ideas and study tips with other ACA and CFAB students online – visit www.icaew.com/studentcommunity.

Go to www.icaew.com/students and look under student societies, to find your local society and find out what additional support they offer.

If you need further information on studying, please refer to the Study Guide for each subject. This includes information on planning your studies. These can be found at www.icaew.com/students

Call +44 (0) 1908 248040 or email studentsupport@icaew.com with non-technical queries.

Watch the ICAEW website for future support initiatives.

4 Syllabus and learning outcomes

Covered in chapter

1 Maintaining financial records

Candidates will be proficient in the use of double entry accounting techniques and the maintenance of accounting records.

In the assessment, candidates may be required to:

(a)	Specify why an entity maintains financial records and prepares financial statements	1
(b)	Identify the sources of information for the preparation of accounting records and financial statements	3, 4
(c)	Record and account for transactions and events resulting in income, expenses, assets, liabilities and equity in accordance with the appropriate basis of accounting and the laws, regulations and accounting standards applicable to the financial statements	1-4, 7-13
(d)	Record and account for changes in the ownership structure and ownership interests in an entity	11, 13
(e)	Prepare a trial balance from accounting records and identify the uses of the trial balance.	5, 6

2 Adjustments to accounting records and financial statements

Candidates will be able to identify and correct omissions and errors in accounting records and financial statements.

In the assessment, candidates may be required to:

(a)	Identify omissions and errors in accounting records and financial statements and demonstrate how the required adjustments will affect profits and/or losses	6
(b)	Correct omissions and errors in accounting records and financial statements using control account reconciliations and suspense accounts	6
(c)	Prepare an extended trial balance	5, 6, 7-13
(d)	Prepare journals for nominal ledger entry and to correct errors in draft financial statements.	4, 6

3 Preparing financial statements

Candidates will be able to specify the components of financial statements, and prepare and present non-complex accounts for sole traders, partnerships and limited companies.

In the assessment, candidates may be required to:

(a)	Identify the main components of a set of financial statements and specify their purpose and interrelationship	2, 7-13
(b)	Specify the key aspects of the accrual basis of accounting, cash accounting and break-up basis of accounting	1
(c)	Prepare and present a statement of financial position, income statement and statement of cash flows (or extracts therefrom) from the accounting records and trial balance in a format which satisfies the information requirements of the entity.	5, 7-13

4.1 Technical knowledge

The tables contained in this section show the technical knowledge in the disciplines of financial reporting, audit and assurance, ethics and taxation covered in the ACA syllabus by module.

For each individual standard the level of knowledge required in the relevant Professional Stage module and at the Advanced Stage is shown.

The knowledge levels are defined as follows:

Level D

An awareness of the scope of the standard.

Level C

A general knowledge with a basic understanding of the subject matter and training in its application sufficient to identify significant issues and evaluate their potential implications or impact.

Level B

A working knowledge with a broad understanding of the subject matter and a level of experience in the application thereof sufficient to apply the subject matter in straightforward circumstances.

Level A

A thorough knowledge with a solid understanding of the subject matter and experience in the application thereof sufficient to exercise reasonable professional judgement in the application of the subject matter in those circumstances generally encountered by Chartered Accountants.

Key to other symbols:

→   the knowledge level reached is assumed to be continued

Financial Reporting

Title	Professional Stage			Advanced Stage
	Accounting	Financial Accounting	Financial Reporting	
Preface to International Financial Reporting Standards		A	→	→
Conceptual Framework for Financial Reporting	C	A	→	→
IAS 1 Presentation of Financial Statements	B	A	→	→
IAS 2 Inventories		A	→	→
IAS 7 Statement of Cash Flows	C	B	A	→
IAS 8 Accounting Policies, Changes in Accounting Estimates and Errors		A	→	→
IAS 10 Events after the Reporting Period		A	→	→
IAS 11 Construction Contracts			A	→
IAS 12 Income Taxes			C	A
IAS 16 Property, Plant and Equipment		A	→	→
IAS 17 Leases		A	→	→
IAS 18 Revenue		A	→	→
IAS 19 Employee Benefits				A

Title	Professional Stage			Advanced Stage
	Accounting	Financial Accounting	Financial Reporting	
IAS 20 Accounting for Government Grants and Disclosure of Government Assistance			A	→
IAS 21 The Effects of Changes in Foreign Exchange Rates				A
IAS 23 Borrowing Costs			A	→
IAS 24 Related Party Disclosures			A	→
IAS 26 Accounting and Reporting by Retirement Benefit Plans				D
IAS 27 Consolidated and Separate Financial Statements		B	A	→
IAS 28 Investments in Associates		B	A	→
IAS 29 Financial Reporting in Hyperinflationary Economies				D
IAS 31 Interests in Joint Ventures			A	→
IAS 32 Financial Instruments: Presentation		C	A	→
IAS 33 Earnings per Share			B	A
IAS 34 Interim Financial Reporting				A
IAS 36 Impairment of Assets		B	A	→
IAS 37 Provisions, Contingent Liabilities and Contingent Assets		A	→	→
IAS 38 Intangible Assets		B	A	→
IAS 39 Financial Instruments: Recognition and Measurement		C	B	A
IAS 40 Investment Property			A	→
IAS 41 Agriculture				D
IFRS 1 First-Time Adoption of IFRS				A
IFRS 2 Share-based Payment				A
IFRS 3 Business Combinations		B	B	A
IFRS 4 Insurance Contracts				D
IFRS 5 Non-current Assets Held for Sale and Discontinued Operations		B	A	→
IFRS 6 Exploration for and Evaluation of Mineral Resources				D
IFRS 7 Financial Instruments: Disclosures			B	A
IFRS 8 Operating Segments			A	→
IFRS 9 Financial Instruments				C
IFRS for SMEs				C

Ethics Codes and Standards

Ethics Codes and Standards	Level	Professional Stage modules
IFAC Code of Ethics for Professional Accountants (parts A, B and C and Definitions)	A	Assurance Business and Finance Law Principles of Taxation
ICAEW Code of Ethics	A	Audit and Assurance Business Strategy Financial Reporting Taxation
APB Ethical Standards 1-5 (revised) Provisions Available to Small Entities (revised)	A	Assurance Audit and Assurance

5 Faculties and special interest groups (SIGs)

The faculties and SIGs are specialist bodies within the ICAEW which offer members networking opportunities, influence and recognition within clearly defined areas of technical expertise. As well as providing accurate and timely technical analysis, they lead the way in many professional and wider business issues through stimulating debate, shaping policy and encouraging good practice. Their value is endorsed by over 40,000 members of the Institute who currently belong to one or more of the seven faculties:

- Audit and Assurance
- Corporate Finance
- Finance and Management
- Financial Reporting
- Financial Services
- Information Technology
- Tax

For example, the Financial Reporting Faculty is the focus for chartered accountants working in financial reporting. It represents the Institute on financial reporting matters, making representations to the government and other authorities, and public pronouncements on major issues affecting the profession. It is a free standing body with its own constitution.

The SIGs provide practical support, information and representation for chartered accountants working within a range of industry sectors, including:

- Charity and Voluntary sector
- Entertainment and Media
- Farming and Rural Business
- Forensic
- Healthcare
- Interim Management
- Non-Executive Directors
- Public Sector
- Solicitors
- Tourism and Hospitality
- Valuation

ACA and CFAB students can register for provisional faculty membership of one of the seven faculties free of charge. ACA students can also register for free membership of a SIG. To register and find out more, visit the student website at www.icaew.com/students and click on student support and services.

6   ICAEW publications for further reading

ICAEW produces publications and guidance for its students and members on a variety of technical and business topics. This list of publications has been prepared for students who wish to undertake further reading in a particular subject area and is by no means exhaustive. You are not required to study these publications for your exams. For a full list of publications, or to access any of the publications listed below, visit the Technical & Business Topics section of the ICAEW website at www.icaew.com.

ICAEW no longer prints a Members Handbook. ICAEW regulations, standards and guidance are available at www.icaew.com/regulations. This area includes regulations and guidance relevant to the regulated areas of audit, investment business and insolvency as well as materials that was previously in the handbook.

The TECH series of technical releases are another source of guidance available to members and students. Visit www.icaew.com/technicalreleases for the most up-to-date releases.

Audit and Assurance Faculty – www.icaew.com/aaf

- **Right First Time with the Clarified ISAs**, ICAEW 2010, ISBN 978-0-85760-063-9

  Clarified ISAs provide many opportunities for practitioners in terms of potential efficiencies, better documentation, better reporting to clients, and enhanced audit quality overall.

  This modular guide has been developed by ICAEW's ISA implementation sub-group to help medium-sized and smaller firms implement the clarified ISAs and take advantage of these opportunities. This modular guide is designed to give users the choice of either downloading the publication in its entirety, or downloading specific modules on which they want to focus.

- **Quality Control in the Audit Environment**, ICAEW 2010, ISBN 0-497-80857-605-5

  The publication identifies seven key areas for firms to consider. Illustrative policies and procedures are provided for selected aspects of each key area, including some examples for sole practitioners. The guide also includes an appendix with answers to a number of frequently asked questions on the standard.

- **The Audit of Related Parties in Practice** ICAEW 2010, ISBN 978-1-84125-565-6

  This practical guide to the audit of related party relationships and transactions is set in the context of the significant change in approach that is required under the revised ISA and highlights the importance of planning, the need to involve the entire audit team in this, to assign staff with the appropriate level of experience to audit this area and upfront discussions with the client to identify related parties.

- **Alternatives to Audit** ICAEW, 2009, ISBN 978-1-84152-819-9

  In August 2006, the ICAEW Audit and Assurance Faculty began a two-year consultation on a new assurance services (the ICAEW Assurance Service), an alternative to audit based on the idea of limited assurance introduced by the International Auditing and Assurance Standards Board (IAASB). This report presents findings from the practical experience of providing the ICAEW Assurance Service over the subsequent two years and views of users of financial information that help in assessing the relevance of the service to their needs.

- **Companies Act 2006 supplement** ICAEW, 2009, ISBN 978-1-84152-639-3

  This updated supplement originally published in December 2006, provides a brief summary of the key sections in the Companies Act 2006 which relate directly to the rights and duties of auditors. It covers the various types of reports issued by auditors and provides a comparison to the requirements and regulations in the Companies Act 1985 and Companies Act 1989. It is designed to be a signposting tool for practitioners and identifies the other pieces of guidance issued by ICAEW, APB, FRC, POB and others to support implementation of the Act, along with transitional provisions arising from the Act.

- **Auditing in a group context: practical considerations for auditors** ICAEW, 2008, ISBN 978-1-84152-628-7

  The guide describes special considerations for auditors at each stage of the group audit's cycle. While no decisions have been taken on UK adoption of the IAASB's clarity ISAs, the publication also covers matters in the IAASB's revised and redrafted 'ISA 600 Special Considerations - Audits of Group Financial Statements (Including the Work of Component Auditors)'. The revised publication contains suggestions for both group auditors and component auditors.

Corporate Finance Faculty – www.icaew.com/corpfinfac

- **Private equity demystified –an explanatory guide** Second Edition, Financing Change Initiative, ICAEW, March 2010, John Gilligan and Mike Wright

  This guide summarises the findings of academic work on private equity transactions from around the world. Hard copies of the abstract and full report are free and are also available by download from www.icaew.com/thoughtleadership

- **Best Practice Guidelines**

  The Corporate Finance Faculty publishes a series of guidelines on best-practice, regulatory trends and technical issues. Authored by leading practitioners in corporate finance, they are succinct and clear overviews of emerging issues in UK corporate finance. www.icaew.com/corpfinfac

- **Corporate Financier magazine**, ISSN 1367-4544

  The award-winning *Corporate Financier* magazine is published ten times a year for members, stakeholders and key associates of ICAEW's Corporate Finance Faculty.

  Aimed at professionals, investors and company directors involved in corporate finance, it covers a wide range of emerging regulatory, commercial and professional development issues.

  The magazine includes features, news, analysis and research, written by experts, experienced editors and professional journalists.

  In 2011, three major themes were introduced: Innovation & Corporate Finance; Financing Entrepreneurship; and Deal Leadership.

Corporate governance – www.icaew.com/corporategovernance

- **The UK Corporate Governance Code 2010**

  The UK Corporate Governance Code (formerly the Combined Code) sets out standards of good practice in relation to board leadership and effectiveness, remuneration, accountability and relations with shareholders. All companies with a Premium Listing of equity shares in the UK are required under the Listing Rules to report on how they have applied the UK Corporate Governance Code in their annual report and accounts.

  The first version of the UK Corporate Governance Code was produced in 1992 by the Cadbury Committee. In May 2010 the Financial Reporting Council issued a new edition of the Code which applies to financial years beginning on or after 29 June 2010.

  The UK Corporate Governance Code contains broad principles and more specific provisions. Listed companies are required to report on how they have applied the main principles of the Code, and either to confirm that they have complied with the Code's provisions or – where they have not – to provide an explanation.

- **Internal Control: Revised Guidance on Internal Control for Directors on the Combined Code (Now the UK Corporate Governance Code)**

  Originally published in 1999, the Turnbull guidance was revised and updated in October 2005, following a review by the Financial Reporting Council. The updated guidance applies to listed companies for financial years beginning on or after 1 January 2006.

- **The FRC Guidance on Audit Committees** (formerly known as the Smith Guidance)

  First published by the Financial Reporting Council in January 2003, and most recently updated in 2010. It is intended to assist company boards when implementing the sections of the UK Corporate Governance Code dealing with audit committees and to assist directors serving on audit committees in carrying out their role. Companies are encouraged to use the 2010 edition of the guidance with effect from 30 April 2011

- **The UK Stewardship Code**

  The UK Stewardship Code was published in July 2010. It aims to enhance the quality of engagement between institutional investors and companies to help improve long-term returns to shareholders and the efficient exercise of governance responsibilities by setting out good practice on engagement with investee companies to which the Financial Reporting Council believes institutional investors should aspire.

  A report summarising the actions being taken by the Financial Reporting Council and explaining how the UK Stewardship Code is intended to operate was also published in July 2010.

Corporate responsibility – www.icaew.com/corporateresponsibility

- **Sustainable Business** January 2009

  The new thought leadership prospectus acts as a framework for the work that ICAEW do in sustainability/corporate responsibility. It argues that any system that is sustainable needs accurate and reliable information to help it learn and adapt, which is where the accounting profession plays an important role. A downloadable pdf is available at www.icaew.com/sustainablebusiness

- **Environmental issues in annual financial statements** ICAEW, May 2009, ISBN 978-1-84152-610-2

  This report is a joint initiative with the Environment Agency. It is aimed at business accountants who prepare, use or audit the financial statements in statutory annual reports and accounts, or who advise or sit on the boards of the UK companies and public sector organisations. It offers practical advice on measuring and disclosing environmental performance. A downloadable pdf is available at www.icaew.com/sustainablebusiness

- **ESRC seminar series – When worlds collide: contested paradigms of corporate responsibility**

  ICAEW, in conjunction with the British Academy of Management, won an Economic and Social Research Council grant to run a seminar series which aims to bring academics and the business community together to tackle some of the big challenges in corporate responsibility. www.icaew.com/corporateresponsibility

- **The Business Sustainability Programme (BSP)**

  The Business Sustainability Programme is an e-learning package for accountants and business professionals who want to learn about the business case for sustainability. The course is spread across five modules taking users from definitions of sustainability and corporate responsibility, through case studies and finally towards developing an individually tailored sustainability strategy for their business. The first two modules are free to everyone. For more information and to download a brochure visit www.icaew.com/bsp

Ethics – www.icaew.com/ethics

- **Code of Ethics** (part of icaew.com/regulations)

  The Code of Ethics helps ICAEW members meet these obligations by providing them with ethical guidance. The Code applies to all members, students, affiliates, employees of member firms and, where applicable, member firms, in all of their professional and business activities, whether remunerated or voluntary.

- **Instilling integrity in organisations** ICAEW June 2009

  Practical guidance aimed at directors and management to assist them in instilling integrity in their organisations. This document may also be helpful to audit firms discussing this topic with clients and individuals seeking to address issues in this area with their employers.

- **Reporting with Integrity** ICAEW May 2007, ISBN 978-1-84152-455-9

  This publication brings ideas from a variety of disciplines, in order to obtain a more comprehensive understanding of what is meant by integrity, both as a concept and in practice. Moreover, because this report sees reporting with integrity as a joint endeavour of individuals, organisations and professions, including the accounting profession, the concept of integrity is considered in all these contexts.

Finance and Management Faculty – www.icaew.com/fmfac

- **Finance's role in the organisation** November 2009, ISBN 978-1-84152-855-7

  This considers the challenges of designing successful organisations, written by Rick Payne, who leads the faculty's finance direction programme.

- **Investment appraisal** SR27: December 2009, ISBN 978-1-84152-854-4

  This special report looks at the key issues and advises managers on how they can contribute effectively to decision making and control during the process of investment appraisal.

- **Starting a business** SR28: March 2010, ISBN 978-1-84152-984-2

  This report provides accountants with a realistic and motivational overview of what to consider when starting a business.

- **Developing a vision for your business** SR30: September 2010, ISBN 978-0-85760-054-7

  This special report looks at what makes a good vision, the benefits of having one, the role of the FD in the process, leadership, storytelling and the use of visions in medium-sized businesses.

- **Finance transformation – the outsourcing perspective** SR31: December 2010, ISBN 978-0-85760-079-0

  The authors of this outsourcing special report share their expertise on topics including service level agreements, people management, and innovation and technology

Financial Services Faculty – www.icaew.com/fsf

- **Audit of banks: lessons from the crisis**, (Inspiring Confidence in Financial Services initiative) ICAEW, June 2010 ISBN 978-0-85760-051-6

  This research has looked into the role played by bank auditors and examined improvements that can be made in light of lessons learned from the financial crisis. The project has included the publication of stakeholder feedback and development of a final report

- **Measurement in financial services**, (Inspiring Confidence in Financial Services initiative) ICAEW, March 2008, ISBN 978-1-84152-546-4

  This report suggests that more work is required on matching measurement practices in the financial services industry to the needs of different users of financial information, despite the fact that the financial services industry has the greatest concentration of measurement and modelling skills of any industry. A downloadable pdf is available at www.icaew.com/thoughtleadership

- **Skilled Persons' Guidance – Reporting Under s166 Financial Services and Markets Act 2000 (Interim Technical Release FSF 01/08)**

  This interim guidance was issued by ICAEW in April 2008 as a revision to TECH 20/30 to assist chartered accountants and other professionals who are requested to report under s166 Financial Services and Markets Act 2000. A downloadable pdf is available at www.icaew.com/technicalreleases

Financial Reporting Faculty – www.icaew.com/frfac

- **EU Implementation of IFRS and the Fair Value Directive** ICAEW, October 2007, ISBN 978-1-84152-519-8

  The most comprehensive assessment to date of compliance with the requirements of IFRS and the overall quality if IFRS financial reporting.

The Financial Reporting Faculty makes available to students copies of its highly-regarded factsheets on UK GAAP and IFRS issues, as well as its journal, *By All Accounts*, at www.icaew.com/frfac

Information Technology Faculty – www.icaew.com/itfac

The IT Faculty provides ongoing advice and guidance that will help students in their studies and their work. The online community (http://www.ion.icaew.com/itcountshome) provides regular free updates as well as a link to the faculty's Twitter feed which provides helpful updates and links to relevant articles. The following publications should also be of interest to students:

- **Business Continuity and Management – an introductory guide** ICAEW, 2010, ISBN 978-0-85760-080-6

  Business Continuity and Management provides a proven corporate discipline which helps small businesses to plan for, respond to, cope with and recover from sudden, unexpected and often traumatic events. By following the steps in this guide and focusing on the consequences of disruption, asking yourselves 'what if' more often than 'how much' you can reap significant benefits.

- **Cloud Computing – A guide for business managers** ICAEW, April 2010, ISBN 987-0-85760-000-4

  This publication outlines what is meant by cloud computing and how business people can take advantage of what it has to offer.

- **Information security – an essential today** ICAEW, December 2009, ISBN 978-1-84152-853-3

  This publication outlines what businesses should be doing to ensure the information assets of their businesses are properly identified, protected and secured. It introduces the information security management framework, ISO 27001, which can be used to implement verifiable system of information security.

Tax Faculty – www.icaew.com/taxfac

The Tax Faculty runs a Younger Members Tax Club which provides informal presentations, discussions and socialising. All young professionals interested in tax are welcome to attend. See the website for more details www.icaew.com/taxfac

- **Tax news service**

  You can keep up with the tax news as it develops on the Tax Faculty's news site www.icaew.com/taxnews. And you can subscribe to the free newswire which gives you a weekly round up. For more details visit www.icaew.com/taxfac

- **Demystifying XBRL**

  This booklet, produced jointly by KPMG, the Tax Faculty and the Information Technology Faculty, explains exactly what iXBRL is all about and what must be done in order to e-file corporation tax returns using the new standard.

CHAPTER 1

Introduction to accounting

Introduction

Examination context

Topic List

Learning objectives

Tick off

- Specify why an entity maintains financial records and prepares financial statements

- Record and account for transactions in accordance with the laws, regulations and accounting standards applicable to the financial statements

- Specify the key aspects of the accrual basis of accounting, cash accounting and break-up basis of accounting

Specific syllabus learning outcomes are: 1a, c, 3b

Syllabus links

The material in this chapter will be developed further in this paper, and then in the Financial Accounting and Financial Reporting papers later in the Professional stage.

Examination context

Questions on topics in this chapter will be knowledge-type multiple choice questions. In the exam you may be required to:

- Identify capital as opposed to revenue expenditure
- Specify the distinctions between the different qualitative characteristics
- Identify the principles that relate to each qualitative characteristic
- Identify the different interests of stakeholders

1 The purpose of accounting information

Section overview

- Accounting is a way of recording, analysing and summarising the transactions of an entity.

- The three main types of business entity are sole traders, partnerships and companies.

- Users who need financial information include: managers, owners, customers, suppliers, lenders, employees, trade unions, HM Revenue and Customs, financial analysts and advisers, government agencies and the public.

- Managers and (present and potential) owners are the prime users of published financial statements.

- People need financial information on a company to make economic decisions, to assess managers' stewardship of the company's resources, and to assess the level, timing and certainty of its future cash flows.

1.1 What is accounting?

Accounting is a way of recording, analysing and summarising transactions of an entity (a term we shall use to describe any business organisation).

- The transactions are **recorded** in 'books of original entry' (see Chapter 3).
- The transactions are then **analysed** and posted to the ledgers (see Chapter 4).
- Finally the transactions are **summarised** in the financial statements (see Chapter 5).

One of the roles of an accountant is to measure the revenue and expenditure of an entity and, if it is a business, its profit. This is not as straightforward as it may seem and in later chapters we will look at some theoretical and practical difficulties.

1.2 Types of business entity

There are three main types of profit-making business entity.

- Sole traders
- Partnerships
- Limited liability companies

Sole traders are people who work for themselves. Examples include a local shopkeeper, plumber or hairdresser. The term sole trader refers to the **ownership** of the business; sole traders can have employees.

Partnerships occur when two or more people decide to share the risks and rewards of a business together. Examples include an accountancy, medical or legal practice. A partnership can take one of two forms: a **general partnership** (like two or more sole traders) and a Limited Liability Partnership LLP (more like a company).

Limited liability companies are incorporated to take advantage of 'limited liability' for their owners (shareholders). This means that, while sole traders (always) and partners (usually) are **personally responsible** for the amounts owed by their businesses, the owners (shareholders) of a limited liability company are only responsible for the **amount to be paid for their shares**.

1.3 The objective of financial statements

The *Conceptual Framework for Financial Reporting* (from now on referred to as the *Conceptual Framework*) was issued by the International Accounting Standards Board (IASB) in September 2010 and it superseded the *Framework for the Preparation and Presentation of Financial Statements*.

You should note that the IASB is currently in the process of updating its conceptual framework via a project being conducted in stages. Only the first stage of the project had been completed at the date of writing of this Study Manual.

The *Conceptual Framework* sets out concepts that underlie the preparation and presentation of financial statements for a wide range of users, many of whom have to rely on financial statements as their major source of financial information on an entity. In reality key user groups will vary between large and small entities. However, the *Conceptual Framework* focuses on larger entities.

Why do businesses need to produce accounting information in the form of financial statements? If a business is being run efficiently, why should it have to go through all the bother of accounting procedures in order to produce financial information? The *Conceptual Framework* states that:

'The objective of general purpose financial reporting is to provide financial information about the reporting entity that is useful to existing and potential investors, lenders and other creditors in making decisions about providing resources to the entity.'

In other words, a business should produce information about its activities because there are user groups who want or need to know that information in order to make **economic decisions**.

When making economic decisions, users need to assess:

- The ability of the business to generate cash, and
- The timing and certainty of cash flows.

Whether the business can generate cash of the right amount determines whether it can:

- Pay its employees and suppliers
- Meet interest payments
- Repay loans
- Pay something to its owners

The objective stated above from the *Conceptual Framework* is concerned with financial reporting in general. It is International Accounting Standard 1 (IAS 1) *Presentation of Financial Statements* (revised in September 2007) that provides the objective of financial statements. It states that 'the objective of financial statements is:

- To provide information about the financial position, financial performance and cash flows of an entity that is useful to a wide range of users in making economic decisions.'

IAS 1 also states that 'the financial statements also:

- Show the results of **management's stewardship** of the resources entrusted to it, and

- Assists users of financial statements in **predicting the entity's future cash flows** and, in particular, their timing and certainty.'

Large businesses are of interest to a greater variety of people and so we will consider the case of a large public company, whose shares can be purchased and sold on a stock exchange.

1.4 Who needs financial information?

The following people are likely to be interested in financial information about a large company with listed shares.

- **Managers/directors** appointed by the company's owners to supervise the day to day activities of the company. They need information about the company's present and future financial situation. This enables them to manage the business efficiently (exercising the stewardship function) and to make effective decisions about matters such as pricing, output, employment and financing.

- **Owners of the company** (shareholders) want to assess management performance. They want to know how profitable the company's operations are and how much profit they can afford to withdraw from the business for their own use.

- **Trade contacts** include suppliers who provide goods on credit and customers who purchase goods or services. **Suppliers** want to know about the company's ability to pay its debts; **customers** need to know that the company is a secure source of supply, so that repeat purchases and after-sales care will be available.

- **Finance providers** include banks which allow the company to operate an overdraft, or provide longer term loan finance secured on the company's assets. A bank wants to ensure that the company is able to keep up loan payments.

- **HM Revenue and Customs (HMRC)** want to know about business profits in order to assess the company's tax liabilities.

- **Employees** have an interest in the company's financial situation, because their careers and remuneration depend on it.

- **Financial analysts and advisers** need information for their clients or audience. For example, stockbrokers need information to advise investors; credit agencies want information to advise potential suppliers of goods to the company; and journalists need information for their reading public.

- **Government agencies** are interested in the efficient allocation of resources and therefore in the activities of enterprises. They also require information in order to provide a basis for national statistics.

- **The public**. Business entities affect members of the public in a variety of ways. For example, they may make a substantial contribution to a local economy by providing employment and using local suppliers. Another important factor is the effect of an entity on the natural environment, for example as regards pollution.

Accounting information is summarised in financial statements to satisfy the **information needs** of these different groups. Not all will be equally satisfied.

Managers of a business need the most information, to help them make planning and control decisions. They have greater access to business information, because they are able to review internally produced statements. Managers can obtain extra information through the **cost and management accounting system**.

Interactive question 1: Accounting information   [Difficulty level: Intermediate]

It is easy to see how 'internal' people get hold of accounting information. A manager, for example, can just go along to the accounts department and ask the staff there to prepare whatever accounting statements she needs. But external users of accounts cannot do this. How, in practice, can a business contact or a financial analyst access accounting information about a company?

See **Answer** at the end of this chapter.

In addition to management information, additional financial statements are prepared for the benefit of other user groups, who may demand particular information.

- **HMRC** will receive information to make tax assessments.
- A **bank** might demand a cash flow forecast as a pre condition of granting an overdraft.

The **International Accounting Standards Board (IASB)** is responsible for issuing **International Accounting Standards** and **International Financial Reporting Standards** (IASs and IFRSs) and these require companies to publish certain additional information. Accountants, as members of professional bodies, are placed under an obligation to ensure that company financial statements conform to the requirements of IAS/IFRS, where relevant.

Over time, **generally accepted accounting practice** has developed in the UK to form **UK GAAP**. Many companies, as well as sole traders and partnerships, prepare their accounting information following UK GAAP rather than IFRS.

Note. In this Study Manual, we will refer to the collective body of standards issued by the IASB as IASs.

1.4.1 Not-for-profit entities

It is not only businesses that need to prepare financial statements. **Charities and clubs**, for example, prepare financial statements every year. Financial statements also need to be prepared for **government (public sector) organisations**.

1.5 Users and their information needs

As well as identifying the objectives of financial reporting the *Conceptual Framework* identifies users of financial statements and their specific information needs.

Below we consider those users identified by the *Conceptual Framework* along with other potential users of financial statements, as well as the aspects of financial statements they are likely to be interested in.

- **Investors** (current and potential owners) are the providers of risk capital for the company, so they are interested in the **risk** to their capital presented by the investment, and the **return** they will get for taking that risk. They need information to help them determine whether they should buy, hold or sell shares. Owners are also interested in information which enables them to assess the ability of the entity to pay dividends.

- **Employees** and their representative groups need information about the stability and profitability of their employers, so they can assess the entity's ability to provide remuneration, retirement benefits and employment opportunities.

- **Lenders** need information that enables them to determine whether their loans, and the interest attached to them, will be paid when due.

- **Suppliers and other creditors** need information that enables them to determine whether amounts owing to them will be paid. Trade creditors are likely to be interested in an entity over a shorter period than lenders, unless they are dependent upon the continuation of the entity as a major customer.

- **Customers** need information about the entity's continuance, especially when they have a long-term involvement with, or are dependent on, the entity.

- **Governments and their agencies** have the needs listed in section 1.4. They also require information in order to regulate the activities of entities, and determine taxation policies.

- **Public**. Members of the public have the needs listed in section 1.4, that is they wish to see how the company will be able to continue employing local people and using local suppliers. Financial statements may assist the public by providing information about the trends and recent developments in the prosperity of the entity and the range of its activities.

The management of a reporting entity will be interested in financial information about the entity but does not need to rely on general purpose financial reports because it is able to obtain the financial information it needs internally.

Therefore instead of being thought of as users of the financial statements, management are primarily responsible for the **preparation and presentation** of the financial statements.

2 The main financial statements

Section overview

- Financial statements prepared under IASs collectively comprise a statement of financial position, a statement of comprehensive income including an income statement, a statement of changes in equity, a statement of cash flows, notes and (in certain circumstances) a revised statement of financial position from an earlier period.

- IAS 1 (revised) *Presentation of Financial Statements* sets out the form and content of the financial statements.

IAS 1 *Presentation of Financial Statements* (revised in September 2007) identifies a complete set of financial statements for a reporting period (typically a year) as comprising:

- a **statement of financial position** as at the end of the reporting period (as we shall see in Chapter 12, under UK GAAP this is called a **balance sheet**),

- a statement of comprehensive income for the reporting period, which can be in a two-part format including a separate **income statement** (as we shall see in Chapter 12, under UK GAAP this is called a **profit and loss account**),

- a statement of changes in equity for the reporting period,

- a **statement of cash flows** for the reporting period,

- notes comprising a **summary of significant accounting policies** and other explanatory information, and

- a statement of financial position as at the beginning of the earliest comparative period when an entity applies an accounting policy retrospectively, makes a restatement of items in its financial statements, or reclassifies items.

In this Study Manual we are only concerned with the **statement of financial position**, the **income statement** part of the statement of comprehensive income, the **statement of cash flows** and the **summary of accounting policies note.**

IAS 1 (revised) makes it clear that an entity may use titles for the statements other than those used in the Standard. Many entities will no doubt continue to use the term '**balance sheet**' instead of 'statement of financial position', '**income statement**' instead of 'statement of comprehensive income' and '**cash flow statement**' instead of 'statement of cash flows'. However in this Study Manual we shall use the IAS 1 (revised) terminology until Chapter 12, when we shall use the terminology of financial statements prepared under UK GAAP ('balance sheet' and 'profit and loss account').

2.1 Statement of financial position

Definitions

Statement of financial position: A *list* of all the *assets controlled* and all the *liabilities owed* by a business as at a particular date: it is a snapshot of the **financial position** of the business at a particular moment. Monetary amounts are attributed to assets and liabilities. It also quantifies the amount of the owners' interest in the company: **equity.**

Equity: The amount invested in a business by the owners (IAS 1 (revised) refers to 'owners' rather than 'equity holders' or 'shareholders').

Assets and liabilities are explained in more detail in Chapter 2. However, the sum of the assets will always be equal to the sum of the liabilities plus equity/capital.

There are a number of factors affecting a company's financial position at any one time which include:

(a) The **economic resources** it controls (cash, labour, materials, machinery, skills)
(b) Its **financial structure** (whether it is funded by owners, lenders, suppliers, or by all three)
(c) Its **liquidity** (short-term availability of cash) and **solvency** (long-term access to funds)
(d) Its **adaptability** to changes in its operating environment

The *Conceptual Framework* focuses on how information about the nature and amounts of an entity's **economic resources** and **claims** (liabilities) can help users to identify the reporting entity's financial strengths and weaknesses.

In particular it points out that information about the nature and amounts of an entity's economic resources and claims can help users to assess:

- The entity's liquidity and solvency
- The entity's need for additional financing; and
- How successful the entity is likely to be in obtaining that financing

Additionally by gaining knowledge of the economic resources a business controls, users will be in a better position to predict the **entity's ability to generate cash in the future**.

Information about an entity's financial structure and liquidity/solvency can also help financial statement users.

Factor	Information on this helps users
Financial structure	• To predict future borrowing needs
	• To predict how future profits and cash flows will be distributed among owners and lenders
	• To predict how successfully it will be able to raise future finance
Liquidity/solvency	• To predict its ability to meet financial commitments as they fall due

2.2 Income statement

In the UK, the income statement part of the statement of comprehensive income is called the profit and loss account.

Definition

Income statement: A statement displaying items of **income** and **expense** in a **reporting period** as components of **profit or loss for the period**. The statement shows whether the business has had more income than expense (a profit for the period) or *vice versa* (a loss for the period).

The **reporting period** chosen will depend on the purpose for which the statement is produced. The income statement which forms part of the published annual financial statements of a **limited liability company** will usually be for the period of a **year**, commencing from the date of the previous year's financial statements. On the other hand, **management** might want to keep a closer eye on a company's profitability by making up **quarterly, monthly, weekly or even daily** statements.

The *Conceptual Framework* sets out how information about the business's financial performance, ie its profits or losses, is needed by users.

- To **understand the return** that the entity has produced on its economic resources.

- To assess how well **management has discharged its responsibilities** to make efficient and effective use of the reporting entity's resources

- To help predict the business's **future returns** on its economic resources

The link between the statement of financial position and the statement of comprehensive income is provided by the **statement of cash flows** and the **statement of changes in equity**. These are covered in detail later in your professional studies. However, you will find an introduction to the statement of cash flows in Chapter 13. The statement of cash flows shows the actual cash flowing into and paid out of the business.

2.3 Presentation of financial statements

Both the statement of financial position and the income statement are **summaries of accumulated data**. For example, the income statement shows a figure for revenue earned from selling goods and services to customers. This is the total revenue earned from all sales made during the period. An accountant devises methods of recording such transactions, so as to produce summarised financial statements from them.

The statement of financial position and the income statement form the basis of financial statements for most businesses. For limited liability companies, other information by way of statements (such as the **statement of cash flows** and the **statement of changes in equity**) and notes is required by statute and accounting standards.

3 The regulation of accounting

Section overview

- Financial statements are regulated by legislation, the application of judgement using established accounting concepts, accounting and financial reporting standards, generally accepted accounting practice (GAAP) and the need for fair presentation (or a true and fair view).

A number of factors have shaped the **development of accounting**.

The regulatory framework of accounting, and the technical aspects of the changes made, will be covered later in this Study Manual and in your professional studies. The purpose of this section is to give a **general picture** of some of the factors which have shaped accounting. We will concentrate on the financial statements of limited liability companies, as these are the ones most closely regulated by statute or otherwise.

The following factors can be identified.

- Legislation
- Accounting concepts and individual judgement
- Accounting standards
- Generally accepted accounting practice (GAAP)
- True and fair view/fair presentation

3.1 Legislation

Limited liability companies are required by the Companies Act 2006 to prepare and publish financial statements annually. Their form and content are regulated by legislation but must comply with **accepted accounting and financial reporting standards**. For listed groups this means compliance with IAS and IFRS. Non-listed companies may follow UK standards which are gradually converging with international ones.

3.2 Accounting concepts and individual judgement

Many figures in financial statements are derived from the **application of judgement** in applying **fundamental accounting concepts**.

Different people exercising their judgement on the same facts could arrive at very different conclusions.

Interactive question 2: Value of reputation　　　　　[Difficulty level: Intermediate]

An accountancy training firm has an excellent **reputation** amongst students and employers. How would you value this?

See **Answer** at the end of this chapter.

Other examples of areas where the judgement of different people may vary are as follows.

- **Valuation of buildings** in times of changing property prices.

- **Research and development** (R&D): is it right to treat this only as an expense? In a sense it is an investment to generate future revenue.

- **Brands** such as 'Snickers' or 'iPod'. Are they assets in the same way that a fork lift truck is an asset?

Working from the same data, different groups of people may produce very different financial statements, but if judgement is completely unregulated, there will be no comparability between the financial statements of different organisations. This will be all the more significant in cases where deliberate manipulation occurs, in order to present financial statements in the most favourable light.

We shall come back to accounting concepts and conventions in section 5 of this chapter.

3.3 Accounting standards

To deal with some of this subjectivity, and to achieve comparability between different organisations, **accounting standards** were developed at both a UK level by the Accounting Standards Board (ASB) and at an international level, by the IASB. In this Study Manual we are concerned with parts of IAS 1 *Presentation of Financial Statements* (as revised in September 2007). We also cover the *Conceptual Framework.*

3.4 Generally Accepted Accounting Practice (GAAP)

GAAP, as a term, has sprung up in recent years and signifies all the rules, from whatever source, which govern accounting. UK GAAP rules derive from:

- The Companies Act 2006
- UK and international accounting and financial reporting standards
- Statutory requirements in other countries (particularly the US)
- Stock exchange listing requirements

We shall look at UK GAAP in Chapter 12, since it only applies to (some) unlisted companies.

3.5 True and fair view/faithful representation

Financial statements are required to give a **true and fair view** or **present fairly in all material respects** the financial results of the entity. These terms are not defined and tend to be decided in courts of law on the facts.

- The *Conceptual Framework* states that if financial information is to be useful, it must be relevant and faithfully represent what it purports to represent.

- The Companies Act 2006 requires that the financial statements should give a **true and fair view** of the financial position of the entity at a particular point in time.

- In terms of IAS 1 (revised), financial statements should present fairly the financial position and performance, and the cash flows, of the entity. This requires faithful representation of the effects of transactions.

4 Qualitative characteristics of useful accounting information

Section overview

- Financial information should be **relevant** and **faithfully represent** what it purports to represent. The usefulness of financial information is enhanced if it is comparable, verifiable, timely and understandable.

What type of information then should financial statements contain? What should its main qualities be from the user's point of view?

4.1 The fundamental qualitative characteristics

The *Conceptual Framework* identifies the fundamental qualitative characteristics to be **relevance** and **faithful representation**. Information must be **both** relevant and faithfully represented to be useful.

- **Relevance.** Relevant financial information is capable of making a difference in the decisions made by users. Information may be capable of making a difference in a decision even if some users choose not to take advantage of it or are already aware of it from other sources.

Financial information can make a difference to decisions if it has:

- **Predictive value**. It can be used to predict future outcomes.

- **Confirmatory value.** It provides feedback about previous evaluations (it confirms whether past predictions were reasonable).

Information's relevance is affected by its nature and **materiality**. (We shall come back to materiality; for now you can think of it as 'important'). You should note that information may become less relevant if there is undue delay in its reporting.

- **Faithful representation**. If information is to be useful, it must represent faithfully the transactions and other events it purports to represent. A faithful representation will be:

  - **Complete**. All information necessary for a user to understand the transactions or events being depicted is included.

  - **Neutral** (unbiased)

  - **Free from error**. Free from error in the context of faithful representation **does not mean** the information is perfectly accurate in all respects. Instead it means there are no errors or omissions in the description of it and the process used to produce the reported information has been selected and applied with no errors in the process.

4.2 Enhancing qualitative characteristics

According to the *Conceptual Framework* information that is relevant and faithfully represented can be enhanced by the following 'enhancing' qualitative characteristics:

- **Comparability**. Comparability is the qualitative characteristic that enables users to identify and understand similarities in, and differences among, items. Information should be produced so that valid comparisons can be made with information from previous periods and with information produced by other entities (for example, the financial statements of similar companies operating in the same line of business). Comparability should not be confused with **consistency**. Applying consistency (using the same methods for the same items) is a means of achieving comparability (comparability is the goal).

- **Verifiability**. Verifiability helps to assure users that information is a faithful representation of the transactions or events it purports to represent. If information is verifiable it essentially means that it can be proven, for example you may be able to check it is true by examination, inspection or comparison. The *Conceptual Framework* states that 'verifiability means that different knowledgeable and independent observers could reach consensus, although not necessarily complete agreement, that a particular depiction is a faithful representation'.

- **Timeliness**. Timeliness means having information available to decision-makers in time to be capable of influencing their decisions. As a general rule older information is less useful than recent information. However, you should note that some information may still be timely for a long time after the end of a reporting period. This is true of information for users of financial information who need to identify and assess trends.

- **Understandability**. Information is understandable if it is classified, characterised and presented clearly and concisely. When considering whether information is understandable you should bear in mind that financial reports are prepared for users who have a **reasonable knowledge of business and economic** activities.

5 Accounting concepts and conventions

Section overview

- The fundamental assumptions behind ledger accounting and the preparation of financial statements are contained in IAS 1 (revised) and the *Conceptual Framework.*

- IAS 1 (revised) is concerned with the presentation of financial statements so that they are comparable across time and with other companies.

- The objective of financial statements is to provide useful information to users making economic decisions. To achieve this information must be presented fairly or faithfully, which generally means it should be presented in accordance with IASs.

- Each entity needs to select and apply accounting policies in order to present its financial statements. The result will be information that is relevant and faithfully represents what it purports to represent.

Many accounting procedures are operated automatically by people who have never questioned whether alternative methods exist which have equal validity. In fact the procedures in common use imply the acceptance of certain concepts which are by no means self evident, nor are they the only possible concepts which could be used to build up an accounting framework.

Our next step is to look at some of the more important concepts which are used in preparing financial statements.

We begin by considering the **fundamental assumptions** which are the subject of IAS 1 (revised) *Presentation of Financial Statements* (and which are also covered in the *Conceptual Framework*).

5.1 Fair presentation

In this section we look at the general requirements of IAS 1 (revised)'s **assumptions**. The rest of IAS 1 (revised), on the format and content of financial statements will be covered in Chapter 11 when we look in detail at the preparation of company financial statements.

5.1.1 Objectives and scope of IAS 1 (revised)

The main objective of IAS 1 (revised) is:

'to prescribe the basis for presentation of general purpose financial statements, to ensure comparability both with the entity's financial statements of previous periods and with the financial statements of other entities.'

IAS 1 (revised) applies to all **general purpose financial statements** prepared and presented in accordance with International Financial Reporting Standards (IFRSs – this refers to IASs as well, the collective term that we use in this Study Manual). General purpose financial statements are those intended to meet the needs of users who are not in a position to demand reports tailored to meet their particular information needs.

5.1.2 Purpose of financial statements

The **objectives of financial statements** are:

- To provide information about the financial position, performance and cash flows of an entity that is useful to a wide range of users in making **economic decisions**

- To show the result of **management's stewardship** of the resources entrusted to it

- To assist users in **predicting the entity's future cash flows** and, in particular, their timing and certainty

To fulfil these objectives, financial statements must provide information about the entity's:

- Assets
- Liabilities
- Equity
- Income and expenses (including gains and losses)
- Other changes in equity
- Cash flows

As defined in Chapter 2, these are called the **elements of financial statements**

A complete set of financial statements includes:

- Statement of financial position
- Income statement (part of the statement of comprehensive income)

Covered in the *Accounting* syllabus

- Accounting policies note
- Statement of changes in equity
- Statement of cash flows
- Explanatory notes

Covered in the *Financial Accounting* and *Financial Reporting* syllabuses

- A further statement of financial position from an earlier period where there has been retrospective application of an accounting policy, a reclassification or a retrospective restatement – issues that we shall come back to in Chapter 11

Preparation of the financial statements is the responsibility of the **board of directors**. IAS 1 (revised) also recognises the value of a **financial review** by management and the production of any other reports and statements which may aid users, but these fall outside the *Accounting* syllabus scope.

5.1.3 Fair presentation and compliance with IASs

Most importantly, financial statements should **present fairly** the financial position, financial performance and cash flows of an entity. **Applying IASs** is presumed to result in fair presentation.

Definition

Fair presentation: The faithful representation of the effects of transactions, other events and conditions in accordance with the *Conceptual Framework*.

The following points made by IAS 1 (revised) expand on this principle.

- Compliance with IASs should be explicitly stated in a note to the financial statements

- All relevant IASs must be followed if compliance with IASs is disclosed

- Use of an inappropriate accounting treatment cannot be rectified either by disclosure of accounting policies or notes/explanatory material

IAS 1 (revised) states what is required for a fair presentation.

- Selection and application of **accounting policies**

- **Presentation of information** in a manner which provides relevant, reliable, comparable and understandable information

- **Additional disclosures** where required to enable users to understand the impact of particular transactions, events and conditions on the entity's financial position and performance.

5.1.4 Departures from IASs

There may be (very rare) circumstances when management decides that compliance with a requirement of an IAS would be so misleading that financial statements would not meet their objectives. **Departure from the IAS** may therefore be required to achieve a fair presentation. The following should be disclosed in such an event.

- Management confirmation that the financial statements fairly present the entity's financial position, performance and cash flows

- Statement that all IASs have been complied with *except* in respect of departure from individual IASs, required to achieve a fair presentation

- Details of the nature of the departure, why the IAS treatment would be misleading, and the treatment adopted

- Financial effect of the departure

5.2 Going concern (IAS 1 (revised))

Definition

Going concern: The entity is viewed as continuing in operation for the foreseeable future. It is assumed that the entity has neither the intention nor the necessity of liquidation or ceasing to trade.

This concept assumes that, when preparing a normal set of financial statements, the business will **continue to operate** in approximately the same manner for the foreseeable future (at least the next 12 months). In particular the entity will not go into liquidation or cease trading, or have no realistic alternative but to liquidate or cease trading.

When an entity is not a going concern its assets are **valued at their 'break up' value**: the amount they would sell for (their **net realisable value**) if they were sold off individually in a forced sale and the business were broken up. Since this forced sale is necessary because the business has foreseen problems in the next 12 months, financial statements prepared on a break-up basis will contain neither non-current assets nor non-current liabilities. All assets will be deemed to be for sale and all liabilities will be treated as becoming due within 12 months of the date of the statement of financial position.

Interactive question 3: Going concern   [Difficulty level: Intermediate]

A retailer commences business on 1 January and buys 20 washing machines, each costing £100. During the year he sells 17 machines at £150 each. How should the remaining machines be valued at 31 December in the following circumstances?

(a) He is forced to close down his business at the end of the year and the remaining machines will realise only £60 each in a forced sale.

(b) He intends to continue his business into the next year.

See **Answer** at the end of this chapter.

If the going concern assumption is not followed, that fact must be disclosed, together with:

- The **basis** on which the financial statements have been prepared.
- The **reasons** why the entity is not considered to be a going concern.

When there is uncertainty as to whether the entity is a going concern, this should be disclosed along with the nature of the uncertainty.

5.3 Accrual basis of accounting (IAS 1 (revised))

An entity should prepare its financial statements, except for cash flow information, using the accrual basis of accounting.

Definition

Accrual basis of accounting: Items are recognised as assets, liabilities, equity, income and expenses (the elements of financial statements) when they satisfy the definitions and recognition criteria for those elements in the *Conceptual Framework*.

Entities should prepare their financial statements on the basis that transactions are recorded in them, not as the cash is paid or received (**cash accounting**), but as the income or expenses are **earned or incurred** in the reporting period to which they relate.

According to the accrual basis, when computing profit **income earned must be matched against the expenses incurred in earning it**.

Worked example: Accrual basis

Emma purchases 20 T-shirts in her first month of trading (May) at a cost of £5 each on credit. She sells all of them on credit for £10 each. Emma has therefore made a profit of £100, by matching the income (£200) earned against the cost (£100) of acquiring them.

If, however, Emma only sells 18 T-shirts, it is incorrect to charge her income statement with the cost of 20 T-shirts, as she still has two T-shirts in hand. If she sells them in June, she is likely to make a profit on the sale. Therefore, only the purchase cost of 18 T-shirts (£90) should be matched with her sales income (£180), leaving her with a profit of £90.

Her statement of financial position will look like this at the end of May.

	£
Assets	
Inventory (two T-shirts at cost, ie 2 × £5)	10
Receivables (18 × £10)	180
	190
Capital and liabilities	
Proprietor's capital (profit for the period)	90
Payables (20 × £5)	100
	190

However, if Emma had decided to give up selling T-shirts at the end of May, then the going concern assumption would no longer apply and the two T-shirts in the statement of financial position should be at their break up valuation, not cost. Similarly, if the two unsold T-shirts are unlikely to be sold at more than their cost of £5 each (say, because of damage or a fall in demand) then they should be recorded on the statement of financial position at their **net realisable value** (ie the likely eventual sales price less any expenses incurred to make them saleable) rather than cost.

In this example, the concepts of **going concern and accrual are linked**. Since the business is assumed to be a going concern, it is possible to carry forward the cost of the unsold T-shirts as a charge against profits of the next period.

5.4 Consistency of presentation (IAS 1 (revised))

To maintain consistency, the presentation and classification of items in the financial statements should **stay the same from one period to the next**, unless:

* There is a significant change in the **nature of the operations,** or a review of the financial statements indicates a **more appropriate presentation.**

* A change in presentation is **required by an IAS.**

By having consistent presentation the **comparability** of financial statements is enhanced, both over a period of time, and also between different companies.

5.5 Materiality and aggregation (IAS 1 (revised))

Definition

Material: Omissions or misstatements of items are material if they could, individually or collectively, influence the economic decisions of users taken on the basis of the financial statements. **Materiality** depends on the size and nature of the omission or misstatement judged in the surrounding circumstances. The size or the nature of an item, or a combination of both, could be the determining factor.

Each **material class of similar items** shall be presented **separately** in the financial statements. Items of a dissimilar nature or function shall be presented separately unless they are immaterial.

A specific disclosure requirement in an IAS need **not** be satisfied if the information is immaterial.

The *Conceptual Framework* links materiality particularly to the qualitative characteristic of **relevance**.

Financial statements result from processing large numbers of transactions or other events that are then **aggregated** into classes according to their nature or function, such as 'revenue', 'purchases', 'trade receivables' and 'trade payables'. The final stage in the process of aggregation and classification is the presentation of condensed and classified items on the face of the statement of financial position or income statement. If an item is not individually material it is aggregated with other items on the face of financial statements, though it may be separately classified in the notes.

There is no absolute measure of materiality. In relation to **materiality by size** it is common to apply a convenient rule of thumb (for example material items are those with a value greater than 5% of net profits). However some items are regarded as particularly sensitive and therefore as being **material by nature**. Even a very small misstatement of such an item is taken as a material error; an example is the amount of remuneration paid to directors of a company.

5.6 The business entity concept

This concept has already been discussed in the context of the **separate entity principle**: that accountants regard a business as a separate entity, distinct from its owners or managers. The concept applies whether the business is a limited liability company (and so recognised in law as a separate entity), a sole trader or a partnership (in which case the business is not legally recognised as separate from its owners).

5.7 The historical cost convention

A basic principle of accounting is that the monetary amount at which **items are normally measured in financial statements is at historical cost**, ie at the amount which the business paid to acquire them. An important advantage of this concept is that the objectivity of financial statements is maximised: there is usually a **source document** to prove the amount paid to purchase an asset or pay an expense.

Definition

Historical cost: Transactions are recorded at their cost when they occurred.

It is easier to deal with costs when measuring items, rather than with 'values', as valuations tend to be subjective and to vary according to what the valuation is for.

Worked example: Cost or valuation

A company acquires a machine to manufacture its products. The company expects to use the machine for four years. At the end of two years the company is preparing a statement of financial position and has to decide what monetary amount to give the machine (the *Framework* refers to this process as 'measurement').

Numerous possibilities can be considered.

- The original cost (historical cost) of the machine

- Half of the historical cost, on the ground that half of its useful life has expired

- The amount the machine might fetch on the secondhand market (**realisable value**)

- The amount needed to replace the machine with an identical machine (**replacement cost**)

- The amount needed to replace the machine with a more modern machine incorporating the technological advances of the previous two years

- The machine's economic value, ie the amount of the profits it is expected to generate for the company during its remaining life (**present value**)

All of these valuations have something to commend them, but the great advantage of the first two is that they are based on a figure (the machine's historical cost) which is **objectively verifiable**.

There are many problems associated with the use of historical cost valuations but these are outside the scope of the *Accounting* syllabus.

Interactive question 4: Accounting concepts   [Difficulty level: Intermediate]

(a) Your office equipment will be used, on average, for five years, so you charge 20% of its cost as depreciation each year in your income statement . This year your business profitability is down and you think you can squeeze an extra year's life out of your equipment. Is it acceptable not to make any charge this year?

(b) You have recently paid £4.95 for a waste paper bin which should be used for about five years. Should you treat it as a non-current asset?

See **Answer** at the end of this chapter.

6 Capital and revenue items

Section overview

- Capital and revenue income and expenditure must be distinguished from each other.

6.1 Capital and revenue expenditure

Definition

Capital expenditure: Expenditure which results in the acquisition of long-term assets, or an improvement or enhancement of their earning capacity.

Long-term assets are those which will be kept in the entity for more than one year.

- Capital expenditure is not charged as an expense in the income statement (although a '**depreciation**' charge will usually be made to write off the capital expenditure gradually over time; depreciation expense is shown in the income statement).

- Capital expenditure on long-term assets appears in the statement of financial position.

Definition

Revenue expenditure: Expenditure which is incurred either

- For **trade purposes**. This includes purchases of raw materials or items for resale, expenditure on wages and salaries, selling and distribution expenses, administrative expenses and finance costs, or

- To maintain the **existing earning capacity** of long-term assets.

Revenue expenditure is charged to the income statement of a period, provided that it relates to the trading activity and sales of that particular period.

Worked example: Revenue expenditure

If a business buys ten steel bars for £200 (£20 each) and sells eight of them during a reporting period, it will have two steel bars left at the end of the period. The full £200 is revenue expenditure but only £160 is the cost of the goods sold during the period. The remaining £40 (cost of two units) will be included in the statement of financial position as 'inventory' valued at £40.

Worked example: Capital expenditure

A business purchases a building for £300,000. It then adds an extension to the building at a cost of £100,000. After a few months the building needs to have a few broken windows mended, its floors polished and some missing roof tiles replaced. These cleaning and maintenance jobs cost £900.

In this example, the original purchase (£300,000) and the cost of the extension (£100,000) are **capital expenditure**, because they are incurred to acquire and then improve a long-term asset. The other costs of £900 are **revenue expenditure**, because these merely maintain the building and thus its 'earning capacity'.

Capital expenditure can include costs incurred in bringing a long-term asset to its final condition and location, such as legal fees, duties and carriage costs borne by the asset's purchaser, plus installation costs. Repair, maintenance and staff costs in relation to long-term assets are **revenue expenditure**.

6.2 Capital income and revenue income

Definition

Capital income: Proceeds from the sale of non current assets.

The profits (or losses) from the sale of long-term assets are included in the income statement for the reporting period in which the sale takes place. For instance, the business may sell machinery or property which it no longer needs.

Definition

Revenue income: Income derived from

- The sale of trading assets, such as goods held in inventory
- The provision of services
- Interest and dividends received from business investments

6.3 Capital transactions

The categorisation of capital and revenue items given above does not mention raising **additional funds from the owner(s) of the business**, or raising and repaying **loans**.

- These transactions add to the cash assets of the business and create corresponding capital or liabilities (loans).

- When a loan is repaid, it reduces the liabilities (loan) and the assets (cash).

None of these transactions would be reported through the income statement.

6.4 Why is the distinction between capital and revenue items important?

Calculating profit for any reporting period depends on the correct and consistent **classification** of revenue or capital items. You must get used to the terminology here as these words appear in the accounting and financial reporting standards themselves.

Interactive question 5: Capital or revenue? [Difficulty level: Intermediate]

State whether each of the following items should be classified as 'capital' or 'revenue' expenditure or income.

(a) The purchase of a property (eg an office building)

(b) Property depreciation

(c) Solicitors' fees in connection with the purchase of property

(d) The costs of adding extra memory to a computer

(e) Computer repairs and maintenance costs

(f) Profit on the sale of an office building

(g) Revenue from sales paid for by credit card

(h) The cost of new machinery

(i) Customs duty charged on machinery when imported into the country

(j) The 'carriage' costs of transporting the new machinery from the supplier's factory to the premises of the business purchasing it

(k) The cost of installing the new machinery in the premises of the business

(l) The wages of the machine operators

See **Answer** at the end of this chapter.

Summary

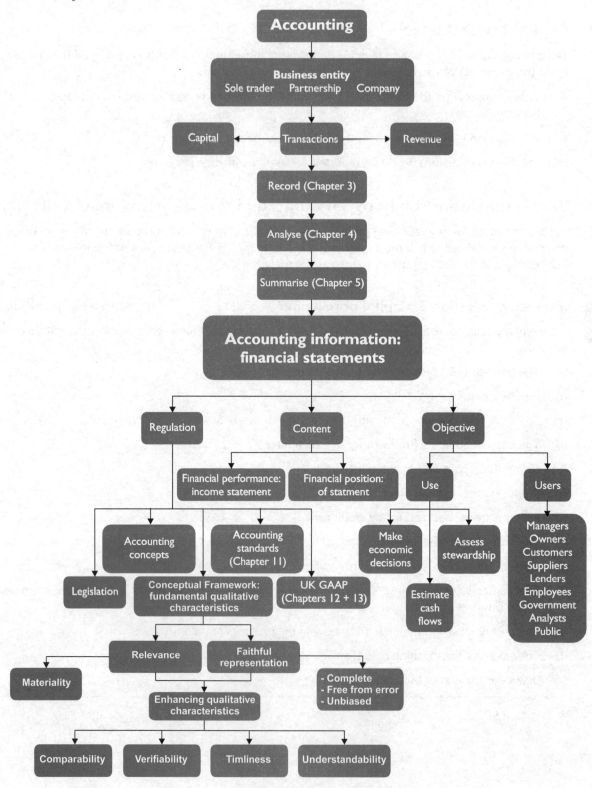

Self-test

Answer the following questions.

1   An entity's transactions are recorded first in

   A   Books of original entry
   B   Ledger accounts
   C   The income statement
   D   The statement of financial position

2   Liability for the debts of the business does **not** fall on

   A   A sole trader
   B   Partners in a general partnership
   C   A limited liability company
   D   Owners of a limited liability company

3   According to IAS 1 (revised) which of the following does **not** represent an objective of financial statements?

   A   To provide information to investors in making economic decisions
   B   To provide information to managers in making business decisions
   C   To show the results of management's stewardship of the resources entrusted to it
   D   To help users predict the entity's future cash flows

4   Which one of the following issues in an entity's financial statements is likely to be of most interest to an entity's lender?

   A   Whether the entity has paid a dividend
   B   Whether the entity will repay a loan when it falls due
   C   Whether the entity will continue to be able to employ people
   D   Whether the entity patronises local suppliers

5   A statement of financial position is best described as:

   A   A snapshot of the entity's financial position at a particular point in time
   B   A record of an entity's financial performance over a period of time
   C   A list of all the income and expenses of the entity at a particular point in time
   D   A list of all the assets and liabilities of the entity over a period of time

6   In applying fundamental accounting concepts the preparers of financial information are also using

   A   Legislation
   B   Accounting standards
   C   Judgement
   D   Financial reporting standards

7   Which of the following is **not** a source of the accounting rules embodied in UK GAAP?

   A   The Companies Act 2006
   B   UK accounting standards
   C   Listing requirements of the London Stock Exchange
   D   Accounting requirements of an entity's US parent company

8   Which of the following factors have **not** influenced financial reporting?

   A   National legislation
   B   Economic factors
   C   Accounting standards
   D   GAAP

9   Materiality is an entity-specific aspect of which qualitative characteristic?

    A   Relevance
    B   Understandability
    C   Faithful representation
    D   Comparability

10   Which of the following is an item of capital expenditure?

    A   Cost of goods sold
    B   Purchase of a machine
    C   Repairs to a machine
    D   Wages cost

Now, go back to the Learning Objectives in the Introduction. If you are satisfied that you have achieved these objectives, please tick them off.

1 The purpose of accounting information

- The objective of general purpose financial reporting is to provide financial information about the reporting entity that is useful to existing and potential investors, lenders and other creditors in making decisions about providing resources to the entity.

  Conceptual Framework Para OB2

- To provide information about the financial position, performance and cash flows of an entity that is useful to a wide range of users in making economic decisions

  IAS 1 (revised) para 9

- To show the results of management's stewardship of the resources entrusted to it

  IAS 1 (revised) para 9

- Assists users of the financial statements in predicting the entity's future cash flows and, in particular, their timing and certainty

  IAS 1 (revised) para 9

2 The main financial statements

- Information about the nature and amounts of an entity's economic resources and claims can help users to assess the entity's liquidity and solvency, its need for additional financing and how successful the entity is likely to be in obtaining that financing

  Conceptual Framework para OB13

- Information about a reporting entity's financial performance is needed by users to understand the return that the entity has produced on its economic resources. Information about the return the entity has produced provides an indication of how well management has discharged its responsibilities to make efficient and effective use of the reporting entity's resources. Information about the variability and components of that return is also important, especially in assessing the uncertainty of future cash flows.

  Conceptual Framework para OB16

3 The regulation of accounting

- A statement of financial position, an statement of comprehensive income, a statement of changes in equity, a statement of cash flows, notes and (in certain circumstances) a revised statement of financial position from an earlier period

  IAS 1 (revised) para 10

  IAS 1 (revised) para 15;

- Fair presentation/faithful representation

  Conceptual Framework paras QC12 - QC16

4 The qualitative characteristics of useful financial information

- Fundamental qualitative characteristics: relevance and faithful representation

- Enhancing qualitative characteristics: comparability, verifiability, timeliness and understandability.

  Conceptual Framework paras QC6-QC34

5 Objectives and scope of IAS 1 (revised)

- To prescribe the basis for presentation of general purpose financial statements, to ensure comparability both with the entity's financial statements of previous periods and with the financial statements of other entities

  IAS 1 (revised) para 1

- To be applied to all general purpose financial statements prepared and presented in accordance with International Financial Reporting Standards (IFRSs)

  IAS 1 (revised) para 2

- General purpose financial statements are those intended to meet the needs of users who are not in a position to demand reports tailored to meet their particular information needs

  IAS 1 (revised) para 7

6   The purpose of financial statements

- To provide information about the financial position, performance and cash flows of an entity that is useful to a wide range of users in making economic decisions

  IAS 1 (revised) para 9

  - To show the results of management's stewardship of the resources entrusted to it

  - To assist users in predicting the entity's future cash flows and, in particular, their timing and certainty

  - To provide information about the entity's assets, liabilities, equity, income and expenses (including gains and losses), other changes in equity and cash flows

7   Components of financial statements

- A statement of financial position at the end of the reporting period, an income statement, an accounting policies note, a statement of changes in equity, a statement of cash flows, explanatory notes and a statement of financial position at an earlier date where there has been retrospective application, retrospective restatement or reclassification

  IAS 1 (revised) para 10

8   Fair presentation (IAS 1 (revised))

- The faithful representation of the effects of transactions, other events and conditions in accordance with the definitions and recognition criteria in the *Framework*. The application of IASs, with additional disclosure when necessary, is presumed to result in financial statements that achieve a fair presentation.

  IAS 1 (revised) para 15

- Compliance with IASs must be explicit and complete

  IAS 1 (revised) para 16

- For there to be fair presentation:

  IAS 1 (revised) para 17

  - Accounting policies must be selected and applied

  - Information must be presented in a manner which provides relevant, reliable, comparable and understandable information

  - To enable users to understand the impact of particular transactions, events and conditions on the entity's financial position and performance additional disclosures may be required

- Use of an inappropriate accounting treatment cannot be rectified either by disclosure of accounting policies or notes/explanatory material

  IAS 1 (revised) para 18

- In some circumstances departure from the IASs may be required to achieve a fair presentation

  IAS 1 (revised) para 23

9   Underlying assumptions

- Financial statements shall be prepared on a **going concern** basis unless management either intends to liquidate the entity or to cease trading, or has no realistic alternative but to do so. Assessment of whether the going concern assumption is appropriate must take into account all available information for at least 12 months from the end of the reporting period. Any uncertainty must be disclosed.

  IAS 1 (revised) para 25 and 26

- An entity should prepare its financial statements using the **accrual basis** of accounting, recognising the elements of financial statements in line with the *Framework*

  IAS 1 (revised) para 27 and 28

- To maintain **consistency**, the presentation and classification of items in the financial statements should stay the same from one period to the next, unless there is significant change in the nature of the operations, or a review of the financial statements indicates a more appropriate presentation, or a change in presentation is required by an IAS

  IAS 1 (revised) para 45

- Omissions or misstatements of items are material if they could, individually or collectively, influence the economic decisions of users taken on the basis of the financial statements. **Materiality** depends on the size and nature of the omission or misstatement judged in the surrounding circumstances. The size or the nature of an item, or a combination of both, could be the determining factor

IAS 1 (revised)
para 7

- Each material class of similar items shall be presented separately in the financial statements. Items of a dissimilar nature or function shall be presented separately unless they are immaterial, but a specific disclosure requirement in an IAS need not be satisfied if the information is immaterial

IAS 1 (revised)
para 29 and 31

Answer to Interactive question 1

Limited liability companies (though not other forms of business such as general partnerships) are required to make certain accounting information public. This is done by filing information centrally, as a Companies Act 2006 requirement.

Answer to Interactive question 2

The firm may have relatively little in the form of things you can touch, perhaps a building, desks and chairs. If you simply drew up a statement of financial position showing the cost of the things owned, then the business would not seem to be worth much, yet its income earning potential might be high. This is true of many service organisations where the people are among the most valuable assets, but justifying their exact value is extremely problematic.

Answer to Interactive question 3

(a) If the business is to be closed down, the remaining three machines must be valued at the amount they will realise in a forced sale, ie 3 × £60 = £180.

(b) If the business is regarded as a going concern, the machines unsold at 31 December will be valued as an asset at cost, 3 × £100 = £300.

Answer to Interactive question 4

(a) No, because of the need for consistency. Once the depreciation policy has been established, it should not be changed without good cause.

(b) No, because of the materiality concept. The cost of the bin is very small. Rather than cluttering up the statement of financial position for five years, treat the £4.95 as an expense in this year's income statement.

Answer to Interactive question 5

(a) Capital expenditure

(b) Depreciation is revenue expenditure

(c) Legal fees associated with purchasing a property may be added to the purchase price and classified as capital expenditure

(d) Capital expenditure (enhancing an existing long-term asset)

(e) Revenue expenditure (restoring an existing long-term asset)

(f) Capital income (net of the costs of sale)

(g) Revenue income

(h) Capital expenditure

(i) If customs duties are borne by the purchaser of the long-term asset, they should be added to the purchase cost of the machinery and classified as capital expenditure

(j) If carriage costs are paid for by the purchaser of the long-term asset, they should be included in the cost of the long-term asset and classified as capital expenditure

(k) Installation fees of a long-term asset are also added to cost and classified as capital expenditure

(l) Revenue expenditure

1 A Books of original entry form the primary record of transactions. These are analysed and posted to the ledger accounts and summarised in the financial statements, including the income statement and the statement of financial position

2 D Sole traders and partners bear full liability for the debts of the business entity, as does a limited liability company itself. The liability of the shareholders or owners for the debts of a company is, however, limited

3 B IAS 1 (revised) identifies A, C and D as an objective The use of accounting information by managers in making business decisions is not identified as an objective.

4 B A is of interest to investors; C is of interest to employees, D is of interest to suppliers.

5 A A statement of financial position is a list of assets and liabilities which represent the entity's financial position at a particular point in time. D is wrong because it refers to 'a period of time'; C refers to income and expenses, not assets and liabilities; B defines the income statement

6 C Many figures in financial statements are derived from the application of judgement in putting fundamental accounting concepts into practice

7 D UK GAAP relates to *generally* accepted accounting practice; the rules applied as a result of internal requirements can therefore not be part of GAAP

8 B Economic factors do not influence the development of financial reporting; all the others do (see section 3)

9 A Information is material if omitting or misstating it could influence the decisions of the users. If information is deemed material then it is relevant to the users. The *Conceptual Framework* states that materiality is an entity-specific aspect of relevance.

10 B This results in the acquisition of a long-term asset. All the others are revenue expenditure

CHAPTER 2

The accounting equation

Introduction

Examination context

Topic List

Summary and Self-test

Technical reference

Answers to Interactive questions

Answers to Self-test

Introduction

Learning objectives

- Record and account for transactions and events resulting in income, expenses, assets, liabilities and capital in accordance with the appropriate basis of accounting and the laws, regulations and accounting standards applicable to the financial statements

- Identify the main components of a set of financial statements and specify their purpose and interrelationship

Specific syllabus learning outcomes are: 1c, 3a

Syllabus links

The material in this chapter will be developed further in this paper, and then in the Financial Accounting and Financial Reporting papers later in the Professional stage.

Examination context

Questions on the topics in this chapter will be set as multiple choice questions, some of which may involve calculations so that the correct answer can be selected.

In the exam you may be required to:

- Identify and manipulate the accounting equation

- Specify transactions affecting the elements of financial statements: assets, liabilities, capital, income and expenditure

1 Assets, liabilities and the business entity concept

Section overview

- An asset is a resource controlled by the entity as a result of past events from which future economic benefits are expected to flow.

- Assets may be held for the long-term (non-current assets) or for the short term as trading assets (current assets).

- A liability is a present obligation arising from past events, the settlement of which is expected to result in an outflow of resources from the business embodying economic benefits.

- Liabilities may be current or non-current.

- A business entity is a separate entity from its owners from an accounting point of view, whatever the legal position may be.

1.1 Assets and liabilities

Definition

Asset: The *Conceptual Framework* states that an asset is a resource controlled by the entity as a result of past events from which future economic benefits are expected to flow to the entity. **Assets are key elements of financial statements**.

Examples of assets:

- **Land and buildings:** factories, office buildings, storage and distribution centres (warehouses)

- **Motor vehicles**

- **Plant and machinery**

- **Fixtures and fittings:** computer equipment, office furniture and shelving

- **Cash:** in a bank account or held as notes and coins

- **Inventory:** goods held in store awaiting sale to customers, and raw materials and components held in store by a manufacturing business for use in production

- **Receivables (or debtors):** amounts owed by customers and others to the entity

Some assets are held and used in operations for a long time. An office building is occupied by administrative staff for years; similarly, a machine has a productive life of many years before it wears out. These are long-term or **non-current assets**.

Other assets are held for only a short time. A newsagent, for example, has to sell his newspapers on the same day that he gets them. The quicker a business sells goods, the more profit it is likely to make, provided, of course, that the goods are sold at a higher price than what it cost the business to acquire them. Short-term assets are called **current assets**.

Definition

Liability: The *Conceptual Framework* states that a liability is a present obligation arising from past events, the settlement of which is expected to result in an outflow from the entity of resources embodying economic benefits. **Liabilities are key elements of financial statements**.

Examples of liabilities:

- A **bank loan** or **overdraft**. The liability is the amount eventually repaid to the bank.

- **Payables (or creditors)**: amounts owed to suppliers for goods purchased but not yet paid for (purchases 'on credit'). For example, a boatbuilder buys some timber on credit from a timber merchant, so that the boatbuilder does not pay for the timber until some time after it has been delivered. Until the boatbuilder pays what he owes, the timber merchant is a creditor for the amount owed.

- **Taxation** owed to the government. A business pays tax on its profits but there is a gap in time between when a business declares its profits (and becomes liable to pay tax) and the payment date.

1.1.1 A note on terminology in this Study Manual

For most of this Study Manual we shall be employing the terminology used in IASs. Financial statements prepared under UK GAAP (for most sole traders and partnerships, and for many smaller companies) use different terminology as follows:

IAS term	UK GAAP term
Non-current asset	Fixed asset
Inventory	Stock
Receivables	Debtors
Payables	Creditors
Statement of financial position	Balance sheet
Income statement	Profit and loss account

To make explanations of basic accounting straightforward, we shall use some sole traders in examples using international terminology. In Chapter 13 however we shall show a set of sole trader financial statements using the UK GAAP format that is currently more likely to apply to sole traders in practice.

1.2 The business as a separate entity

You may have wondered whether an intangible entity, such as a business, can own assets or have liabilities in its own name. There are two aspects to this question: the **strict legal position** and the **convention adopted by accountants**.

Many businesses are carried on in the form of **limited liability companies**. The owners of a limited company are its shareholders, who may be few in number (as with a small, family owned company) or very numerous (as with a large public company whose shares are listed on a stock exchange).

The law recognises a **company as a legal entity**, quite separate from its owners. A company may, in its own name, acquire assets, incur debts, and enter into contracts. If a company's assets became insufficient to meet its liabilities, the company as a separate entity becomes 'insolvent'. However, the owners of the company are not usually required to pay the debts from their own private resources: the debts are not debts of the owners, but of the company.

The case is different when a business is carried on by an individual (a sole trader). There is **no legal separation** between a **sole trader** and the business he/she runs. In most **partnerships–**, there is also no legal distinction.

 Worked example: Sole trader

Rodney Quiff starts business as a hairdresser, trading under the business name 'Quiff's Hair Salon'. The law recognises no distinction between Rodney Quiff, the individual, and the business known as 'Quiff's Hair Salon'. Any debts of the business which cannot be met from business assets must be met from Rodney's personal resources.

However in **accounting, any business is treated as a separate entity from its owner(s)**. This applies whether or not the business is recognised in law as a separate entity, ie it applies whether the business is carried on by a company or by a sole trader. This is known as the **business entity concept** (or separate entity concept, or just entity concept).

Definition

Business entity concept: A business is a separate entity from its owner.

Although this may seem illogical and unrealistic you must try to appreciate it, as it is the basis of a fundamental rule of accounting, which is that the **liabilities** plus the **capital** of the business must always equal its **assets**. We will look at this rule in more detail later in this chapter, but a simple example now will clarify the idea of a business as a separate entity from its owners.

Worked example: The business as a separate entity

On 1 July 20X6, Liza Doolittle opened a flower stall. She had saved up £2,500 and opened a business bank account with this amount.

When the business commences, an accountant's picture can be drawn of what it **owns** and what it **owes**. The business begins by owning the cash that Liza has put into it, £2,500.

The business is a separate entity in accounting terms. It has obtained assets, in this example cash, from Liza Doolittle. It therefore **owes this amount of money to Liza**. If Liza changed her mind and decided not to go into business, the business would be dissolved by the 'repayment' of cash to Liza.

The amount owed by a business to its owners is known as (equity) **capital**.

Definition

Capital: The *Conceptual Framework* states that capital (which it calls **equity** in the context of a company, as we shall see in Chapter 11) is the residual interest in the assets of the entity after deducting all its liabilities. **Equity is a key element of financial statements**.

2 The accounting equation

Section overview

- The basic accounting equation states that assets = capital + liabilities.
- Capital is the amount that the entity owes to its owners.

2.1 What is the accounting equation?

Definition

Accounting equation: ASSETS = CAPITAL + LIABILITIES.

We will use an example to illustrate the **accounting equation**, ie the rule that the assets of a business will at all times equal its liabilities plus capital. This is also known as the **balance sheet equation**.

2.2 Assets = capital + liabilities

Worked example: Assets = capital

The business began by owning the **cash** that Liza has put into it, £2,500. The business is a separate entity in accounting terms and so it owes the money to Liza as **capital**.

In accounting, **capital** is an investment of money (funds) with the intention of earning a return. A business owner invests capital with the intention of earning **profit**. As long as that money is invested, accountants will treat the capital as money owed to the owner by the business.

When Liza Doolittle sets up her business:

	£
Cash at bank	2,500
Capital invested	2,500

We can express Liza's initial accounting equation as follows:

For Liza Doolittle, as at 1 July 20X6:

Assets	=	Capital	+	Liabilities
£2,500 (cash at bank)	=	£2,500	+	£0

Worked example: Different types of asset = capital

Liza purchases a market stall from Len Turnip for £1,800.

She also purchases some flowers from a trader in the wholesale market, at a cost of £650.

This leaves £50 in cash, after paying for the stall and goods for resale, out of the original £2,500. Liza keeps £30 in the bank and holds £20 in small change for trading. She is now ready for her first day of market trading on 3 July 20X6.

The assets and liabilities of the business have now altered, and at 3 July, before trading begins, the state of her business is as follows.

Assets		=	Capital	+	Liabilities
	£				
Stall	1,800	=	£2,500	+	£0
Flowers	650				
Cash at bank	30				
Cash in hand	20				
	2,500				

The stall and the flowers are physical items, but they must be given a money value. This money value is usually what they cost the business (called **historical cost** in accounting terms).

Definition

Historical cost: Transactions are recorded at their cost when they were incurred.

2.3 Where do profits/losses fit into the accounting equation?

Worked example: Assets = capital + profit

On 3 July Liza sells all her flowers for £900 cash.

Since Liza has sold goods costing £650 to earn income of £900, we can say that she has **earned a profit of £250 on the day's trading**.

Profits are added to the owner's capital. In this case, the £250 belongs to Liza Doolittle. However, so long as the business retains the profits and does not pay anything out to its owner, the **retained profits** are accounted for as an **addition to the owner's capital**.

Assets		=	Capital		+	Liabilities
	£			£		
Stall	1,800		Original investment	2,500		
Flowers	0					
Cash in hand and at			Retained profit			
bank (30+20+900)	950		(900–650)	250		
	2,750			2,750	+	£0

We can re arrange the accounting equation to help us to calculate the capital balance.

Assets – liabilities (net assets) = Capital

At the beginning and end of 3 July 20X6, Liza Doolittle's financial position was as follows.

		Net assets	=	Capital
(a)	At the beginning of the day:	£(2,500 – 0) = £2,500		£2,500
(b)	At the end of the day:	£(2,750 – 0) = £2,750		£2,750

There has been an increase of £250 in net assets, which is the amount of profit earned during the day.

Definitions

Profit: The excess of income over expenses.

Loss: The excess of expenses over income.

Income: Increases in economic benefits over a period in the form of inflows or increases of assets, or decreases of liabilities, resulting in increases in equity/capital (*Conceptual Framework*). It can include both revenue and gains. **Income is a key element of financial statements**.

Expenses: Decreases in economic benefits over a period in the form of outflows or depletion of assets, or increases in liabilities, resulting in decreases in equity/capital (*Conceptual Framework*). **Expense is a key element of financial statements**.

Thus: **Profits** are **added** to owner's capital
        Losses are **deducted** from owner's capital

Note that the *Conceptual Framework* identifies **income** and **expenses**, and **assets, liabilities** and **equity**, as the **elements of financial statements**. Each element represents a class of transactions or other events that are grouped together according to their economic characteristics.

2.4 Appropriation of profits: sole trader drawings

The owner of a sole tradership does not get paid a wage; they '**draw out**' or **appropriate** some of their capital as drawings.

Definition

Drawings: Money and goods taken out of a business by its owner.

Worked example: Assets = capital + profit − drawings

Business owners, like everyone else, need income for living expenses. Liza therefore decides to pay herself £180 in 'wages'.

The payment of £180 is regarded by Liza as a fair reward for her day's work and she might think of the sum as 'wages'. However, the £180 she draws is not an expense to be deducted in arriving at the figure of net profit because any amounts paid by a business to its owner are treated by accountants as **withdrawals or appropriations of profit** and **not as expenses** incurred by the business. In the case of Liza's business, the true position is:

	£
Net profit earned by the business	250
Less profit withdrawn by Liza	(180)
Net profit **retained** in the business	70

Profits are capital as long as they are retained in the business. Once they are **appropriated,** the business suffers a reduction in capital.

The withdrawals of profit are taken in cash, and so the business loses £180 of its cash assets. After the withdrawal has been made, the accounting equation would be restated.

(a)

Assets		=	Capital		+	Liabilities
	£			£		
Stall	1,800		Original investment	2,500		
Goods	0		Retained profit			
Cash (950 − 180)	770		(250 − 180)	70		
	2,570			2,570	+	£0

(b) Alternatively

Net assets		=	Capital
£(2,570 − 0)		=	£2,570

The increase in net assets since trading operations began is now only £(2,570 − 2,500) = £70, which is the amount of the retained profits.

Worked example: Assets = capital

On 10 July Liza purchases flowers for cash, at a cost of £740. She decides to employ her cousin Ethel for a wage of £40 for the day.

On 10 July Liza and Ethel sold all their flowers for £1,100 cash. Liza paid Ethel £40 and drew out £200 for herself.

After the purchase of the goods for £740 the accounting equation is:

Assets		=	Capital		+	Liabilities
	£					
Stall	1,800					
Flowers	740					
Cash (770 − 740)	30					
	2,570	=		£2,570	+	£0

On 10 July, all the flowers are sold for £1,100 cash, and Ethel is paid £40. The profit for the day is calculated as follows:

	£	£
Sales		1,100
Less cost of goods sold	740	
Ethel's wage	40	
		(780)
Profit		320

Assets		=	Capital		+	Liabilities	
	£			£			
Stall	1,800		At beginning of 10 July	2,570			
Flowers	0		Profits earned on				
Cash (30 + 1,100 – 40)	1,090		10 July	320			
	2,890	=		2,890	+		£0

After Liza has withdrawn £200 in cash, retained profits will be only £(320 – 200) = £120.

Assets		=	Capital		+	Liabilities	
	£			£			
Stall	1,800		At beginning of 10 July	2,570			
Flowers	0		Retained profits for				
Cash (1,090 – 200)	890		10 July	120			
	2,690	=		2,690	+		£0

Interactive question 1: Capital   [Difficulty level: Easy]

Fill in the missing words.

Capital = ... less ....

See **Answer** at the end of this chapter.

3 Credit transactions

Section overview

- A creditor is any person to whom the entity owes money.

- A trade payable is a creditor which has arisen following a purchase on credit by the entity.

- A trade payable is a liability of the entity.

- A debtor is any person who owes money to the entity.

- A trade receivable is a debtor that has arisen following a sale on credit by the entity.

- A trade receivable is an asset of the entity.

- The matching or accruals concept requires that income is matched with the expenses incurred in earning it. This concept is the reason why we account for credit transactions before they are realised in the form of cash.

3.1 Trade payables (creditors)

Definition

Creditor: Person to whom a business owes money.

A **trade creditor** is a person to whom a business owes money for trading debts. In the accounts of a business, debts still outstanding which arise from the purchase from suppliers of materials, components or goods for resale are called **trade payables**.

A business does not always pay immediately for goods or services it buys. It is common business practice to make credit purchases, with a promise to pay within 30/60/90 days, of the date of the bill or 'invoice' for the goods. For example, A buys goods costing £2,000 on credit from B, B sends A an invoice for £2,000, dated 1 March, with credit terms that payment must be made within 30 days. If A then delays payment until 31 March, B will be a creditor of A between 1 and 31 March for £2,000. From A's point of view, the amount owed to B is a **trade payable.**

A trade payable is a **liability** of a business. When the debt is finally paid, the trade payable 'disappears' as a liability and the balance of cash at bank and in-hand decreases.

3.2 Trade receivables (debtors)

Definition

Debtor: Person who owes money to the business.

Suppose that C sells goods on credit to D for £6,000 on terms that the debt must be settled within two months of the invoice date, 1 October. D will be a debtor of C for £6,000 from 1 October until the date payment is made. In the accounts of the business, amounts owed by debtors are called **trade receivables**.

A debtor is an **asset** of a business. When the debt is finally paid, the debtor 'disappears' as an asset, to be replaced by 'cash at bank and in hand'.

Worked example: Assets = capital + liabilities

Look at the consequences of the following transactions in the week to 17 July 20X6. (See Worked example: Assets = capital for the situation as at the end of 10 July.)

(a) Liza Doolittle realises that she is going to need more money in the business and so she makes the following arrangements.

    (i) She invests a further £250 of her own capital.

    (ii) She persuades her Uncle Henry to lend her £500. Uncle Henry tells her that she can repay the loan whenever she likes, but in the meantime, she must pay him interest of £5 each week at the end of the market day. They agree that it will probably be quite a long time before the loan is eventually repaid.

(b) She decides to buy a van to pick up flowers from her supplier and bring them to her market stall. She finds a car dealer, Laurie Loader, who agrees to sell her a van on credit for £700. Liza agrees to pay for the van after 30 days' trial use.

(c) During the week, Liza's Uncle George telephones her to ask whether she would sell him some garden furniture. Liza tells him that she will look for a supplier. She buys what Uncle George has asked for, paying £300 in cash. Uncle George accepts delivery of the goods and agrees to pay £350, but he asks if she can wait until the end of the month for payment. Liza agrees.

(d) Liza buys flowers costing £800. Of these purchases £750 are paid in cash, with the remaining £50 on seven days' credit. Liza decides to use Ethel's services again, at an agreed wage of £40 for the day.

(e) On 17 July, Liza sells all her goods, for £1,250 (cash). She decides to withdraw £240 for her week's work. She also pays Ethel £40 in cash. She decides to make the interest payment to her Uncle Henry the next time she sees him.

(f) There are no van expenses for the week.

Solution

Deal with transactions one at a time in chronological order. (In practice, it is possible to do one set of calculations which combines all transactions.)

(a) **The addition of Liza's extra capital and Uncle Henry's loan**

An investment analyst might call Uncle Henry's loan a capital investment, on the grounds that it will probably be for the long term. Uncle Henry is not the owner of the business, however, even though he has made an investment in it. He would only become an owner if Liza offered him a partnership in the business, and she has not done so. To the business, Uncle Henry is a long term creditor, and it is appropriate to define his investment as a liability and not business capital.

The accounting equation after £(250 + 500) = £750 cash is put into the business will be:

Assets		=	Capital		+	Liabilities	
	£			£			£
Stall	1,800		As at end of 10 July	2,690		Loan	500
Goods	0		Additional capital	250			
Cash (890 + 750)	1,640						
	3,440	=		2,940	+		500

(b) The purchase of the van (cost £700) on credit

Assets		=	Capital		+	Liabilities	
	£			£			£
Stall	1,800		As at end of 10 July	2,690		Loan	500
Van	700		Additional capital	250		Payables	700
Cash	1,640						
	4,140	=		2,940	+		1,200

(c) The sale of goods to Uncle George on credit (£350) which cost the business £300 (cash paid)

Assets		=	Capital		+	Liabilities	
	£			£			£
Stall	1,800		As at end of 10 July	2,690		Loan	500
Van	700		Additional capital	250		Payables	700
Receivable	350		Profit on sale to				
Cash (1,640 – 300)	1,340		Uncle George				
			(350 – 300)	50			
	4,190	=		2,990	+		1,200

(d) After the purchase of goods for the weekly market (£750 paid in cash and £50 of purchases on credit)

Assets		=	Capital		+	Liabilities	
	£			£			£
Stall	1,800		As at end of 10 July	2,690		Loan	500
Van	700		Additional capital	250		Payables	
Goods (750 + 50)	800		Profit on sale to			(van)	700
Receivable	350		Uncle George	50		Payables	
Cash (1,340 – 750)	590					(goods)	50
	4,240	=		2,990	+		1,250

(e) After market trading on 17 July

Goods costing £800 earned income of £1,250 in cash. Ethel's wages were £40 (paid), Uncle Henry's interest charge is £5 (not paid yet) and drawings were £240 (paid). The profit for 17 July may be calculated as follows, taking the full £5 of interest as a cost on that day.

	£	£
Sales		1,250
Cost of goods sold	800	
Wages	40	
Interest	5	
		(845)
Profit earned on market trading on 17 July		405
Profit on sale of goods to Uncle George		50
Profit for the week		455
Drawings		(240)
Retained profit		215

Assets		£	=	Capital		£	+	Liabilities		£
Stall		1,800		As at end of 10 July		2,690		Loan		500
Van		700		Additional capital		250		Payables		
Goods (800 – 800)		0		Profits retained		215		(van)		700
Receivable		350						Payables		
Cash (590 +								(goods)		50
1,250 – 40 – 240)		1,560						Payables		
								(interest		
								payment)		5
		4,410	=			3,155	+			1,255

3.3 Accruals concept

The **accruals** (or matching) **concept** requires that income earned is matched with the expenses incurred in earning it.

In Liza's case, we have 'matched' the income earned with the expenses incurred in earning it. So in part (e), we included all the costs of the goods sold of £800, even though £50 had not yet been paid in cash. Also the interest of £5 was deducted from income, even though it had not yet been paid.

Interactive question 2: The accounting equation   [Difficulty level: Intermediate]

How would each of these transactions affect the accounting equation in terms of increase or decrease in asset, capital or liability?

(a) Purchasing £800 worth of goods on credit
(b) Paying the telephone bill £25
(c) Selling £450 worth of goods for £650
(d) Paying £800 to a supplier

See **Answer** at the end of this chapter.

We shall look now at how the business entity concept and accruals together result in the statement of financial position.

4 The statement of financial position

Section overview

- The statement of financial position shows the entity's financial position at a particular moment in time.

- The statement of financial position represents the accounting equation: assets are in one half and capital and liabilities in the other.

- The more detailed accounting equation, represented in the IAS 1 format for the statement of financial position, states that non-current assets + current assets = capital + profit – losses – drawings + non-current liabilities + current liabilities.

- Net assets = assets – liabilities, therefore net assets = capital.

- A non-current asset is acquired for long term use in the business, with a view to earning profits from its use, either directly or indirectly.

- Non-current assets may be tangible (with a physical reality) or intangible.

- Current assets are either cash or items which are held by the entity to be turned into cash shortly.

- Capital comprises opening capital + capital introduced + profits – losses – drawings of capital/profits taken by the owners.

- Non-current liabilities are payable after one year, such as secured loans.

- Current liabilities are payable within one year, such as trade payables and bank overdrafts.

4.1 What is a statement of financial position?

The business's **statement of financial position** shows its financial position at a given moment in time. It contains three key **elements of financial statements: liabilities, capital and assets** at that moment. It is a 'financial snapshot', since it captures on paper a still image of something which is dynamic and continually changing. Typically, a statement of financial position is prepared at the end of the reporting period to which the financial statements relate.

A statement of financial position is very similar to the accounting equation. In fact, the only **differences between a statement of financial position and an accounting equation** are:

- The manner or **format** in which the liabilities and assets are presented and
- The extra **detail** which is usually contained in a statement of financial position

The details shown in a statement of financial position will not be described in full in this chapter. Instead we will make a start in this chapter and add more detail in later chapters as we go on to look at other ideas and methods in accounting.

A statement of financial position is divided into two halves, and is presented in either of the following ways.

- **Capital and liabilities** in one half and **assets** in the other (the IAS 1 (revised) format that we adopt in this Study Manual)

- **Capital** in one half and **net assets** in the other (the UK GAAP format for the balance sheet that is looked at in Chapters 12 and 13).

Definition

Net assets: Assets less liabilities

In this Study Manual we will follow the assets = capital + liabilities format given by IAS 1 (revised) *Presentation of Financial Statements*.

NAME OF BUSINESS
STATEMENT OF FINANCIAL POSITION AS AT (DATE)

	£
Assets (item by item)	X
Capital	X
Liabilities	X
	X

The total value in one half of the statement of financial position equals the total value in the other half. Since each half of the statement of financial position has an equal value, one side **balances** the other.

Capital, liabilities and assets are usually shown in some detail in a statement of financial position. The following paragraphs describe the sort of detail we might expect to find.

4.2 Capital (sole trader)

The sole trader's capital is usually analysed into its component parts.

	£	£
Capital at the beginning of the reporting period (ie **capital brought forward**)		X
Add additional **capital introduced** during the period		X
		X
Add profit earned during the period (or **less losses** incurred in the period)	X	
Less **drawings**	(X)	
Retained profit for the period		X
Capital as at the end of the reporting period (ie **capital carried forward**)		X

'**Brought forward**' means that the amount is brought forward from the previous period. Similarly, '**carried forward**' means carried forward to the next period. The carried forward amount at the end of one period is therefore the brought forward amount of the next period.

4.2.1 Equity (company)

The capital or equity side of a company's **statement of financial position** is more complicated than a sole trader's. We shall look at it in detail in Chapter 11.

4.3 Liabilities

A distinction is required by IAS 1 (revised) in the statement of financial position between **non-current liabilities** and **current liabilities**.

- **Current liabilities** are debts which are payable within one year
- **Non-current liabilities** are debts which are payable after one year

4.3.1 Non-current liabilities

Definition

Non-current liability: A debt which is not payable within one year. Any liability which is not current must be non-current.

Examples of non-current liabilities:

- **Loans** which are not repayable for more than one year, such as a bank loan or a loan from an individual to a business.

- **Loan stock or debentures.** These are common with limited companies. Loan stocks or debentures are securities issued by a company at a fixed rate of interest. They are repayable on agreed terms by a specified date in the future. Holders of loan stocks are therefore lenders of money to a company. Their interests, including security for the loan, are protected by the terms of a trust deed. If the loan is repayable over several years then the portion repayable within one year is shown as a current liability (see below)

4.3.2 Current liabilities

Definition

Current liabilities: Debts of the business that must be paid within **one year**, or within the entity's normal operating cycle, or that are held to be traded.

Examples of current liabilities:

- **Loans** repayable within **one year**, including the element of a long term loan that is repayable within one year

- A bank **overdraft**, which is usually **repayable on demand**

- **Trade payables** represent suppliers to which the business owes money for goods or services bought on credit as part of the business's trading activities

- **Other payables** are due to anyone else to whom the business owes money, such as HM Revenue and Customs (HMRC) in respect of VAT, pension trustees in respect of pension contributions, and employees in respect of unpaid remuneration, for example sales commissions

- **Taxation payable** to HMRC with respect to corporation tax on the company's profits.

- **Accruals.** These are expenses already incurred by the business, for which no invoice has yet been received, or for which the date of payment has not yet arrived. An example of accrued charges is the cost of gas or electricity used. If a business ends its accounting year on 31 December, but does not expect its next quarterly gas bill until the end of January, there will be two months of accrued gas charges to record in the statement of financial position as a liability. Accruals will be described more fully in Chapter 7.

4.4 Assets

The statement of financial position distinguishes between **non-current assets** and **current assets** (again as required by IAS 1 (revised)).

- **Non-current assets** are acquired for **long-term** use within the business. They are normally valued at cost less accumulated depreciation.

- **Current assets** are expected to be converted into cash within **one year**.

4.4.1 Non-current assets

Definition

Non-current assets: Assets acquired for continuing use within the business, with a view to earning income or making profits from their use, either directly or indirectly, over more than one reporting period.

Non-current assets in the statement of financial position usually comprise:

- **Property, plant and equipment** (ie 'tangible' assets)
- **Intangible non-current assets** such as goodwill
- **Long-term investments**

A non-current asset is not acquired for sale to a customer.

- In a manufacturing industry, a production machine is a non-current asset, because it makes goods which are then sold.

- In a service industry, equipment used by employees giving service to customers is a non-current asset (eg the equipment used in a garage, or furniture in a hotel).

- Less obviously factory premises, office furniture, computer equipment, company cars, delivery vans or pallets in a warehouse are all non-current assets.

To be classed as a non-current asset in the business's statement of financial position, an item must satisfy two further conditions.

- It must be **used by the business**. For example, the owner's own house would not normally appear on the business statement of financial position.

- The asset must have a 'life' in use of **more than one reporting period** or year.

A **tangible non-current asset** is a physical asset that can be touched. All of the examples of non-current assets mentioned above are 'tangible' assets. They are often referred to as **property, plant and equipment**.

Intangible non-current assets are assets which do not have a physical existence; they cannot be 'touched'. An example is a **patent**, which protects an idea, and **goodwill**.

An **investment** can also be a non-current asset. Company A might invest in another company, B, by purchasing some of B's shares. These investments will earn income for A in the form of dividends paid out by B. If the investments are purchased by A with a view to holding on to them for more than one year, they would be classified as non-current assets of A.

In this chapter, we shall restrict our attention to **tangible non-current assets**.

4.4.2 Non-current assets and depreciation

Non-current assets are held and used by a business for a number of years, but they wear out or lose their usefulness in the course of time. Every tangible non-current asset has a limited life. The only exception is **freehold land**, although this too can be exhausted if it is used by extractive industries (eg mining).

The financial statements of a business reflect that the cost of a non-current asset is gradually consumed as the asset wears out. This is done by gradually 'writing off' the asset's cost in the income statement over several reporting periods. For example, in the case of a machine costing £1,000 and expected to wear out after ten years, it is appropriate to reduce the value in the statement of financial position by £100 each year. This process is known as **depreciation**.

If a statement of financial position were drawn up four years after the asset was purchased, the amount of depreciation accumulated over four years would be 4 * £100 = £400. The machine would then appear in the statement of financial position as follows.

	£
Machine at original cost	1,000
Less accumulated depreciation	(400)
Carrying amount *	600

* ie the value of the asset in the books of account, net of accumulated depreciation. After ten years the asset would be fully depreciated and would appear in the statement of financial position with a carrying amount of zero.

The amount that is written off over time does not have to be the full cost of the asset if it is expected to have a resale – or 'residual' – value at the end of its useful life.

Interactive question 3: Residual value　　　　　　　　　　　　[Difficulty level: Exam standard]

Suppose a business buys a car for £10,000. It expects to keep the car for three years and then to sell it for £3,400. How much depreciation should be accounted for in each year of the car's useful life?

See **Answer** at the end of this chapter.

We shall study non-current assets in detail in Chapter 10.

4.4.3 Current assets

Current assets take one of the following forms.

(a) Items owned by the business with the intention of **turning them into cash in a short time**, usually within one year (see the worked example below).

(b) **Cash**, including money in the bank, owned by the business.

These assets are 'current' in the sense that they are continually flowing through the business; they are always realisable in the near future.

Definition

Current asset: An asset is current when it is expected to be realised in, or intended for sale or consumption in, the entity's normal operating cycle, or it is held for being traded, or it is expected to be realised within 12 months of the date of the statement of financial position, or it is cash or a cash equivalent.

Worked example: Current assets

David Wickes runs a business selling cars. He purchases a showroom, which he stocks with cars for sale. He obtains the cars from a manufacturer and pays for them in cash on delivery.

- If he sells a car in a **cash sale**, the goods are immediately converted into cash. The cash can then be used to buy more cars for re sale.

- If he sells a car in a **credit sale**, the car will be given to the customer, who then becomes a trade receivable. Eventually, the customer will pay what they owe and David Wickes will receive cash. Once again, the cash can then be used to buy more cars for re-sale.

Current assets are as follows.

- The cars (goods) held in **inventory** for re-sale are current assets, because David Wickes intends to sell them within one year in the normal course of trade.

- Any **trade and other receivables** are current assets, if they will be paid within the usual cash operating cycle of less than one year.

- **Cash** is a current asset.

Interactive question 4: Asset classification   [Difficulty level: Intermediate]

Identify which of the following assets falls into the non-current category and which should be treated as current. Could any be treated as either?

Asset	Business	Current or non-current
Van	Delivery firm	
Machine	Manufacturing company	
Car	Car trader	
Investment	Any	

See **Answer** at the end of this chapter.

Cars are current assets for David Wickes because he is in the business of buying and selling them, ie he is a car trader. If he also has a car which he keeps and uses for business purposes, this car would be a non-current asset. The distinction between a non-current asset and a current asset is not what the asset is physically, but for what **purpose it is obtained and used** by the business.

There are some other categories of current asset.

- **Short term investments**. These are stocks and shares of other businesses, owned with the intention of selling them in the near future. For example, if a business has a lot of spare cash for a short time, its managers might decide to invest short-term in the stock exchange. The shares will later be sold when the business needs the cash. If share prices rise in the meantime, the business will make a profit from its short term investment. Such shares must be readily realisable (ie easy to sell) to be short-term.

- **Prepayments**. These are amounts of money paid by the business in one reporting period for benefits which have not yet been enjoyed, but which will be enjoyed within the next reporting period. For example, a business pays an annual insurance premium of £240, and the premium is payable annually in advance on 1 December. If the business has an accounting year end of 31 December, it will pay £240 on 1 December but only enjoy one month's insurance cover by the year end. The remaining 11 months' cover (£220 cost, at £20 per month) will be enjoyed in the next year. The prepayment of £220 is shown in the statement of financial position, at 31 December, as a current asset. Prepayments will be described more fully in Chapter 7.

4.4.4 Trade and other receivables

A receivable can be due from **anyone** who owes the business money. For example, if a business makes an insurance claim, the insurance company is a receivable for the money payable on the claim. If the business makes loans to staff to buy rail season tickets, staff are receivables for the amount outstanding.

A distinction can be made between two types of receivable.

- **Trade receivables** represent customers who owe money for goods or services bought on credit in the course of the trading activities of the business.

- **Other receivables** are due from anyone else owing money to the business, such as an insurance company, HMRC for VAT, or employees for season ticket loans.

5 Preparing the statement of financial position

Section overview

- The statement of financial position lists out and totals non-current plus current assets, then it lists out and totals capital plus non-current liabilities plus current liabilities.

5.1 How is a basic statement of financial position prepared?

We shall now look at how the various types of assets and liabilities are shown in a business's statement of financial position (IAS 1 (revised) format). You might like to attempt to prepare it yourself from the information provided before reading the solution which follows.

Worked example: Statement of financial position

Prepare a statement of financial position for Sunken Arches as at 31 December 20X6, given the information below.

	£
Capital as at 1 January 20X6	51,100
Profit for the year to 31 December 20X6	8,000
Premises, carrying amount at 31 December 20X6	50,000
Motor vehicles, carrying amount at 31 December 20X6	9,000
Fixtures and fittings, carrying amount at 31 December 20X6	8,000
Non-current loan	25,000
Bank overdraft *	2,000
Inventories	16,000
Trade receivables	500
Cash in hand *	100
Trade payables	1,200
Drawings	4,000
Accrued costs of rent	600
Prepayment of insurance premium	300

* A shop might have cash in its cash registers, but an overdraft at the bank.

Solution

SUNKEN ARCHES
STATEMENT OF FINANCIAL POSITION AS AT 31 DECEMBER 20X6

	£	£
ASSETS		
Non-current assets		
Property, plant and equipment		
Premises		50,000
Fixtures and fittings		8,000
Motor vehicles		9,000
		67,000
Current assets		
Inventories	16,000	
Trade and other receivables	500	
Prepayments	300	
Cash and cash equivalents	100	
		16,900
Total assets		83,900

	£	£
CAPITAL AND LIABILITIES		
Capital		
As at 1 January 20X6	51,100	
Profit for the year	8,000	
Less drawings	(4,000)	
At 31 December 20X6		55,100
Non-current liabilities		
Long-term borrowings		25,000
Current liabilities		
Short-term borrowings (bank overdraft)	2,000	
Trade and other payables	1,200	
Accrued costs	600	
		3,800
Total capital and liabilities		83,900

The layout is in the preferred format from IAS 1 (revised), adapted for a sole trader, and we will use it throughout this Study Manual, for sole traders as well as companies, until we look at UK GAAP in Chapters 12 and 13.

Interactive question 5: Preparing a statement of financial position 1

[Difficulty level: Intermediate]

You are given the following information about Liza Doolittle at the end of her first full month of trading, 31 July 20X6:

	£
Capital at 1 July 20X6	2,500
Additional capital introduced	250
Profit for the month	3,620
Stall at cost	1,800
Van at cost	700
Drawings in month	960
Loan	50
Inventories	1,250
Cash in hand	20
Trade payables	675
Cash at bank	1,475
Trade receivables	890

Requirement

Prepare a statement of financial position for Liza Doolittle as at 31 July 20X6.

See **Answer** at the end of this chapter.

6 The income statement

Section overview

- The income statement sets out the entity's financial performance over a period of time.

- It matches income and expenses to arrive at a figure for profit or loss.

- Trading income less the costs of trading represents gross profit.

- Gross profit less expenses represents net profit.

- Net profit per the income statement is added to the capital section in the statement of financial position; drawings are deducted as appropriations of profit in order to arrive at the owner's total capital.

6.1 What is the income statement?

The **income statement** is a statement in which two key **elements of financial statements – income** and **expenses** – are matched to arrive at profit or loss. Many businesses distinguish between:

- **Gross profit** earned on trading (revenue less cost of sales)
- **Net profit** after other income and expenses.

In the first part of the income statement **revenue** from selling goods is compared with direct costs of acquiring or producing the goods sold to arrive at a **gross profit** figure. From this, deductions are made in the second half of the statement (which we will call the **expenses** section) in respect of indirect costs (overheads). Additions may also be made to gross profit in respect of **non-trading income**.

Gross profit	=	revenue from sales, less cost of sales
Net profit	=	gross profit less expenses plus non-trading income

Business owners want to know how much profit or loss has been made, but there is only limited information value in the profit figure. In order to exercise financial control effectively, managers must know how much revenue and other income has been earned, what costs have been, and whether the performance of sales or the control of costs appears to be satisfactory.

The income statement **matches income earned to the expenses of earning that income**. This is why prepayments and accrued expenses appear in the financial statements. **Prepayments** are excluded from expenses in the income statement and are included in receivables in the statement of financial position, because they relate to future periods.

Accrued expenses are added to expenses in the income statement and shown as payables in the statement of financial position, because they relate to the current period but have not been paid as cash in the period.

6.1.1 Gross profit

Gross profit is the difference between:

- The value of sales revenue and
- The purchase or production cost of the goods sold: **cost of sales**

In a retail business, the cost of the goods sold is **their purchase cost** from suppliers. In a manufacturing business, the production cost of goods sold is the **cost of raw materials** in the finished goods, plus **labour costs** required to make the goods, plus an amount of production 'overhead' costs. In many types of business the cost of sales also includes:

- The cost of employing those people directly involved in making or providing a service

- Maintenance and depreciation on non-current assets used directly in making sales, plus losses on their disposal

Gross profit represents the profit made directly from the sale of goods or services. It can be represented as a percentage of revenue, called the **gross profit margin**.

$$\textbf{Gross profit margin} = \frac{\text{Gross profit}}{\text{Re venue}} \times 100$$

The gross profit margin can be used to compare the results of different periods to see how well the costs of sales are being controlled as revenue changes. It can also be used to compare the results of different businesses in the same industry.

We shall see more about margin in Chapter 9.

6.1.2 Net profit

The second part of the income statement shows the **net profit** for the reporting period. The net profit is:

Gross profit	X
Plus any other income from sources other than the sale of goods	X
Minus other business expenses, not included in the cost of goods sold	(X)
	X

Income from other sources will include:

- Profit on disposals of non-current assets

- Dividends or interest received from investments

- Rental income from property owned but not otherwise used by the business

- Amounts due in respect of insurance claims

- **Discounts received** from suppliers for early payment of their debt. (See under administrative costs below for a brief explanation of discounts.)

Business expenses not directly related to cost of sales appear in the income statement under one of three headings.

- **Distribution costs.** Expenses associated with selling and delivering goods to customers. They include the following.

  - Salaries, wages and sales commission of employees

  - Marketing costs (eg advertising and sales promotion expenses)

- The costs of running and maintaining delivery vans, including **depreciation** on these and any **losses** on their disposal

- **Administrative costs.** Expenses of providing management and administration for the business. Examples include:

    - Management and office staff salaries

    - Rent and local business or property taxes

    - Insurance

    - Telephone and postage

    - Printing and stationery

    - Heating and lighting

    - Discounts allowed to customers for early payment of their debt. For example, a business sells goods to a customer for £100 and offers a 5% discount for payment in cash. If the customer takes the discount, record revenue at the full £100, with an administrative cost for discounts allowed of £5. Discounts are described more fully in Chapter 3.

    - Irrecoverable debts written off. Sometimes customers fail to pay what they owe and a business has to decide at some stage that there is now no prospect of ever being paid. The debt has to be written off as 'irrecoverable'. The amount of the debt written off is charged as an expense in the income statement. Irrecoverable debts are also described more fully in Chapter 8.

    - The cost of running and maintaining other non-current assets such as office buildings, plus depreciation and losses on disposal of these.

- **Finance costs.** These include:

    - Interest on loans
    - Bank overdraft interest

As far as possible, items of expense should be grouped (distribution costs, administrative expenses, and finance costs) but this is not something that you need worry about at this stage.

Worked example: Preparing an income statement

On 1 June 20X5, Jock Heiss commenced trading as an ice cream salesman, using a van.

(a) He borrowed £2,000 from his bank, and the interest cost of the loan was £25 per month.

(b) He rented the van for £1,000 for three months. Running expenses for the van averaged £300 per month.

(c) He hired an assistant for £100 per month.

(d) His main business was to sell ice cream to customers in the street, but he also did special catering for business customers, supplying ice creams for office parties. Sales to these customers were usually on credit.

(e) For the three months to 31 August 20X5, his total sales were as follows.

    (i)   Cash sales   £8,900
    (ii) Credit sales   £1,100

(f) He purchased his ice cream from a local manufacturer, Floors Co. The purchase cost in the three months to 31 August 20X5 was £6,200, and at 31 August he had sold every item. He still owed £700 to Floors Co for unpaid purchases on credit.

(g) One of his credit sale customers has gone bankrupt (insolvent), owing Jock £250. Jock has decided to write off the debt in full, with no prospect of getting any of the money owed.

(h) He used his own home for his office work. Telephone and postage expenses for the three months to 31 August were £150, which he paid in cash.

(i) During the period he paid himself £300 per month.

An income statement can be presented in various formats, but here we will use a vertical format similar to the one used in IAS 1 (revised). (It is not exactly the same.)

JOCK HEISS
INCOME STATEMENT
FOR THE THREE MONTHS ENDED 31 AUGUST 20X5

	£	£
Revenue (8,900 + 1,100)		10,000
Cost of sales		(6,200)
Gross profit		3,800
Expenses		
Wages (3 × 100)	300	
Van rental	1,000	
Van expenses (3 × 300)	900	
Irrecoverable debt written off	250	
Telephone and postage	150	
Interest charges (3 × 25)	75	
		(2,675)
Net profit		1,125

6.2 Relationship between the income statement and the statement of financial position

- **Net profit** is the profit for the period. For a sole trader it is transferred to the statement of financial position as an addition to the owner's capital. A net loss would be transferred as a deduction from capital in the statement of financial position.

- **Drawings** are **appropriations of profit** and not expenses. They must **not** be included in the income statement. The payments that Jock Heiss makes to himself (£900) are shown as **deductions from capital** in the statement of financial position.

- The cost of sales is £6,200, even though £700 of the costs have not yet been paid for. The £700 owed to Floors Co will be shown in the balance sheet as a trade payable. This is an example of the **accruals concept**.

Interactive question 6: Preparing a statement of financial position 2
[Difficulty level: Intermediate]

Prepare a statement of financial position as at 31 August 20X5 for Jock Heiss, using the information from the Worked example above.

See **Answer** at the end of this chapter.

Summary and Self-test

Summary

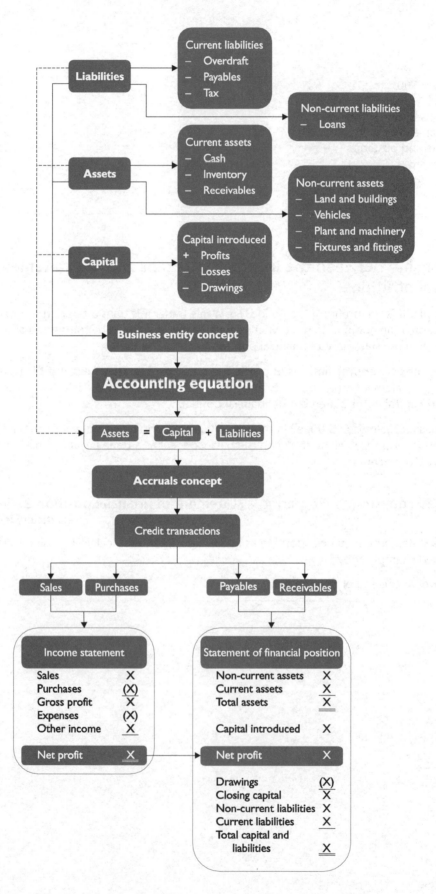

Self-test

Answer the following questions.

1   Which of the following is an asset?

   A   A trade payable   C   Drawings
   B   A loan   D   A prepayment

2   Which of the following is a liability?

   A   Depreciation   C   Cash at bank
   B   An accrual   D   Plant and machinery

3   Capital is the amount:

   A   The entity's owners owe to it   C   The entity owes to its creditors
   B   The entity's customers owe to it   D   The entity 'owes' to its owners

4   Which of the following are assets of an entity?

   A   Trade payables   D   Cash in hand
   B   Trade receivables   E   Funds introduced by the owner
   C   Bank overdraft

5   Which of the following best describes the accruals concept?

   A   Assets are matched with liabilities   C   Expenses are matched with assets
   B   Income is matched with expenses   D   Income is matched with liabilities

6   Which of the following is a non-current liability?

   A   A bank overdraft   C   A mortgage repayable in five years' time
   B   A bank loan repayable within a year   D   A trade payable

7   The statement of financial position sets out the entity's

   A   Financial position over a period of time
   B   Financial performance over a period of time
   C   Financial position at one point in time
   D   Financial performance at one point in time

8   Which of the following expenses is included in cost of sales?

   A   Sales people's salaries   C   Overdraft interest
   B   Management salaries   D   Cost of raw material

9   A business has sales of £100,000, cost of sales of £60,000 and expenses of £20,000. The gross profit margin is:

   A   60%   C   20%
   B   40%   D   80%

10 Which figure from a sole trader's income statement would appear in its statement of financial position?

   A   Gross profit   C   Revenue
   B   Drawings   D   Net profit

Now, go back to the Learning Objectives in the Introduction. If you are satisfied you have achieved the objectives, please tick them off.

Technical reference

- Basic format of the statement of financial position and income statement

  IAS 1 (revised) IG

- Elements of financial statements

  Conceptual Framework paras 4.2 to 4.3

- Definition of asset, liability, equity

  Conceptual Framework para 4.4

- Definition of income, expense

  Conceptual Framework para 4.25

- Current/non-current distinction in the statement of financial position

  IAS 1 (revised) paras 60/61

- Definition of current asset

  IAS 1 (revised) para 66

- Definition of current liability

  IAS 1 (revised) para 69

Answer to Interactive question 1

Assets = capital + liabilities. Therefore capital = assets – liabilities

Answer to Interactive question 2

(a)	Increase in liabilities (payables)	£800
	Increase in assets (inventory)	£800
(b)	Decrease in assets (cash)	£25
	Decrease in capital (an expense reduces profit)	£25
(c)	Decrease in assets (inventory)	£450
	Increase in assets (cash)	£650
	Increase in capital (profit)	£200
(d)	Decrease in liabilities (payables)	£800
	Decrease in assets (cash)	£800

Answer to Interactive question 3

The point in this case is that the car has a residual value of £3,400. It would be inappropriate to account for depreciation in such a way as to write off the asset completely over three years; the aim should be to account only for its loss of value (£10,000 – £3,400 = £6,600), which suggests depreciation of £2,200 per year.

Answer to Interactive question 4

Asset	Business	Current or non-current
Van	Delivery firm	Non-current
Machine	Manufacturing company	Non-current
Car	Car trader	Current
Investment	Any	Either*

* The classification of the investment will depend on the purpose for which it is held. If the intention is to make a non-current investment it will be a **non-current asset**, but if it is a short-term way of investing spare cash it will be a **current asset**.

Answer to Interactive question 5

LIZA DOOLITTLE
STATEMENT OF FINANCIAL POSITION AS AT 31 JULY 20X6

	£	£
ASSETS		
Non-current assets		
Stall		1,800
Van		700
		2,500
Current assets		
Inventories	1,250	
Trade receivables	890	
Cash in hand	20	
Cash at bank	1,475	
		3,635
Total assets		6,135
CAPITAL AND LIABILITIES		
Capital		
Opening capital	2,500	
Additional capital introduced	250	
		2,750
Profit for month	3,620	
Less: drawings	(960)	
		2,660
		5,410
Non-current liabilities		
Loan		50
Current liabilities		
Trade payables		675
Total capital and liabilities		6,135

Answer to Interactive question 6

JOCK HEISS
STATEMENT OF FINANCIAL POSITION AS AT 31 AUGUST 20X5

	£
ASSETS	
Current assets	
Trade receivables (1,100 – 250)	850
Cash at bank and in hand	
(2,000 + 8,900 – (6,200 – 700) – 300 – 1,000 – 900 – 150 – 75 – 900)	2,075
Total assets	2,925
CAPITAL AND LIABILITIES	
Capital	
Opening capital	0
Net profit	1,125
Drawings	(900)
Closing capital	225
Non-current liabilities	
Loan	2,000
Current liabilities	
Trade payables	700
Total capital and liabilities	2,925

Answers to Self-test

1   D   A and B are liabilities; C is an appropriation of profit

2   B   C and D are assets, depreciation is an expense and a reduction in the value of an asset

3   D   B is an asset while C is a liability; A is the wrong way round. A better way of thinking of capital is that it is the owners' residual interest in the entity's net assets.

4   B and D. A and C are current liabilities; E is capital

5   B   The accruals concept is best described as the matching of income with expenses

6   C   The mortgage is repayable in over a year's time and, therefore, is a non-current liability. The bank overdraft is repayable on demand, a trade payable is usually paid within a year and the bank loan is repayable within one year, so these are all current liabilities.

7   C   B describes the income statement accurately

8   D   The others are examples of selling expenses (A), administration expenses (B) and finance cost (C)

9   B   Gross profit margin $= \dfrac{\text{Gross profit}}{\text{Sales}} \times 100\% = \dfrac{(100,000 - 60,000)}{100,000} \times 100\% = 40\%$

10   D   Gross profit (A) and revenue (C) are included in the calculation of net profit; drawings are appropriations of net profit that appear in the statement of financial position only

CHAPTER 3

Recording financial transactions

Introduction

Learning objectives

Tick off

- Identify the sources of information for the preparation of accounting records and financial statements

- Record transactions and events resulting in income, expenses, assets, liabilities and equity

Specific syllabus learning outcomes are: 1b, c

Syllabus links

The material in this chapter will be developed further in this paper, and then in the Financial Accounting and Financial Reporting papers later in the Professional stage.

Examination context

Questions on the topics in this chapter will be set as multiple choice questions, some of which may involve calculations so that the correct answer can be selected.

In the exam you may be required to:

- Specify source documents for the accounting system
- Identify the purpose of books of original entry
- Identify the books of original entry in which specific transactions are recorded
- Identify an accurate description of the petty cash imprest system
- Calculate net or gross pay, or the amounts owed to HMRC

1 Source documents for recording financial transactions

Section overview

- Credit sales make use of sales orders, delivery notes to the customer and sales invoices (which is the source document that is then recorded).

- Credit purchases make use of purchase orders, goods received notes and sales invoices from the supplier (which become purchase invoices to be recorded).

- Invoices show, among other things, what has been sold at what price. Trade discounts and VAT are also shown, so that the total reflects the full amount that remains to be paid.

- Credit notes are negative invoices.

1.1 What are source documents used for?

Whenever a business transaction takes place involving sales or purchases, receiving or paying money, or owing or being owed money, it is usual for the transaction to be recorded on a **source document**. These documents are the source of all information recorded by a business, but only invoices and credit notes are source documents for the accounting system.

CREDIT SALE		CREDIT PURCHASE	
Receive sales order from customer	Sales order (received from customer)	Purchase order	Send purchase order to supplier
Prepare goods and delivery note; deliver to customer	Delivery note	Goods received note	Receive goods with supplier's delivery note; prepare goods received note (GRN)
Prepare sales invoice and send to customer SOURCE DOCUMENT FOR ACCOUNTING SYSTEM	Sales invoice	Purchase invoice (received from supplier)	Receive purchase invoice from supplier, and match to GRN SOURCE DOCUMENT FOR ACCOUNTING SYSTEM

In many businesses a customer writes out or signs a **sales order** for goods or services he requires. Similarly, a business will place **purchase orders** with other businesses for goods or services, such as material supplies.

While sales and purchase orders are very important from a practical point of view, they are **not** treated as source documents for recording financial transactions in the business accounts.

1.2 Invoices

Invoices are used to record transactions which have been made on credit. This is where goods or services are supplied but payment is not made straight away as there is a 'period of credit' before they are actually due for payment.

- When a business sells goods or services on credit to a customer, it sends out a **sales invoice**. The invoice details should match the sales order details. The invoice is a request for the customer to pay what is owed.

- When a business buys goods or services on credit it receives a **purchase invoice** from the supplier. The details on the invoice should match the details on the purchase order.

An **invoice** may relate to a sales or purchase order. **Invoices are source documents for credit transactions**.

Most **sales invoices** are numbered, so that the business can keep track of all the **sales invoices** it sends out. Information usually shown on an invoice includes the following.

- Invoice number

- Name and address of seller and purchaser

- Sale date

- Product/service description

- Quantity and unit price of what has been sold (eg 20 pairs of shoes at £25 a pair)

- Details of trade or bulk discount, if any (eg 10% reduction in cost if buying over 100 pairs of shoes)

- Total invoice amount including (usually) VAT details

- The date by which payment is due, and other terms of sale

- A tear-off remittance advice, for the customer to send to the business along with payment so that the business can identify what outstanding amounts are being settled.

Purchase invoices received will show exactly the same details as a sales invoice – because it is of course the supplier's sales invoices to us! Most businesses will give unique reference numbers to purchase invoices received so that they can be 'tracked' within the business.

1.3 Credit notes

Suppose China Supplies sent out a sales invoice to a customer (a shop) for 20 dinner plates, but the person creating the invoice accidentally typed in a total of £162.10, instead of £62.10. The shop has been **overcharged** by £100. What is China Supplies to do?

Another shop received 15 plates from China Supplies but found that they had all been broken in the post. Although the shop has received an invoice for, say, £45.60, it has no intention of paying it because the plates were substandard. Again, what is China Supplies to do?

The answer is that China Supplies sends out a **credit note**. It will be made out in the same way as an invoice, but with a 'credit note number' instead of a 'sales invoice number'.

Definition

Credit note: A document issued to a customer relating to returned goods, or refunds when a customer has been overcharged for whatever reason. It can be regarded as a **negative invoice**. **It is a source document for credit transactions**.

1.3.1 Debit notes

A **debit note** might be issued to a supplier as a means of formally requesting a credit note from that supplier. A debit note is **not a source document**.

1.4 Delivery notes

When goods or services are delivered to a customer in respect of a sale, they are usually accompanied by a **delivery note** prepared by the seller. This sets out:

- The goods/service delivered
- The quantities delivered
- The date of the delivery and
- The delivery address

The delivery note is most often prepared with reference to the sales order. Once the delivery is complete the delivery note is used to provide information for creating the **sales invoice**. The delivery note is **not** a source document for credit transactions.

1.5 Goods received notes

A **goods received note** (GRN) records a receipt of goods purchased, most commonly in a warehouse. They may be used in addition to suppliers' delivery notes. Often the accounts department will ask to see the GRN before paying a purchase invoice. Even where GRNs are not routinely used, the details of a delivery from a supplier which arrives without a delivery note must always be recorded. A GRN is **not** a source document for credit transactions.

Interactive question 1: Credit note [Difficulty level: Easy]

Fill in the blanks.

'China Supplies sends out a .... to a credit customer in order to correct an error where a customer has been overcharged on a ....'

See **Answer** at the end of this chapter.

1.6 VAT

Value added tax (VAT) is a sales tax added to most sales invoices in the UK. Details for calculating and recording VAT are discussed in Chapter 4. As well as the sale or purchase amount, the business also normally needs to record VAT on each invoice or credit note. This amount will ultimately be paid to or received from HMRC.

1.7 Other source documents

So far we have only considered source documents for initial recording of sales and purchases on credit, ie sales and purchase invoices and credit notes. Other source documents for transactions involving settlement of credit transactions (by cheque, debit card or transfer), cash, wages and other matters are also used, as we shall see.

2 Books of original entry

Section overview

- Books of original entry record information about a transaction shown in a source document.

- The key books of original entry are sales and purchases day books, the cash book, the petty cash book, the journal and the payroll.

2.1 What are books of original entry used for?

Source documents need to be summarised, as otherwise the business might forget to ask for some money, forget to pay some, or pay something twice. It needs to keep records of transactions as documented in invoices and credit notes. Such records are made in **books of original (or prime) entry**.

Definition

Books of original entry: The records in which the business first records transactions.

The main books of original entry are:

- Sales day book
- Purchases day book
- Cash book

- Petty cash book
- The payroll
- The journal

To help you visualise what is going on, this chapter describes books of original entry as if they are actual books written by hand. In fact, books of original entry are nearly always computer files. However, the principles remain the same whether they are manual or computerised.

3 Sales and purchases day books

Section overview

- Sales invoices and credit notes are recorded in the sales day book.
- The sales day book is usually analysed to show the types of sale and VAT.
- Purchase invoices and credit notes are recorded in the purchases day book.
- The purchases day book is usually analysed to show the types of purchase and VAT.

Invoices and credit notes are recorded in **day books**.

3.1 Sales day book

Definition

Sales day book: The book of original entry in respect of credit sales, including both invoices and credit notes.

The sales day book lists all invoices and credit notes sent out to customers. An extract from a sales day book might look like this.

SALES DAY BOOK

Date	Invoice/credit note number	Customer	Total £
20X0			
Jan 10	I 247	Jones & Co	107.04
	I 248	Smith Co	88.32
	CN 004	Alex & Co	(32.16)
	I 249	Enor College	1,291.68
			1,454.88

Most businesses 'analyse' their sales. For example, this business sells boots and shoes. The invoice to Smith Co was entirely boots, the credit note to Alex & Co was entirely shoes, and the other two invoices were a mixture of both. All contained an element of VAT. We look at VAT in detail in Section 9 of Chapter 4 and in particular we cover VAT rates in Section 9.3 of Chapter 4. However at this stage you should note that VAT is typically charged at a rate of 20% of the related sales value and is analysed separately on sales invoices. A separate column is used in the sales day book to account for VAT.

The analysed sales day book might look like this.

SALES DAY BOOK   Folio: SDB 48

Date	Invoice/credit note number	Customer	Total £	VAT £	Boots £	Shoes £
20X0						
Jan 10	I 247	Jones & Co	107.04	17.84	50.00	39.20
	I 248	Smith Co	88.32	14.72	73.60	–
	CN 004	Alex & Co	(32.16)	(5.36)	–	(26.80)
	I 249	Enor College	1,291.68	215.28	800.30	276.10
			1,454.88	242.48	923.90	288.50

The analysis gives business managers useful information which helps them to decide how best to run the business. It also fulfils in part their duty to record and account for VAT.

3.2 Purchases day book

Definition

Purchases day book: The book of original entry in respect of credit purchases, including both invoices and credit notes.

An extract from a purchases day book might look like this. VAT on purchases is also separately analysed on purchase invoices and a VAT column is included in the purchase day book.

PURCHASE DAY BOOK   Folio: PDB 37

Date	Invoice/credit note number	Supplier	Total £	VAT £	Purchases £	Expenses £
20X8						
Mar 15	I 4192	Cook	321.60	53.60	268.00	–
	CN 048	Butler	(30.24)	(5.04)	(25.20)	–
	I 4193	Telcom	119.04	19.84	–	99.20
	I 4194	Show	102.24	17.04	85.20	–
			512.64	85.44	328.00	99.20

In the 'invoice/credit note number' column a number is allocated by the business; the purchases day book records **other people's invoices**, which have all sorts of different numbers which it cannot usually record.

The purchases day book analyses invoices and credit notes which have been received. In this example, two of the invoices and the credit note related to goods which the business intends to re sell (called simply 'purchases') and the third invoice was a phone bill. All included VAT.

4 Cash book

Section overview

- The cash book records all payments from and receipts into the entity's bank account.
- Payments and receipts may be via cash, cheque, card payment, BACS transfer or online transfer.
- Ideally, payments and receipts should be evidenced by a remittance advice as the source document.
- The cash book is analysed to show the types of payment and receipt, and any VAT.
- Discount allowed and received is recorded in memorandum columns in the cash book.

Definition

Cash book: The book of original entry for receipts and payments in the business's bank account.

4.1 What is the cash book used for?

The cash book is used to record money received and paid out by the business through the business **bank account**. This could be money received on the business premises in notes, coins and cheques, and subsequently paid into the bank. The source documents for such items are usually remittance advices, which identify what is being settled. There are also receipts and payments made by card, bank transfer, standing order, direct debit and online transfer, plus bank interest and charges made directly by the bank. The source documents for such items are remittance advices or receipts, though the first the business may know of some transactions is when they appear on the business's bank statement.

Some cash, in notes and coins, is usually kept on the business premises in order to make occasional payments for odd items of expense. This cash is usually accounted for separately in a **petty cash book**.

One part of the cash book records cash receipts, and another part records payments. The best way to see how the cash book works is to follow through an example.

Worked example: Cash book

At the beginning of 1 September 20X7, Robin Plenty had £900 in the bank.

On 1 September, Robin had the following receipts and payments.

(a) Cash sale: receipt of £96 (including VAT of £16)
(b) Payment from credit customer Hay £380
(c) Payment from credit customer Been £720
(d) Payment from credit customer Seed £140
(e) Cheque received as a short term loan from Len Dinger £1,800
(f) Cash sale: receipt of £144 (including VAT of £24)
(g) Cash received for sale of machine £200 (no VAT)
(h) Payment to supplier Kew £120
(i) Payment to supplier Hare £310
(j) Payment of telephone bill £384 (including VAT of £64)
(k) Payment of gas service charge £288 (including VAT of £48)
(l) £100 in cash withdrawn from bank for petty cash
(m) Payment of £1,500 to Hess for new plant and machinery (no VAT)

The receipts part of the cash book for 1 September would look like this.

CASH BOOK (RECEIPTS)

Date	Narrative	Total receipts £	VAT £	Receivables £	Cash sales £	Other £
20X7						
1 Sept	Balance b/d*	900				
	Cash sale (a)	96				
	Receivables: Hay (b)	380				
	Receivables: Been (c)	720				
	Receivables: Seed (d)	140				
	Loan: Len Dinger (e)	1,800				
	Cash sale (f)	144				
	Sale of non-current assets (g)	200				
	Total	4,380				

* 'b/d' = brought down (ie brought forward)

There is usually space on the right hand side of the cash book so that the receipts can be analysed – for example, 'VAT', '(cash from) receivables', 'cash sales' and 'other (receipts)'.

The cash received in the day amounted to £3,480. Added to the £900 at the start of the day, this comes to £4,380. This is not the amount to be carried forward to the next day, because first we have to subtract all the payments made on 1 September.

The payments part of the cash book for 1 September would look like this.

CASH BOOK (PAYMENTS)

Date	Narrative	Total payment £	VAT £	Payables £	Petty cash £	Wages £	Other £
20X7							
1 Sept	Payables: Kew (h)	120					
	Payables: Hare (i)	310					
	Telephone bill (j)	384					
	Service charge bill (k)	288					
	Petty cash (l)	100					
	Machinery purchases (m)	1,500					
	Total payments	2,702					
	Balance c/d (4,380 – 2,702)	1,678					
	Total	4,380					

The analysis on the right would be under headings like 'VAT', '(payments to) payables', '(payments into) petty cash', 'wages' and 'other (payments)'.

Payments during 1 September totalled £2,702. We know that the total of receipts was £4,380. That means that there is a balance of £4,380 – £2,702 = £1,678 to be 'carried down' to the start of the next day. As you can see this 'balance carried down' is noted at the end of the payments column, so that the total receipts and total payment columns show the same figure of £4,380 at the end of 1 September.

With analysis columns completed, the cash book given in the example above would look as follows.

CASH BOOK (RECEIPTS)

Date	Narrative	Total receipts £	VAT £	Receivables £	Cash sales £	Other £
20X7						
1 Sept	Balance b/d	900				
	Cash sale (a)	96	16		80	
	Receivables: Hay (b)	380		380		
	Receivables: Been (c)	720		720		
	Receivables: Seed (d)	140		140		
	Loan: Len Dinger (e)	1,800				1,800
	Cash sale (f)	144	24		120	
	Sale of non-current assets (g)	200				200
		4,380	40	1,240	200	2,000

CASH BOOK (PAYMENTS)

Date	Narrative	Total payment £	VAT £	Payables £	Petty cash £	Wages £	Other £
20X7							
1 Sept	Payables: Kew (h)	120		120			
	Payables: Hare (i)	310		310			
	Telephone bill (j)	384	64				320
	Service charge bill (k)	288	48				240
	Petty cash (l)	100			100		
	Machinery purchases (m)	1,500					1,500
	Total payments	2,702	112	430	100	–	2,060
	Balance c/d						
	(4,380 – 2,702)	1,678					
		4,380					

4.2 VAT in the cash book

In the cash book VAT was included in only the cash sales and the telephone and service charge payments. There are two reasons:

- Some transactions did not fall under the scope of VAT at all (the sale of non-current assets, the loan receipt, the petty cash payment and the purchase of machinery).

- For all other transactions the VAT had already been recorded in the sales or purchases day book. Subsequent receipts from customers or payments to suppliers are simply of the total amount owed.

The cash book only records VAT in respect of receipts or payments which:

- Fall under the scope of VAT, and
- Are not recorded in any other book of original entry, because they are not credit transactions.

4.3 Discounts in the cash book

Discounts may be offered in respect of credit transactions.

- A **discount allowed** arises when a business records one amount as being due from a customer, but then allows the customer to pay slightly less in full settlement (in return for the customer paying early).

- A **discount received** arises when a business records one amount as being due to a supplier, but then receives notice from the supplier that slightly less can be paid in full settlement (again, usually in return for paying early).

When a receipt is for less than the total amount owed by the customer, the amount of the discount (the difference between the amount owed and the receipt) is recorded in a special 'memorandum' column of the cash book.

Worked example: Discount allowed

Suppose that in the example above, Hay's payment of £380 was in full settlement of an invoice that had been recorded at £385 in total in the sales day book. The cash book would be written up as follows, with an additional 'discount allowed' column.

Date	Narrative	Total receipts £	VAT £	Receivables £	Cash sales £	Other £	Discount allowed £
	Receivables: Hay	380		380			5

There is usually a vertical line to separate discounts, as the discount column is not included in the addition to the total receipts column (it is not 'cross-cast').

Worked example: Discount received

Suppose now that, in the example above, the payment to Kew of £120 was in full settlement of an invoice which had been recorded in the purchases day book at £123 in total. The cash book would be written up as follows, with an additional 'discount received' column.

CASH BOOK (PAYMENTS)

Date	Narrative	Total payments £	VAT £	Payables £	Petty cash £	Wages £	Other £	Discount received £
	Payables: Kew	120		120				3

5 Petty cash book

Section overview

- The petty cash book records all payments out of and receipts into petty cash.

- Petty cash is the cash (notes and coins) that an entity keeps on the premises for incidental expenditure.

- Under an imprest system, petty cash is kept at a fixed 'float' amount, which is made up of notes, coins and vouchers representing payments from and receipts of petty cash.

- The amount of notes and coins used to 'top up' petty cash will be equal to the total of the vouchers issued for petty cash receipts and payments.

- The petty cash book is analysed to record the different types of petty cash expense plus VAT on petty cash purchases.

5.1 What is the petty cash book used for?

Most businesses keep a small amount of 'petty cash' on the premises to make occasional small payments in cash, eg staff refreshments, postage stamps, taxi fares, etc. This is often called the **cash float** or **petty cash**. Petty cash can also be the resting place for occasional small receipts, eg cash paid by a visitor to make a phone call, etc.

Definition

Petty cash book: The book of original entry for small payments and receipts of cash.

Petty cash transactions – including VAT on payments where relevant – still need to be recorded, otherwise petty cash could be abused for personal expenses or even stolen.

There are usually more payments than receipts, and petty cash must be 'topped up' from time to time with cash from the business bank account. A typical layout is as follows.

PETTY CASH BOOK

Receipts £	Date	Narrative	Payments £	VAT £	Milk £	Postage £	Travel £	Other £
	20X7							
250	1 Sept	Bal b/d						
		Milk bill	25		25			
		Postage stamps	5			5		
		Taxi fare	10				10	
		Flowers for sick staff	15					15
		Bal c/d	195					
250			250	0	25	5	10	15

Under what is called the **imprest system**, the amount of money in petty cash is kept at an agreed sum or 'float' (say £250). Expense items are recorded on vouchers as they occur, so that at any time:

	£
Cash still held in petty cash	195
Plus vouchers for payments (25 + 5 + 10 + 15)	55
Must equal the agreed sum or float	250

The total float is made up regularly (to £250, or whatever the agreed sum is) by means of a cash payment from the bank account into petty cash. The amount of the 'top up' into petty cash will be the total of the voucher payments since the previous top up.

Interactive question 2: Books of original entry   [Difficulty level: Intermediate]

State which books of original entry the following transactions would be entered into.

(a)   Your business pays A Brown (a supplier) a cheque for £450.00.
(b)   You send D Smith (a customer) an invoice for £650.
(c)   Your accounts manager asks you for £12 to buy envelopes.
(d)   You receive an invoice from A Brown for £300.
(e)   You pay D Smith £500 by online transfer.
(f)   F Jones (a customer) returns goods valued £250.
(g)   You return goods to J Green valued £504.
(h)   F Jones pays you a cheque for £500.

See **Answer** at the end of this chapter.

6 The payroll

Section overview

- The payroll is the book of original entry for wages and salaries costs.

- The amount actually paid to employees is called net pay; this is less than gross pay since the employer pays over what the employee owes to HMRC (for income tax under PAYE, and employees' NI) and the pension trustees (for any pension contribution) directly.

- Gross payroll cost is more than employees' gross pay since the employer has to pay additional employment tax (employer's NI) to HMRC plus additional pension contributions to the pension trustees.

6.1 What is the payroll used for?

Definition

Payroll: The book of original entry for recording staff costs.

The payroll records all the individual amounts that appear on employees' payslips, namely:

- Gross pay to employees

    - PAYE income tax
    - Employee's NI contributions
    - Employee's pension contributions
    - Net pay (cash paid to employees)

- Additional costs for the employer:

    - Employer's NI contributions
    - Pension contributions

Gross pay is **not** the amount paid to the employee. The employer needs to make deductions from gross pay before **paying net pay to the employee**.

Worked example: Payroll

Sunny Climes Ltd employs three people: Anja earns £36,000 a year, Mark earns £33,000 a year and Dipak earns £30,000 a year. The gross pay in September for each employee is as follows.

	£
	£
Anja	3,000
Mark	2,750
Dipak	2,500

However, these are not the amounts that each employee will receive. Sunny Climes Ltd first of all has to deduct income tax from gross pay under the PAYE scheme to be paid to HMRC. It deducts National Insurance (employee NI) from gross pay, again to be paid to HMRC. As it runs a pension scheme, it has to deduct each employee's pension contribution, to be paid to pension fund trustees.

	Deductions				
	PAYE	NI	Pension	Net pay	Gross pay
	£	£	£	£	£
Anja	550	250	150	2,050	3,000
Mark	500	230	135	1,885	2,750
Dipak	460	210	125	1,705	2,500
	1,510	690	410	5,640	8,250

Deductions + Net pay = Gross pay

The employees will receive the net pay; this amount will be shown in the cash book.

The employer has deducted amounts the employees owe to other people from the gross pay the employer owes to them. This is not the end of the story however; the employer also owes additional NI to HMRC, and pension contributions of its own to the trustees, over and above the amount of gross pay. The final payroll will be as follows.

	PAYE £	Deductions Employee NI £	Pension £	Net pay £	Gross pay £	Employer NI £	Employer Pension £	Total payroll cost £
Anja	550	250	150	2,050	3,000	310	200	3,510
Mark	500	230	135	1,885	2,750	265	180	3,195
Dipak	460	210	125	1,705	2,500	230	165	2,895
	1,510	690	410	5,640	8,250	805	545	9,600

Gross pay + Employer NI + Employer pension = Total payroll cost

The total payroll cost for Sunny Climes Ltd is £9,600. This is paid out as follows:

	£
Employees (net pay)	5,640
HMRC: Income tax PAYE	1,510
HMRC: Employee and employer NI (690 + 805)	1,495
Pension trustees: Employee and employer pension (410 + 545)	955
Total payroll cost	9,600

Interactive question 3: Payroll

[Difficulty level: Exam standard]

Fantab Ltd has 10 employees who had gross pay of £190,000 per annum between them in 20X4. In that year, Fantab Ltd made net pay payments to employees of £129,200, and paid £20,900 to the pension trustees. Its total payroll cost was £220,400. How much did Fantab Ltd pay to HMRC in respect of NI and PAYE?

See **Answer** at the end of this chapter.

7 The journal

Section overview

- The journal records transactions that are not recorded in any other book of original entry.

7.1 What is the journal used for?

The final book of original entry is the **journal**. This is the record of transactions which do not appear in any of the other books of original entry. **Non-current asset purchases are usually recorded via the journal**.

Summary

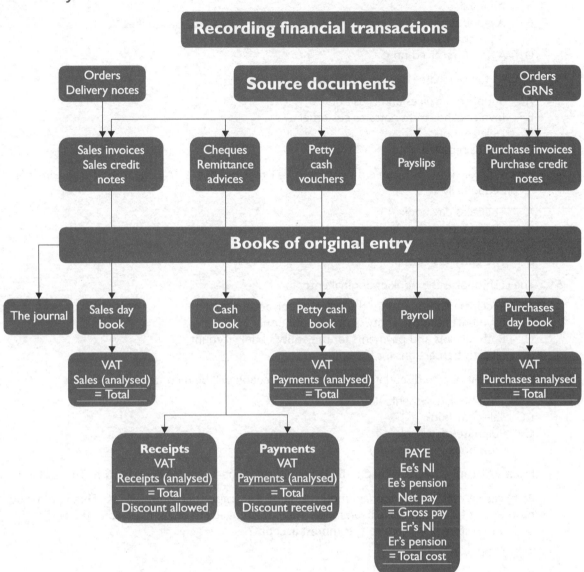

Recording financial transactions

- Orders
  Delivery notes
- **Source documents**
- Orders
  GRNs

- Sales invoices
  Sales credit
  notes
- Cheques
  Remittance
  advices
- Petty
  cash
  vouchers
- Payslips
- Purchase invoices
  Purchase credit
  notes

Books of original entry

- The journal
- Sales day
  book
- Cash
  book
- Petty cash
  book
- Payroll
- Purchases
  day book

VAT
Sales (analysed)
= Total

VAT
Payments (analysed)
= Total

VAT
Purchases analysed
= Total

Receipts
VAT
Receipts (analysed)
= Total
Discount allowed

Payments
VAT
Payments (analysed)
= Total
Discount received

PAYE
Ee's NI
Ee's pension
Net pay
= Gross pay
Er's NI
Er's pension
= Total cost

CHAPTER

3

Self-test

Answer the following questions.

1   Sales orders are source documents that are recorded in the sales day book. True or false?

2   When an entity returns goods to a supplier it will expect to receive from the supplier

    A   An invoice
    B   A credit note
    C   A purchase order
    D   A goods received note

3   What is the purchases day book used to record?

    A   Suppliers' invoices and credit notes
    B   Invoices and credit notes to customer
    C   Delivery notes
    D   Goods received notes

4   If a credit sale is made by an entity which is VAT registered, the VAT due from the customer is recorded initially in

    A   The sales day book
    B   The purchases day book
    C   The cash book
    D   The petty cash book

5   The cash book is the book of original entry for

    A   Receipts of amounts into the entity's bank account only
    B   Payments from the entity's bank account only
    C   Both receipts and payments for the entity's bank account
    D   All cash transactions for the entity

6   The amount of cash discount allowed on a transaction will be recorded initially in the

    A   Cash book (payments side)
    B   Sales day book
    C   Purchases day book
    D   Cash book (receipts side)

7   Input VAT cannot be reclaimed if the expenditure has been made via petty cash. True or false?

8   Petty cash is controlled under an imprest system. The imprest amount is £100. During a period, payments totalling £53 have been made. How much needs to be reimbursed at the end of the period to restore petty cash to the imprest account?

    A   £100
    B   £53
    C   £47
    D   £50

9   The cost of employer's NI is part of a company's

    A   Net pay
    B   Gross pay
    C   Gross wages and salaries cost
    D   Corporation tax charge

10 A transaction which does not involve payroll, cash or credit transactions is likely to be recorded in

    A   The cash book
    B   The petty cash book
    C   The sales day book
    D   The journal

Now, go back to the Learning Objectives in the Introduction. If you are satisfied you have achieved the objectives, please tick them off.

Answer to Interactive question 1

Credit note; sales invoice

Answer to Interactive question 2

(a) Cash book
(b) Sales day book
(c) Petty cash book
(d) Purchases day book
(e) Cash book
(f) Sales day book
(g) Purchases day book
(h) Cash book

Answer to Interactive question 3

	£
Total payroll cost	220,400
Employees (net pay)	(129,200)
Pension trustees	(20,900)
Amount paid to HMRC	70,300

Answers to Self-test

1   False. The sales invoice is recorded in the sales day book

2   B   An invoice (A) is received in respect of the original purchase, after a purchase order (C) has been placed and a goods received note (D) has been created in respect of the delivery of goods

3   A   Customers' invoices and credit notes (B) are recorded in the sales day book. Delivery notes and goods received notes (C and D) are not recorded directly in any day books

4   A   VAT on credit sales is recorded in the sales day book initially (A), not the purchase day book (B) which relates to credit purchases, nor the cash book (C) which records the receipt from the customer when they settle the bill. The petty cash book (D) is not normally a book of original entry in respect of credit sales

5   C   The cash book records *both* receipts *and* payments via the bank account. It does not record all cash transactions since the petty cash book records petty cash transactions

6   D   Cash discount is allowed to customers, so it will be first recorded not when the invoice is recorded in the sales day book (B) but when cash is received from the customer. Discounts received would be recorded in the cash book (payments side) (A)

7   False. Petty cash books often have a column for VAT on small items of expenditure

8   B   Under the imprest system, a reimbursement is made of the amount of the vouchers (or payments made) for the period

9   C   The cost of employer's NI is added to gross pay (B) (which includes net pay (A)) to form the gross wages and salaries cost. Payroll taxes are not included in the company's corporation tax charge (D)

10   D   The journal records items which are not recorded in any other book of original entry

CHAPTER 4

Ledger accounting and double entry

Introduction

Examination context

Topic List

Learning objectives

- Identify the sources of information for the preparation of accounting records and financial statements

- Record and account for transactions and events resulting in income, expenses, assets, liabilities and equity

- Prepare journals for nominal ledger entry

Specific syllabus learning outcomes are: 1b, c; 2d

Syllabus links

The material in this chapter will be developed further in this paper, and then in the Financial Accounting and Financial Reporting papers later in the Professional stage.

Examination context

Questions on the topics in this chapter will be set as multiple choice questions, some of which may involve calculations so that the correct answer can be selected. Very often double entry questions are phrased in terms of preparing a journal.

In the exam you may be required to:

- Identify the effect of debit and credit entries in ledger accounts for the elements of financial statements

- Specify the double entry needed to record particular transactions

- Identify how to post transactions to both the nominal and memorandum ledgers

- Identify entries in ledger accounts for VAT, payables and receivables

- Use ledger accounts to identify balancing figures

1 Ledger accounts

Section overview

- Ledger accounts summarise all the individual transactions listed in the books of original entry.
- Records should be kept in ledger accounts in chronological order, with cumulative totals built up.

1.1 Why do we need ledger accounts?

A business is continually making transactions, eg buying and selling. To prepare an income statement and a statement of financial position on completion of every individual transaction would be a time consuming and cumbersome administrative task.

If a business records and **analyses** the transactions it makes, assets it acquires and liabilities it incurs then, when the time comes to prepare an income statement and a statement of financial position, the relevant information can be taken from those records.

The **records of transactions, assets and liabilities** should be kept in the following ways.

- In **chronological order**, and **dated** so that transactions can be related to a particular period of time.

- Built up in **cumulative totals**.

  - Day by day (eg total sales on Monday, total sales on Tuesday)
  - Week by week
  - Month by month
  - Year by year

The first step in this process is to list all the transactions in various books of original entry, as we have seen. Now we will look at the method used to **analyse** these records: **ledger accounting** and **double entry**.

2 The nominal ledger

Section overview

- The nominal ledger is the accounting record which analyses all the entity's financial records.

- Ledger accounts for each type of transaction can take the form of a T account, the left hand side is the debit side, and the right hand side is the credit side.

2.1 What is the nominal ledger used for?

Definition

Nominal ledger: An accounting record which analyses the financial records of a business.

The nominal ledger contains details of assets, liabilities, capital, income and expenditure, and so profit and loss. It consists of a large number of different **ledger accounts**, each account having its own purpose or 'name' and an identity or code.

There may be various subdivisions, whether for convenience, ease of handling, confidentiality, security, or to meet the needs of computer software design. For example, the ledger may be split alphabetically, with different clerks responsible for sections A-F, G-M, N-R and S-Z. This can help to reduce fraud, as there would have to be collusion between the different section clerks.

Examples of ledger accounts in the nominal ledger include:

- Plant and machinery at cost (non-current asset)
- Motor vehicles at cost (non-current asset)
- Plant and machinery, provision for accumulated depreciation (deduction from non-current asset)
- Motor vehicles, provision for accumulated depreciation (deduction from non-current asset)
- Owner's capital (capital)
- Inventories – raw materials (current asset)
- Inventories – finished goods (current asset)
- Total trade receivables (current asset)
- Total trade payables (current liability)
- Wages and salaries (expense)
- Rent and local taxes (expense)
- Advertising expenses (expense)
- Bank charges (expense)
- Motor expenses (expense)
- Telephone expenses (expense)
- Sales (income)
- Total cash/bank overdraft (current asset/liability)

When it comes to drawing up the financial statements, the income and expense ledger accounts will together form the income statement, while the asset, capital and liability ledger accounts go into the statement of financial position.

2.2 The format of a ledger account

If a ledger account were to be kept in an actual book, rather than as a computer record, it would look like this.

ADVERTISING EXPENSES

Date	Narrative	Ref.	£	Date	Narrative	Ref.	£
20X6	JFK Agency for quarter to 31 March	PL 348	2,500				

There are two sides to the account, with an account heading on top. The lines form a 'T', so it is convenient to think in terms of **'T' accounts**.

- On top of the account is its name.
- There is a left hand, or **debit** side.
- There is a right hand, or **credit** side.

NAME OF ACCOUNT

	£		£
Debit side		Credit side	

3 Double entry bookkeeping

Section overview

- The principle of double entry bookkeeping is that, for each transaction, every debit has a credit.
- Debit entries increase assets and expenses, and decrease liabilities, capital and income.
- Credit entries increase liabilities, capital and income, and decrease assets and expenses.
- A receipt of cash is a debit in the cash ledger account.
- A payment of cash is a credit in the cash ledger account.
- A credit sale is recorded as debit receivables (increase asset), credit sales (increase income).
- A credit purchase is recorded as debit purchases (increase expenses), credit payables (increase liabilities).
- Discount allowed to customers is credited to receivables along with payments received, and debited to a discount allowed ledger account.
- Discounts received from suppliers is debited to payables along with payments made, and credited to a discount received ledger account.

Definition

Double entry bookkeeping: Each transaction has an equal but opposite effect. Every accounting event must be entered in ledger accounts both as a debit and a credit.

3.1 Dual effect (duality concept)

Double entry bookkeeping is the method used to transfer totals from the **books of original entry** into the **nominal ledger**.

Central to this process is the idea that every transaction has two effects, the **dual effect** (also known as the **duality concept**). This feature is not something peculiar to business. If you were to purchase a car for £1,000 cash, for instance, you would be affected in two ways.

- You own a car worth £1,000.
- You have £1,000 less cash.

If instead you got a bank loan to make the purchase:

- You own a car worth £1,000.
- You owe the bank £1,000.

A month later if you pay a garage £50 to have the exhaust repaired:

- You have £50 less cash.
- You have incurred a repairs expense of £50.

Ledger accounts, with their debit and credit sides, are kept in a way which allows the two sided nature of every transaction to be recorded. This is known as **double entry bookkeeping**, because **every transaction is recorded twice in the ledger accounts**.

CHAPTER

4

Ledger accounting and double entry

81

3.2 The rules of double entry bookkeeping

A **debit entry** will:

•	Increase an asset	•	Decrease a liability
•	Increase an expense	•	Decrease capital
		•	Decrease income

A **credit entry** will:

•	Decrease an asset	•	Increase a liability
•	Decrease an expense	•	Increase capital
		•	Increase income

The basic rule, which must always be observed, is that **every financial transaction gives rise to two accounting entries, one a debit and the other a credit**. The total value of debit entries in the nominal ledger is therefore always equal to the total value of credit entries. Which account receives the credit entry and which receives the debit entry depends on the nature of the transaction.

- An **increase** in an **expense** (eg a purchase of stationery) or an **increase in an asset** (eg a purchase of office furniture) is a **debit**.

- An **increase** in **income** (eg a sale) or an **increase in a liability** (eg buying goods on credit) or **capital** is a **credit**.

- A **decrease** in an **asset** (eg making a cash payment) or a **decrease in an expense** is a **credit**.

- A **decrease** in a **liability** (eg paying a creditor) or **capital** or **income** is a **debit**.

In terms of 'T' accounts, for assets, liabilities and capital:

ASSET		LIABILITY		CAPITAL	
£	£	£	£	£	£
DEBIT	CREDIT	DEBIT	CREDIT	DEBIT	CREDIT
Increase	Decrease	Decrease	Increase	Decrease	Increase

For income and expenses, think about profit. Profit retained in the business increases capital. Income increases profit and expenses decrease profit.

INCOME		EXPENSE	
£	£	£	£
DEBIT	CREDIT	DEBIT	CREDIT
Decrease	Increase	Increase	Decrease

Interactive question 1: Debits and credits   [Difficulty level: Intermediate]

Complete the following table relating to the transactions of a bookshop. (The first two are done for you.)

(a) Purchase of books on credit

•	Payables increase	CREDIT	payables	(increase in liability)
•	Purchases increase	DEBIT	purchases	(increase in expense)

(b) Purchase of cash register by cheque

•	Own a cash register	DEBIT	non-current asset	(increase in asset)
•	Cash at bank decreases	CREDIT	cash at bank	(decrease in asset)

(c) Payment received from a credit customer

- Receivables decrease
- Cash at bank increases

(d) Sell books for cash

- Revenue increases
- Cash at bank increases

See **Answer** at the end of this chapter.

3.3 Double entry for cash transactions

A good starting point is the cash account, ie the nominal ledger account in which receipts and payments of cash are recorded, or posted, from the book of original entry, the cash book.

- A cash **payment** is a **credit** entry in the cash account. Here **cash is decreasing**. Cash may be paid out, for example to pay an expense (such as insurance) or to purchase an asset (such as a machine). The matching debit entry is therefore made in the appropriate expense or asset account.

- A cash **receipt** is a **debit** entry in the cash account. Here **cash is increasing**. Cash might be received, for example, by a retailer who makes a cash sale. The credit entry would then be made in the revenue account (and the VAT account if relevant).

Worked example: Cash transactions

In the cash book, the following transactions have been recorded (ignore VAT for now).

(a) A cash sale (ie a receipt) of £250
(b) Payment of a rent bill totalling £150
(c) Buy some goods for cash of £100
(d) Buy some shelves for cash of £200

How would these four transactions be entered (or 'posted') to the ledger accounts, and to which ledger accounts should they be posted? Remember each transaction will be posted twice, in accordance with double entry rules.

Solution

(a) The two sides of the transaction are:

- £250 cash is received (debit cash account).
- Sales increase by £250 (credit sales account).

CASH ACCOUNT

	£		£
Sales a/c	250		

SALES ACCOUNT

	£		£
		Cash a/c	250

(The cash account entry is cross referenced to the sales account and *vice versa*. This enables a person looking at one of the ledger accounts to trace where the other half of the double entry is found.)

(b) The two sides of the transaction are:

- Cash is paid (credit entry in the cash asset account).
- Rent expense increases by £150 (debit entry in the rent expense account).

CASH ACCOUNT

	£		£
		Rent a/c	150

RENT ACCOUNT

	£		£
Cash a/c	150		

(c) The two sides of the transaction are:

- Cash is paid (credit entry in the cash asset account).
- Purchases increase by £100 (debit entry in the purchases expense account).

CASH ACCOUNT

	£		£
		Purchases a/c	100

PURCHASES ACCOUNT

	£		£
Cash a/c	100		

(d) The two sides of the transaction are:

- Cash is paid (credit cash account).
- Assets – in this case, shelves – increase by £200 (debit shelves account).

CASH ACCOUNT

	£		£
		Shelves a/c	200

SHELVES ACCOUNT

	£		£
Cash a/c	200		

If all four of these transactions related to the same business, the cash account of that business would end up looking as follows.

CASH ACCOUNT

	£		£
Sales a/c	250	Rent a/c	150
		Purchases a/c	100
		Shelves a/c	200

3.4 Double entry for credit transactions

Not all transactions are settled immediately. A business can purchase goods or non-current assets on credit terms, so that suppliers would be trade payables until settlement was made in cash. Equally, the business might grant customers credit terms, so they would then be trade receivables of the business. No entries can be made in the cash book when a credit transaction occurs, because no cash has been received or paid.

Instead of the cash account we use **receivables and payables accounts**. When a business acquires goods or services on credit, the credit entry is posted from the purchases day book to a 'trade payables' account instead of the cash account. The debit entry is posted to the expense or asset account, exactly as in the case of cash transactions. Similarly, when a sale is made to a credit customer, entries posted from the sales day book are a debit to the trade receivables account (instead of cash account), and a credit to the sales revenue account.

3.4.1 Double entry when credit transactions are entered into

Worked example: Double entry for credit transactions

Recorded in the sales day book and the purchases day book for a business are the following transactions.

(a) The business sells goods on credit to Mr A for £2,000.
(b) The business buys goods on credit from B Ltd for £100.

How and where are these transactions posted in the ledger accounts from the books of original entry?

Solution

(a)

TRADE RECEIVABLES (MR A)

	£		£
Sales a/c	2,000		

SALES ACCOUNT

	£		£
		Trade receivables a/c (Mr A)	2,000

(b)

TRADE PAYABLES (B LTD)

	£		£
		Purchases a/c	100

PURCHASES ACCOUNT

	£		£
Trade payables a/c (B Ltd)	100		

3.4.2 Double entry when cash is paid by customers or to suppliers

What happens when a credit transaction is eventually settled in cash? Suppose that, in the example above, the business paid £100 to B Ltd one month after the goods were acquired, recorded in the cash book. The two sides of this new transaction are:

(a) Cash is paid (credit entry in the cash account).
(b) The amount owing to trade payables is reduced (debit entry in the trade payables account).

CASH ACCOUNT

	£		£
		Trade payables a/c (B Ltd)	100

TRADE PAYABLES (B LTD)

	£		£
Cash a/c	100		

If we now bring together the two parts of this example, the original purchase of goods on credit and the eventual settlement in cash, we find that the accounts appear as follows.

CASH ACCOUNT

	£		£
		Trade payables a/c (B Ltd)	100

PURCHASES ACCOUNT

	£		£
Trade payables a/c (B Ltd)	100		

TRADE PAYABLES (B LTD)

	£		£
Cash a/c	100	Purchases a/c	100

The two entries in trade payables cancel each other out, indicating that no money is owing to B Ltd. A cash account credit entry of £100 and a debit purchases account entry of £100 remain. These are the same as the entries used to record a **cash** purchase of £100. This is what we would expect: after the business has paid off its trade payables, it is in exactly the same position as if it had made a cash purchase, and the accounting records reflect this.

Similar reasoning applies when a customer settles a debt. In the example above, when Mr A pays his debt of £2,000 and it is recorded in the cash book, the two sides of the transaction are:

(a) Cash is received (debit entry in the cash account).
(b) The amount owed by trade receivables is reduced (credit entry in the trade receivables account).

CASH ACCOUNT

	£		£
Trade receivables (Mr A)	2,000		

TRADE RECEIVABLES (MR A)

	£		£
		Cash a/c	2,000

The accounts recording this sale to, and payment by, Mr A now appear as follows.

CASH ACCOUNT

	£		£
Trade receivables (Mr A)	2,000		

SALES ACCOUNT

	£		£
		Trade receivables a/c (Mr A)	2,000

	£		£
Sales a/c	2,000	Cash a/c	2,000

The two trade receivables entries cancel each other out, while the entries in the cash at bank account and sales account reflect the same position as if the sale had been made for cash (see above).

Interactive question 2: Debits and credits [Difficulty level: Intermediate]

Identify the debit and credit entries in the following transactions (ignore VAT).

(a) Bought a machine on credit from A, cost £8,000.
(b) Bought goods on credit from B, cost £500.
(c) Sold goods on credit to C, value £1,200.
(d) Paid D (a credit supplier) £300.
(e) Collected £180 from E, a credit customer.
(f) Paid net pay £4,000.
(g) Received rent bill of £700 from landlord G.
(h) Paid rent of £700 to landlord G.
(i) Paid insurance premium £90.

See **Answer** at the end of this chapter.

3.4.3 Double entry for discounts

In Chapter 3 we saw how discounts allowed to customers and received from suppliers are recorded in a memorandum column of the cash book. This means that **neither the debit nor the credit entry is made in the cash account**; instead, the memorandum column is used to post the double entry to two nominal ledger accounts, as follows.

- Discounts allowed to customers

  DEBIT   Discounts allowed (administrative expense account)
  CREDIT   Trade receivables

The discount allowed reduces the balance owed by customers, so it is a **credit** in the receivables asset account. The other side of the entry is as a **debit** to the discount allowed expense account.

- Discounts received from suppliers

  DEBIT   Trade payables
  CREDIT   Discount received (other income account)

The discount received reduces the liability to suppliers, so it is a **debit** in the payables liability account. The other side of the entry is as a **credit** in the discount received income account.

Interactive question 3: Ledger entries [Difficulty level: Intermediate]

Ron Knuckle set up a business selling fitness equipment. He put £7,000 of his own money into a business bank account (transaction A) and in his first period of trading, the following transactions occurred.

Transaction		£
B	Paid rent of shop for the period	3,500
C	Purchased equipment (inventories) on credit	5,000
D	Loan from bank	1,000
E	Purchase of shop fittings (for cash)	2,000
F	Sales of equipment: cash	10,000
G	Sales of equipment: on credit	2,500
H	Payments for trade payables (discount received £50)	4,950
I	Receipt from trade receivables (discount allowed £20)	2,480
J	Interest on loan (paid)	100
K	Other expenses (all paid in cash)	1,900
L	Drawings	1,500

Ignore VAT.

Prepare the ledger accounts for Ron Knuckle by opening up the following accounts and completing them:

- Cash at bank
- Capital
- Loan
- Purchases
- Trade payables
- Rent
- Shop fittings

- Sales
- Trade receivables
- Discount received
- Discount allowed
- Loan interest
- Other expenses
- Drawings

See **Answer** at the end of this chapter.

---

4 The journal

Section overview

- Journal entries have a particular format that you should use.

- Journals can be used to record any type of financial transaction, in which case the journal acts as the book of original entry for that transaction.

- Journals are particularly useful for recording internal transfers between ledger accounts.

4.1 What are journal entries used for?

The **journal** records transactions not recorded in any other book of original entry, such as credit purchases of **non-current assets**. In particular the **journal** keeps a record of **unusual movements between ledger accounts**. It is used to record any double entries made which do not arise from the other books of original entry, such as when errors are discovered and need to be corrected.

Whatever type of transaction is being recorded, the **format of a journal entry** is as follows.

Date	Debit £	Credit £
Account to be debited	X	
Account to be credited		X

Narrative to explain the transaction

In due course, the ledger accounts will be written up to include the transactions listed in the journal.

A **narrative explanation** should accompany each journal entry. It is required for audit and control, to indicate the purpose and authority of every transaction which is not first recorded in a book of original entry.

Worked example: Journal entries to record transactions

The following is a summary of the transactions of Hair by Fiona Middleton hairdressing business, of which Fiona is the sole owner.

1 January	Put in cash of £2,000 as capital
	Purchased brushes and combs for cash £50
	Purchased hair driers from Gilroy Ltd on credit £150
30 January	Paid three months rent to 31 March £300
	Collected and paid in takings £600
31 January	Gave Mrs Sullivan a perm, highlights etc on credit £80
31 January	Took out £100 for personal expenses

Show the transactions by means of journal entries.

Solution

JOURNAL

				£	£
1 January	DEBIT	Cash at bank		2,000	
	CREDIT	Fiona Middleton – capital account			2,000
	Initial capital introduced				
1 January	DEBIT	Brushes and combs account (non-current asset)		50	
	CREDIT	Cash at bank			50
	The purchase for cash of brushes and combs				
1 January	DEBIT	Hair dryer account (non-current asset)		150	
	CREDIT	Trade payables (Gilroy Ltd)			150
	The purchase on credit of hair driers as non-current assets				
30 January	DEBIT	Rent expense account		300	
	CREDIT	Cash at bank			300
	The payment of rent to 31 March				
30 January	DEBIT	Cash at bank		600	
	CREDIT	Sales revenue account			600
	Cash takings				
31 January	DEBIT	Trade receivables		80	
	CREDIT	Sales revenue account			80
	The provision of hair treatment on credit				
31 January	DEBIT	Drawings		100	
	CREDIT	Cash at bank			100
	Owner's drawings				

4.2 Journal entries to correct errors

Errors corrected by the journal must be **capable of correction by means of double entry** in the ledger accounts. In other words, the error must not have caused total debits and total credits to be unequal.

Special rules, covered in Chapter 6, apply to correcting errors which broke the rule of double entry.

5 The petty cash imprest system

Section overview

- The double entry for transactions recorded in the petty cash book works in the same way as the cash book.

5.1 Double entry for petty cash transactions

In Chapter 3, we saw how the petty cash book was used to operate the imprest system. It is now time to see how the **double entry** works.

A business starts with a cash float (imprest) on 1.3.20X7 of £250. This will be a payment from cash at bank to petty cash:

DEBIT	Petty cash	£250	
CREDIT	Cash at bank		£250

Suppose five payments were made out of petty cash during March 20X7, none of which attracted VAT. The petty cash book might look as follows.

Total receipts £	Date	Narrative	Total payments £	Postage £	Travel £
250.00	1.3.X7	Cash			
	2.3.X7	Stamps	12.00	12.00	
	8.3.X7	Stamps	10.00	10.00	
	19.3.X7	Travel	16.00		16.00
	23.3.X7	Travel	5.00		5.00
	28.3.X7	Stamps	11.50	11.50	
250.00			54.50	33.50	21.00

At the end of each month (or at any other suitable interval) the total payments in the petty cash book are **posted** to nominal ledger accounts. This just means that the totals of the columns are entered as appropriate debit and credit entries in the ledger accounts. For March 20X7, £33.50 would be **debited** to the postage account and £21.00 to the travel account. The total payments of £54.50 are **credited** to the petty cash account. This completes the double entry.

		£	£
DEBIT	Postage	33.50	
DEBIT	Travel	21.00	
CREDIT	Petty cash		54.50

Next, the cash float needs to be topped up to the imprest amount by a payment of £54.50 from the main bank account:

DEBIT	Petty cash	£54.50	
CREDIT	Cash at bank		£54.50

So double entry rules have been satisfied, and the petty cash book for the month of March 20X7 will look like this.

Receipts £	Date	Narrative	Payments £	Postage £	Travel £
250.00	1.3.X7	Cash			
	2.3.X7	Stamps	12.00	12.00	
	8.3.X7	Stamps	10.00	10.00	
	19.3.X7	Travel	16.00		16.00
	23.3.X7	Travel	5.00		5.00
	28.3.X7	Stamps	11.50	11.50	
	31.3.X7	Balance c/d	195.50		
250.00			250.00	33.50	21.00
195.50	1.4.X7	Balance b/d			
54.50	1.4.X7	Cash			

The cash float is back up to (£195.50 + £54.50) = £250 imprest on 1.4.X7, ready for more payments to be made.

The petty cash account in the nominal ledger will be as follows.

PETTY CASH

20X7		£	20X7		£
1.3	Cash	250.00	31.3	Payments	54.50
1.4	Cash	54.50	1.4	Balance c/d	250.00
		304.50			304.50
1.4	Balance b/d	250.00			

Interactive question 4: Petty cash   [Difficulty level: Exam standard]

Summit Glazing operates an imprest petty cash system. The imprest amount is £150.00. At the end of the period the totals of the four analysis columns in the petty cash book were as follows.

	£
Column 1	23.12
Column 2	6.74
Column 3	12.90
Column 4	28.50

How much cash is required to restore the imprest amount?

See **Answer** at the end of this chapter.

6 Day book analysis

Section overview

- When day books are analysed, totals are calculated for each column which are then posted to the ledger accounts that are relevant to that column.

6.1 How are day books posted?

In Chapter 3 we used the following example of four transactions in the sales day book.

SALES DAY BOOK

Date	Invoice/credit note no.	Customer	Total £	VAT £	Boots £	Shoes £
20X0						
Jan 10	I 247	Jones & Co	107.04	17.84	50.00	39.20
	I 248	Smith Co	88.32	14.72	73.60	–
	CN 004	Alex & Co	(32.16)	(5.36)	–	(26.80)
	I 249	Enor College	1,291.68	215.28	800.30	276.10
			1,454.88	242.48	923.90	288.50

The business would open up a 'sale of shoes' account and a 'sale of boots' account as well as a VAT account and the trade receivables account. Then the sales day book totals would be **posted** to the nominal ledger accounts as follows.

		£	£
DEBIT	Trade receivables	1,454.88	
CREDIT	Sale of shoes account		288.50
CREDIT	Sale of boots account		923.90
CREDIT	VAT account		242.48

That is why the analysis of sales is kept. Exactly the same reasoning lies behind the analyses kept in the other books of original entry.

7 The receivables and payables ledgers

Section overview

- Individual ledger accounts for each credit customer (personal accounts) are maintained in the receivables ledger.
- A total receivables account is held in the nominal ledger, called the receivables control account.
- Individual ledger accounts for each credit supplier (personal accounts) are maintained in the payables ledger.
- A total payables account is held in the nominal ledger, called the payables control account.

7.1 Nominal ledger accounts and personal accounts

Nominal ledger accounts relate to types of income, expense, asset, capital and liability – rent, sales, trade receivables, payables and so on – rather than to the person to whom the money is paid or from whom it is received. However, there is also a need for **personal** accounts, most commonly for receivables and payables, and these are contained in the **receivables ledger** and **the payables ledger**. These are **memorandum accounts** only, in memorandum ledgers; they are **not** part of the double entry system. Instead summary **receivables control** and **payables control** accounts are kept in the nominal ledger.

Keeping each credit customer's account separately enables us to identify at any moment how much that customer owes us; similarly, the technique enables us to tell exactly how much we owe each credit supplier. Any disputes with customers or suppliers can thereby be more easily resolved.

7.2 Receivables ledger

The sales day book provides a chronological record of invoices and credit notes sent out by a business to credit customers. This might involve very large numbers of invoices/credit notes per day or per week. The same customer might appear in several different places in the sales day book, for sales made on credit at different times so a customer may owe money on several unpaid invoices. Similarly, the customer may make payments and take discounts at different times.

In addition to keeping a chronological record of invoices/credit notes and cash received/discount allowed, a business should also keep a record of how much money each **individual credit customer** owes, and what this total debt consists of. The need for a **personal account for each customer** is a practical one.

- A customer might ask how much they currently owe. Staff must be able to tell them.
- It is a common practice to send out **statements** to credit customers at the end of each month, showing how much they owe, and itemising new invoices or credit notes sent out and payments received during the month.
- The business managers will want to check the **credit position** of individual customers, and to ensure that no customer is exceeding their credit limit.
- Most important is the need to **match** payments received against debts owed. If a customer makes a payment, the business must be able to set off the payment against the customer's debt and establish how much he still owes on balance.

Definition

Receivables ledger: The memorandum ledger for customers' personal accounts. It is **not** part of the nominal ledger nor the double entry system, but double entry rules apply to the receivables ledger accounts.

Receivables ledger accounts are written up as follows.

- When invoices or credit notes are sent out, entries are made in the sales day book. Each one is then subsequently also entered in the relevant customer account in the receivables ledger: **invoices** on the **debit** side, and **credit notes** on the **credit** side.

- When receipts are debited in the cash book (cash/cheques etc received), each one is also entered in the **credit side** of the relevant customer account.

Each customer account is given a reference or code number, and it is that reference which appears in the **sales day book** and **cash book**.

Here is an example of how a receivables ledger account is laid out. The sales day book reference is SDB 48.

ENOR COLLEGE

		£			A/c no: RL9 £
			10.1.X0	Credit note SDB 48 (CN012)	50.00
Balance b/f		250.00	10.1.X0	Cash CB 48	200.00
10.1.X0	Sales SDB 48 (I 249)	1,291.68	Balance c/d		1,291.68
		1,541.68			1,541.68
11.1.X0	Balance b/d	1,291.68			

7.3 Payables ledger

The payables ledger, like the receivables ledger, consists of a number of personal accounts. These are separate accounts for **each individual supplier**, and they enable a business to keep a continuous record of how much it owes each supplier at any time.

Definition

Payables ledger: The memorandum ledger for suppliers' personal accounts. It is **not** part of the nominal ledger nor part of the double entry system, but double entry rules apply to the payables ledger accounts.

After entries are made in the purchases day book and cash book, they are also made in the relevant supplier account in the payables ledger. Entries are **posted** to the supplier's personal accounts in the payables ledger from the books of original entry (the purchases day book and the cash book).

Here is an example of how a payables ledger account is laid out.

COOK

		£			A/c no: PL 31 £
15.3.X8	Cash CB 48	100.00		Balance b/f	200.00
	Balance c/d	421.60	15.3.X8	Invoice I 4192 PDB 37	321.60
		521.60			521.60
			16.3.X8	Balance b/d	421.60

7.4 Control accounts for the receivables and payables ledgers

Having personal accounts for every customer and supplier in the nominal ledger can become very unwieldy, so:

- **Details** of transactions are posted from the book of original entry using double entry principles to the memorandum **receivables and payables ledgers**, and

- Only **totals** are posted from books of original entry to **nominal ledger** control accounts as part of the double entry system

We shall return to control accounts in Chapter 6.

8 Accounting for discounts

Section overview

- Trade discount reduces the goods total amount on an invoice. It is not recorded separately anywhere in the accounting system.

- Cash discount is recorded only when it reduces the amount paid by the business (discount received) or received by it (discount allowed).

- Discount received from suppliers is recorded on the payments side of the cash book. It is debited to payables control and credited to discounts received (an income account).

- Discount allowed to customers is recorded on the receipts side of the cash book. It is debited to discounts allowed (an expense account) and credited to receivables control.

Definition

Discount: A reduction in the price of goods below the amount at which those goods would normally be sold to other customers.

There are two types of discount: trade discount and cash discount.

8.1 Trade discount

Definition

Trade discount: A reduction in the cost of goods, owing to the nature of the trading transaction. It usually results from buying goods in bulk. It is deducted from the list price of goods sold, to arrive at a final sales figure. **There is no separate ledger account for trade discount.**

8.1.1 Examples of trade discount

- A customer is quoted a price of £1 per unit for a particular item, but a lower price of 95p per unit if the item is bought in quantities of 100 units or more at a time. This is sometimes called **bulk discount**.

- An important customer or a regular customer is offered a discount on all the goods they buy, regardless of the size of each individual order, because the total volume of their purchases over time is so large.

8.2 Cash discount

Definition

Cash discount: A reduction in the amount payable in return for immediate payment in cash, or for payment within an agreed period. There are separate ledger accounts for cash discounts: one for discount allowed to customers, and one for discount received from suppliers.

For example, a supplier charges £1,000 for goods, but offers a discount of 5% if the goods are paid for immediately in cash.

8.3 Accounting for trade discount

A trade discount is a reduction in the amount of money initially demanded on an invoice.

- If a trade discount is received by a business for goods purchased from a supplier, the amount of money demanded from the business by the supplier will be net of discount (ie it will be the normal sales value less the discount).

- If a trade discount is given by a business for goods sold to a customer, the amount of money demanded of the customer by the business will be after deduction of the discount.

Trade discount should therefore be accounted for as follows.

- **Trade discounts received** should be **deducted from the gross cost of purchases** by the supplier. The cost of purchases in the payables ledger will be stated at gross cost minus discount, ie the invoiced amount.

- **Trade discounts allowed** should be **deducted from the gross sales price** by the business, so that revenue will be reported at invoice value net of trade discount, ie the invoiced amount.

8.4 Accounting for cash discount received

Whether to take advantage of a cash discount for prompt payment is a matter of **financing policy**.

Worked example: Taking cash discount

If the business receives, say, £80 cash discount for paying a debt of £2,000 early, we account for this as follows:

- In the purchases account, we debit the invoiced price of £2,000, and the subsequent financing decision about accepting the cash discount is ignored. The credit is to trade payables.

- When we pay (£2,000 – £80) = £1,920 and take the discount, we **credit** cash and **debit** trade payables with £1,920.

- To account for the discount we **debit** trade payables £80, so eliminating the £2,000 debt entirely, and **credit** £80 to the discount received account (an income account).

Interactive question 5: Discounts I [Difficulty level: Easy]

Soft Supplies Co recently purchased from Hard Imports Co 10 printers originally priced at £200 each. A 10% trade discount was negotiated together with a 5% cash discount if payment was made within 14 days. Calculate the following.

(a) The total of the trade discount
(b) The total of the cash discount

See **Answer** at the end of this chapter.

8.5 Accounting for cash discount allowed

The same principle is applied in accounting for cash discounts allowed to customers. Goods are sold at a trade price, and the offer of a discount on that price is a matter of financing policy for the business.

Interactive question 6: Discounts II [Difficulty level: Intermediate]

You are required to prepare the income statement of Seesaw Timber Merchants for the year ended 31 March 20X6, given the following information.

	£
Purchases at gross cost	120,000
Trade discounts received	4,000
Cash discounts received	1,500
Cash sales	34,000
Credit sales at invoice price	150,000
Cash discounts allowed	8,000
Distribution costs	32,000
Administrative expenses	40,000
Drawings by owner, Tim Burr	22,000

See **Answer** at the end of this chapter.

9 Accounting for VAT

Section overview

- VAT on sales (output VAT) is debited to receivables as part of the posting from the sales day book and credited to the VAT liability account (it is owed to HMRC).

- VAT on purchases (input VAT) is debited to the VAT liability account (it is due from HMRC) and credited to payables as part of the posting from the purchases day book.

- The net amount of VAT owed to HMRC is paid to HMRC regularly.

9.1 What is VAT?

VAT is an indirect tax on the supply of goods and services. Tax is collected at each transfer point in the chain from prime producer to final consumer. Eventually, the consumer bears the tax in full and any tax paid earlier in the chain can be recovered by a registered trader who paid it.

Worked example: VAT

A manufacturing company, A Ltd, purchases raw materials at a cost of £1,000 plus VAT at the standard rate of 20%. From the raw materials A Ltd makes finished products which it sells to a retail outlet, B plc, for £1,600 plus VAT at 20%. B plc sells the products to customers at a total price of £2,000 plus VAT at 20%. How much VAT is paid at each stage in the chain?

Solution

	Value of goods sold £	VAT 20% £
Supply to A Ltd (A Ltd pays £200 VAT but recovers it)	1,000	200
Value added by A Ltd	600	
Sale to B plc (B plc pays £320 VAT but recovers it)	1,600	320
Value added by B plc	400	
Sale to 'consumers' (customers pay £400 VAT, and cannot recover it)	2,000	400

9.2 How is VAT collected?

Although it is the final consumer who eventually bears the full VAT of £400, the sum is **collected and paid by the traders who make up the chain**, provided they are registered for VAT. Each trader must assume that his customer is the final consumer:

- He must collect and pay over VAT at the appropriate rate on the full sales value (known as **output tax**) of the goods sold.

- He is normally entitled to reclaim VAT paid on his own purchases of goods, expenses and non-current assets (known as **input tax**) and so makes a net payment to the HMRC equal to the tax on value added by himself.

In the example above, the supplier of raw materials collects from A Ltd output VAT of £200, all of which he pays over to HMRC. When A Ltd sells goods to B plc, output VAT is charged at the rate of 20% on £1,600 = £320. Only £120, however, is paid by A Ltd to HMRC, because the company is entitled to deduct input tax of £200 suffered on its own purchases. Similarly, B plc must charge its customers £400 in output VAT, but need only pay over to HMRC the net amount of £80 after deducting the £320 input VAT suffered on its purchase from A Ltd.

9.3 Registered and non-registered persons

Traders whose sales (outputs) are below a certain level need not register for VAT although they may do so voluntarily. Unregistered traders neither charge VAT on their outputs nor are entitled to reclaim VAT on their inputs. They are in the same position as a final consumer.

All outputs of registered traders are either taxable or exempt. Traders carrying on **exempt activities** (such as banks) cannot charge VAT on their outputs and consequently cannot reclaim VAT paid on their inputs.

Taxable outputs are chargeable at one of **three rates**.

- **Zero rate** (on books and newspapers for instance)
- **Reduced rate** (5% on domestic fuel)
- **Standard rate**: 20%

HMRC identifies supplies falling into each category. **Persons carrying on taxable activities** (even activities taxable at zero rate) **are entitled to reclaim VAT paid on their inputs.**

Some traders carry on a **mixture of taxable and exempt activities**. Such traders need to apportion the VAT suffered on inputs and **can usually only reclaim the proportion of input tax that relates to taxable outputs.**

Most traders account quarterly to HMRC for VAT.

- The most usual position is to have to pay the net balance to HMRC (when output tax exceeds input tax) ie HMRC is a payable.

- A trader who makes zero-rated supplies will have paid more input tax than it has received output tax, so will recover cash from HMRC, ie HMRC is a receivable.

9.4 Accounting for VAT

As a general principle the treatment of VAT in the trader's ledger accounts should reflect the trader's role as tax collector, so **VAT should not be included in income or in expenses, whether of a capital or a revenue nature**.

9.4.1 Irrecoverable VAT

Where the **trader suffers irrecoverable VAT** as a cost, as in the following cases, VAT should be included as an expense. (It cannot be claimed as input tax.)

- **Persons not registered** for VAT will suffer VAT on inputs as a cost. This will increase their expenses and the cost of any non-current assets they purchase.

- **Registered persons** who also carry on **exempted activities** may have a residue of input VAT which falls directly on them. In this situation the costs to which this residue applies will be inflated by the **irrecoverable VAT**.

- **Non-deductible inputs will be borne** by all traders.

  - VAT on **cars** purchased and used in the business is not reclaimable (VAT on a car acquired new for resale, ie by a car trader, is reclaimable).

  - VAT on **business entertaining** is not deductible as input tax other than VAT on entertaining staff.

Where VAT is not recoverable it must be regarded as part of the cost of the items purchased and included in the income statement or statement of financial position as appropriate.

9.5 VAT and discounts

VAT is charged on the goods or services total on an invoice (or credit note) net of both:

- Trade discount and
- Cash discount.

This general principle is carried to the extent that where a discount is offered at the point of sale, VAT is charged on the amount net of the offered discount **even where it is subsequently not taken up**.

Worked example: VAT and discounts

Matt sells usually sells goods at £130 each, he gives Anil a trade discount of £10 so he sells goods to Anil for £120. He also offers a cash discount of 5% for prompt payment. Matt is registered for VAT. This means that £120 × 5% = £6 cash discount is available.

How much output VAT should Matt include on Anil's invoice?

Solution

If the discount had not been offered output VAT of £120 × 20% = £24.00 would be due. But because of the discount, Matt's sales invoice will show:

INVOICE

	£
List price	130.00
Trade discount	(10.00)
Goods value	120.00
VAT (120 × 95% × 20%)	22.80
Invoice total	142.80
Cash discount available (£120 × 5%)	£6.00

If Anil takes up the discount, he need only pay £136.80 in full settlement (£142.80 – £6), but even if he does not take the discount, the amount of VAT is not adjusted.

9.6 VAT and irrecoverable debts

Most registered persons are obliged to record VAT when a supply is made or received (effectively when a sales invoice is raised or a purchase invoice recorded). This may have the effect that **output tax has to be paid to HMRC before it has all been received from customers**. If an amount due from a customer is subsequently written off as irrecoverable, the VAT element may not be recoverable from HMRC for some time after the sale.

9.7 Summary of accounting entries for VAT

In Chapter 3 we saw how VAT is initially recorded in the books of original entry. Let's summarise it now.

(a) **Sales revenue** shown in the income statement must **exclude output VAT**. However trade receivables will **include** VAT, as they reflect the total amount due from customers. The sales day book is the book of original entry for VAT on credit sales.

The double entry posted from the sales day book for sales of £500,000 on credit is:

		£	£
DEBIT	Trade receivables a/c (including VAT, called **gross**)	600,000	
CREDIT	Sales a/c (excluding VAT, called **net**)		500,000
	VAT a/c (20% × £500,000) – output tax		100,000

(b) **Expenses** shown in the income statement must **exclude input VAT**. However, trade payables will **include** input VAT, as they reflect the total amount payable to suppliers. The purchases day book is the book of original entry for VAT on credit purchases. The double entry posted from the purchases day book for purchases of £400 is:

		£	£
DEBIT	Purchases expense (net)	400	
	VAT a/c (20% × £400) – input tax	80	
CREDIT	Trade payables (gross)		480

(c) Sales revenue received and expenses paid as cash transactions in the cash book or petty cash book must have the VAT recorded in these books of original entry, and then posted as above in (a) and (b).

(d) **Irrecoverable VAT** on expenses or non-current assets must be **included in the cost** of the expense or non-current asset in the income statement or statement of financial position.

(e) The net amount due to HMRC should be included in **other payables** (or **other receivables**) in the statement of financial position.

9.8 Calculating VAT from a gross amount

If you are told that an amount **includes VAT** at 20% (a gross amount), you can calculate the VAT element by multiplying the gross amount by 20%/120% or 1/6. Therefore the net amount will always be 5/6 of the gross element.

Worked example: VAT calculation

A sale of £200 attracts VAT at 20%, ie £40. The gross amount is £240. To get back to the VAT element:

£240 × 1/6 = £40

Interactive question 7: VAT
[Difficulty level: Exam standard]

Mussel is preparing financial statements for the year ended 31 May 20X9. Included in its statement of financial position as at 31 May 20X8 was a balance for VAT due from HMRC of £15,000.

Mussel's summary income statement for the year to 31 May 20X9 is as follows.

	£'000
Revenue (net) (all standard rated)	500
Purchases (net) (all standard rated)	(120)
Gross profit	380
Expenses (see note)	(280)
Net profit	100

	£'000
Note: expenses	
Wages and salaries (exempt of VAT)	162
Entertainment expenditure (£40 + irrecoverable VAT £8)	48
Other (net) (all standard rated at 20%)	70
	280

In respect of VAT payments of £5,000, £15,000 and £20,000 have been made in the year to HMRC and a repayment of £12,000 was received.

Requirement

What is the balance for VAT in the statement of financial position as at 31 May 20X9? Assume a 20% standard rate of VAT. (Hint: Use a T account for VAT.)

See **Answer** at the end of this chapter.

Summary

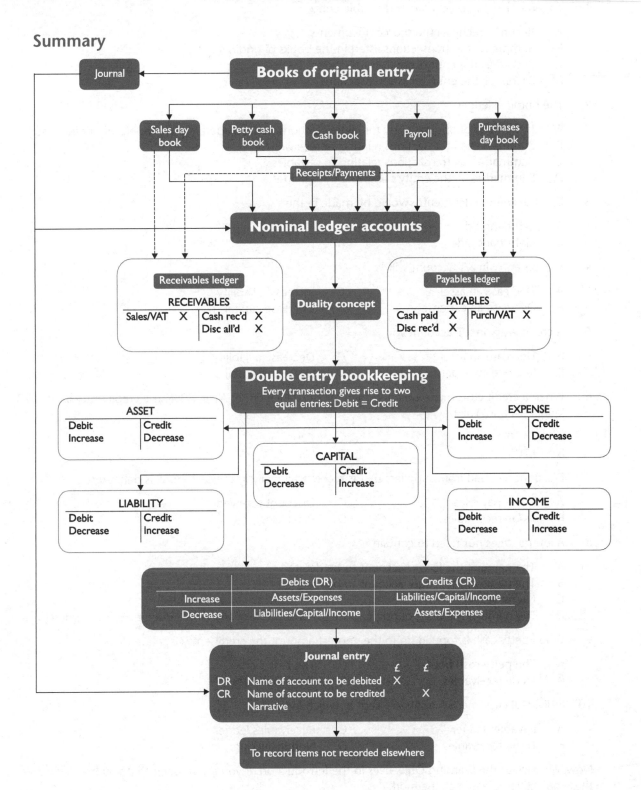

Self-test

Answer the following questions.

1   Together ledger accounting and double entry

    A   Record directly all the source documents
    B   Summarise the transactions listed in the books of original entry
    C   Record all the entity's credit transactions
    D   Record all the entity's cash transactions

2   The nominal ledger

    A   Is the book of original entry for all transactions not recorded in other books of original entry
    B   Summarises all transactions relating to receivables
    C   Summarises all transactions relating to payables
    D   Summarises all the entity's financial transactions

3   In a T account a debit entry would be made in the

    A   Left hand side
    B   Right hand side

4   A debit entry in a T account will

    A   Decrease an asset   C   Increase a liability
    B   Decrease an expense   D   Decrease capital

5   A credit entry in a T account will

    A   Decrease an asset   C   Decrease a liability
    B   Increase an expense   D   Decrease capital

6   When a credit customer pays an invoice for £120 including VAT at 20%, the credit entry in the VAT ledger account will be

    A   £120   C   £20
    B   £100   D   Nil

7   Discount received from suppliers that is recorded initially in the cash book is debited to

    A   Trade payables   C   Discount received
    B   Trade receivables   D   Purchases

8   A journal does **not** need to contain

    A   The name of the ledger account to be debited
    B   The name of the ledger account to be credited
    C   Narrative
    D   The name of the book of original entry where the relevant source document is recorded

9   When petty cash is topped up to the imprest amount the credit entry is made to

    A   The petty cash book   C   The cash book
    B   Trade receivables   D   Trade payables

10 Individual customer accounts are kept in which ledger?

    A   Payables ledger   C   Receivables ledger
    B   Trade receivables   D   Nominal ledger

Now, go back to the Learning Objectives in the Introduction. If you are satisfied that you have achieved these objectives, please tick them off.

Answer to Interactive question 1

(c)   Payment received from a credit customer

- Receivables decrease CREDIT Receivables (decrease in asset)
- Cash at bank increases DEBIT Cash at bank (increase in asset)

(d)   Sell books for cash

- Revenue increases CREDIT Sales (increase in income)
- Cash at bank increases DEBIT Cash at bank (increase in asset)

Answer to Interactive question 2

			£	£
(a)	DEBIT	Machine account (non-current asset)	8,000	
	CREDIT	Trade payables		8,000
(b)	DEBIT	Purchases account	500	
	CREDIT	Trade payables		500
(c)	DEBIT	Trade receivables	1,200	
	CREDIT	Sales		1,200
(d)	DEBIT	Trade payables	300	
	CREDIT	Cash at bank		300
(e)	DEBIT	Cash at bank	180	
	CREDIT	Trade receivables		180
(f)	DEBIT	Wages account	4,000	
	CREDIT	Cash at bank		4,000
(g)	DEBIT	Rent account	700	
	CREDIT	Trade payables		700
(h)	DEBIT	Trade payables	700	
	CREDIT	Cash at bank		700
(i)	DEBIT	Insurance expense	90	
	CREDIT	Cash at bank		90

Answer to Interactive question 3

In this answer we have calculated the balancing figure on the cash at bank account. We shall come back to this in Chapter 5. For now, just make sure that you completed all the necessary steps correctly.

CASH AT BANK

	£		£
Capital (A)	7,000	Rent (B)	3,500
Bank loan (D)	1,000	Shop fittings (E)	2,000
Sales (F)	10,000	Trade payables (H)	4,950
Trade receivables (I)	2,480	Bank loan interest (J)	100
		Other expenses (K)	1,900
		Drawings (L)	1,500
			13,950
		Balancing figure (the amount of cash left over after payments have been made) – carried down	6,530
	20,480		20,480
Debit balance brought down	6,530		

CAPITAL (RON KNUCKLE)

	£		£
		Cash at bank (A)	7,000

BANK LOAN

	£		£
		Cash at bank (D)	1,000

PURCHASES

	£		£
Trade payables (C)	5,000		

TRADE PAYABLES

	£		£
Cash at bank (H)	4,950	Purchases (C)	5,000
Discount received (H)	50		
	5,000		5,000

RENT

	£		£
Cash at bank (B)	3,500		

SHOP FITTINGS

	£		£
Cash at bank (E)	2,000		

SALES

	£		£
		Cash at bank (F)	10,000
		Trade receivables (G)	2,500

TRADE RECEIVABLES

	£		£
Sales (G)	2,500	Cash at bank (I)	2,480
		Discount allowed (I)	20
	2,500		2,500

DISCOUNT RECEIVED

	£		£
		Trade payables (H)	50

DISCOUNT ALLOWED

	£		£
Trade receivables (I)	20		

BANK LOAN INTEREST

	£		£
Cash at bank (J)	100		

OTHER EXPENSES

	£		£
Cash at bank (K)	1,900		

DRAWINGS ACCOUNT

	£		£
Cash at bank (L)	1,500		

(a) If you want to make sure that this solution is complete, you should go through the transactions A to L and tick off each of them twice in the ledger accounts, once as a debit and once as a credit. When you have finished, all transactions in the 'T' account should be ticked, with only totals and the balancing figure in the cash at bank account left over.

(b) In fact, there is an easier way to check that the solution to this sort of problem does 'balance' properly, which we will see in Chapter 5.

(c) On asset, capital and liability accounts, the debit or credit balance represents the amount of the asset, capital or liability outstanding at the period end. For example, on the cash at bank account, debits exceed credits by £6,530 and so there is a balance on the credit side carried down to be a debit balance of cash in hand of £6,530. On the capital account, there is a credit balance of £7,000 and so the business owes Ron £7,000.

(d) The balances on the income and expense accounts represent the total of each type of income or expense for the period. For example, sales revenue for the period totals £12,500.

Answer to Interactive question 4

£71.26. This is the total amount of cash that has been used.

Answer to Interactive question 5

(a) £200 (£200 × 10 × 10%)
(b) £90 (£200 × 10 × 90% × 5%)

Answer to Interactive question 6

SEESAW TIMBER MERCHANTS
INCOME STATEMENT
FOR THE YEAR ENDED 31 MARCH 20X6

	£	£
Revenue (150,000 + 34,000)		184,000
Purchases (120,000 – 4,000)		(116,000)
Gross profit		68,000
Discounts received		1,500
Expenses		
Distribution costs	32,000	
Administrative expenses including discount allowed (40,000 + 8,000)	48,000	
		(80,000)
Net loss transferred to the statement of financial position		(10,500)

Answer to Interactive question 7

VAT

	£		£
Balance b/d	15,000	Output tax – (£500,000 × 20%)	100,000
Input tax – Purchases (£120,000 × 20%)	24,000	Cash received from HMRC	12,000
Input tax – Other expenses (£70,000 × 20%)	14,000		
Cash paid to HMRC (5,000 + 15,000 + 20,000)	40,000		
Balance c/d	19,000		
	112,000		112,000
		Balance b/d	19,000

Therefore there is a balance **owing to** HMRC of £19,000, which is shown on the statement of financial position as an **other payable**.

1   B   The nominal ledger contains summaries of both cash and credit transactions (C and D). Source documents are recorded directly in books of original entry, not the nominal ledger (A)

2   D   The nominal ledger contains summaries of transactions relating to both receivables and payables (B and C) as well as other transactions. Answer (A) describes the journal

3   A   A credit entry is made in the right hand side

4   D   Answers A, B and C all describe credit entries

5   A   Answers B, C and D all describe debit entries

6   D   The VAT is recorded in the VAT account when the invoice is first entered in the sales day book, not when the customer pays

7   A   The double entry is debit trade payables, credit discount received (C). It has no effect on purchases (D) nor on trade receivables (B)

8   D   The journal is the book of original entry. Items A, B and C are all required in a journal entry, though narrative is often omitted when the journal is routine

9   C   The double entry is debit petty cash (A), credit cash at bank. Trade receivables and payables (B and D) are unaffected

10   C   The receivables ledger contains the individual customer accounts. The nominal ledger (D) contains the trade receivables account (B) which is the **total** of all the individual customer accounts. The payables ledger contains individual suppliers' accounts

CHAPTER 5

Preparing basic financial statements

Introduction

Examination context

Topic List

Summary and Self-test

Answers to Interactive questions

Answers to Self-test

Learning objectives

- Prepare a trial balance from accounting records and identify the uses of a trial balance ☐

- Prepare an extended trial balance ☐

- Prepare and present a statement of financial position, income statement and statement of cash flows (or extracts therefrom) from the accounting records and trial balance in a format which satisfies the information requirements of the entity ☐

Specific syllabus learning outcomes are: 1e; 2c; 3c

Syllabus links

The material in this chapter will be developed further in this paper, and then in the Financial Accounting and Financial Reporting papers later in the Professional stage.

Examination context

Questions on the topics in this chapter will be set as multiple choice questions, some of which may involve calculations so that the correct answer can be selected.

In the exam you may be required to:

- Specify the nature of items in the statement of financial position: non-current and current assets, non-current and current liabilities, and capital

- Identify the correct balances on ledger accounts

- Identify how ledger account balances would appear in the trial balance

- Use a profit and loss ledger account to calculate gross or net profit

- Use the extended trial balance to calculate figures for basic financial statements

1 Balancing ledger accounts

Section overview

- A ledger account is balanced by totalling both sides of the account, then subtracting the smaller amount from the larger one and inserting this as a balance on the side which had the smaller total.

At the end of a reporting period such as a month or a year, a balance is extracted for each nominal ledger account.

- All debits and credits, including opening balances, on the account are totalled
- If total debits exceed total credits there is a *debit* balance on the account
- If total credits exceed total debits the account has a *credit* balance

Look back at Ron Knuckle's ledger accounts in the answer to Interactive question 3 in Chapter 4. There was very little balancing to do

- Both trade payables and trade receivables balance off to zero
- The cash at bank account has a debit balance of £6,530 (total debits exceed total credits)
- The total on the sales account is £12,500, which is a credit balance

Otherwise, the accounts have only one entry each, so there is no totalling to do to arrive at the balance on each account.

2 The trial balance

Section overview

- The balances at the end of a period on all the nominal ledger accounts are listed on a trial balance: debit balances appear in the debit column and credit balances in the credit column. When added up, the two columns should be equal.

- Extracting a trial balance serves as a check that certain types of error have not occurred in posting the accounts.

- The trial balance does not in itself detect errors of omission, commission or principle, nor compensating errors.

- An initial trial balance can be adjusted with journals using an extended trial balance to create an income statement and statement of financial position.

Definition

Trial balance: A list of nominal ledger balances shown in debit and credit columns, as a method of testing the accuracy of double entry bookkeeping. The trial balance is not part of the double entry system.

To draw up a trial balance, you need a set of ledger accounts. For the sake of convenience, we will continue to use Ron Knuckle's accounts, which we drew up in Chapter 4.

2.1 Listing ledger account balances in the trial balance

If double entry principles have been correctly applied throughout the period, total credit balances will equal total debit balances and so the totals will balance. Here are the balances on Ron Knuckle's accounts.

C H A P T E R

5

	Debit £	Credit £
Cash at bank	6,530	
Capital		7,000
Bank loan		1,000
Purchases	5,000	
Trade payables		0
Rent	3,500	
Shop fittings	2,000	
Sales		12,500
Trade receivables	0	
Discount received		50
Discount allowed	20	
Bank loan interest	100	
Other expenses	1,900	
Drawings	1,500	
	20,550	20,550

It does not matter in what order the various accounts are listed in the trial balance.

2.2 What if the trial balance fails to balance?

If the two column totals on the trial balance are not equal, there must be an **error** in recording transactions in the ledger accounts, or in the addition of the trial balance.

Even if the trial balance balances, the following error types may still have arisen in the ledger accounts.

- **Omission errors**: a transaction is completely omitted, either in the nominal ledger, or the trial balance itself, so neither a debit nor a credit is made.

- **Commission errors**: a debit or credit is posted to the correct side of the nominal ledger, but to a **wrong account**. For example, wages paid are debited to the rent account instead of the wages account.

- **Compensating errors**: one error is exactly cancelled by another error elsewhere.

- **Errors of principle**, such as cash from receivables being debited to trade receivables and credited to cash at bank instead of the other way round.

We shall come back to these errors, and to what happens when the trial balance fails to balance, in Chapter 6.

2.3 Making adjustments after the trial balance is extracted

We often need to make adjustments after all ledger balances have been calculated and listed on the trial balance. **Adjustment journals** are needed for this.

Worked example: Trial balance and adjustment journals

As at 31.3.20X7, a business, which is not registered for VAT, has the following nominal ledger balances.

	Balance £
Bank loan	12,000
Cash at bank	11,700
Capital	13,000
Rent	1,880
Trade payables	11,200
Purchases	12,400
Sales	34,600
Other payables	1,620
Trade receivables	12,000
Bank loan interest	1,400
Other expenses	11,020
Non-current assets	22,020

On 31.3.X7 the business made the following transactions after the balances listed above had been calculated.

- Bought materials for £1,000, half for cash and half on credit
- Made sales of £1,040, £800 of which were on credit
- Paid wages to shop assistants of £260 in cash

Draw up a trial balance showing the balances as at the end of 31.3.X7.

Solution

To draw up an **initial trial balance** we split the original balances into debit and credit balances. You need to use your knowledge of assets, capital, liabilities, expenses and income for this.

	Dr £	Cr £
Bank loan		12,000
Cash at bank	11,700	
Capital		13,000
Rent	1,880	
Trade payables		11,200
Purchases	12,400	
Sales		34,600
Other payables		1,620
Trade receivables	12,000	
Bank loan interest	1,400	
Other expenses	11,020	
Non-current assets	22,020	
	72,420	72,420

Next prepare journals for the transactions on 31.3.X7.

			£	£
(a)	DEBIT	Purchases	1,000	
	CREDIT	Cash at bank		500
		Trade payables		500
(b)	DEBIT	Cash at bank	240	
		Trade receivables	800	
	CREDIT	Sales		1,040
(c)	DEBIT	Other expenses	260	
	CREDIT	Cash at bank		260

Now we can produce the final trial balance

	Dr £	Cr £
Bank loan		12,000
Cash at bank (11,700 + 240 – 500 – 260)	11,180	
Capital		13,000
Rent	1,880	
Trade payables (11,200 + 500)		11,700
Purchases (12,400 + 1,000)	13,400	
Sales (34,600 + 1,040)		35,640
Other payables		1,620
Trade receivables (12,000 + 800)	12,800	
Bank loan interest	1,400	
Other expenses (11,020 + 260)	11,280	
Non-current assets	22,020	
	73,960	73,960

2.4 The extended trial balance

An alternative way of presenting this information is to use an extended trial balance. This has debit and credit columns for the initial trial balance, plus debit and credit columns for adjustment journals. A revised trial balance is then created by cross-casting horizontally.

- To a **debit balance** in the TB, add debits and subtract credits from the adjustment columns. If the result is positive, insert it in the debit column of the revised trial balance. If it is negative, insert it in the credit column of the revised trial balance.

- To a **credit balance** in the TB, subtract debits and add credits. If the answer is positive, insert it in the credit column of the revised trial balance. If it is negative, insert it in the debit column of the revised trial balance.

Ledger balance	Trial balance		Adjustments		Revised trial balance	
	Debit	Credit	Debit	Credit	Debit	Credit
	£	£	£	£	£	£
Bank loan		12,000				12,000
Cash at bank	11,700		240	760*	11,180	
Capital		13,000				13,000
Rent	1,880				1,880	
Trade payables		11,200		500		11,700
Purchases	12,400		1,000		13,400	
Sales		34,600		1,040		35,640
Other payables		1,620				1,620
Trade receivables	12,000		800		12,800	
Bank loan interest	1,400				1,400	
Other expenses	11,020		260		11,280	
Non-current assets	22,020				22,020	
	72,420	72,420	2,300	2,300	73,960	73,960

* 500 + 260

We shall see how a complete extended trial balance works later in this chapter.

3 Preparing the income statement

Section overview

- To prepare the income statement, all the income and expense account balances are transferred to a new ledger account in the nominal ledger, called the profit and loss ledger account. The balance on this account is the net profit/(loss) for the period.

- The information summarised in the profit and loss ledger account is then transferred into the vertical income statement format to show: revenue, cost of sales, gross profit, expenses and net profit/(loss).

3.1 Preparing the profit and loss ledger account

The first step in preparing the income statement is to create a new ledger account in the nominal ledger, called the **profit and loss ledger account**. To this account all the ledger account balances relating to the income statement, both income and expense, are transferred. The profit and loss ledger account is part of the double entry system, so the basic rule of double entry still applies: every debit must have an equal and opposite credit entry.

The profit and loss ledger account contains the same information as the income statement, and there are very few differences between the two. However, the income statement lays the information out differently.

The first step is to **identify** the ledger accounts which relate to income and expenses. For Ron Knuckle, these accounts consist of purchases, rent, sales, discount allowed and received, bank loan interest, and other expenses.

Next, we transfer these balances to the profit and loss ledger account. For example, the balance on the purchases account is £5,000 DR. To transfer this balance, we write £5,000 on the credit side of the purchases account, and £5,000 on the debit side of the profit and loss ledger account. Now the balance on the purchases account has been moved to the profit and loss ledger account.

If we do the same thing with all the separate accounts of Ron Knuckle dealing with income and expenses, the result is as follows. (When we transfer or 'clear' these accounts to the profit and loss ledger account (P&L a/c) we double underline both sides of the ledger account we are transferring from to show that the balance is now zero.)

PURCHASES

	£		£
Trade payables	5,000	P&L a/c	5,000

RENT

	£		£
Cash at bank	3,500	P&L a/c	3,500

SALES

	£		£
P&L a/c	12,500	Cash at bank	10,000
		Trade receivables	2,500
	12,500		12,500

DISCOUNT RECEIVED

	£		£
P&L a/c	50	Trade payables	50

DISCOUNT ALLOWED

	£		£
Trade receivables	20	P&L a/c	20

BANK LOAN INTEREST

	£		£
Cash at bank	100	P&L a/c	100

OTHER EXPENSES

	£		£
Cash at bank	1,900	P&L a/c	1,900

PROFIT AND LOSS LEDGER ACCOUNT (P&L a/c)

	£		£
Purchases	5,000	Sales	12,500
Rent	3,500	Discount received	50
Discount allowed	20		
Bank loan interest	100		
Other expenses	1,900		
Net profit for the period	2,030		
	12,550		12,550

The balance on the profit and loss ledger account is the net profit for the period.

3.2 Preparing the income statement

The items in the profit and loss ledger account are the same items that we need to draw up the income statement.

- Sales and purchases are included in gross profit
- All other income is added, and all other expenses are deducted, to arrive at net profit

Interactive question 1: Income statement   [Difficulty level: Intermediate]

Draw up Ron Knuckle's income statement.

See **Answer** at the end of this chapter.

4 Preparing the statement of financial position

Section overview

- To prepare the statement of financial position, the profit and loss ledger account balance is transferred to the capital ledger account.

- All the remaining balances (on the asset, capital and liabilities accounts) in the nominal ledger are then listed out in the vertical format statement of financial position to show: non-current and current assets (total assets), which are equal to capital plus non-current and current liabilities (total capital and liabilities).

4.1 Transferring net profit/loss to the capital account

The owner's capital comprises any cash introduced, plus any profits made by the business, less any drawings. At the stage we have now reached, these three elements are contained in different ledger accounts: cash introduced of £7,000 appears in the capital account; drawings of £1,500 appear in the drawings account; and the profit made by the business is represented by the £2,030 credit balance on the profit and loss account. To determine the closing capital balance we combine these in the **capital account**.

DRAWINGS

	£		£
Cash at bank	1,500	Capital a/c	1,500

PROFIT AND LOSS LEDGER ACCOUNT

	£		£
Purchases	5,000	Sales	12,500
Rent	3,500	Discount received	50
Bank loan interest	100		
Other expenses	1,900		
Discount allowed	20		
Capital a/c	2,030		
	12,550		12,550

CAPITAL

	£		£
Drawings	1,500	Cash at bank	7,000
Balance c/d	7,530	P&L a/c	2,030
	9,030		9,030
		Balance b/d	7,530

4.2 Preparing the statement of financial position

We now just have the cash, capital, bank loan, trade payables, non-current assets and trade receivables accounts.

These accounts represent assets, capital and liabilities of the business (not income and expenses) so their balances are **carried down** in the books of the business. This means that they become **opening balances** for the next reporting period.

The conventional method of ruling off a ledger account at the end of a reporting period and carrying down the balance to the next accounting period is illustrated by Ron Knuckle's bank loan account.

BANK LOAN ACCOUNT

	£		£
Balance carried down (c/d)	1,000	Cash at bank	1,000
		Balance brought down (b/d)	1,000

Ron Knuckle therefore begins the new reporting period with a credit balance brought down of £1,000 on the loan account.

- A **credit balance brought down** denotes a liability.
- A **debit balance brought down** denotes an asset.

Interactive question 2: Statement of financial position   [Difficulty level: Intermediate]

Complete Ron Knuckle's simple statement of financial position.

See **Answer** at the end of this chapter.

5 Preparing basic financial statements

Section overview

- To prepare the income statement and statement of financial position together, you need to follow through methodically the steps involved:

    - Calculate balances on all nominal ledger accounts

    - Prepare trial balance

    - Transfer income and expense balances to the profit and loss ledger account and calculate net profit/(loss)

    - Prepare income statement

    - Transfer profit and loss ledger account and drawings balance to capital account

    - Prepare statement of financial position

We can now work through a full example of preparing a set of basic financial statements. This is by far the most important example in the Study Manual so far. It covers all the accounting steps from entering up ledger accounts to preparing the income statement and statement of financial position. **You must try this example yourself first**, before carefully following through the solution.

Worked example: Preparing financial statements

A business is established with capital of £2,000 paid by the owner into a business bank account, which has an overdraft facility. During the first year's trading, the following transactions occurred:

	£
Purchases of goods for resale, on credit	4,300
Payments to suppliers	3,600
Sales, all on credit	5,800
Payments from customers	3,200
Non-current assets purchased for cash	1,500
Other expenses, all paid in cash	900

Prepare ledgers accounts, an income statement for the year and a statement of financial position as at the end of the year.

Solution

The first thing to do is to open ledger accounts. The accounts needed are: cash at bank; capital; trade payables; purchases; non-current assets; sales; trade receivables; other expenses.

The next step is to perform the double entry bookkeeping for each transaction. Normally you would write them straight into the accounts, but to make this example easier to follow, they are listed below.

		Debit	Credit
(a)	Establishing business (£2,000)	Cash at bank	Capital
(b)	Credit purchases (£4,300)	Purchases	Trade payables
(c)	Payments to suppliers (£3,600)	Trade payables	Cash at bank
(d)	Credit sales (£5,800)	Trade receivables	Sales
(e)	Payments from customers (£3,200)	Cash at bank	Trade receivables
(f)	Non-current assets (£1,500)	Non-current assets	Cash at bank
(g)	Other (cash) expenses (£900)	Other expenses	Cash at bank

So far, the ledger accounts will look like this.

CASH AT BANK

	£		£
Capital	2,000	Trade payables	3,600
Trade receivables	3,200	Non-current assets	1,500
		Other expenses	900

CAPITAL

	£		£
		Cash at bank	2,000

TRADE PAYABLES

	£		£
Cash at bank	3,600	Purchases	4,300

PURCHASES

	£		£
Trade payables	4,300		

NON-CURRENT ASSETS

	£		£
Cash at bank	1,500		

SALES

	£		£
		Trade receivables	5,800

TRADE RECEIVABLES

	£		£
Sales	5,800	Cash at bank	3,200

OTHER EXPENSES

	£		£
Cash at bank	900		

Next we balance the ledger accounts and draw up a trial balance to make sure the double entry is accurate.

	Dr £	Cr £
Cash at bank		800
Capital		2,000
Trade payables		700
Purchases	4,300	
Non-current assets	1,500	
Sales		5,800
Trade receivables	2,600	
Other expenses	900	
	9,300	9,300

Next the balances relating to income and expenses (ie sales, other income, purchases and other expenses) are cleared to a profit and loss ledger account. At this point, the ledger accounts will be as follows.

CASH AT BANK

	£		£
Capital	2,000	Trade payables	3,600
Trade receivables	3,200	Non-current assets	1,500
Balance c/d	800	Other expenses	900
	6,000		6,000
		Balance b/d	800*

* A credit balance b/d on the cash at bank ledger account means that this cash item is a liability, not an asset. This indicates a bank overdraft of £800.

PROFIT AND LOSS LEDGER ACCOUNT

	£		£
Purchases account	4,300	Sales	5,800
Gross profit c/d	1,500		
	5,800		5,800
Other expenses	900	Gross profit b/d	1,500
Net profit (transferred to capital account)	600		
	1,500		1,500

CAPITAL

	£		£
Balance c/d	2,600	Cash at bank	2,000
		P&L a/c (net profit)	600
	2,600		2,600
		Balance b/d	2,600

TRADE PAYABLES

	£		£
Cash at bank	3,600	Purchases	4,300
Balance c/d	700		
	4,300		4,300
		Balance b/d	700

PURCHASES ACCOUNT

	£		£
Trade payables	4,300	P&L a/c	4,300

NON-CURRENT ASSETS

	£		£
Cash at bank	1,500	Balance c/d	1,500
Balance b/d	1,500		

SALES

	£		£
P&L a/c	5,800	Trade receivables	5,800

TRADE RECEIVABLES

	£		£
Sales	5,800	Cash at bank	3,200
		Balance c/d	2,600
	5,800		5,800
Balance b/d	2,600		

OTHER EXPENSES

	£		£
Cash at bank	900	P&L a/c	900

The income statement and statement of financial position are as follows.

Income statement

	£
Sales	5,800
Cost of sales (purchases)	(4,300)
Gross profit	1,500
Expenses	(900)
Net profit	600

Statement of financial position

	£	£
Assets		
Non-current assets		1,500
Current assets		
Trade receivables		2,600
Total assets		4,100
Capital and liabilities		
Capital		
At start of period	2,000	
Net profit for period	600	
At end of period		2,600
Current liabilities		
Bank overdraft	800	
Trade payables	700	
		1,500
Total capital and liabilities		4,100

Interactive question 3: Profit and loss ledger account   [Difficulty level: Intermediate]

Polly had the following transactions in her first year of trading as a beauty therapist visiting clients at home.

1.1.X1	Opened a bank account with £400. Took out bank loan for £5,000, and agreed an overdraft limit of the same amount
1.1.X1	Bought car for £2,500 cash. Insured it for £300 cash. Bought other equipment for £1,500, and consumable items for £500, both on credit
During year:	Charged customers £15,945, all on credit.
During year:	Purchased further consumables for £3,690 on credit, and diesel for car for £650 in cash.
During year:	Took £1,250 in cash from ATMs for herself
By end of year:	Received £12,935 from customers and paid £3,250 to suppliers

Prepare Polly's ledger accounts including a profit and loss ledger account, and draw up an income statement and statement of financial position in respect of her first year of trading.

See **Answer** at the end of this chapter.

6 The extended trial balance (ETB)

Section overview

- We can prepare the income statement and statement of financial position without a separate profit and loss ledger account if we use the extended trial balance (ETB).

- The ETB cross-casts from the trial balance and any adjusting journals straight to debit and credit columns for the income statement (all income and expense items) and the statement of financial position (all asset, liability and capital items).

- If the entity has made a profit this is shown in the debit column for the income statement, and in the credit column for the statement of financial position.

- If the entity has made a loss this is shown in the credit column for the income statement, and in the debit column for the statement of financial position.

In section 2.4 we saw how the extended trial balance (ETB) helped us to adjust an initial trial balance to create a revised one. The full way in which we use the ETB is to help us draw up an income statement and statement of financial position, **without the need to create a profit and loss ledger account**.

Worked example: Extended trial balance

Taking the revised trial balance from section 2.4 and using it as the trial balance column of the ETB, we 'extend' it across so that:

- All the income and expense items are taken into the appropriate debit and credit columns of the income statement

- A net profit for the year is calculated in the debit column of the income statement

- This net profit is inserted in the credit column of the statement of financial position to complete the double entry

- All the other items are taken to the appropriate debit and credit columns of the statement of financial position. Note that we take the opening capital balance and the drawings balance straight from the trial balance to the statement of financial position

- All columns are added up to ensure the double entry has been carried out properly

- The income statement and statement of financial position in IAS 1 (revised) format are prepared from the relevant columns of the ETB

Solution

Ledger balance	Revised trial balance		Income statement		Statement of financial position	
	Debit	Credit	Debit	Credit	Debit	Credit
	£	£	£	£	£	£
Bank loan		12,000				12,000
Cash at bank	11,180				11,180	
Capital		13,000				13,000
Rent	1,880		1,880			
Trade payables		11,700				11,700
Purchases	13,400		13,400			
Sales		35,640		35,640		
Other payables		1,620				1,620
Trade receivables	12,800				12,800	
Bank loan interest	1,400		1,400			
Other expenses	11,280		11,280			
Non-current assets	22,020		27,960	35,640	22,020	
Net profit			7,680			7,680
	73,960	73,960	35,640	35,640	46,000	46,000

Income statement

	£	£
Revenue		35,640
Cost of sales		
Purchases		(13,400)
Gross profit		22,240
Expenses		
Other expenses	11,280	
Rent	1,880	
Finance costs (interest)	1,400	
		(14,560)
Net profit		7,680

Statement of financial position

	£	£
Non-current assets		22,020
Current assets		
Trade receivables	12,800	
Cash at bank	11,180	
		23,980
Total assets		46,000
Capital and liabilities		
Opening capital		13,000
Net profit for year (from income statement)		7,680
Drawings		0
Closing capital		20,680
Non-current liabilities		
Bank loan		12,000
Current liabilities		
Trade payables	11,700	
Other payables	1,620	
		13,320
Total capital and liabilities		46,000

CHAPTER 5

Interactive question 4: Extended trial balance [Difficulty level: Intermediate]

Prepare an extended trial balance for Polly, for whom we prepared an income statement and statement of financial position in Interactive question 3.

See **Answer** at the end of this chapter.

Summary

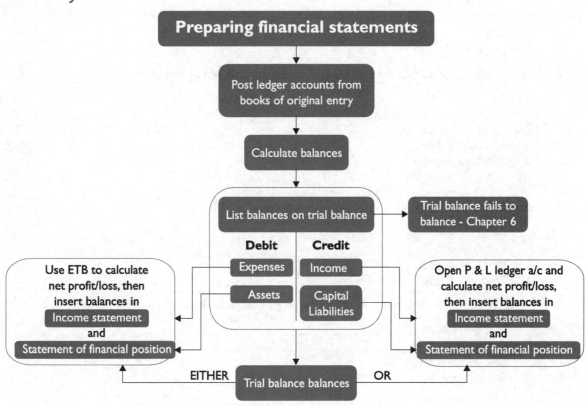

C
H
A
P
T
E
R

5

Self-test

Answer the following questions.

1 In a period, sales are £140,000, purchases £75,000 and other expenses £25,000. What is the figure for net profit to be transferred to the capital account?

    A   £40,000
    B   £65,000
    C   £75,000
    D   £140,000

2 During March, Chan had the following items in the cash at bank account.

	£
Balance at 1 March (overdrawn)	500
Receipts from receivables	12,000
Payments to payables	7,000
Payments for expenses	3,000
Cash drawn for own use	1,200

What is the balance on Chan's cash at bank account on 31 March?

    A   Debit   £300
    B   Credit   £300
    C   Debit   £1,300
    D   Credit   £1,300

3 Which **three** of the following items will be listed as a credit balance on a trial balance?

    A   Trade payables
    B   Purchases
    C   Discounts received
    D   Sundry expenses
    E   Capital
    F   Drawings

4 Select whether the following balances will be in the debit or the credit columns of the trial balance.

	Debit	Credit
Machinery	☐	☐
Trade payables	☐	☐
Drawings	☐	☐
Discount allowed	☐	☐
Revenue	☐	☐
Discount received	☐	☐
Bank overdraft	☐	☐
Rental income	☐	☐

5 When an error in a debit entry is cancelled out by an error in a credit entry, this is called

    A   A commission error
    B   A compensating error
    C   An omission error
    D   An error of principle

6   An error has led to Erica's trial balance failing to balance. This could have been caused by an error of commission.

☐ True

☐ False

7   The balance on Tim's loan account is £1,200. He has just realised that a £100 loan repayment that he made during the year was posted from the cash book to drawings. On the loan account line of the extended trial balance, adjusting for this mistake will mean:

A   A credit entry in the adjustments columns and a credit balance of £1,100 in the statement of financial position columns

B   A debit entry in the adjustments columns and a credit balance of £1,100 in the statement of financial position columns

C   A credit entry in the adjustments columns and a credit balance of £1,300 in the statement of financial position columns

D   A debit entry in the adjustments columns and a credit balance of £1,300 in the statement of financial position columns

8   Manny has a net loss of £400. This should be

A   Credited to the profit and loss ledger account and debited to the capital account
B   Debited to the profit and loss ledger account and credited to the capital account
C   Credited to the profit and loss ledger account and debited to the drawings account
D   Debited to the profit and loss ledger account and credited to the drawings account

9   At 31 December 20X6 Richard's total assets are £20,376 and his non-current liabilities are £10,000. If his current liabilities are £6,290 then his capital balance at 31 December 20X6 must be

A   £4,086
B   £16,666
C   £24,086
D   £36,666

10   The income statement columns on Jude's ETB are £57,390 for the debit column and £84,928 for the credit column. What final entry does Jude need to make?

A   Credit £27,538 net profit
B   Credit £27,538 net loss
C   Debit £27,538 net profit
D   Debit £27,538 net loss

Now, go back to the Learning Objectives in the Introduction. If you are satisfied that you have achieved these objectives, please tick them off.

Answer to Interactive question 1

RON KNUCKLE: INCOME STATEMENT FOR FIRST TRADING PERIOD

	£	£
Revenue (= sales)		12,500
Cost of sales (= purchases)		(5,000)
Gross profit		7,500
Other income: discount received		50
Expenses		
Rent	3,500	
Discount allowed	20	
Bank loan interest	100	
Other expenses	1,900	
		(5,520)
Net profit (the balance on the profit and loss ledger account)		2,030

Answer to Interactive question 2

RON KNUCKLE

STATEMENT OF FINANCIAL POSITION AT END OF FIRST TRADING PERIOD

Assets	£
Non-current assets	2,000
Current assets	
Cash at bank	6,530
Total assets	8,530
Capital and liabilities	
Owner's capital	7,530
Non-current liabilities	
Bank loan	1,000
Total capital and liabilities	8,530

Answer to Interactive question 3

CASH AT BANK

		£			£
1.1.X1	Capital	400	1.1.X1	Insurance	300
1.1.X1	Loan	5,000	1.1.X1	Non-current assets	2,500
31.12.X1	Trade receivables	12,935	31.12.X1	Car expenses	650
			31.12.X1	Drawings	1,250
			31.12.X1	Trade payables	3,250
			31.12.X1	C/d	10,385
		18,335			18,335
31.12.X1	B/d	10,385			

CAPITAL

		£			£
31.12.X1	Drawings	1,250	1.1.X1	Cash at bank	400
31.12.X1	C/d	9,955	31.12.X1	P&L account	10,805
		11,205			11,205
			31.12.X1	B/d	9,955

LOAN

		£			£
31.12.X1	C/d	5,000	1.1.X1	Cash at bank	5,000
		5,000			5,000
			31.12.X1	B/d	5,000

NON-CURRENT ASSETS (NCA)

		£			£
1.1.X1	Cash at bank	2,500	31.12.X1	C/d	4,000
1.1.X1	Trade payables	1,500			
		4,000			4,000
31.12.X1	B/d	4,000			

TRADE PAYABLES

		£			£
31.12.X1	Cash at bank	3,250	1.1.X1	NCA	1,500
31.12.X1	C/d	2,440	1.1.X1	Purchases	500
			31.12.X1	Purchases	3,690
		5,690			5,690
			31.12.X1	B/d	2,440

INSURANCE

		£			£
1.1.X1	Cash at bank	300	31.12.X1	P&L account	300
		300			300

CAR EXPENSES

		£			£
31.12.X1	Cash at bank	650	31.12.X1	P&L account	650
		650			650

PURCHASES

		£			£
1.1.X1	Trade payables	500	31.12.X1	P&L account	4,190
31.12.X1	Trade payables	3,690			
		4,190			4,190

SALES

		£			£
31.12.X1	P&L account	15,945	31.12.X1	Trade receivables	15,945
		15,945			15,945

TRADE RECEIVABLES

		£			£
31.12.X1	Sales	15,945	31.12.X1	Cash at bank	12,935
			31.12.X1	C/d	3,010
		15,945			15,945
31.12.X1	B/d	3,010			

DRAWINGS

		£			£
31.12.X1	Cash at bank	1,250	31.12.X1	Capital	1,250
		1,250			1,250

PROFIT AND LOSS LEDGER ACCOUNT

		£			£
31.12.X1	Purchases	4,190	31.12.X1	Sales	15,945
31.12.X1	Car expenses	650			
31.12.X1	Insurance	300			
31.12.X1	Capital	10,805			
		15,945			15,945

POLLY: INCOME STATEMENT FOR YEAR ENDED 31 DECEMBER 20X1

	£
Revenue	15,945
Cost of sales	
Purchases	(4,190)
Gross profit	11,755
Expenses	
Car expenses	(650)
Insurance	(300)
Net profit	10,805

POLLY: STATEMENT OF FINANCIAL POSITION AS AT 31 DECEMBER 20X1

	£	£
Non-current assets		4,000
Current assets		
Trade receivables	3,010	
Cash at bank	10,385	
		13,395
Total assets		17,395
Capital and liabilities		
Opening capital		400
Profit for year		10,805
Drawings		(1,250)
Closing capital		9,955
Non-current liabilities		
Bank loan		5,000
Current liabilities		
Trade payables		2,440
Total capital and liabilities		17,395

Answer to Interactive question 4

Ledger balance	Trial balance Debit £	Trial balance Credit £	Income statement Debit £	Income statement Credit £	Statement of financial position Debit £	Statement of financial position Credit £
Cash at bank	10,385				10,385	
Opening capital		400				400
Loan		5,000				5,000
Non-current assets	4,000				4,000	
Trade payables		2,440				2,440
Insurance	300		300			
Car expenses	650		650			
Purchases	4,190		4,190			
Sales		15,945		15,945		
Trade receivables	3,010				3,010	
Drawings	1,250				1,250	
Net profit			10,805			10,805
	23,785	23,785	15,945	15,945	18,645	18,645

1 A

PROFIT & LOSS LEDGER ACCOUNT

	£		£
Purchases	75,000	Sales	140,000
Gross profit c/d	65,000		
	140,000		140,000
Other expenses	25,000	Gross profit b/d	65,000
Net profit – to capital a/c	40,000		
	65,000		65,000

B is the **gross** profit figure, while C is the figure for purchases and D is the figure for sales.

2 A

CASH AT BANK

	£		£
Receivables	12,000	B/d	500
		Payables	7,000
		Expenses	3,000
		Drawings	1,200
		C/d	300
	12,000		12,000
B/d	300		

3 A, C, E Purchases, sundry expenses and drawings are all debit balances

4

	Debit	Credit
Machinery	✓	
Trade payables		✓
Drawings	✓	
Discount allowed	✓	
Revenue		✓
Discount received		✓
Bank overdraft		✓
Rental income		✓

5 B A commission error (A) occurs when the double entry is complete, but the entries are made in the wrong account(s). An omission error (C) occurs when a transaction is completely omitted from the accounting records. An error of principle (D) occurs when the double entry is performed but the wrong treatment is applied to a transaction. With all four errors the trial balance will still balance.

6 False. An error of commission does not lead to the trial balance failing to balance.

7 B The £100 payment was debited to drawings from cash. It needs to be credited to drawings and debited to the loan account, leading to a reduction in the loan balance on the statement of financial position to £1,100.

8 A A net loss is debited to the capital account, reducing the owner's interest in the business, and is credited to the profit and loss ledger account.

9 A £20,376 – £10,000 – £6,290 = £4,086

10 C The difference between the two columns is a debit, so this must appear in the debit column of the income statement as a net profit; a credit entry would make it a net loss.

CHAPTER 6

Control accounts, errors and omissions

Introduction

Examination context

Topic List

Summary and Self-test

Answers to Interactive questions

Answers to Self-test

Introduction

Learning objectives

Tick off

- Prepare a trial balance from accounting records and identify the uses of a trial balance

- Identify omissions and errors in accounting records and financial statements and demonstrate how the required adjustments will affect profits or losses

- Correct omissions and errors in accounting records and financial statements using control account reconciliations and suspense accounts

- Prepare an extended trial balance

- Prepare journals for nominal ledger entry and to correct errors in draft financial statements

Specific syllabus learning outcomes are: 1e; 2a, b, c, d

Syllabus links

The accuracy of financial statements is the bedrock on which the rest of your studies for this paper, and for Financial Accounting and Financial Reporting, are built.

Examination context

Questions on the topics in this chapter will be set as multiple choice questions, some of which may involve calculations so that the correct answer can be selected. Very often double entry questions are phrased in terms of preparing a journal.

In the exam you may be required to:

- Identify distinctions between errors that cause trial balance imbalances and those that do not

- Identify a journal to correct errors

- Calculate a suspense account balance

- Identify the correct journal to clear a suspense account

- Identify the effects of correcting errors on draft gross or net profit

- Use the techniques of bank reconciliations to identify the correct cash at bank balance in the financial statements

- Use reconciliation techniques to identify the correct receivables and payables balances in the financial statements

1 What are control accounts?

Section overview

- Control accounts in the nominal ledger for receivables and payables record **total** amounts in respect of all customers/suppliers.

- The memorandum receivables and payables ledgers record each transaction for individual customers and suppliers in their personal accounts. These are not part of the double entry system if control accounts are maintained.

- The total of all the balances in each memorandum ledger should equal the balance on the relevant control account.

In Chapter 4 when we looked at the memorandum receivables and payables ledgers (ie the ledgers containing personal accounts for customers and suppliers, which are not part of the nominal ledger double entry system) we briefly introduced the idea of **control accounts**.

Definitions

Control account: Nominal ledger account in which a record is kept of the total value of a number of similar individual items. Control accounts are used chiefly for trade receivables and payables.

- A **receivables control account** is a nominal ledger account in which records are kept of transactions involving all receivables in total. The balance on the receivables control account at any time will be the total amount due to the business from all its credit customers.

- A **payables control account** is a nominal ledger account in which records are kept of transactions involving all payables in total, and the balance on this account at any time will be the total amount owed by the business to all its credit suppliers.

Control accounts are also kept for wages and salaries, cash, VAT and non-current assets. The most important idea to remember, however, is that a control account is an account which keeps a total record for a collective item (eg receivables), which in reality consists of many individual items (eg individual trade receivables).

1.1 Control accounts (nominal ledger) and personal accounts (memorandum ledgers)

The amount owed by each credit customer is a balance on their personal account in the receivables ledger, which as we saw in Chapter 4 is a memorandum ledger only, outside the double entry system of the nominal ledger. The amount owed by all the credit customers together (ie all the trade receivables) is the balance on the **receivables control account**.

At any time the **balance on the receivables control account** should be **equal** to the **sum of the individual personal account balances** on the **receivables ledger**.

Most customers will have a **debit balance** on their personal account in the receivables ledger, as they owe the business money for goods/services supplied. Sometimes a customer may have a **credit balance**, perhaps because it has overpaid the business, or paid for goods and then returned some. While credit balances will show up on the receivables ledger balances quite clearly, the balance on the receivables control account in the nominal ledger is an aggregate balance and will always be a debit balance.

Worked example: Receivables control account

A business has three trade receivables: A Arnold owes £80, B Bagshaw owes £310 and C Cloning owes £200.

Receivables ledger personal accounts

	£
A Arnold	80
B Bagshaw	310
C Cloning	200
	590

The balance on the nominal ledger receivables control account should be the total, £590.

What has happened here is that three entries of £80, £310 and £200 were first entered into the sales day book. They were posted individually to the three personal accounts of Arnold, Bagshaw and Cloning in the receivables ledger, but these are not part of the double entry system.

Later, the **total** of £590 was posted from the sales day book to the nominal ledger, which is the double entry system:

		£	£
DEBIT	Receivables control account	590	
CREDIT	Sales		590

2 Operating control accounts

Section overview

- Individual entries in receivables and payables ledgers are summarised and posted to relevant control accounts in the nominal ledger.

- For sales: debit receivables, credit sales & VAT.

- For receipts from customers and discount allowed: credit receivables, debit cash/discount allowed.

- For purchases: credit payables, debit purchases & VAT.

- For payments to suppliers and discount received: debit payables, credit cash/discount received.

- Other entries in receivables accounts: credit receivables, debit payables (contra with payables ledger); credit receivables, debit irrecoverable debts (debt written off); debit receivables, credit cash (customer's cheque dishonoured, or refund to customer).

- Other entries in payables accounts: credit payables, debit cash (refund from supplier); debit payables, credit receivables (contra with receivables ledger).

- The wages control account is used as a clearing account for all the postings from the payroll; at the end of each period the balance should be zero.

The two most important **control accounts** are those for **receivables** and **payables**. They are part of the double entry system; the receivables and payables ledger are memorandum ledgers only.

2.1 Accounting for receivables

Transactions involving receivables are accounted for by posting from books of original entry to both the personal accounts in the receivables ledger, and the receivables control account in the nominal ledger. Reference numbers are shown in the accounts to illustrate cross-referencing as follows:

- SDB refer to a sales day book page
- RL refer to a receivables ledger account
- NL refer to a nominal ledger account
- CB refer to a cash book page

Worked example: Accounting for receivables

At 1 July 20X2, the Outer Business Company (not registered for VAT) had no trade receivables. During July, the following transactions affecting credit sales and customers occurred.

(a) July 3: invoiced A Arnold for the sale on credit of hardware goods: £100

(b) July 11: invoiced B Bagshaw for the sale on credit of electrical goods: £150

(c) July 15: invoiced C Cloning for the sale on credit of hardware goods: £250

(d) July 10: received payment from A Arnold of £90, in settlement of his debt in full, having taken a permitted cash discount of £10 for payment within seven days

(e) July 18: received a payment of £72 from B Bagshaw in part settlement of £80 of his debt; a cash discount of £8 was allowed for payment within seven days of invoice

(f) July 28: received a payment of £120 from C Cloning, who was unable to claim any discount

(g) July 31: received notice that B Bagshaw had become insolvent, so no more payments could be expected from him. The balance of his debt was to be 'written off' as irrecoverable (£70)

Account numbers:

RL 4   A Arnold
RL 9   B Bagshaw
RL 13   C Cloning
NL 1   Cash at bank
NL 6   Receivables control account
NL 7   Discount allowed
NL 21   Sales: hardware
NL 22   Sales: electrical
NL 30   Irrecoverable debts expense

First we indicate in the sales day book where the column totals are to be posted, using the nominal ledger account code, and 'Dr' for debit and 'Cr' for credit. We also note where each invoice total is to be posted in the receivables ledger.

SALES DAY BOOK

SDB 35

Date 20X2	Name	Receivables ledger ref	Total £	Hardware £	Electrical £
July 3	A Arnold	RL 4 Dr	100.00	100.00	
11	B Bagshaw	RL 9 Dr	150.00		150.00
15	C Cloning	RL 13 Dr	250.00	250.00	
			500.00	350.00	150.00
			NL 6 DR	NL 21 CR	NL 22 CR

Note: The personal accounts in the receivables ledger are usually debited on the day the invoices are sent out. The double entry in the nominal ledger accounts might be made at the end of each day, week or month; here it is made at the end of the month, by posting from the sales day book as follows.

			£	£
DEBIT	NL 6	Receivables control	500	
CREDIT	NL 21	Sales: hardware		350
	NL 22	Sales: electrical		150

Next we do the same for the cash book. Remember that discounts allowed and received are recorded in the cash book as a book of original entry only; they are not included in the cross-cast total column.

CASH BOOK EXTRACT
RECEIPTS – JULY 20X2

Date 20X2	Narrative	Receivable ledger ref	Total £	Discount allowed £	Receivables control £
July 10	A Arnold	RL 4 CR	90.00	10.00	90.00
18	B Bagshaw	RL 9 CR	72.00	8.00	72.00
28	C Cloning	RL 13 CR	120.00	–	120.00
			282.00	18.00	282.00
			NL 1 DR	NL 6 CR	NL 6 CR
				NL 7 DR	

Note: Posting discount allowed and cash separately to the receivables control account and to each receivables ledger personal account allows us to cross-check postings more easily.

At the end of July, the cash book is posted to the nominal ledger.

			£	£
DEBIT	NL 1	Cash at bank	282.00	
	NL 7	Discount allowed	18.00	
CREDIT	NL 6	Receivables control (282 + 18)		300.00

B Bagshaw's irrecoverable debt has to be removed from the nominal ledger account, via the journal, using a special nominal ledger expense account called **irrecoverable debt expense**. The credit entry will also be posted from the journal to B Bagshaw's personal account in the receivables ledger.

		£	£
DEBIT	NL 30 Irrecoverable debt expense	70	
CREDIT	NL 6 Receivables control (RL 9)		70

The personal accounts in the receivables ledger are not part of the double entry system, but will look as follows after the postings from the sales day book, the cash book and the journal.

MEMORANDUM RECEIVABLES LEDGER
A ARNOLD
A/c no: RL 4

Date 20X2	Narrative	Ref.	£	Date 20X2	Narrative	Ref.	£
July 3	Sales	SDB 35	100.00	July 10	Cash	CB 23	90.00
					Discount	CB 23	10.00
			100.00				100.00

B BAGSHAW
A/c no: RL 9

Date 20X2	Narrative	Ref.	£	Date 20X2	Narrative	Ref.	£
July 11	Sales	SDB 35	150.00	July 18	Cash	CB 23	72.00
					Discount	CB 23	8.00
				July 31	Irrecoverable Debt	Jnl	70.00
			150.00				150.00

C CLONING
A/c no: RL 13

Date 20X2	Narrative	Ref.	£	Date 20X2	Narrative	Ref.	£
July 15	Sales	SDB 35	250.00	July 28	Cash	CB 23	120.00
				July 31	Balance	c/d	130.00
			250.00				250.00
Aug 1	Balance	b/d	130.00				

In the nominal ledger, the total accounting entries are made from the books of original entry to the ledger accounts at the end of the month.

NOMINAL LEDGER (EXTRACT)
RECEIVABLES CONTROL ACCOUNT

A/c no: NL 6

Date	Narrative	Ref.	£	Date	Narrative	Ref.	£
20X2				20X2			
July 31	Sales	SDB 35	500.00	July 31	Cash	CB 23	282.00
				July 31	Discount allowed	CB 23	18.00
				July 31	Irrecoverable debt	Jnl	70.00
				July 31	Balance	c/d	130.00
			500.00				500.00
Aug 1	Balance	b/d	130.00				

So at 31 July the closing balance on the receivables control account (£130) is the same as the total of the individual balances on the personal accounts in the receivables ledger (£0 + £0 + £130).

The other nominal ledger accounts are written up as follows.

DISCOUNT ALLOWED

A/c no: NL 7

Date	Narrative	Ref.	£	Date	Narrative	Ref.	£
20X2							
July 31	Receivables	CB 23	18.00				

CASH AT BANK ACCOUNT

A/c no: NL 1

Date	Narrative	Ref.	£	Date	Narrative	Ref.	£
20X2							
July 31	Cash received	CB 23	282.00				

Note that discount allowed is **not** posted to the cash at bank account. It only affects the discount allowed and receivables control account.

SALES: HARDWARE

A/c no: NL 21

Date	Narrative	Ref.	£	Date	Narrative	Ref.	£
				20X2			
				July 31	Receivables	SDB 35	350.00

SALES: ELECTRICAL

A/c no: NL 22

Date	Narrative	Ref.	£	Date	Narrative	Ref.	£
				20X2			
				July 31	Receivables	SDB 35	150.00

IRRECOVERABLE DEBTS

A/c no: NL 30

Date	Narrative	Ref.	£	Date	Narrative	Ref.	£
20X2							
July 31	Receivables	Jnl	70.00				

The trial balance at 31 July 20X2 – for the nominal ledger only – is as follows.

TRIAL BALANCE

	Debit £	Credit £
Cash (all receipts)	282	
Receivables	130	
Discount allowed	18	
Irrecoverable debts	70	
Sales: hardware		350
Sales: electrical		150
	500	500

The trial balance is shown here to emphasise the point that a trial balance **includes** the balance on the control account, but **excludes** the balance on the personal accounts in the receivables ledger.

2.2 Accounting for payables

Refer back to revise the entries made in the purchases day book, the payables ledger personal accounts and the payables control account in the nominal ledger. Such entries are mirror images of the way we account for receivables, though there will be no irrecoverable debt entries in the payables accounts.

2.3 Entries in receivables/payables control accounts

Typical entries in the receivables and payables control accounts are set out below. The reference 'Jnl' indicates that the transaction is first entered in the journal before posting to the control account and other accounts indicated.

Definitions

Contra: When a person or business is both a customer and a supplier, amounts owed by and owed to the person may be 'netted off' by means of a **contra**:

DEBIT	Payables control account (and personal account in the payables ledger)
CREDIT	Receivables control account (and personal account in the receivables ledger)

Irrecoverable debt: When a debt owed by a customer will never be paid, the total amount is removed from receivables:

DEBIT	Irrecoverable debt expense
CREDIT	Receivables control account (and personal account in the receivables ledger)

Dishonoured cheque: When a customer's cheque is paid into the business's bank but the customer's bank refuses to honour payment of it, it is 'written back' (the original entry is reversed) so as to remove the receipt of the cheque from the books and recreate the debt that has still not been paid:

DEBIT	Receivables control account (and personal account in the receivables ledger)
CREDIT	Cash

RECEIVABLES CONTROL ACCOUNT

	Ref.	£		Ref.	£
Opening balance	b/d	6,800	Cash received	CB	52,250
Sales/VAT	SDB	51,590	Discounts allowed	CB	1,250
Dishonoured cheques from customers	Jnl	1,000	Contra with payables ledger	Jnl	150
Refunds paid to customers	CB	110	Irrecoverable debts	Jnl	300
			Balance	c/d	5,550
		59,500			59,500
Balance	b/d	5,550			

* Sometimes customers overpay and are left with a credit balance on their personal accounts. This can be settled by the business refunding the overpayments in cash.

PAYABLES CONTROL ACCOUNT

	Ref.	£		Ref.	£
Cash paid	CB	29,840	Opening balance	b/d	8,230
Discounts received	CB	30	Purchases/VAT	PDB	30,940
Contra with receivables ledger	Jnl	150	Refunds received from suppliers*	CB	20
Closing balance	c/d	9,170			
		39,190			39,190
			Balance	b/d	9,170

* As with refunds to customers, so too the business may receive a refund in cash from a supplier regarding an overpayment.

As we saw above, posting from the journal to the receivables (or payables) ledgers and to the nominal ledger may be effected at the same time, as in the following example, where C Cloning has returned goods with a sales value of £50.

Journal entry	Ref.	£	£
DEBIT Sales: hardware	NL 21	50	
CREDIT Receivables control	NL 6		50
C Cloning (personal account)	RL 13		50
Return of hardware goods			

Here is an example of a journal recording the contra entry in respect of Perch Ltd.

Journal entry	Ref.	DR £	CR £
DEBIT Payables control	NL 14	150	
CREDIT Receivables control	NL 6		150
Perch Ltd: payables ledger a/c	PL 82	150	
Perch Ltd: receivables ledger a/c	RL 49		150

Contra between Perch Ltd's receivables and payables ledger accounts.

Interactive question 1: Payables control account   [Difficulty level: Exam standard]

A payables control account contains the following entries:

	£
Bank	79,500
Credit purchases	83,200
Discount received	3,750
Contra with receivables control account	4,000
Balance c/d at 31 December 20X8	12,920

There are no other entries in the account. What was the opening balance brought down at 1 January 20X8?

See **Answer** at the end of this chapter.

Interactive question 2: Receivables control account   [Difficulty level: Exam standard]

The total of the balances in a company's receivables ledger is £800 more than the debit balance on its receivables control account. Which one of the following errors could by itself account for the discrepancy?

A   The sales day book total column has been undercast by £800

B   Cash discounts totalling £800 have been omitted from the nominal ledger

C   One receivables ledger account with a credit balance of £800 has been treated as a debit balance in the list of balances

D   The cash receipts book has been undercast by £800

See **Answer** at the end of this chapter.

Figure 6.1 should help you now to see how the receivables ledger and receivables control account are used. Note that A overpaid by £20 in error, while B only paid part of what he owed.

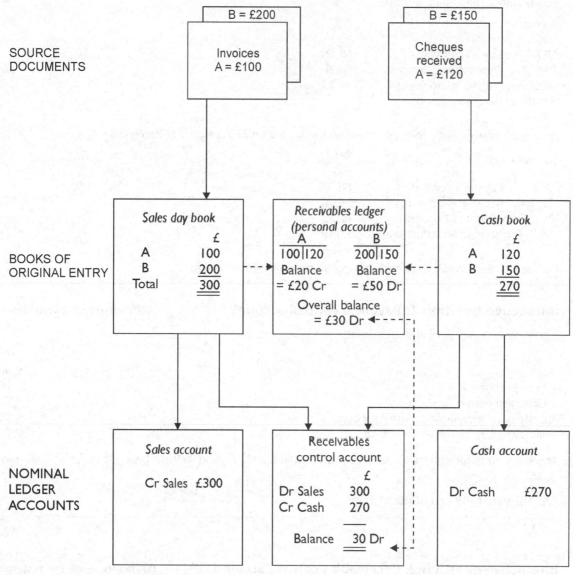

Figure 6.1 Accounting for receivables

The total of the balances on the receivables ledger (ie the personal account balances of A and B added up) equals the balance on the receivables control account.

Interactive question 3: Receivables and payables control accounts
[Difficulty level: Exam standard]

For Exports Co on 1 October 20X8 the receivables ledger balances were £8,024 debit and £57 credit, and the payables ledger balances on the same date were £6,235 credit and £105 debit. These balances have been checked and are correct.

For the year ended 30 September 20X9 the following particulars are available.

	£
Sales	62,514
Purchases	39,439
Cash from credit customers	55,212
Cash to credit suppliers	37,307
Discount received	1,475
Discount allowed	2,328
Irrecoverable debts written off	326
Cash received in respect of debit balances in payables ledger (refunds from suppliers)	105

	£
Amount due from customer as shown by receivables ledger, offset against amount due to the same firm as shown by payables ledger (settlement by contra)	434

What are the balances as at 30 September 20X9 on:

(a) Receivables control account
(b) Payables control account?

See **Answer** at the end of this chapter.

2.4 Accounting for wages: the wages control account

In Chapter 3 we looked at payroll as a book of original entry for the total costs of employing and paying staff. We now look at how payroll is accounted for in the nominal ledger, and how the wages control account is used:

- To maintain the accuracy of payroll double entry
- To identify errors in payroll double entry

 Worked example: Ledger accounting for payroll

The payroll looked at in Chapter 3 was as follows:

	PAYE	Deductions Ees' NI	Ees' pension	Net pay	Gross pay	Er's NI	Er's pension	Total payroll cost
	£	£	£	£	£	£	£	£
Anja	550	250	150	2,050	3,000	310	200	3,510
Mark	500	230	135	1,885	2,750	265	180	3,195
Dipak	460	210	125	1,705	2,500	230	165	2,895
	1,510	690	410	5,640	8,250	805	545	9,600

When using the **wages control account** the objective is that at the end of the process the account balance clears to zero: it is a clearing account. This will affirm that the double entry has been made correctly, though compensating errors could still exist.

The first step is to account for net pay. Net pay is gross pay less deductions; we could debit it straight to the nominal ledger wages expense account, but instead we 'collect' all the entries in the wages control account:

		£	£
DEBIT	Wages control account	5,640	
CREDIT	Cash at bank		5,640
	Payment of net pay to staff		

The next step is to record those amounts which will be paid to outside agencies on behalf of employees. All employees' wages deductions have to be paid eventually to either HMRC or pension trustees, so at some point these will need to be credited to liability accounts – but where will the debit go to? Again, the answer is initially to the wages control account:

		£	£
DEBIT	Wages control account (1,510 + 690 + 410)	2,610	
CREDIT	HMRC (1,510 + 690)		2,200
	Pension trustee		410
	Deductions from pay		

Finally we record the amounts which are payable to external agencies directly by the entity. The employers' NI and pension contributions also need to be credited to liability accounts – but where will the debit go to? Again, the answer is initially to the wages control account:

		£	£
DEBIT	Wages control account (805 + 545)	1,350	
CREDIT	HMRC		805
	Pension trustee		545
	Additional employer costs		

After these entries have been made the wages control account will look like this:

WAGES CONTROL ACCOUNT

	£		£
Cash at bank (net pay)	5,640	Balance	9,600
HMRC (PAYE)	1,510		
HMRC (Ees' NIC)	690		
Pension trustee (Ees' pension)	410		
HMRC (Er's NIC)	805		
Pension trustee (Er's pension)	545		
	9,600		9,600

The wages control account balance represents the total payroll cost to the business, which should be a debit in its wages expense account. Therefore the final entry to bring the wages control account to zero is;

		£	£
DEBIT	Wages expense	9,600	
CREDIT	Wages control		9,600
	Total payroll costs for period		

We could have omitted the wages control account entirely and just done one big journal as follows:

		£	£
DEBIT	Wages expense (gross pay + er's NI and er's pension)	9,600	
CREDIT	Cash at bank (net pay)		5,640
	HMRC (PAYE + ees' NI + er's NI)		3,005
	Pension trustee (ees' and er's)		955
	Total payroll costs for period		

Many businesses use a wages control account so that the accuracy of the initial postings can be verified before making the final posting to wages expense.

3 The purpose of control accounts

Section overview

- Control accounts duplicate in summary form the individual entries in the memorandum ledgers: provide a check on the accuracy of postings; help to locate errors; provide an internal check; allow a total balance to be extracted quickly and easily; keep the number of nominal ledger accounts to a minimum.

- The receivables and payables ledger control accounts must be reconciled to the list of individual balances on the relevant memorandum ledger: strike a balance on all personal accounts; total the balances in the memorandum ledger; compare this total with the control account balance; identify reasons for failure to agree; prepare reconciliation statement; draw up correcting journals and post.

3.1 Why do we use control accounts?

- They help **check the accuracy** of entries made in the personal accounts. With hundreds of entries to make it is very easy to make a mistake posting entries. Figures can get **transposed**. Some entries might be **omitted** altogether, so that an invoice or a payment transaction does not appear in a personal account as it should. By performing (i) and (ii) below, it is possible to identify the fact that such errors have been made.

    (i)   The receivables control account balance is compared with the total of individual balances on the personal accounts in the receivables ledger.

    (ii) The payables control account balance is compared with the total of individual balances on the personal accounts in the payables ledger.

- They help us **locate errors** in postings promptly. If a clerk fails to record an invoice or a payment in a personal account, or makes a transposition error, it would be difficult to locate the error or errors at the end of a year, say, given the number of transactions. By using the control account regularly, a comparison with the individual balances in the receivables or payables ledger can be made for every week or day of the month, and the error found much more quickly than if control accounts did not exist.

- They **provide an internal check** where there is a separation of clerical (bookkeeping) duties. The person posting entries to the control accounts will act as a check on the different person(s) whose job it is to post entries to the receivables and payables ledger accounts.

- They **provide total receivables and payables balances** more quickly for producing a trial balance or statement of financial position. A single balance on a control account is extracted more simply and quickly than individual balances in the receivables or payables ledger.

- They keep the number of accounts in the trial balance down to a **manageable size**, since the personal accounts are memorandum accounts only.

In computerised systems receivables and payables ledgers are often used without separate control accounts. In such systems, the receivables or payables ledger printouts produced by the computer constitute the list of individual balances as well as providing the total control account balance.

Unless told otherwise in the exam, you should assume that a control account is part of the nominal ledger, with individual personal accounts kept in memorandum ledgers.

3.2 Balancing and agreeing control accounts with the memorandum ledgers

The control accounts should be **balanced regularly** and the balance **agreed** with the sum of the individual customers' or suppliers' balances extracted from the receivables or payables ledgers respectively.

The balance on the control account **may not agree** with the sum of balances extracted, for one or more of the following reasons.

- The **total column in the book of original entry may be miscast** so an **incorrect amount** is **posted** to the control account (ie adding up incorrectly the total value of invoices, receipts or payments).

  Effect:

  - The nominal ledger debit and credit postings will balance, as both nominal ledger accounts will be incorrect

  - The control account balance will not agree with the (correct) sum of individual balances extracted from the receivables ledger or payables ledger.

  Correction:

  - A journal entry must be made in the nominal ledger to correct the control account and the corresponding sales/VAT or expense/VAT accounts.

- An incorrect amount may be posted to an individual's personal account from the book of original entry to the memorandum ledger, eg a sale to C Cloning of £250 might be posted to his account as £520.

  Effect:

  - The nominal ledger would not be affected, as £250 would be correctly included in the total of the sales day book and posted

  - The receivables ledger would be incorrect, since it contains a transposition error in recording £250 as £520. It is too high.

  - The two would not agree

  Correction:

  - The sum of the memorandum ledger balances must be corrected, so in this case the total will decrease by £270. No entry in the nominal ledger is required.

- A transaction may be **recorded in the control account** and *not* **in the memorandum ledger**, or *vice versa*. This requires an entry in the ledger that has been missed out, which means a double entry posting if the control account has to be corrected, and a single entry if it is the individual's personal account in the memorandum ledger that is at fault.

- The list of balances extracted from the memorandum ledger may be **incorrectly extracted or miscast**. This would involve simply correcting the total of the balances.

Worked example: Agreeing control account balance with the ledger

Reconciling the control account balance with the sum of the balances extracted from the receivables ledger should be done in two stages, though these stages can be completed simultaneously.

(1) Correct the total of the balances extracted from the memorandum ledger. (The errors must be located first of course.)

	£	£
Receivables ledger total		
Original total extracted		15,320
Add difference arising from transposition error on		
SDB posting of invoice (£95 written as £59)		36
		15,356
Less		
Credit balance of £60 extracted as a debit balance (£60 × 2)	120	
Overcast of list of balances	90	
		(210)
		15,146

(2) Bring down the balance on the control account, and adjust or post the account with correcting entries.

RECEIVABLES CONTROL ACCOUNT

	£		£
Balance before adjustments	15,091	Cash book: posting omitted	10
Undercast of total invoices issued		Credit note: Individual posting from SDB	
in sales day book	100	omitted from control account	35
		Balance c/d (now in agreement	
		with the corrected total of	
		individual balances in (1))	15,146
	15,191		15,191
Balance b/d	15,146		

Interactive question 4: Receivables control account   [Difficulty level: Intermediate]

April Showers sells goods on credit to most of its customers and maintains a receivables control account. For the year to 30 October 20X3 the accountant discovers that the total of all personal accounts in the receivables ledger is £12,802, whereas the receivables control account balance is £12,550.

The following errors are discovered.

(a) Sales for the week ending 27 March 20X3 amounting to £850 had been omitted from the control account.

(b) A customer's debit balance of £300 had not been included in the list of balances.

(c) Cash received of £750 had been entered in a personal account as £570.

(d) Discount allowed totalling £100 had not been entered in the control account.

(e) A personal account debit balance had been undercast by £200.

(f) A contra item of £400 with the payables ledger had not been entered in the control account.

(g) An irrecoverable debt of £500 had not been entered in the control account.

(h) Cash received of £250 had been debited to a personal account.

(i) Discounts received of £50 had been debited to Bell's receivables ledger account.

(j) A Credit note for £200 had been omitted from the casting of the sales day book.

(k) Cash received of £80 had been credited to a personal account as £8.

(l) A cheque for £300 received from a customer and entered in the control account and personal account had been dishonoured by the bank, but no adjustment had been made in the control account.

Requirements

(a) Prepare a corrected receivables control account, bringing down the amended balance as at 1 November 20X3.

(b) Prepare a statement showing the adjustments that are necessary to the list of personal account balances so that it reconciles with the amended receivables control account balance.

See **Answer** at the end of this chapter.

4 The cash at bank account, the cash book and the bank statement

Section overview

- The cash at bank account in the nominal ledger is the control account for the cash book, although often they are one and the same.

- The cash at bank account, the cash book and the bank statement all reflect transactions through the business's bank account.

In many businesses, the **cash book** (comprising both receipts and payments) acts as both the book of original entry for all transactions affecting the bank account, and as the nominal ledger account for cash at bank.

Where there is a separate **cash at bank account** in the nominal ledger, making sure that its balance at the end of a period agrees with the balance carried down on the cash book at the same time is a useful accuracy and completion check.

In the case of cash at bank, there is another important control check: agreeing the **cash book balance** in the business's ledger accounts with the balance reported to it by the **bank statement**.

4.1 The cash book and the cash at bank account

So far in this Study Manual we have seen that:

- The **cash book** is the book of original entry for all transactions related to the company's bank account

- The **cash at bank** account is the nominal ledger account (part of the double entry system) that is the permanent record of the business's bank transactions

In some accounting systems the cash at bank account is posted only monthly or so from the cash book, with totals:

| DR | Cash at bank (with cash received) | CR | Corresponding income, asset, liability and capital accounts |
| CR | Cash at bank (with cash paid) | DR | Corresponding expense, asset, liability and capital accounts |

Once these postings have been made the business can be sure that its nominal ledger accounts are up to date, but in practice there is a lot of work involved in getting the cash book right before the postings can be made. This is because the cash book is essentially a record of what goes on in the business's bank account, and there are quite often discrepancies that need to be resolved, with the help of the bank statement.

In practice, it is common for the cash book to be treated as a ledger account in that balances are regularly extracted. The business always wants to know its cash balance, as this is a vital asset.

4.2 The bank statement

Definition

Bank statement: A record of transactions on the business's bank account maintained by the bank in its own books.

4.2.1 Mirror image of the cash book

The bank statement is the mirror image of the cash book:

- Cash is an **asset** (a debit balance) in the business's ledger accounts. As far as the bank is concerned it owes the business money. Thus every item recorded as a debit in the business's books – a **positive bank balance, and any receipts of cash** – will be shown as a **credit on the bank statement**.

- When cash is a **liability** (a credit balance) in the business's books, as far as the bank is concerned it is owed money. Thus every credit entry in the business's books – a **negative bank balance, and any payments of cash** – will be shown as a **debit on the bank statement**.

4.2.2 Disagreement with the cash book

It is rare for the balance as shown on the bank statement to be the same as that on the cash book.

There are five common explanations for **differences between cash book and bank statement.**

- **Error**. Errors in calculation, or recording revenue and payments, may have been made in the business cash book, by the bank, or by both.

- **Unrecorded bank charges or bank interest**. The bank might charge interest or make charges for its services, which the customer is not informed about and so cannot record until the bank statement is received.

- **Automated payments and receipts**. Payments processed automatically by the banking system (direct debits and standing orders), and receipts processed automatically, may be shown on the bank statement, but not yet recorded in the cash book.

- **Dishonoured cheques**. When a customer sends in a cheque and it is banked, the business debits the cash book. However, it may be returned unpaid or 'dishonoured' by the customer's bank, usually because the customer has insufficient funds. The dishonour of the cheque will appear on the bank statement and will need to be 'written back' in the ledger accounts:

DEBIT	Receivables	£X
CREDIT	Cash at bank	£X

- **Timing differences**

  - There may be some **cheques received**, recorded in the cash book and paid into the bank, but which have not yet been 'cleared' (paid by the bank) and added to the account by the bank. So although the business's records show that some cash has been added to the account, it has not yet been acknowledged by the bank – although it will be soon, once the cheque has cleared.

  - Similarly, the business might have made some **payments by cheque**, and reduced the balance in the cash book accordingly, but the person who receives the cheque might not bank it for a while. Even when it is banked, it takes a day or two for the bank to process it and for the money to be deducted from the account.

All these differences need to be identified and eradicated, using the **bank reconciliation** process.

5 The bank reconciliation

Section overview

- The cash book needs to be regularly reconciled to the bank statement.

- The cash book and bank statement usually fail to agree because of: errors in the cash book or by the bank; bank charges and interest not entered in the cash book; automated payments and receipts not entered in the cash book; customers' cheques dishonoured or returned unpaid by the bank, not entered in the cash book; timing differences between the cash book and the bank statement (the cash book is usually more up-to-date: unpresented cheques and uncredited lodgements).

- Often correcting or additional entries are needed in the cash book as a result of the bank reconciliation; the bank statement then agrees/reconciles with the corrected cash book balance once timing differences are taken into account.

Definition

Bank reconciliation: A comparison of a bank statement (sent monthly, weekly or even daily by the bank) with the cash book. Differences between the balance on the bank statement and the balance in the cash book should be identified and satisfactorily reconciled.

When doing a bank reconciliation, you will have to look for the following items on the bank statement and in the cash book.

(a) **Errors in the cash book**, such as transposition errors (eg writing £36 and £63) or cheques sent out but omitted from the cash book. The correct amount appears on the bank statement and the cash book must be updated.

(b) **Corrections and adjustments to the cash book**

    (i) Payments made into or from the bank account by way of debit card, standing order, direct debit or online transfer which have not yet been entered in the cash book.

    (ii) Bank interest and bank charges, not yet entered in the cash book.

    (iii) Dishonoured cheques not yet entered in the cash book.

(c) **Errors in the bank statement**, such as transposition errors, payments or receipts recorded twice or interest and fees deducted incorrectly. The correct amount appears in the cash book and the balance per the bank statement must be corrected.

(d) **Items reconciling the correct cash book balance to the bank statement (timing differences)**

    (i) Cheques paid out by the business and credited in the cash book which have not yet been presented to the bank, or 'cleared', and so do not yet appear on the bank statement. These are known as '**unpresented cheques**'.

    (ii) Cheques received by the business, paid into the bank and debited in the cash book, but which have not yet been cleared and entered in the bank account, and so do not yet appear on the bank statement. These are known as '**uncleared lodgements**'.

Worked example: Bank reconciliation 1

At 30 September 20X6, the balance in Wordsworth Co's cash book was £805.15 debit. A bank statement on 30 September 20X6 showed Wordsworth Co to be in credit at the bank by £1,112.30.

On investigation of the difference, it was established that:

(a) The cash book had been undercast by £90.00 on the debit side.
(b) Cheques paid in but not yet credited by the bank were £208.20.
(c) Cheques drawn not yet presented to the bank were £425.35.

We need to show the correction to the cash book, then prepare a statement reconciling the balance per the bank statement to the balance per the cash book.

Solution

(a)

	£
Cash book balance brought forward	805.15
Add	
Correction of undercast	90.00
Corrected cash book balance	895.15

(b)

	£
Balance per bank statement	1,112.30
Add	
Uncleared lodgements	208.20
	1,320.50
Less	
Unpresented cheques	(425.35)
Balance per corrected cash book	895.15

Worked example: Bank reconciliation II

At his year end of 30 June 20X0, Cook's cash book showed that he had an overdraft of £300 on his current account at the bank. A bank statement as at 30 June 20X0 showed that Cook has an overdraft of £35.

On checking the cash book and the bank statement you find the following.

(a) Cheques drawn, amounting to £500, had been entered in the cash book but had not yet been presented.

(b) Cheques received, amounting to £400, had been entered in the cash book, but had not yet been credited by the bank.

(c) On instructions from Cook on 30 June 20X0 the bank had transferred £60 interest received on his savings account to his current account, but it only recorded the transfer on 5 July 20X0. This amount was credited in the cash book on 30 June 20X0.

(d) Bank charges of £35 shown in the bank statement had not been entered in the cash book.

(e) The payments side of the cash book had been undercast by £10.

(f) Dividends received of £200 had been paid direct into the bank and not entered in the cash book.

(g) A cheque for £50 from Sunil was recorded and banked on 24 June. This was returned unpaid on 30 June and then shown as a debit on the bank statement. No entry has been made in the cash book for the unpaid cheque.

(h) A cheque issued to Jones for £25 was replaced when it was more than six months old, at which time it had become 'out of date' and the bank would have refused to pay it. It was entered again in the cash book, no other entry being made. Both cheques were included in the total of unpresented cheques shown above.

We need to make the appropriate adjustments in the cash book, then prepare a statement reconciling the amended balance with that shown in the bank statement.

Solution

The errors to correct in the cash book are given in notes (c), (e), (f), (g) and (h) of the problem. Bank charges (note (d)) also call for an adjustment.

Item (c) is rather complicated. The transfer of interest from the deposit to the current account was given as an instruction to the bank on 30 June 20X0, probably because that is Cook's year end and he wants to make sure that all transactions are recorded. Since the correct entry should have been to debit the current account (and credit the deposit account) the correction in the cash book should be to debit the current account with $2 \times £60 = £120$ – ie to cancel out the incorrect credit entry in the cash book, and then to make the correct debit entry. However, the bank does not record the transfer until 5 July, and so it will not appear in the bank statement.

Item (h) also requires explanation. Two cheques have been paid to Jones, but one is now cancelled. Since the cash book is credited whenever a cheque is paid, it should be debited whenever a cheque is cancelled. The amount of unpresented cheques should be reduced by the amount of the cancelled cheque.

CASH BOOK

		£			£
20X0			*20X0*		
Jun 30	Savings interest 60 × 2(c)	120	Jun 30	Balance b/d	300
	Dividends paid direct			Bank charges (d)	35
	to bank (f)	200		Correction of undercast (e)	10
	Cheque issued to Jones			Dishonoured cheque (g)	50
	cancelled (h)	25			
	Balance c/d	50			
		395			395

BANK RECONCILIATION STATEMENT AT 30 JUNE 20X0

	£	£
Balance per bank statement		(35)
Add Outstanding lodgements	400	
Savings interest not yet credited	60	
		460
		425
Less Unpresented cheques	500	
Less cheque to Jones cancelled	(25)	
		(475)
Balance per corrected cash book		(50)

In a bank reconciliation you should begin with the balance shown by the bank statement and end with the balance shown by the corrected cash book. This corrected cash book balance will appear in the statement of financial position as 'cash at bank'.

In answering an exam question however, you should expect to work the other way round on occasion.

Interactive question 5: Bank reconciliation I   [Difficulty level: Exam standard]

A bank reconciliation statement is being prepared. Using the table select the effect of each of the following on the closing balance shown by the bank statement of £388 in hand. (The closing balance shown by the cash book is £106 in hand.) Tick **one** box for each finding.

		Increase	Decrease	No effect
A	The bank has made a mistake in crediting the account with £110 belonging to another customer – an error not yet rectified.	☐	☐	☐
B	£120 received by the bank under a standing order arrangement has not been entered in the cash book.	☐	☐	☐
C	Cheques totalling £5,629 have been drawn, entered in the cash book and sent out to suppliers but they have not been presented for payment.	☐	☐	☐
D	Cheques totalling £5,577 have been received and entered in the cash book but not yet credited in the bank statements.	☐	☐	☐

See **Answer** at the end of this chapter.

Interactive question 6: Bank reconciliation II [Difficulty level: Exam standard]

Tilfer's bank statement shows £715 direct debits and £353 investment income not recorded in the cash book. The bank statement does not show a customer's cheque for £875 entered in the cash book on the last day of the reporting period. The cash book has a credit balance of £610.

What balance appears on the bank statement?

See **Answer** at the end of this chapter.

6 Types of error in accounting

Section overview

- Errors can be classified as: errors of commission or omission, compensating errors, errors of principle and transposition errors.

- Many errors in the ledger accounts are detected during the control account reconciliation and bank reconciliation processes.

There are **five broad types of error** as follows.

- **Transposition** errors
- Errors of **omission**
- Errors of **principle**
- Errors of **commission**
- **Compensating errors**

Once an error has been detected, it needs to be put right.

- If the correction **involves a double entry** in the nominal ledger accounts, then it is recorded via an **entry** in the journal.

- When the error **breaks the rule of double entry**, then it is corrected via a journal entry using a **suspense account** to complete the double entry.

6.1 Transposition errors

Definition

Transposition errors: When two digits in an amount are accidentally recorded the wrong way round.

- A sale is credited in the sales account as £6,843, but has been incorrectly debited in the receivables control account as £6,483. In consequence total debits will not equal to total credits: credits will exceed debits by 6,843 – 6,483 = 360. You can often detect a transposition error by checking whether the difference between debits and credits can be divided exactly by 9 (£360 ÷ 9 = £40).

6.2 Errors of omission

Definition

Error of omission: Failing to record a transaction at all, or making a debit or credit entry, but not the corresponding double entry.

- A business receives an invoice from a supplier for £250, and the transaction is omitted from the books. As a result, both total debits **and** credits will be wrong by £250.

- A business receives an invoice from a supplier for £300, the payables control account is credited but no debit entry is made. In this case, the total credits would not equal total debits (because total debits are £300 less than they ought to be).

6.3 Errors of principle

Definition

Error of principle: Making a double entry in the belief that the transaction is being entered in the correct accounts, but subsequently finding out that the accounting entry breaks the 'rules' of an accounting principle or concept. A typical example of such an error is to treat revenue expenditure incorrectly as capital expenditure.

- Machine repairs costing £150 (which should be treated as revenue expenditure) are debited to the cost of a non-current asset (capital expenditure). Although total debits still equal total credits, the repairs account is £150 understated and the cost of the non-current asset is £150 overstated.

- A business owner takes £280 cash out of the till for his personal use. The bookkeeper incorrectly debits sales by £280, when they should have debited drawings. This is an error of principle, so that drawings and sales are both understated by £280.

6.4 Errors of commission

Definition

Errors of commission: A mistake is made in recording transactions in the ledger accounts.

- **Putting a debit entry or a credit entry in the wrong account.** Telephone expenses of £540 are debited to the electricity expense account, an error of commission. Although total debits and credits balance, telephone expenses are understated by £540 and electricity expense is overstated by the same amount.

- **Casting errors (adding up).** Daily credit sales in the sales day book of £28,425 are incorrectly added up ('miscast') as £28,825. This amount is credited to sales and debited to receivables control. Although total debits and total credits are still equal, the nominal ledger is incorrect by £400. Note that if the correct individual entries are made in the receivables ledger, the total on the list of balances will be right, but it will not agree with the receivables control account balance.

6.5 Compensating errors

Definition

Compensating errors: Errors which are, coincidentally, equal and opposite to one another.

Compensating errors hide trial balance errors.

- Administrative expenses of £2,822 are entered as £2,282 in the administrative expenses ledger account. At the same time, income of £8,931 is shown in the sales account as £8,391. Both debits and credits are £540 too low, and the mistake would not be apparent when the trial balance is cast.

7 Correcting errors

Section overview

- Errors which have not caused an imbalance are corrected via journals.

- Errors which have broken the rules of double entry bookkeeping and result in the trial balance failing to balance can be corrected by (1) setting up a suspense account and then (2) clearing it with correcting journals.

- A suspense account may also be deliberately set up when a bookkeeper does not know where to put one side of an entry.

- Suspense accounts are always temporary and should never appear in financial statements; these should not be prepared until the errors have been corrected and the suspense account has been cleared.

- Some corrections of errors will result in adjustments to a draft profit calculated while there were still errors in the accounts.

Errors which leave total debits and credits in the ledger accounts in balance can be corrected just using **journal entries**.

Where errors mean that the trial balance does not balance, a **suspense account** has to be opened first, later cleared by a **journal entry**.

7.1 Journal entries

The journal requires a debit and an equal credit entry for each correction.

- If total debits equal total credits before a journal entry is made then they will still be equal after the journal entry is made, as would be the case if, for example, the original error was a debit wrongly posted as a credit and vice versa.

- If total debits and total credits are unequal before a journal entry is made, then they will still be unequal (by the same amount) after it is made.

Worked example: Correcting errors with journal entries

A bookkeeper accidentally posts an invoice for £40 to the local property taxes account instead of to the electricity account. A trial balance is drawn up. Total debits are £40,000 and total credits are £40,000. A journal entry is made to correct the misposting error as follows.

DEBIT	Electricity account	£40	
CREDIT	Local property taxes account		£40

To correct a misposting of £40 from the local property taxes account to electricity account

After the journal has been posted, total debits and credits will still be equal at £40,000.

Now suppose that, because of some error which has not yet been detected, total debits were originally £40,000 but total credits were £39,900. If the same journal correcting the £40 is put through, total debits will remain £40,000 and total credits will remain £39,900. Total debits were different by £100 **before** the journal, and they are still different by £100 **after** the journal.

This means that **journals alone can only be used to correct errors which require both a credit and (an equal) debit adjustment**.

In a question which requires a 'correcting journal'

- Work out **first** what the original entry was
- **Then** what the original entry should have been
- And **finally** what the correcting entry should be

Interactive question 7: Journal entries   [Difficulty level: Intermediate]

Write out the journal entries which would correct these errors.

(a) A business receives an invoice for £250 from a supplier which was omitted from the books entirely.

(b) Repairs worth £150 were incorrectly debited to the non-current asset (machinery) account instead of the repairs account.

(c) The bookkeeper of a business reduces cash sales by £280 because he was not sure what the £280 represented. In fact, it was drawings.

(d) Telephone expenses of £540 are incorrectly debited to the electricity account.

(e) A page in the sales day book has been added up to £28,425 instead of £28,825.

See **Answer** at the end of this chapter.

7.2 Suspense accounts

Definition

Suspense account: An account showing a balance equal to the difference in a trial balance.

A suspense account is a **temporary** account which can be opened for the following reasons.

- A trial balance is drawn up which **does not balance** (ie total debits do not equal total credits).

- The bookkeeper of a business knows where to post one side of a transaction, **but does not know where to post the other side**. For example, a cash payment must obviously be credited to cash, but the bookkeeper may not know what the payment is for, and so will not know which account to debit. To complete the double entry, he debits suspense

In both these cases, a **suspense account** is opened up until the problem is resolved.

7.3 Using a suspense account when the trial balance does not balance

When an error has occurred which results in an imbalance between total debits and total credits in the ledger accounts:

Step 1
Open a suspense account with the amount of the imbalance

Step 2
Use a journal entry to clear the suspense account and correct the error. It is good practice for the correcting side of the double entry to appear first in the journal, then the suspense account entry.

Worked example: Suspense account

An accountant draws up a trial balance and finds that total debits exceed total credits by £162.

He knows that there is an error somewhere, but for the time being he opens a **suspense account** with a credit balance of £162. This serves two purposes.

- As the suspense account now exists, the accountant will not forget that there is an error (of £162) to be sorted out.

- Now that there is a credit of £162 in the suspense account, the trial balance balances.

When the cause of the £162 discrepancy is tracked down, it is corrected by means of a **journal entry**. Suppose the error was an omitted credit of £162 to the purchases account. The correcting journal entry is:

CREDIT	Purchases		£162
DEBIT	Suspense a/c	£162	

To close off suspense a/c and correct error of omission

Worked example: Suspense account and transposition error

Instead of entering the correct amount of £37,453 in the sales account, a bookkeeper entered £37,543 Trade receivables were posted correctly, so on the trial balance **credits exceeded debits** by £(37,543 – 37,453) = £90.

Step 1
Equalise the total debits and credits by posting a **debit** of £90 to the suspense account.

Step 2
Correcting journal entry: sales need to be reduced, and the suspense account needs to be cleared.

DEBIT	Sales	£90	
CREDIT	Suspense a/c		£90

To close off suspense a/c and correct transposition error

Worked example: Error of omission

A cheque payment of £250 was correctly credited to the cash account, but the bookkeeper omitted to debit the expense account. On the trial balance, credits exceeded debits by £250.

Step 1
Debit £250 to the suspense account, to equalise the total debits and total credits.

Step 2

Correcting journal entry: expenses need to be increased, and the suspense account cleared.

DEBIT	Expense account	£250	
CREDIT	Suspense a/c		£250

To close off suspense a/c and correct error of omission

Worked example: Error of commission

A cheque received for £460 is debited to cash but also debited to receivables control, instead of being credited.

The total debit balances now exceed the total credits by 2 * £460 = £920.

Step 1

Make a credit entry of £920 in a suspense account, to equalise debits and credits.

Step 2

Correcting journal entry: decrease trade receivables, and clear the suspense account.

CREDIT	Trade receivables		£920
DEBIT	Suspense a/c	£920	

To close off suspense a/c and correct error of commission

7.4 Using a suspense account to complete the double entry

When a bookkeeper does not know where to post one side of a transaction, it can be temporarily recorded in a suspense account. A typical example is when the business receives cash through the post from a source which cannot be determined. The double entry in the accounts would be a debit in the cash book, and a credit to a suspense account.

Worked example: Not knowing where to post a transaction

Windfall Garments banks a cheque for £620 from R J Beasley. The business has no idea who this person is, nor why he should be sending £620. The bookkeeper opens a suspense account:

DEBIT	Cash	£620	
CREDIT	Suspense a/c		£620

It transpires that the cheque was in payment for a debt owed by the Haute Couture Corner Shop and paid out of the owner's personal bank account. The suspense account can now be cleared, as follows.

CREDIT	Trade receivables		£620
DEBIT	Suspense a/c	£620	

7.5 Suspense accounts might contain several items

All errors and unidentifiable postings in a reporting period are merged together in the suspense account; until the cause of each error is discovered, the bookkeeper is unlikely to know exactly how many errors there are.

An exam question might give you a suspense account balance, together with information to make corrections which will leave a nil balance on the suspense account and correct balances on the nominal ledger accounts.

7.6 Suspense accounts are temporary

It must be stressed that a **suspense account should only be temporary**. Postings to a suspense account are only made when the bookkeeper doesn't know yet what to do, or when an error has occurred. **There should be no suspense account when it comes to preparing the income statement and statement of financial position. The suspense account should be cleared and all correcting entries made before the final financial statements are drawn up.**

7.7 Adjustment of profits for errors

Correcting errors can affect either the statement of financial position, the income statement, or sometimes both. An error of omission corrected by debiting sales and crediting suspense with £90 meant that sales decreased, so gross profit was reduced by £90 as a result of the error being corrected.

If there are still errors to be corrected after the trial balance and initial income statement and statement of financial position have been prepared, then corrections will alter those draft financial statements.

You may need to demonstrate how draft financial statements are affected by error corrections by calculating:

- How much gross or net profit is increased or reduced as a result of error correction
- The final gross or net profit after the error correction

Interactive question 8: Errors [Difficulty level: Exam standard]

At T Down & Co year end, the trial balance contained a suspense account with a credit balance of £1,040.

Investigations revealed the following errors.

(i) A sale of goods on credit for £1,000 had been omitted from the sales account.

(ii) Delivery and installation costs of £240 on a new item of plant had been recorded as revenue expenditure in the distribution costs account.

(iii) Cash discount of £150 had been taken on paying a supplier, JW, even though the payment was made outside the time limit. JW is insisting that £150 is still payable.

(iv) A raw materials purchase of £350 had been recorded in the purchases account as £850, but the trade payables account was correctly written up.

(v) The purchases day book included a credit note for £230 as an invoice in the total column. The correct entry was made in the purchases account.

Requirements

(a) Prepare journal entries to correct *each* of the above errors. Narratives are *not* required.

(b) Open a suspense account and show the corrections to be made.

(c) Before the errors were corrected, T Down & Co's gross profit was calculated at £35,750 and the net profit for the year at £18,500. Calculate the revised gross and net profit figures after correction of the errors.

See **Answer** at the end of this chapter.

8 Correcting errors via the ETB

Section overview

- The journals which correct errors and make other adjustments can be put through the adjustments columns of the extended trial balance.

In Chapter 5 we saw how an extended trial balance made the preparation of the income statement and statement of financial position easier and more clear-cut. The ETB is also useful when recording correcting journals made at the final stages of preparing financial statements, after the initial trial balance has been prepared. This is especially the case where a suspense account had to be used to make the trial balance agree.

As well as debit and credit columns for the TB, the income statement and the statement of financial position, in a full ETB we include debit and credit columns for adjustments between the TB and the income statement; we don't bother with a revised TB, as we initially used in Chapter 5. Instead the entries in the adjustment columns just get included in the cross-casting to the income statement and statement of financial position columns.

Worked example: Error correction on the ETB

Handle extracted a trial balance and created a suspense account. He inserted the TB on his extended trial balance as follows:

Ledger balance	Trial balance		Adjustments		Income statement		Statement of financial position	
	Debit	Credit	Debit	Credit	Debit	Credit	Debit	Credit
	£	£	£	£	£	£	£	£
Cash at bank	5,415							
Opening capital		10,000						
Loan		5,000						
Non-current assets	30,000							
Trade payables		18,689						
Expenses	6,781							
Purchases	21,569							
Sales		38,974						
Trade receivables	9,445							
Suspense		6,400						
Drawings	5,853							
Net profit								
	79,063	79,063						

Handle has now discovered the following matters:

(a) An amount of £1,000 was credited on the bank statement in the year and entered in the cash book, but no other entry was made as the bookkeeper did not know what the receipt was in respect of. Handle tells you it was a payment on account from a major customer.

(b) A non-current asset was purchased on credit just before the year end, for £9,300. This was incorrectly entered in the trade payables account via a journal as £3,900, but the correct entry was made in non-current assets.

To correct these errors Handle uses the following journals:

			£	£
(a)	CREDIT	Trade receivables		1,000
	DEBIT	Suspense	1,000	
(b)	CREDIT	Trade payables		5,400
	DEBIT	Suspense	5,400	

These are entered in the adjustments columns of the ETB, which is then cross-cast to produce Handle's income statement and statement of financial position:

Ledger balance	Trial balance		Adjustments		Income statement		Statement of financial position	
	Debit £	Credit £	Debit £	Credit £	Debit £	Credit £	Debit £	Credit £
Cash at bank	5,415						5,415	
Opening capital		10,000						10,000
Loan		5,000						5,000
Non-current assets	30,000						30,000	
Trade payables		18,689		5,400				24,089
Expenses	6,781				6,781			
Purchases	21,569				21,569			
Sales		38,974				38,974		
Trade receivables	9,445			1,000			8,445	
Suspense		6,400	6,400					
Drawings	5,853						5,853	
Net profit					10,624			10,624
	79,063	79,063	6,400	6,400	38,974	38,974	49,713	49,713

No balance remains on the suspense account.

Summary (1/2)

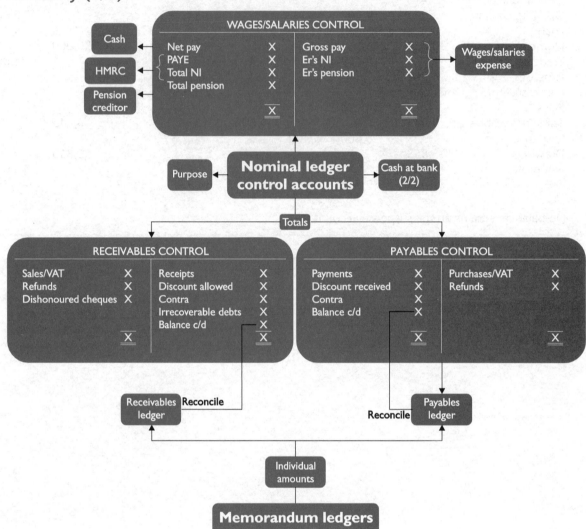

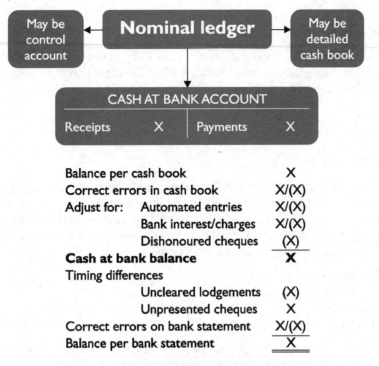

Nominal ledger

May be control account

May be detailed cash book

CASH AT BANK ACCOUNT

| Receipts | X | Payments | X |

Balance per cash book	X
Correct errors in cash book	X/(X)
Adjust for: Automated entries	X/(X)
Bank interest/charges	X/(X)
Dishonoured cheques	(X)
Cash at bank balance	**X**
Timing differences	
Uncleared lodgements	(X)
Unpresented cheques	X
Correct errors on bank statement	X/(X)
Balance per bank statement	X

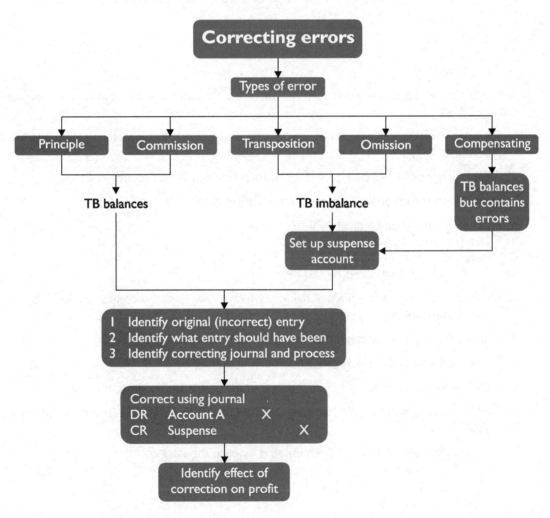

Correcting errors

Types of error

Principle   Commission   Transposition   Omission   Compensating

TB balances

TB imbalance

TB balances but contains errors

Set up suspense account

1   Identify original (incorrect) entry
2   Identify what entry should have been
3   Identify correcting journal and process

Correct using journal
DR   Account A   X
CR   Suspense   X

Identify effect of correction on profit

Self-test

Answer the following questions.

1   On its receivables control account A Co has: sales £125,000, cash received £50,000, discounts allowed £2,000. The balance carried down is £95,000. What was the opening balance at the beginning of the period?

   A   £22,000 debit
   B   £22,000 credit
   C   £18,000 debit
   D   £20,000 debit

2   A bank statement shows a balance of £1,200 in credit. An examination of the statement shows a £500 cheque paid in per the cash book but not yet on the bank statement and a £1,250 cheque paid out but not yet on the statement. In addition the cash book shows the owner's correct calculation of savings interest of £50 which should have been received, but which is not on the statement. What is the balance per the cash book?

   A   £1,900 overdrawn
   B   £500 overdrawn
   C   £1,900 in hand
   D   £500 in hand

3   Sales of £460 have been debited to purchases, although the correct entry has been made to receivables control. The balance on the suspense account that needs to be set up is for:

   A   £460 debit
   B   £460 credit
   C   £920 debit
   D   £920 credit

4   Sutton & Co had a difference on its trial balance. After investigation the following errors were discovered.

   1   A sales invoice for £500 was mis-read by the clerk as £600 and entered as such into the ledger accounts.

   2   Bank charges of £145 had been debited to the cash at bank account as £154.

   How much was the original difference on the trial balance?

   A   Debits greater than credits by £9
   B   Debits greater than credits by £199
   C   Debits greater than credits by £299
   D   Credits greater than debits by £91

5   Gresham & Sons has drawn up a trial balance which shows credits greater than debits by £250. Which **two** of the following are possible explanations for this difference?

   A   Rent paid of £250 had been credited to the rent account

   B   The debit side of the trial balance had been undercast by £250

   C   Cash drawings of £125 had been debited to the cash and drawings accounts

   D   £250 paid for motor repairs had been debited to the motor vehicles (non-current assets) account

   E   A sales invoice for £250 had been entered twice in the sales account

6   The trial balance of Z Ltd as extracted from the books has a difference of £812, and this has been posted to the credit of a suspense account. Some errors, as set out below, have now been discovered.

1   The year end bank overdraft of £756 has been entered in the trial balance as a debit balance.

2   The total of discounts receivable for the last month of the year of £13,400 has been posted to the discounts receivable account as £14,300.

3   A purchase invoice totalling £2,015 has been correctly credited to the control account, but this amount has been debited to light and heat.

After correction of these errors, what is the remaining balance brought down on the suspense account?

A   £1,815 DR
B   £200 CR
C   £956 CR
D   £1,424 CR

7   On reconciling the purchases control account with the list of payables ledger balances, the accountant of Moore discovered that there were two reconciling items.

1   A purchase invoice from Polly totalling £158 had been entered on her account as £258, but was correctly entered in the purchases day book.

2   The purchases day book had been undercast by £100.

To complete the reconciliation, which of the following should happen?

			£	£
A	DR	Purchases	200	
	CR	Payables ledger control account		200
B	DR	Payables ledger control account	100	
	CR	Purchases		100
	and reduce the amount shown as owed to Polly and the list of balances by £100		
C	DR	Payables ledger control account	200	
	CR	Purchases		200
	and reduce the amount shown as owed to Polly and the list of balances by £100		
D	DR	Purchases	100	
	CR	Payables ledger control account		100
	and reduce the amount shown as owed to Polly and the list of balances by £100		

8   Due to a fault in the company's computer software East Cowes Ltd's purchases day book was undercast by £8,800, and its sales day book was undercast by £3,800. In addition, debit balances of £580 had been omitted from the list of sales ledger balances, credit balances of £280 omitted from the list of payables ledger balances, and contras of £750 had not been entered anywhere in the books. After the correction of these errors East Cowes Ltd's profit will

A   Decrease by £5,000
B   Decrease by £4,700
C   Decrease by £3,400
D   Increase by £5,000

9   On 31 January 20X8 Randall's cash book for its current account showed a credit balance of £150 which did not agree with the bank statement balance. In performing the reconciliation the following points come to light.

	£
Not recorded in the cash book	
Bank charges	36
Transfer from savings account to current account	500
Not recorded on the bank statement	
Unpresented cheques	116
Uncleared lodgements	630

It was also discovered that the bank had debited Randall's account with a cheque for £400 in error. This should have been debited to Hopkirk's account.

What was the original balance on the bank statement?

A   £200 DR
B   £428 DR
C   £600 CR
D   £1,600 CR

10   A bank reconciliation statement for Worth Ltd at 31 December 20Y1 is in course of preparation. In the light of the information given below, compute the final balance shown by the cash book.

1   Overdrawn balance per bank statement is £1,019.

2   An amount of £250 credited in the bank statement under a standing order arrangement has not been entered in the cash book.

3   Cheques drawn and entered but not presented total £2,467.

4   Bank charges of £1,875 debited by the bank have not been entered in the cash book.

5   Cash and cheques received and entered but not credited in the bank statement total £4,986.

6   An uncorrected bank error has resulted in a cheque for £397 debited to Worth's account instead of to the account of the drawer.

The final balance shown by the cash book, after making all necessary corrections, should be

A   £6,831 DR
B   £3,141 DR
C   £1,897 DR
D   £228 DR

Now, go back to the Learning Objectives in the Introduction. If you are satisfied that you have achieved these objectives, please tick them off.

Answer to Interactive question 1

PAYABLES CONTROL ACCOUNT

	£		£
Bank payments	79,500	Balance b/d (balancing figure)	16,970
Discount received	3,750	Purchases	83,200
Contra with receivables	4,000		
Balance c/d	12,920		
	100,170		100,170

Answer to Interactive question 2

A   The total of sales invoices in the day book is debited to the control account. If the total is understated by £800, the debits in the control account will also be understated by £800. Options B and D would have the opposite effect: credit entries in the control account would be understated. Option C would lead to a discrepancy of 2 × £800 = £1,600.

Answer to Interactive question 3

(a)   RECEIVABLES CONTROL ACCOUNT

20X8		£	20X9		£
Oct 1	Balances b/d (8,024 – 57)	7,967	Sept 30	Cash received from credit customers	55,212
20X9				Discount allowed	2,328
Sept 30	Sales	62,514		Irrecoverable debts written off	326
				Contra	434
				Balance c/d	12,181
		70,481			70,481

(b)   PAYABLES CONTROL ACCOUNT

20X8		£	20X8		£
Sept 30	Cash paid to credit suppliers	37,307	Oct 1	Balance b/d (6,235 – 105)	6,130
	Discount received	1,475	20X9		
	Contra	434	Sept 30	Purchases	39,439
	Balance c/d	6,458		Cash refund	105
		45,674			45,674

Answer to Interactive question 4

(a)   RECEIVABLES CONTROL ACCOUNT

	£		£
Uncorrected balance b/d	12,550	Discount omitted (d)	100
Sales omitted (a)	850	Contra entry omitted (f)	400
Bank: cheque dishonoured (l)	300	Irrecoverable debt omitted (g)	500
		Credit note omitted (j)	200
		Amended balance c/d	12,500
	13,700		13,700
Balance b/d	12,500		

Note: Items (b), (c), (e), (h), (i) and (k) are matters affecting the personal accounts of customers. They have no effect on the control account.

(b) STATEMENT OF ADJUSTMENTS TO LIST OF BALANCES

	£	£
Original total of list of balances		12,802
Add: debit balance omitted (b)	300	
debit balance undercast (e)	200	
		500
		13,302
Less: transposition error (c): understatement of cash received	180	
cash debited instead of credited (2 × £250) (h)	500	
discounts received wrongly debited to Bell (i)	50	
understatement of cash received (k)	72	
		(802)
Corrected total on list of balances		12,500

Answer to Interactive question 5

A Decrease
B No effect. Adjustment to cash book.
C Decrease
D Increase

CASH

	£		£
b/d	106	c/d	226
Standing order	120		
	226		226

	£
Balance per bank statement	388
Unpresented cheques	(5,629)
Uncleared lodgements	5,577
Bank error	(110)
Balance per cash account	226

Answer to Interactive question 6

	£	£
Balance per cash book		(610)
Items on statement, not in cash book		
Direct debits	(715)	
Investment income	353	
		(362)
Corrected balance per cash book		(972)
Item in cash book not on statement:		
Customer's cheque (uncleared lodgements)		(875)
Balance per bank statement		(1,847)

Answer to Interactive question 7

(a) DEBIT   Purchases   £250
    CREDIT   Trade payables   £250

A transaction previously omitted

(b) DEBIT   Repairs account   £150
    CREDIT   Non-current asset (machinery) a/c   £150

The correction of an error of principle: repairs costs incorrectly added to non-current asset costs

(c)   DEBIT   Drawings   £280

       CREDIT   Sales   £280

An error of principle, in which sales were reduced to compensate for cash drawings not accounted for

(d)   DEBIT   Telephone expense   £540

       CREDIT   Electricity expense   £540

Correction of an error of commission: telephone expenses wrongly charged to the electricity account

(e)   DEBIT   Trade receivables   £400

       CREDIT   Sales   £400

The correction of a casting error in the sales day book
(£28,825 – £28,425 = £400)

Answer to Interactive question 8

(a)

				DR £	CR £
(i)	DEBIT	Suspense a/c		1,000	
	CREDIT	Sales			1,000
(ii)	DEBIT	Non-current asset		240	
	CREDIT	Distribution costs			240
(iii)	DEBIT	Discount received		150	
	CREDIT	Trade payables			150
(iv)	DEBIT	Suspense a/c		500	
	CREDIT	Purchases			500
(v)	DEBIT	Trade payables		460	
	CREDIT	Suspense a/c			460

(b)

SUSPENSE A/C

		£		£
(i)	Sales	1,000	End of year balance	1,040
(iv)	Purchases	500	(vi) Trade payables	460
		1,500		1,500

(c)

	£
Gross profit originally reported	35,750
Sales omitted (i)	1,000
Incorrect recording of purchases (iv)	500
Adjusted gross profit	37,250
Net profit originally reported	18,500
Adjustments to gross profit £(37,250 – 35,750)	1,500
Cash discount incorrectly taken (iii)	(150)
Non-current asset costs wrongly classified	240
Adjusted net profit	20,090

1 A   RECEIVABLES CONTROL

	£		£
Bal b/f (bal figure)	22,000	Cash	50,000
Sales	125,000	Discounts allowed	2,000
		Bal c/f	95,000
	147,000		147,000

If you had answer B, you reversed the double entry and so produced a payables control account. In answer D, you omitted the discounts allowed figure; while in answer C you put discounts allowed on the debit instead of the credit side of the control account.

2 D

	£	£
Balance per bank statement		1,200
Add outstanding lodgements	500	
deposit interest not yet credited	50	550
		1,750
Less unpresented cheques		(1,250)
Balance per cash book		500

3 D Sales of £460 have been debited to accounts receivable and also £460 has been debited to purchases. Therefore the trial balance needs a credit of 2 × £460 = £920 to balance.

4 C **1** This error will not lead to a difference in the trial balance. Both receivables and sales will be overstated.

2 The cash at the bank account has been debited (it should have been credited) with £154, bank charges debited with £145 therefore £299 more debits than credits.

5 B and E

	Should have	Have	Result
A	DR Rent £250 CR Bank £250	CR Rent £250 CR Bank £250	£500 more CRs than DRs
B	–	–	£250 more CRs than DRs
C	DR Drawings £125 CR Bank £125	DR Bank £125 DR Drawings £125	£250 more DRs than CRs
D	DR Repairs £250 CR Bank £250	DR Non-current assets £250 CR Bank £250	DRs = CRs (even though entry is wrong in principle)
E	DR Receivables £250 CR Sales £250	DR Receivables £250 CR Sales £500	£250 more CRs than DRs

6 B   SUSPENSE

	£		£
Bank overdraft (2 × 756)	1,512	Opening balance	812
C/d (β)	200	Discounts	900
	1,712		1,712

7 D 1 As purchases day book entry is correct, subsequent double entry is correct. Personal account is incorrect.

2 Double entry incorrect.

8 A

	Bookkeeping	Effect on profit
		£
Undercast of purchase day book	DR Purchases	– 8,800
	CR Purchase ledger control account	
Undercast of sales day book	DR Sales ledger control account	
	CR Sales	+ 3,800
		– 5,000

Contras will not affect the profit for the year, whilst errors in the sales and purchase ledgers, not being part of the double entry system, cannot do so.

9 C

CASH AT BANK ACCOUNT

	£		£
		Balance b/d	150
Transfer from savings a/c	500	Charges	36
		Balance c/d	314
	500		500

	£
Balance per cash book	314
Add unpresented cheques	116
Less uncleared lodgements	(630)
Less error by bank*	(400)
Balance per bank statement	**(600)**

* On the bank statement a debit is a payment **out of** the account.

10 C

	£
Balance per bank statement	(1,019) o/d
Cheques not presented	(2,467)
	(3,486)
Amount not credited	4,986
	1,500
Bank error	397
Debit balance per cash book	1,897

CHAPTER 7

Cost of sales, accruals and prepayments

Introduction

Examination context

Topic List

Learning objectives

- Record and account for transactions and events resulting in income, expenses, assets, liabilities and equity in accordance with the appropriate basis of accounting and the laws, regulations and accounting standards applicable to the financial statements

- Prepare an extended trial balance

- Identify the main components of a set of financial statements and specify their purpose and interrelationship

- Prepare and present a statement of financial position, income statement and statement of cash flows (or extracts therefrom) from the accounting records and trial balance in a format which satisfies the information requirements of the entity

Specific syllabus learning outcomes are: 1c, 2c, 3a, 3c

Syllabus links

The material in this chapter will be developed further in this paper, and then in the Financial Accounting and Financial Reporting papers later in the Professional stage.

Examination context

Questions on the topics in this chapter will be set as multiple choice questions, some of which may involve calculations so that the correct answer can be selected. Very often double entry questions are phrased in terms of preparing a journal.

In the exam you may be required to:

- Identify the accounting principles behind cost of sales, accruals and prepayments

- Specify the components of cost of sales in the income statement

- Use margin and mark-up to calculate revenue or cost of sales

- Calculate figures in the statement of financial position for accruals and prepayments of expenditure

- Calculate figures in the statement of financial position for accrued and deferred income (arrears and advances)

- Identify the correct income statement figures for income and expenses

- Identify the effects of accruals and prepayments of income and expenses on gross and net profit in the income statement

- Specify how year-end accruals and prepayments are accounted for on the extended trial balance

1 Cost of sales

Section overview

- Cost of sales comprises:

Opening inventory	X
Purchases	X
Carriage inwards	X
Closing inventory	(X)
Cost of sales	X

- Cost of sales is deducted from revenue to arrive at gross profit.

- When a large amount of purchased or manufactured items are stolen or lost, we remove them from the cost of sales and treat them as an expense, so as not to distort gross profit.

The **cost of sales** is deducted from **revenue** in an entity's **income statement**. Because it results in the **gross profit** it has long been regarded as a key figure in the financial statements.

Definition

Cost of sales: Opening inventory + purchases + carriage inwards – closing inventory = cost of sales. This amount is then deducted from revenue to arise at the business's gross profit.

Inventory, both opening and closing, features in the income statement whereas you might expect it to feature only in the statement of financial position, as an asset. How is this so?

1.1 Unsold goods at the end of a reporting period

Goods might be unsold at the end of a reporting period and so still be **held in inventory**. Under the **accrual concept**, the cost of these goods should not be included in cost of sales, instead it should be carried forward and matched against revenue in subsequent periods.

Worked example: Closing inventory

The Umbrella Shop's financial year ends on 30 September each year. On 1 October 20X4 it had no goods in inventory. During the year to 30 September 20X5, it purchased 30,000 umbrellas costing £60,000 from umbrella suppliers. It resold the umbrellas for £5 each, and sales for the year amounted to £100,000 (20,000 umbrellas). At 30 September there were 10,000 unsold umbrellas left in inventory, valued at cost of £2 each.

Requirement

What was The Umbrella Shop's gross profit for the year?

Solution

It purchased 30,000 umbrellas, but only sold 20,000. Purchase costs of £60,000 and sales of £100,000 do not relate to the same quantity of goods.

The gross profit for the year should be calculated by 'matching' the sales value of 20,000 umbrellas sold with the cost of those 20,000 umbrellas. The cost of sales in this example is therefore the cost of purchases minus the cost of goods in inventory at the year end.

		£	£
Sales (20,000 units at £5)			100,000
Purchases	30,000 units at £2	60,000	
Less closing inventory	(10,000) units at £2	(20,000)	
Cost of sales	20,000 units at £2		(40,000)
Gross profit			60,000

Worked example: Opening and closing inventory

In its next reporting period, 1 October 20X5 to 30 September 20X6, The Umbrella Shop purchased 40,000 umbrellas at a total cost of £95,000, and sold 45,000 umbrellas for £230,000. At 30 September 20X6 it had (10,000 + 40,000 – 45,000) = 5,000 umbrellas left in inventory, which together had cost £12,000.

Requirement

What was The Umbrella Shop's gross profit for the second period?

Solution

In this reporting period, it purchased 40,000 umbrellas to add to the 10,000 it already had in inventory at the start of the year. It sold 45,000, leaving 5,000 umbrellas in inventory at the year end. Once again, gross profit should be calculated by matching the value of 45,000 units of sales with the cost of those 45,000 units.

The cost of sales is the value of the 10,000 umbrellas in inventory at the beginning of the period, plus the cost of the 40,000 umbrellas purchased, less the cost of the 5,000 umbrellas in inventory at the period end.

		£	£
Sales (45,000 units)			230,000
Opening inventory*	10,000 units at £2	20,000	
Add purchases	40,000 units	95,000	
Less closing inventory	(5,000) units	(12,000)	
Cost of sales	45,000 units		(103,000)
Gross profit			127,000

* Taken from the closing inventory value of the previous reporting period.

1.2 Cost of sales

	£
Opening inventory value	X
Add cost of purchases (or, for a manufacturing company, the cost of production)	X
Add cost of carriage inwards (see below)	X
Less closing inventory value	(X)
Equals cost of sales	X

In other words, to match 'sales' and 'cost of sales', it is necessary to adjust the cost of goods **purchased** or **manufactured** to allow for increases or reduction in inventory levels during the period.

Interactive question 1: Gross profit [Difficulty level: Easy]

On 1 January 20X6, Grand Union Food Stores had goods in inventory valued at £6,000. During 20X6 its owner purchased supplies costing £50,000. Sales for the year to 31 December 20X6 amounted to £80,000. The cost of goods in inventory at 31 December 20X6 was £12,500.

Requirement

Calculate the business's gross profit for the year.

See **Answer** at the end of this chapter.

1.3 Carriage inwards and outwards

'Carriage' refers to the **cost of transporting purchased goods** from the supplier to the premises of the business which has bought them. Someone has to pay for these delivery costs: sometimes the supplier pays (in which case the purchaser has no costs to record) and sometimes the purchaser pays. When the purchaser pays, the cost to the purchaser is **carriage inwards** when the goods are coming **into** the business, and **carriage outwards** when the goods are going **out** of the business.

- The **cost of carriage inwards** is added to the **cost of purchases**, and is therefore included in the calculation of cost of sales and gross profit.

- The **cost of carriage outwards** is a distribution cost deducted from gross profit in the **income statement**.

Worked example: Carriage inwards and carriage outwards

Gwyn Tring imports and resells clocks. He pays for the costs of delivering the clocks from his supplier in Switzerland to his shop, called Clickety Clocks, in Wales.

He resells clocks to other traders throughout the country, paying carriage costs for deliveries from his business premises to his customers.

On 1 July 20X5, he had clocks in inventory valued at £17,000. During the year to 30 June 20X6 he purchased more clocks for £75,000. Carriage inwards amounted to £2,000. Sales for the year were £162,100. Other business expenses amounted to £56,000, excluding carriage outwards which cost £2,500. The value of clocks in inventory at the year end was £15,400.

Requirement

Prepare the income statement of Clickety Clocks for the year ended 30 June 20X6.

Solution

CLICKETY CLOCKS
INCOME STATEMENT FOR THE YEAR ENDED 30 JUNE 20X6

	£	£
Revenue		162,100
Opening inventory	17,000	
Purchases	75,000	
Carriage inwards	2,000	
	94,000	
Less closing inventory	(15,400)	
Cost of sales		(78,600)
Gross profit		83,500
Carriage outwards	2,500	
Other expenses	56,000	
		(58,500)
Net profit		25,000

1.4 Inventory written off or written down

A trader might be unable to sell all the goods purchased, because before they can be sold they might:

- Be lost or stolen
- Be damaged and become worthless
- Become obsolete or out of fashion. These might be thrown away, or sold off at a low price

When goods are lost, stolen or thrown away as worthless, the business will make a loss on those goods because their 'sales value' will be nil.

Similarly, when goods lose value because they have become **obsolete** or out of fashion, the business will **make a loss** if their **net realisable value** is less than cost. For example, if goods which originally cost £500 are now obsolete and could only be sold for £150, the business would suffer a loss of £350.

If, at the end of a reporting period, a business still has goods in inventory which are either worthless or worth less than their original cost, the value of the inventories should be **written down** to:

- **Nothing**, if they arc worthless, or
- Their **net realisable value**, if this is less than their original cost.

The cost of inventory written off or written down does not usually cause any problems in calculating the gross profit of a business, because the cost of sales already includes the cost of inventories written off or written down, as the following example shows.

Worked example: Inventories written off and written down

Lucas Wagg ends his financial year on 31 March. At 1 April 20X5 he had goods in inventory valued at £8,800. During the year to 31 March 20X6, he purchased goods costing £48,000. Fashion goods which cost £2,100 were held in inventory at 31 March 20X6, and Lucas Wagg believes that these can only now be sold at a sale price of £400. Goods still held in inventory at 31 March 20X6 (including the fashion goods) had an original purchase cost of £7,600. Sales for the year were £81,400.

Requirement

Calculate Lucas Wagg's gross profit for the year ended 31 March 20X6.

Solution

Initial calculation of closing inventory values:

	At cost £	Realisable value £	Amount written down £
Fashion goods	2,100	400	1,700
Other goods (balancing figure)	5,500		
	7,600		

LUCAS WAGG
GROSS PROFIT FOR THE YEAR ENDED 31 MARCH 20X6

	£	£
Revenue		81,400
Opening inventory	8,800	
Purchases	48,000	
Less closing inventory (400 + 5,500)	(5,900)	
Cost of sales		(50,900)
Gross profit		30,500

By using the figure of £5,900 for closing inventories, the cost of sales automatically includes the inventory write-down of £1,700.

We shall return to the calculation of net realisable value in Chapter 10 of this Study Manual.

1.5 Inventory destroyed or stolen and subject to an insurance claim

Where a **material** amount of inventory has been stolen or destroyed, including their cost in gross profit will give a very distorted idea of the business's basic profitability:

- Purchases will include the cost of goods that could not be sold, so the accrual principle is broken, yet they are not in closing inventory either, so it will look as if the business's gross margin on sales has fallen catastrophically

- There may be an amount of income as a result of an insurance claim, which cannot be included in cost of sales under the 'no offsetting' principle

These problems are overcome by taking the cost of goods stolen or destroyed **out of purchases**, and including it under **expenses**. The insurance claim is treated as **other income** in calculating net profit; if it has not yet been received in the form **of cash** it is disclosed as '**other receivables**' on the statement of financial position.

Worked example: Material amount of inventory stolen

Ethelberta had £15,000 of inventory as at 1 January 20X2. During the year to 31 December 20X2 she purchased inventory for £98,000, incurring carriage inwards of £150. She made sales of £150,000, incurring delivery costs to her customers of £2,400. At 31 December 20X2 she realises that she has inventory costing only £200 left; goods costing £18,000 have been stolen. The insurance company has agreed to pay her claim for 75% of the cost.

We shall prepare Ethelberta's income statement on (a) the basis set out in section 1.5 above, and compare this with (b) the alternative in section 1.4.

Solution

	(a) £	(a) £	(b) £	(b) £
Revenue		150,000		150,000
Opening inventory	15,000		15,000	
Purchases	98,000		98,000	
Carriage inwards	150		150	
Inventory stolen	(18,000)		0	
Closing inventory	(200)		(200)	
Cost of sales		(94,950)		(112,950)
Gross profit		55,050		37,050
Other income (18,000 × 75%)		13,500		13,500
Cost of goods stolen		(18,000)		0
Distribution costs (carriage out)		(2,400)		(2,400)
Net profit		48,150		48,150
Gross profit margin (Gross profit/Revenue)		36.7%		24.7%
Net profit margin (Net profit/Revenue)		32.1%		32.1%

Both treatments result in the same net profit. However, the treatment in (a) matches revenue with the cost of the goods that generated the revenue in gross profit, and also matches the cost of the goods stolen with the insurance receipt in respect of them in arriving at net profit. The treatment in (b) does not match revenue and expense so effectively.

Interactive question 2: Insurance claim [Difficulty level: Exam standard]

Wasa lost inventory that cost £64,500 in a fire. The goods were insured for 60% of their cost.

Requirement

Prepare a journal to account for this in Wasa's books.

See **Answer** at the end of this chapter.

We shall come back to how to account fully for inventories, including material write-offs, in Chapter 9.

2 The principle behind accruals and prepayments

Section overview

- The accrual principle requires that we match expenses with the revenue generated by them.
- We sometimes therefore need to carry forward actual expenditure to a subsequent period (a **prepayment**), or account for expenditure incurred before it is actually paid for (an **accrual**).

Gross profit should be calculated by **matching** revenue and cost of sales. Net profit should be calculated by charging the expenses which relate to that period. For example, in preparing the income statement for a six month period, it would be appropriate to charge six months' expenses for rent, local property taxes, insurance and telephone costs, etc.

However, expenses may not actually be paid for during the period to which they relate.

Worked example: Accrual principle

A business rents a shop for £20,000 per annum and pays the full annual rent on 1 April each year. If we calculate the profit of the business for six months to 30 June 20X7, the correct charge for rent in the income statement is £10,000, even though the rent paid is £20,000 in that period. Similarly, the rent charge in the income statement for the second six months of 20X7 is £10,000, even though no rent is actually paid in that period.

We use the **accrual principle** here to match expenses to the relevant time period.

Definitions

Accruals (accrued expenses): Expenses which are charged against the profit for a particular period, even though they have not yet been paid for.

Prepayments (prepaid expenses): Expenses which have been paid in one reporting period, but are not charged against profit until a later period, because they relate to that later period.

The following examples clarify the principle involved, that **expenses should be matched against income in the period to which they relate**. Accruals and prepayments are the means by which we move charges into the correct reporting period.

- If we pay in this period for something which relates to the next reporting period, we use a **prepayment** to transfer that charge **forward** to the next period.
- If we have incurred an expense in this period which will not be paid for until the next period, we use an **accrual** to bring the charge **back** into this period.

3 Accruals

Section overview

- To set up an accrual

DEBIT	Expense (income statement)	£X	
CREDIT	Accrual (liability on the statement of financial position)		£X

Worked example: Accruals I

Horace Goodrunning ends his motor spares business's reporting period on 28 February each year. His telephone was installed on 1 April 20X6 and he receives his telephone bill quarterly at the end of each quarter. We need to calculate the telephone expense to be charged to the income statement for the year ended 28 February 20X7.

Telephone expense for the three months ended:

	£
30.6.20X6	23.50
30.9.20X6	27.20
31.12.20X6	33.40
31.3.20X7	36.00

All the bills were paid on the final day of each three-month period.

Solution

As at 28 February 20X7, no telephone bill had been received in respect of 20X7 because it was not due for another month. However, the accrual principle means we cannot ignore the telephone expenses for January and February, and so an accrual of £24 is made, being two thirds of the final bill of £36.

The telephone expenses for the year ended 28 February 20X7 are as follows:

	£
1 March – 31 March 20X6 (no telephone)	0.00
1 April – 30 June 20X6	23.50
1 July – 30 September 20X6	27.20
1 October – 31 December 20X6	33.40
1 January – 28 February 20X7 (two months: £36 × 2/3)*	24.00
	108.10

* The charge for the period 1 January – 28 February 20X7 is two thirds of the bill received on 31 March.

The accrual will also appear in the statement of financial position of the business as at 28 February 20X7, as a current liability. The journal to set this up is as follows:

DEBIT	Electricity	£24	
CREDIT	Accrual (current liability)		£24

Interactive question 3: Accruals I   [Difficulty level: Exam standard]

Cleverley started in business as a paper plate and cup manufacturer on 1 January 20X2, preparing financial statements to 31 December 20X2. He is not registered for VAT. Electricity bills received were as follows.

	20X2 £	20X3 £	20X4 £
31 January	–	491.52	753.24
30 April	279.47	400.93	192.82
31 July	663.80	700.94	706.20
31 October	117.28	620.00	156.40

Requirement

What should the electricity charge be for the year ended 31 December 20X2? Prepare a journal to record the accrual or prepayment as at 31 December 20X2.

See **Answer** at the end of this chapter.

4 Prepayments

Section overview

- To set up a prepayment

  DEBIT   Prepayment (asset in the statement of financial position)   £X
  CREDIT   Expense (income statement)   £X

Worked example: Prepayments I

A business opens on 1 January 20X4 in a shop where the rent is £20,000 per year, payable quarterly in advance at the beginning of each three month period. Payments were made as follows.

	£
1 January 20X4	5,000
31 March 20X4	5,000
30 June 20X4	5,000
30 September 20X4	5,000
31 December 20X4	5,000

Requirement

What will the rental charge be for the year ended 31 December 20X4?

Solution

The total amount paid in the year is £25,000. The yearly rental, however, is only £20,000. The last payment was a prepayment as it is a payment in advance for the first three months of 20X5. The charge for 20X4 is therefore:

	£
Paid in year	25,000
Prepayment	(5,000)
	20,000

The double entry for this prepayment is:

DEBIT	Prepayments (current asset)	£5,000	
CREDIT	Rent		£5,000

5 Accounting for accruals and prepayments

Section overview

- Both accruals and prepayments are usually included as current liabilities/assets as they nearly always clear very soon after the end of the reporting period.

- In order not to double count accrued expenditure, or fail to account for prepaid expenditure at all, closing accruals and prepayments must be reversed at the start of the next reporting period:

| DEBIT | Accruals | £X | CREDIT | Expense | £X |
| DEBIT | Expense | £X | CREDIT | Prepayment | £X |

You can see from the double entry shown for both these examples that the other side of the entry is taken to the statement of financial position: an asset or a liability account that are needed only at the end of each reporting period.

- **Prepayments** are included in **current assets** in the statement of financial position as they represent money that has been paid out in advance of the expense being incurred. They usually clear within 12 months of the date of the statement of financial position. The balance on the prepayment ledger account is brought down as a debit balance at the beginning of the next period.

- **Accruals** are included in **current liabilities** as they represent liabilities which have been incurred but for which no invoice has yet been received. They nearly always clear soon after the end of the reporting period. The balance on the accruals account is brought down as a credit balance at the beginning of the next period.

Transaction	DR	CR	Description
Accrual	Expense	Liability (accrual)	Expense incurred in period, not paid/recorded
Prepayment	Asset (prepayment)	(Reduction in) expense	Expense paid/recorded in period, not incurred until next period

5.1 Reversing accruals and prepayments in new period

Prepayments and accruals must be **reversed** by an opening journal in the new period, otherwise the entity will charge itself twice for the same expense (accruals) *or* will never charge itself (prepayments).

Transaction	DR	CR	Description
Reverse accrual	Accrual (opening credit balance on liability account)	Expense (new period)	Reversing accrual of expense set up in previous period
Reverse prepayment	Expense (new period)	Prepayment (opening debit balance on asset account)	Reversing prepayment of expense set up in previous period

Once these **opening journals** are written up, the balance on the accruals and prepayments accounts will be zero. They will not be used again until the end of the new period.

5.1.1 Reversing accruals

We shall use the electricity account from Interactive question 3 above, plus a new accrual ledger account, and see how the accrual is reversed at the beginning of the new period, then a new one is set up at its end.

ACCRUAL ACCOUNT

	£		£
20X2		*20X2*	
31.12 Balance c/d	327.68	31.12 Electricity account	327.68
	327.68		327.68
20X3		*20X3*	
1.1 Electricity account (accrual reversed)	327.68	1.1 Balance b/d	327.68

ELECTRICITY ACCOUNT

		£			£
20X2			*20X2*		
30.4	Cash	279.47	31.12	Income statement	1,388.23
31.7	Cash	663.80			
31.10	Cash	117.28			
31.12	Accrual account	327.68			
		1,388.23			1,388.23
20X3			*20X3*		
31.1	Cash	491.52	1.1	Accrual reversed	327.68
30.4	Cash	400.93	31.12	Income statement	2,387.87
31.7	Cash	700.94			
31.10	Cash	620.00			
31.12	Accrual account	502.16			
		2,715.55			2,715.55

The income statement charge and accrual for 20X3 of £2,387.87 and £502.16 respectively can be checked as follows.

Invoice paid	£	Proportion charged in 20X3	£
31.1.X3	491.52	1/3	163.84
30.4.X3	400.93	all	400.93
31.7,X3	700.94	all	700.94
31.10.X3	620.00	all	620.00
31.1.X4	753.24	2/3	502.16
Charge to income statement in 20X3			2,387.87

5.1.2 Reversing prepayments

Using the rent account from the prepayment worked example, the £5,000 rent prepaid in 20X4 will be reversed by an opening journal in the new period. The rent account will be added to by the payments in 20X5, and then reduced by a journal setting up the prepayment at the end of 20X5 in the same way.

PREPAYMENT ACCOUNT

	£		£
20X4		*20X4*	
31.12 Rent a/c	5,000.00	31.12 Balance c/d	5,000.00
	5,000.00		5,000.00
20X5		*20X5*	
1.1 Balance b/d	5,000.00	1.1 Rent a/c	
		(prepayment reversed)	5,000.00
31.12 Rent a/c	5,000.00	31.12 Balance c/d	5,000.00
	10,000.00		10,000.00

RENT

	£		£
20X4		*20X4*	
In year Cash (5 payments)	25,000.00	31.12 Prepayment a/c	5,000.00
		31.12 Income statement	20,000.00
	25,000.00		25,000.00
20X5		*20X5*	
1.1 Rent a/c (prepayment reversed)	5,000.00	31.12 Prepayment a/c	5,000.00
In year Cash (5 payments)	20,000.00	31.12 Income statement	20,000.00
	25,000.00		25,000.00

Interactive question 4: Accruals II [Difficulty level: level]

Ratsnuffer is a business dealing in pest control. Its owner, Roy Dent, employs a team of eight people who were paid £12,000 per annum each in the year to 31 December 20X5. At the start of 20X6 he raised salaries by 10% to £13,200 per annum each.

On 1 July 20X6, he hired a trainee at a salary of £8,400 per annum.

He pays his work force on the first working day of every month, one month in arrears, so that his employees receive their salary for January on the first working day in February, etc.

Requirements

(a) Calculate the cost of salaries charged in Ratsnuffer's income statement for the year ended 31 December 20X6.

(b) Calculate the amount actually paid in salaries during the year (ie the amount of cash received by the work force).

(c) State the amount of the accrual for salaries which will appear in Ratsnuffer's statement of financial position as at 31 December 20X6.

See **Answer** at the end of this chapter.

Worked example: Prepayments II

The Square Wheels Garage pays fire insurance annually in advance on 1 June each year. The firm's reporting period is the year ended 28 February. From the following record of insurance payments you are required to calculate the insurance charge to the income statement for the 12 month reporting period ended 28 February 20X8.

Insurance paid

	£
1.6.20X6	600
1.6.20X7	700

Solution

		£
(a)	3 months, 1 March – 31 May 20X7 (3/12 × £600) (opening prepayment)	150
(b)	9 months, 1 June 20X7 – 28 February 20X8 (9/12 × £700)	525
	Insurance cost for the year to 28 February 20X8, charged to the income statement	675

At 28 February 20X8 there is a prepayment for insurance, covering the period 1 March – 31 May 20X8. This insurance premium was paid on 1 June 20X7, but only nine months worth of the annual cost is chargeable to the reporting period ended 28 February 20X8. The prepayment of (3/12 × £700) £175 as at 28 February 20X8 will appear as a current asset in the statement of financial position of the Square Wheels Garage.

In the same way, there was a prepayment of (3/12 × £600) £150 in the statement of financial position one year earlier as at 28 February 20X7.

Summary

	£
Prepaid insurance premiums as at 28 February 20X7	150
Add insurance premiums paid 1 June 20X7	700
	850
Less insurance costs charged to the income statement for the year ended 28 February 20X8	(675)
Equals prepaid insurance premiums as at 28 February 20X8 (asset in statement of financial position)	175

Interactive question 5: Accruals and prepayments [Difficulty level: Exam standard]

The Batley Print Shop, which is not registered for VAT, rents a photocopying machine. It makes a quarterly payment as follows:

(a) Three months rental in advance

(b) A charge of 2 pence per copy made during the quarter just ended

The rental agreement began on 1 August 20X4. The first six quarterly bills were as follows.

Bills dated	Rental	Cost of copies taken	Total
	£	£	£
1 August 20X4	2,100	0	2,100
1 November 20X4	2,100	1,500	3,600
1 February 20X5	2,100	1,400	3,500
1 May 20X5	2,100	1,800	3,900
1 August 20X5	2,700	1,650	4,350
1 November 20X5	2,700	1,950	4,650

The bills are paid promptly, as soon as they are received.

Requirements

(a) Calculate the charge for photocopying expenses for the year to 31 August 20X4 and the amount of prepayments and/or accrued charges as at that date.

(b) Calculate the charge for photocopying expenses for the following year to 31 August 20X5, and the amount of prepayments and/or accrued charges as at that date.

See **Answer** at the end of this chapter.

Worked example: Accruals III

Mark opens a shop on 1 May 20X6 to sell camping equipment. The shop rent is £12,000 per annum, payable quarterly in arrears (with the first payment on 31 July 20X6). His reporting period ends on 31 December each year.

The rent ledger account as at 31 December 20X6 will record only two rental payments (on 31 July and 31 October) and there will be two months' accrued rental expenses for November and December 20X6 (£2,000), since the next rental payment is not due until 31 January 20X7.

The charge to the income statement for the period to 31 December 20X6 will be for eight months' rent (May December inclusive), £8,000.

So far, the rent account appears as follows.

RENT ACCOUNT

	£			£
20X6		*20X6*		
31 July Cash	3,000			
31 Oct Cash	3,000	31 Dec	Income statement	8,000

To complete the picture, the accrual of £2,000 has to be put in, to bring the balance on the account up to the full charge for the year. At the beginning of the next year the accrual is reversed.

RENT ACCOUNT

	£			£
20X6		*20X6*		
31 July Cash	3,000			
31 Oct Cash	3,000			
31 Dec Accruals	2,000	31 Dec	Income statement	8,000
	8,000			8,000
		20X7		
		1 Jan	Accrual reversed	2,000

The corresponding credit entry would be cash if rent is paid without the need for an invoice – eg with payment by standing order or direct debit at the bank. If there is always an invoice when rent becomes payable, the double entry would be:

| DEBIT | Rent account | £2,000 | |
| CREDIT | Payables | | £2,000 |

Then when the rent is paid, the ledger entries would be:

| DEBIT | Payables | £2,000 | |
| CREDIT | Cash | | £2,000 |

The rent account for the *next* year to 31 December 20X7, assuming no increase in rent in that year, would be as follows.

RENT ACCOUNT

		£			£
20X7			*20X7*		
31 Jan	Cash	3,000	1 Jan	Accrual reversed	2,000
30 Apr	Cash	3,000			
31 Jul	Cash	3,000			
31 Oct	Cash	3,000			
31 Dec	Accruals	2,000	31 Dec	Income statement	12,000
		14,000			14,000
			20X8		
			1 Jan	Accrual reversed	2,000

A full twelve months' rental charge is taken as an expense to the income statement.

Worked example: Prepayments III

Terry Trunk commences business as a landscape gardener on 1 September 20X5. He immediately decides to join his local trade association, the Confederation of Luton Gardeners, for which the annual membership subscription is £180, payable annually in advance. He paid this amount on 1 September 20X5. In the following year he expects the subscription to rise by £12. Terry decides that his reporting period should end on 30 June each year.

In the first reporting period to 30 June 20X6 (10 months), a full year's membership will have been paid, but only ten twelfths of the subscription should be charged to the period (10/12 × £180 = £150). There is a prepayment of two months of membership subscription (ie 2/12 × £180 = £30).

The journal to set up the prepayment is as follows.

| DEBIT | Prepayment account | £30 | |
| CREDIT | Subscriptions account | | £30 |

The balance on the subscriptions account (£150) should then be taken to the income statement. The balance on the prepayment account will appear as a current asset in the statement of financial position as at 30 June 20X6, and will be reversed on 1 July 20X6.

SUBSCRIPTIONS ACCOUNT

		£			£
20X5			*20X6*		
1 Sept	Cash	180	30 Jun	Income statement	150
			30 Jun	Prepayment	30
		180			180
20X6					
1 Jul	Prepayment reversed	30			

The subscription account for the next reporting period will be:

SUBSCRIPTIONS ACCOUNT

		£			£
20X6			*20X7*		
1 Jul	Prepayment reversed	30	30 Jun	Income statement (bal fig)	190
1 Sept	Cash	192	30 Jun	Prepayment (192 × 2/12)	32
		222			222
20X7					
1 Jul	Prepayment reversed	32			

Interactive question 6: Income statement and statement of financial position
[Difficulty level: Intermediate]

The Umbrella Shop has the following trial balance as at 30 September 20X8.

	£	£
Sales		156,000
Purchases	65,000	
Non-current assets	200,000	
Inventory at 1.10.X7	10,000	
Cash at bank	12,000	
Trade receivables	54,000	
Trade payables		40,000
Distribution costs	10,000	
Cash in hand	2,000	
Administrative expenses	15,000	
Finance costs	5,000	
Carriage inwards	1,000	
Carriage outwards	2,000	
Capital account at 1.10.X7		180,000
	376,000	376,000

The following information is available:

(a) Closing inventory at 30.9.X8 is £13,000, after writing off damaged goods of £2,000.

(b) Included in administrative expenses is machinery rental of £6,000 covering the year to 31 December 20X8.

(c) A late invoice for £12,000 covering rent for the year ended 30 June 20X9 has not been included in the trial balance.

Requirement

Prepare an income statement and statement of financial position for the year ended 30 September 20X8.

See **Answer** at the end of this chapter.

Interactive question 7: Administrative expenses account   [Difficulty level: Exam standard]

Xbat has posted £10,500 from its purchases day book to its administrative expenses ledger account during 20X2, and £250 direct from its cash book. At 31 December 20X2 the business estimates that the year-end accrual should be £100 less than the accrual brought forward, and the prepayment should be £150 less.

Requirement

What is the total cost of administrative expenses in the year ended 31 December 20X2?

See **Answer** at the end of this chapter.

6 The accrual principle and income

Section overview

- The accrual principle also applies to income.

- Accrued income arises when receipt of income (such as rent or subscription) is in arrears at the year end.

- Deferred income arises when income has been received in advance at the end of the reporting period, so it needs to be carried forward and treated as income of the following reporting period.

- Accounting for accrued income

DEBIT	Accrued income (asset in the statement of financial position)	£X
CREDIT	Other income (income statement)		£X

- Accounting for deferred income:

DEBIT	Revenue or other income (income statement)	£X
CREDIT	Deferred income (liability in the statement of financial position)		£X

So far we have concentrated on accrued and prepaid expenses arising from the need to match expenses with the income to which they relate. It is also necessary sometimes to treat income in line with the accruals principle.

- Cash may be received in one period although the actual sale to which it relates occurs in the subsequent period. An example is a **deposit** (or **advance payment**, or **payment on account**) received from a customer on an item which will be delivered in the future. The deposit is banked but until the actual sale is recognised the cash should be treated as still being owing to the customer, not as income. This is known as **deferred income**, a **current liability** in the statement of financial position

- Cash may be received in one period in relation to an event which arose in a previous period. An example is where a supplier makes a **refund** in relation to a purchase in a previous period. This is known as **accrued income**, a **current asset** on the statement of financial position.

The treatment is similar to accruals and prepayments of expenses:

- Calculate the amount of the deferred or accrued income

- At the end of the reporting period, write up a journal which updates the relevant income statement accounts, and which sets up the relevant asset and liability accounts

- At the beginning of the next reporting period, reverse the double entry

Worked example: Deferred and accrued income

Sunrise Carpets sells floor coverings to the public. At the end of its 12 month reporting period,

31 December 20X4, it has recorded as sales £1,200 received from customers as deposits on carpets which are not due to be invoiced until February 20X5. In January 20X5 it records a £500 refund from one of its main suppliers as a result of exceeding the agreed level of custom during 20X4.

Requirement

Prepare journals:

(a) Recording these transactions in the ledger accounts for the reporting period ended 31 December 20X4.

(b) Recording these transactions in the ledger accounts for the reporting period ended 31 December 20X5.

Solution

- The reversal of deferred income in 20X5 is not to an income statement account but to trade receivables. This is because we are dealing with credit transactions: the full amount of the sale will be invoiced in February 20X5 (Debit Receivables, Credit Sales), so the deposit should be credited to trade receivables in the new reporting period in anticipation

- The full amount of purchases was originally invoiced by the supplier in 20X4, so the refund is treated as a deduction from what is owed to the supplier by being debited to trade payables in 20X5.

(a)

			£	£
31.12.X4	DEBIT	Sales	1,200	
	CREDIT	Deferred income (liability)		1,200
		Deposits from customers		
31.12.X4	DEBIT	Accrued income (asset)	500	
	CREDIT	Purchases		500
		Refund from supplier		

(b)

			£	£
1.1.X5	DEBIT	Deferred income (liability)	1,200	
	CREDIT	Trade receivables		1,200
		Reversal of deferred income		
1.1.X5	DEBIT	Trade payables	500	
	CREDIT	Accrued income (asset)		500
		Reversal of accrued income		

Most frequently this situation is seen in relation to subscriptions to clubs or associations, which do not generally maintain a receivables ledger and so just use cash accounting. Some members pay an annual subscription earlier than they need to (in **advance**), and others pay late (in **arrears**). At the end of the year there are bound to be amounts in arrears and amounts paid in advance, but the club will nevertheless need to make sure that the income figure it shows relates only to the actual reporting period. The treatment is as follows.

- Open a subscriptions receivable ledger account.

- Enter all the amounts you know eg annual income or cash received.

- Calculate the balancing figure – in an exam the balancing figure will be the amount you are looking for.

SUBSCRIPTIONS RECEIVABLE

Opening arrears	X	Opening advances	X
Annual income	X	Cash received in year	X
		Irrecoverable amounts	X
Closing advances	X	Closing arrears	X
	X̄		X̄

Interactive question 8: Accrued income   [Difficulty level: Exam standard]

The Drones Club has a reporting period of 12 months to 30 June. Its annual subscription for the year ended 30 June 20X7 was £100, and this rose to £120 per annum for the year to 30 June 20X8. As at 1 July 20X6 the Club's members had paid £2,380 in advance, and were £4,840 in arrears. The Club only has 200 members, and there are no irrecoverable amounts. It received £23,620 in respect of subscriptions in the year to 30 June 20X7, and four members are known to be in arrears at 30 June 20X8.

Requirement

How many members have paid their subscriptions for the reporting period ended 30 June 20X8 in advance?

[Hint: Use the subscriptions receivable T account.]

See **Answer** at the end of this chapter.

You may also encounter deferred income/advances and accrued income/arrears in relation to rent receivable in the exam. Again, a single **rent receivable** ledger account is the best way to make the required calculations.

7 Accruals, prepayments, advances and arrears on the ETB

Section overview

- An adjustment journal for accrued expenses on the ETB debits the expenses line and credits a new accrued line. The debit is added to the income statement expense. The credit is a liability in the statement of financial position.

- Adjustment journal for prepaid expenses: debit new prepayments line, credit expenses line. The debit is an asset in the statement of financial position. The credit is deducted from the income statement expense.

So far we have looked at how accruals and prepayments/advances and arrears are accounted for in the ledger accounts, using closing and opening journals. These are necessary to keep the ledger accounts up-to-date, but from the point of view of preparing the income statement and statement of financial position the procedure can be rather cumbersome. This is because accruals, prepayments, advances and arrears at the period end are usually calculated and accounted for after the initial trial balance has been extracted. A neater way of incorporating the relevant figures is to use the ETB.

- We calculate the amounts of the accrued and prepaid expenses, and the deferred or accrued income, as usual

- We prepare the period-end journals as usual

- We enter these journals in the adjustments columns of the ETB, opening up lines in the statement of financial position column for accruals, prepayments, accrued income and deferred income as necessary

- We include these adjustments in the ETB cross-cast to prepare the financial statements

- We enter the closing journals in the ledger accounts as usual

- We prepare and enter the opening journals

Worked example: Accruals and prepayments on the ETB

Jezebel makes and sells clothing to order. Her reporting period is the 12 months ended 31 December. She has extracted the following trial balance as at 31 December 20X1:

	Debit £	Credit £
Cash at bank	6,541	
Opening capital		15,000
Loan		8,000
Non-current assets	45,000	
Trade payables		16,758
Expenses	10,877	
Purchases	62,975	
Sales		157,632
Other income		0
Trade receivables	22,854	
Drawings	49,143	
	197,390	197,390

She needs to take account of the following matters:

(a) Her quarterly power bills are £822. The last bill she paid was in respect of the quarter ending 31 October 20X1.

(b) Her annual rent bill of £2,970 was paid on 1 May 20X1 in respect of the year to 30 April 20X2.

(c) Sales include £350 received from cash customers in December in respect of items of clothing that Jezebel will complete in January 20X2.

(d) A royalty of £58 is due from a fashion magazine which used Jezebel's products in a fashion shoot. Jezebel wishes to account for this as other/accrued income rather than trade receivables.

We need to complete Jezebel's ETB to calculate her net profit for the reporting period.

Solution

Ledger balance	Trial balance		Adjustments		Income statement		Statement of financial position	
	Debit £	Credit £	Debit £	Credit £	Debit £	Credit £	Debit £	Credit £
Cash at bank	6,541						6,541	
Opening capital		15,000						15,000
Loan		8,000						8,000
Non-current assets	45,000						45,000	
Trade payables		16,758						16,758
Expenses (a),(b)	10,877		548	990	10,435			
Purchases	62,975				62,975			
Sales (c)		157,632	350			157,282		
Other income (d)				58		58		
Trade receivables	22,854						22,854	
Drawings	49,143						49,143	
Accruals								
(822 x 2/3) (a)				548				548
Prepayments								
(2,970 x 4/12) (b)			990				990	
Accrued income (d)			58				58	
Deferred income (c)				350				350
Net profit					83,930			83,930
	197,390	197,390	1,946	1,946	157,340	157,340	124,586	124,586

Summary and Self-test

Summary

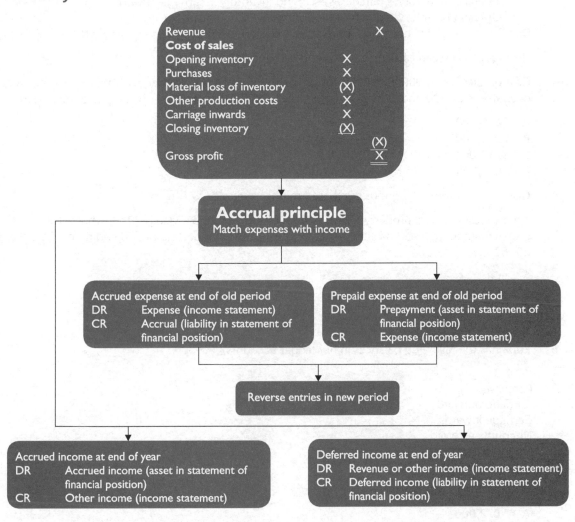

The ETB table:

	Adj DR	Adj CR	IS DR	IS CR	SFP DR	SFP CR
Expense	A	B	A	B		
Income	C	D	C	D		
Accrual		A				A
Prepayment	B				B	
Accrued income (arrears)	D				D	
Deferred income (advances)		C				C

Self-test

Answer the following questions.

1   Which of the following is the correct calculation for cost of sales?

    A   Sales – purchases
    B   Opening inventory + purchases + closing inventory + carriage inwards
    C   Opening inventory + purchases – closing inventory + carriage inwards
    D   Sales – opening inventory - purchases + closing inventory – carriage inwards

2   Distinguish between carriage inwards and carriage outwards.

3   Cost of sales is £14,000. Purchases for the period are £14,000, carriage inwards is £1,000, carriage outwards is £1,500 and closing inventory is £13,000. What was the opening inventory figure?

    A   £10,500
    B   £11,500
    C   £12,000
    D   £13,000

4   Give three reasons why goods purchased might have to be written off.

5   If a business has paid property tax of £1,000 for the year to 31 March 20X9, what is the prepayment in the financial statements for the 12 month reporting period ending on 31 December 20X8?

    A   £0
    B   £250
    C   £750
    D   £1,000

6   Rupa has the following balances in her ledger accounts.

	£
Purchases	75,000
Carriage outwards	800
Carriage inwards	1,000
Discounts received	2,000
Opening inventory	10,000
Closing inventory	12,000

    What is Rupa's cost of sales?

    A   £72,000
    B   £73,000
    C   £74,000
    D   £74,800

7   On 5 May 20X8 Portals pays a rent bill of £1,800 for the eighteen months ended 30 June 20X9.

    What is the charge in the income statement and the entry for rent in the statement of financial position in respect of the 12 month reporting period ended 31 March 20X9?

    A   £1,200 with prepayment of £300
    B   £1,200 with accrual of £600
    C   £1,500 with accrual of £300
    D   £1,500 with prepayment of £300

8   A firm made the following rent payments.

  £9,000 for the six months ended 31 March 20X6
  £12,000 for the six months ended 30 September 20X6
  £11,196 for the 12 months ended 30 September 20X7

  The charge to the income statement for the 12 month reporting period ended 31 December 20X6 was

    A   £13,299
    B   £19,299
    C   £24,897
    D   £22,098

9   Elizabeth paid £2,500 for gas during the reporting period. At the beginning of the period she owed £500; at the end she owed £1,000.

  What charge should have appeared in her income statement for that reporting period?

    A   £2,000
    B   £2,500
    C   £3,000
    D   £3,500

10 At the beginning of September Barney & Co were owed £200 in rent. At the end of September they were owed £400. £800 cash for rent was received during September.

  What entry will be made in the income statement for September for rent receivable?

    A   Debit £600
    B   Debit £1,000
    C   Credit £600
    D   Credit £1,000

Now, go back to the Learning Objectives in the Introduction. If you are satisfied that you have achieved these objectives, please tick them off.

Answer to Interactive question 1

GRAND UNION FOOD STORES

INCOME STATEMENT (EXTRACT) FOR THE YEAR ENDED 31 DECEMBER 20X6

	£	£
Revenue		80,000
Opening inventories	6,000	
Add purchases	50,000	
Less closing inventories	(12,500)	
Cost of sales		(43,500)
Gross profit		36,500

Answer to Interactive question 2

		£	£
DEBIT	Expenses	64,500	
	Other receivables	38,700	
CREDIT	Purchases		64,500
	Other income		38,700

Answer to Interactive question 3

The three invoices received during 20X2 totalled £1,060.55, but this is not the full charge for the reporting period: the November and December electricity charge was not invoiced until the end of January 20X3. To show the correct charge for the reporting period, we **accrue** the charge for November and December based on January's bill. The charge for 20X2 is:

	£
Paid in year	1,060.55
Accrual (2/3 × £491.52)	327.68
	1,388.23

The double entry for the accrual will be:

DEBIT	Electricity account	£327.68	
CREDIT	Accruals		£327.68

Answer to Interactive question 4

(a) *Salaries charge in the income statement year ended 31 December 20X6*

	£
Cost of 8 employees for a full year at £13,200 each	105,600
Cost of trainee for a half year (£8,400/2)	4,200
	109,800

(b) *Salaries actually paid in 20X6*

	£
December 20X5 salaries paid in January (8 employees × £1,000 per month)	8,000
Salaries of 8 employees for January – November 20X6 paid in February – December	
(8 employees × £1,100 per month × 11 months)	96,800
Salary of trainee (for July – November paid in August – December:	
5 months × £700 per month)	3,500
Salaries actually paid	108,300

(c) *Accrued salary as at 31 December 20X6*

(ie costs charged in the Income statement, but not yet paid)

	£
8 employees × 1 month × £1,100 per month	8,800
1 trainee × 1 month × £700 per month	700
	9,500

Summary

	£
Accrued salaries as at 1 January 20X6 (December 20X5 salaries)	8,000
Add salaries cost for 20X6 (Income statement (a))	109,800
	117,800
Less salaries paid (b)	(108,300)
Equals accrued salaries as at 31 December 20X6 (liability in statement of financial position (c))	9,500

SALARIES ACCOUNT

20X6	£	20X6	£
Cash paid	108,300	1.1 Accrual reversed	8,000
31.12 Accrual	9,500	31.12 Income statement	109,800
	117,800		117,800

Answer to Interactive question 5

(a) *Year to 31 August 20X4*

	£
One months' rental (1/3 × £2,100) *	700
Accrued copying charges (1/3 × £1,500) **	500
Photocopying expense (Income statement)	1,200

* From the quarterly bill dated 1 August 20X4
** From the quarterly bill dated 1 November 20X4

There is a prepayment for 2 months' rental (2/3 × £2,100 = £1,400) as at 31 August 20X4, and an accrual for copying charges of £1,500/3 = £500

(b) *Year to 31 August 20X5*

	£	£
Rental from 1 September 20X4 – 31 July 20X5 (11 months at £2,100 per quarter or £700 per month)		7,700
Rental from 1 August – 31 August 20X5 (1/3 × £2,700)		900
Rental charge for the year		8,600
Copying charges:		
1 September – 31 October 20X4 (2/3 × £1,500)	1,000	
1 November 20X4 – 31 January 20X5	1,400	
1 February – 30 April 20X5	1,800	
1 May – 31 July 20X5	1,650	
Accrued charges for August 20X5 (1/3 × £1,950)	650	
		6,500
Photocopying expense (income statement)		15,100

There is a prepayment for 2 months' rental (2/3 × £2,700 = £1,800) as at 31 August 20X5, and an accrual for copying charges of £1,950/3 = £650.

Summary of reporting period 1 September 20X4 – 31 August 20X5

	Rental charges £	Copying costs £
Prepayment as at 31.8.20X4 (2/3 × £2,100)	1,400	
Accrued charge as at 31.8.20X4		(500)
Bills paid during the reporting period		
1 November 20X4	2,100	1,500
1 February 20X5	2,100	1,400
1 May 20X5	2,100	1,800
1 August 20X5	2,700	1,650
Prepayment as at 31.8.20X5 (2/3 × £2,700)	(1,800)	
Accrued charge as at 31.8.20X5		650
Charge to the Income statement for the reporting period	8,600	6,500
Items in the statement of financial position as at 31 August 20X5		
Prepaid rental (current asset)	1,800	
Accrued copying charge (current liability)		650

Answer to Interactive question 6

THE UMBRELLA SHOP
INCOME STATEMENT FOR THE YEAR ENDED 30 SEPTEMBER 20X8

	£	£
Sales		156,000
Opening inventory	10,000	
Purchases	65,000	
Carriage inwards	1,000	
Closing inventory (W1)	(13,000)	
Cost of sales		(63,000)
Gross profit		93,000
Distribution costs (10,000 + 2,000)	12,000	
Administrative expenses (W2)	16,500	
Finance costs	5,000	
		(33,500)
Net profit for the year		59,500

THE UMBRELLA SHOP
STATEMENT OF FINANCIAL POSITION AS AT 30 SEPTEMBER 20X8

	£	£
Assets		
Non-current assets		200,000
Current assets		
Inventory (W1)	13,000	
Trade receivables	54,000	
Prepayments (W4)	1,500	
Cash at bank and in hand (12,000 + 2,000)	14,000	
		82,500
Total assets		282,500
Capital and liabilities		
Owner's capital		
Balance brought forward	180,000	
Profit for the year	59,500	
		239,500
Current liabilities		
Trade payables	40,000	
Accruals (W3)	3,000	
		43,000
Total capital and liabilities		282,500

WORKINGS

(1) **Closing inventory**

As the figure of £13,000 is **after** writing off damaged goods, no further adjustments are necessary. Remember that you are crediting closing inventory to the income statement and the corresponding debit is to the statement of financial position.

(2) **Administrative expenses**

	£
Per trial balance	15,000
Add: accrual (W3)	3,000
Less: prepayment (W4)	(1,500)
	16,500

(3) **Accrual**

	£
Rent for year to 30 June 20X9	12,000
Accrual for period to 30 September 20X8 ($^3/_{12} \times £12,000$)	3,000

(4) **Prepayment**

	£
Machinery rental for the year to 31 December 20X8	6,000
Prepayment for period 1 October to 31 December 20X8 ($^3/_{12} \times £6,000$)	1,500

Answer to Interactive question 7

ADMINISTRATIVE EXPENSES

	£		£
Purchases day book	10,500	Decrease in accruals	100
Cash book	250	Income statement	10,800
Decrease in prepayment	150		
	10,900		10,900

Answer to Interactive question 8

SUBSCRIPTIONS RECEIVABLE

		£			£
1.7.X6	Arrears (accrued income reversed)	4,840	1.7.X6	Advances (deferred income reversed)	2,380
30.6.X7	Income statement (200 × £100)	20,000	Year	Cash	23,620
30.6.X7	Advances (deferred income) bal fig	1,560	30.6.X7	Arrears (4 × £100) (accrued income)	400
		26,400			26,400

Advances total £1,560, which represents 13 members' payments (13 × £120 = £1,560).

1 C Opening inventory + purchases – closing inventory + carriage inwards = cost of sales

2 Carriage inwards is paid on goods coming **into** the business and is added to the cost of purchases

Carriage outwards is paid on goods going **out of** the business to customers and is charged to selling expenses

3 C

	£
Opening inventory value (balancing figure)	12,000
Add purchases (incl carriage inwards)	15,000
	27,000
Less closing inventory	(13,000)
Cost of goods sold	14,000

If you picked A, then you wrongly included carriage outwards in cost of goods sold. If you chose B, then you used the carriage outwards instead of the carriage inwards figure in your calculations. With D, you ignored carriage inwards and outwards altogether!

4
- Goods are stolen or lost
- Goods are damaged
- Goods are obsolete

5 B $^3/_{12} \times £1,000 = £250$

6 C

	£
Opening inventory	10,000
Purchases	75,000
Carriage inwards	1,000
Less Closing inventory	(12,000)
	74,000

7 A

	£
Income statement 12/18 × 1,800	1,200
Closing prepayment: 3/18 × 1,800	300

8 B

	£
Income statement: (3/6 × 9,000) + 12,000 + (3/12 × 11,196)	19,299

9 C

	£
Opening accrual	(500)
Cash paid	2,500
Closing accrual	1,000
	3,000

10 D

RENT RECEIVABLE

	£		£
Other receivables (reversal of opening accrued income)	200	Cash	800
Income statement (bal fig)	1,000	Accrued income	400
	1,200		1,200

CHAPTER 8

Irrecoverable debts and allowances

Introduction

Examination context

Topic List

Summary and Self-test

Answers to Interactive questions

Answers to Self-test

Learning objectives

- Record and account for transactions and events resulting in income, expenses, assets, liabilities and equity in accordance with the appropriate basis of accounting and the laws, regulations and accounting standards applicable to the financial statements

- Prepare an extended trial balance

- Identify the main components of a set of financial statements and specify their purpose and interrelationship

- Prepare and present a statement of financial position, income statement and statement of cash flows (or extracts therefrom) from the accounting records and trial balance in a format which satisfies the information requirements of the entity

Specific syllabus learning outcomes are: 1c, 2c, 3a, 3c

Syllabus links

The material in this chapter will be developed further in this paper, and then in the Financial Accounting and Financial Reporting papers later in the Professional Stage.

Examination context

Questions on the topics in this chapter will be set as multiple choice questions, some of which may involve calculations so that the correct answer can be selected. Very often double entry questions are phrased in terms of preparing a journal.

In the exam you may be required to:

- Identify the accounting principles behind accounting for irrecoverable debts and allowances

- Identify journals for writing off irrecoverable debts, receiving cash in respect of debts previously written off, and setting up or adjusting specific allowances for receivables

- Calculate the figure in the statement of financial position figure for receivables

- Identify the income statement figure for irrecoverable debts expense

- Identify the effects of irrecoverable debts and allowances for receivables on gross and net profit in the income statement

- Specify how year-end irrecoverable debts and allowances for receivables are accounted for on the extended trial balance

1 Irrecoverable debts

Section overview

- Writing off an irrecoverable debt

  DEBIT   Irrecoverable debts expense   £X
  CREDIT Trade receivables   £X

- Accounting for receipt of cash in respect of a debt previously written off:

  DEBIT   Cash   £X
  CREDIT Irrecoverable debts expense   £X

- The fact that a customer's cheque is returned unpaid does not automatically mean the customer's debt should be written off.

Customers who buy goods on credit might fail to pay for them, perhaps out of dishonesty, or because they have gone bankrupt and cannot pay, or because there is a dispute between the parties about the amount payable.

For one reason or another, a business might decide to give up expecting payment of the debt and to **write it off**.

Definitions

Irrecoverable debt: A debt which is not expected to be paid.

Writing off: Charging the cost of the debt against the profit for the period.

1.1 Writing off irrecoverable debts

When a business decides that a particular debt will not be paid, the whole amount of the receivable in question is '**written off**' as an expense in the income statement:

DEBIT   Irrecoverable debts expense (income statement)   £X
CREDIT   Trade receivables (statement of financial position)   £X

Irrecoverable debts written off are presented for as follows.

- **Sales** are shown at their final invoice value in the **income statement**. The sale has been made, expense has been incurred making it and gross profit should be earned. The subsequent failure to collect the debt is a separate administrative matter.

- **Irrecoverable debts** expense is shown as an **administrative expense**.

- The receivable is removed from the receivables control account and ledger.

Suppose an invoice for services rendered to a customer for £300 is never going to be paid. The net effect of the way we account for this as follows:

	£
Revenue (in the income statement)	300
Irrecoverable debt written off (administrative expense)	(300)
	0

Overall however a loss is made on the transaction since the entity has incurred costs in rendering the service, and these will not be recovered. The business has also foregone the profit it could have made on the transaction in selling the good or service to a different customer.

When a debt is written off, the value of the receivable as a current asset is zero. It is no longer recognised as an asset because the business is unlikely to generate any benefits from it.

1.1.1 Irrecoverable debts written off and subsequently paid

An irrecoverable debt which has been written off might be unexpectedly paid.

Whether it is paid in the same reporting period or a subsequent one, the entry is

DEBIT	Cash	£X
CREDIT	Irrecoverable debts expense	£X

We do not need to credit receivables as this has already been done when the debt was initially written off.

Worked example: Irrecoverable debt subsequently paid

We have the following information on Blacksmith's Forge for the year to 31 December 20X5.

	£
Inventory, 1 January 20X5	6,000
Purchases	122,000
Inventory, 31 December 20X5	8,000
Cash sales	100,000
Credit sales	70,000
Discounts allowed	1,200
Discounts received	5,000
Irrecoverable debts expense	9,000
Debts paid in 20X5 which were previously written off as irrecoverable in 20X4	2,000
Other expenses	31,800

We can prepare the income statement as follows:

BLACKSMITH'S FORGE
INCOME STATEMENT FOR THE YEAR ENDED 31.12.20X5

	£	£
Sales (100,000 + 70,000)		170,000
Opening inventory	6,000	
Purchases	122,000	
Less closing inventory	(8,000)	
Cost of sales		(120,000)
Gross profit		50,000
Add discounts received		5,000
		55,000
Expenses		
Discounts allowed	1,200	
Irrecoverable debts expense (9,000 – 2,000)	7,000	
Other expenses	31,800	
		(40,000)
Net profit		15,000

1.2 Dishonoured cheques and irrecoverable debts

We have seen that when a customer's cheque is dishonoured, we **debit trade receivables** (reinstating the debt) and **credit cash** (removing the 'receipt').

In an exam question, unless you are specifically told otherwise, you should NOT automatically treat a dishonoured cheque as an irrecoverable debt. Cheques may be dishonoured for administrative reasons that have nothing to do with a customer's actual inability to pay its debt, so do not presume that it will never be paid.

2 Allowances for receivables

Section overview

- If there is doubt that a specific debt will be recovered an allowance can be made, which is set off against receivables in the statement of financial position.

- On setting up an allowance for irrecoverable debts, and on increasing an existing allowance:

  DEBIT   Irrecoverable debts expense (income statement)   £X
  CREDIT Allowance for receivables (statement of financial position)   £X

- When a smaller allowance is needed at the end of a subsequent reporting period, the entries are reversed:

  DEBIT   Allowance for receivables   £X
  CREDIT Irrecoverable debts expense   £X

Specific debts owed to the business are identified as certain never to be collected when irrecoverable debts are **written off**.

However, because of the risks involved in selling goods on credit, the business may conclude that some other specific debts have a risk of being irrecoverable. We call such balances '**doubtful receivables**'. We leave them as an asset on the statement of financial position, but create an **allowance** (a credit balance) which we set off against the receivable.

Definition

Allowance for receivables: An amount in relation to specific debts that reduces the receivables asset to its prudent valuation in the statement of financial position. It is offset against trade receivables, which are shown at the net amount.

An allowance for receivables provides for potential irrecoverable debts, as a precaution by the business. The business will thereby be more likely to avoid claiming profits which subsequently fail to materialise because some specific debts turn out to be irrecoverable.

- When an allowance is first made, it is charged as an expense in the income statement along with the irrecoverable debt expense for the period in which the allowance is created. The other side of the entry credits an account in the statement of financial position, the **allowance for receivables**. The double entry is:

  DEBIT   Irrecoverable debts expense (income statement – administrative expense)   £X
  CREDIT Allowance for receivables (statement of financial position)   £X

- When an allowance already exists, but is subsequently **increased**, the amount of the **increase** in allowance is **debited to irrecoverable debt expense**, and **credited to the allowance**.

- When an allowance already exists, but is subsequently **reduced**, the amount of the **decrease** in allowance is **credited** to **irrecoverable debt expense** in the income statement for the period in which the reduction in allowance is made, and **debited to the allowance**.

Worked example: Allowance for receivables I

A business commences operations on 1 July 20X4, and in the twelve months to 30 June 20X5 makes credit sales of £300,000 and writes off irrecoverable debts of £6,000. Cash received from customers during the reporting period is £244,000.

	£
Credit sales during the reporting period	300,000
Add receivables at 1 July 20X4	0
Total debts owed to the business	300,000
Less cash received from credit customers	(244,000)
	56,000
Less irrecoverable debts written off	(6,000)
Trade receivables outstanding at 30 June 20X5	50,000

Of these outstanding debts collection of an amount of £5,000 is doubtful.

The business accounts for its irrecoverable and doubtful debts as follows:

		£	£
DEBIT	Irrecoverable debts expense (£6,000 + £5,000)	11,000	
CREDIT	Allowance for receivables		5,000
	Trade receivables		6,000

In the statement of financial position, the value of trade receivables (after the debt write-off, ie £50,000) must be shown with the allowance for receivables netted off.

	£
Total receivables at 30 June 20X5	50,000
Less, allowance for receivables	(5,000)
Amount in the statement of financial position	45,000

Worked example: Allowance for receivables II

Corin Flake owns and runs the Aerobic Health Foods Shop. He commenced trading on 1 January 20X1, selling health foods to customers, most of whom make use of a credit facility that Corin offers. (Customers are allowed to purchase up to £200 of goods on credit but must repay a certain proportion of their outstanding debt every month.)

This credit system initially gives rise to a large number of irrecoverable debts, but experience helps Corin to control them by the third year. Corin Flake's results for his first three years of operations are as follows.

Year to 31 December 20X1

Gross profit	£27,000
Irrecoverable debts written off	£8,000
Debts owed by customers as at 31 December 20X1	£40,000
Allowance for receivables	£1,000
Other expenses	£20,000

Year to 31 December 20X2

Gross profit	£45,000
Irrecoverable debts written off	£10,000
Debts owed by customers as at 31 December 20X2	£50,000
Allowance for receivables	£1,250
Other expenses	£28,750

Year to 31 December 20X3

Gross profit	£60,000
Irrecoverable debts written off	£7,000
Debts owed by customers as at 31 December 20X3	£30,000
Allowance for receivables	£800
Other expenses	£32,850

Requirement

For each of these three reporting periods, calculate the business's net profit, and state the value of trade receivables appearing in the statement of financial position as at 31 December.

Solution

AEROBIC HEALTH FOODS SHOP
INCOME STATEMENT FOR THE YEARS ENDED 31 DECEMBER

	20X1		20X2		20X3	
	£	£	£	£	£	£
Gross profit		27,000		45,000		60,000
Expenses:						
Irrecoverable debts written off	8,000		10,000		7,000	
Increase/decrease in allowance for receivables*	1,000		250		(450)	
Other expenses	20,000		28,750		32,850	
		(29,000)		(39,000)		(39,400)
Net profit/(loss)		(2,000)		6,000		20,600

* We calculate the income statement amount by:

- Preparing a T account for the allowance

- Carrying down the figure that we require at the end of each reporting period's statement of financial position

- Treating the balancing figure in the reporting period as the charge or the write back required in the income statement for that reporting period.

ALLOWANCE FOR RECEIVABLES

		£			£
31.12.X1	Balance c/d	1,000	31.12.X1	Irrecoverable debt expense	1,000
		1,000			1,000
			1.1.X2	Balance b/d	1,000
31.12.X2	Balance c/d	1,250	31.12.X2	Irrecoverable debt expense (bal fig)	250
		1,250			1,250
31.12.X3	Irrecoverable debt expense (bal fig)	450	1.1.X3	Balance b/d	1,250
31.12.X3	Balance c/d	800			
		1,250			1,250
			1.1.X4	Balance b/d	800

VALUE OF TRADE RECEIVABLES IN THE STATEMENT OF FINANCIAL POSITION

	As at 31.12.20X1	As at 31.12.20X2	As at 31.12.20X3
	£	£	£
Total value of receivables	40,000	50,000	30,000
Less allowance for receivables	(1,000)	(1,250)	(800)
Value in the statement of financial position	39,000	48,750	29,200

3 Accounting for irrecoverable debts and receivables allowances

Section overview

- The irrecoverable debts expense account will be debited with debts written off and with increases in allowances for receivables. It will be credited with amounts received in respect of debts written off, and with reductions in receivables allowances.

- The trade receivables account is only affected when it is credited when a debt is written off. It is unaffected by accounting entries related to the allowance for receivables.

3.1 Irrecoverable debts written off: ledger accounting entries

The double entry bookkeeping is split into two separate transactions. To recap:

- When it is decided that a particular debt will not be paid, the customer is no longer called an outstanding receivable, and becomes an irrecoverable debt.

DEBIT	Irrecoverable debts expense account	£X
CREDIT	Trade receivables	£X

In the receivables ledger, personal accounts of the customers whose debts are irrecoverable will be credited off the ledger.

- At the end of the reporting period, the balance on the irrecoverable debt expense account is transferred to the profit and loss ledger account (like all other expense accounts).

DEBIT	Profit and loss ledger account	ƒX
CREDIT	Irrecoverable debts	£X

- Where an irrecoverable debt is subsequently recovered, the accounting entries will be as follows.

DEBIT	Cash	£X
CREDIT	Irrecoverable debts expense account	£X

Interactive question 1: Irrecoverable debts written off   [Difficulty level: Intermediate]

At 1 October 20X5 a business had total outstanding debts of £8,600. During the 12 month reporting period to 30 September 20X6 the following transactions took place.

(a)   Credit sales £44,000.

(b)   Payments from customers £49,000.

(c)   Two debts, for £180 and £420, were declared irrecoverable and the customers are no longer purchasing goods from the company. These are to be written off.

Requirement

Prepare the trade receivables account and the irrecoverable debts account for the reporting period.

See **Answer** at the end of this chapter.

3.2 Allowance for receivables: ledger accounting entries

If particular customers are regarded as being less likely to pay but the debt is not seen as irrecoverable as such, the **trade receivables balance is completely untouched**. An allowance account is set up by the following entries:

DEBIT	Irrecoverable debts expense	£X
CREDIT	Allowance for receivables	£X

When preparing the statement of financial position, the credit balance on the allowance account is deducted from the balance on the receivables account.

In subsequent reporting periods, the allowance will be adjusted as follows.

- Carry down the new allowance required in the allowance for receivables account.

- Calculate the charge or credit to the income statement.

    - If the allowance has **risen**:

        CREDIT   Allowance for receivables   £X
        DEBIT   Irrecoverable debts expense   £X

        with the amount of the increase.

    - If the allowance has **fallen**:

        DEBIT   Allowance for receivables   £X
        CREDIT   Irrecoverable debts expense   £X

        with the amount of the decrease.

Worked example: Accounting entries for allowance for receivables

Alex Gullible has total receivables outstanding at 31 December 20X2 of £28,000. He believes there is a chance that £280 of these balances may not be collected and wishes to make an appropriate allowance. Before now, he has not made any allowance for receivables at all.

On 31 December 20X3 his trade receivables are £40,000. He believes an allowance of £2,000 needs to be made against specific debts in the receivables ledger.

What accounting entries should Alex make on 31 December 20X2 and 31 December 20X3, and what figures for trade receivables will appear in his statements of financial position as at those dates?

Solution

At 31 December 20X2

Alex will make the following entries:

    DEBIT   Irrecoverable debts expense   £280
    CREDIT   Allowance for receivables   £280

In the statement of financial position receivables will appear as follows.

	£
Trade receivables	28,000
Less allowance for receivables	(280)
	27,720

At 31 December 20X3

Following the procedure described above, Alex will calculate as follows.

ALLOWANCE FOR RECEIVABLES

	£		£
Balance c/d (2)	2,000	Balance b/d (1)	280
		Irrecoverable debts expense (3)	1,720
	2,000		2,000

So on completing step (3) he will make the following entries:

    DEBIT   Irrecoverable debts expense   £1,720
    CREDIT   Allowance for receivables   £1,720

In the statement of financial position trade receivables will be shown as follows.

	£
Trade receivables	40,000
Less allowance for receivables	(2,000)
	38,000

In practice, a statement of financial position would normally show only the net figure (£27,720 in 20X2, £38,000 in 20X3).

Worked example: Accounting entries for specific allowance subsequently written off

Alex Gullible has doubts about a customer's ability to pay and makes an allowance for the whole of his debt of £3,000 at 31 December 20X4. During the year ended 31 December 20X5, the customer pays £2,000 and the balance of £1,000 is to be written off as irrecoverable. How is this accounted for during the year ended 31 December 20X5?

Solution

The answer arises in three stages.

1 Set up the allowance
2 Receive cash and write off the balance
3 Write back allowance as a year end adjustment

ALLOWANCE FOR RECEIVABLES

	£		£
Irrecoverable debts	3,000	Specific allowance b/f	3,000

RLCA (EXTRACT)

	£		£
		Cash received	2,000
		Irrecoverable debt	1,000

IRRECOVERABLE DEBTS

	£		£
RLCA	1,000	Allowance for receivables	3,000
I/S	2,000		
	3,000		3,000

So during the year ended 31 December 20X4, £3,000 is charged to the income statement and during the year ended 31 December 20X5, £2,000 is recovered. This leaves a net charge for the two years of £1,000, the amount of the irrecoverable debt.

Interactive question 2: Receivables allowance　　　　[Difficulty level: Exam standard]

Horace Goodrunning realises that his business will suffer an increase in customers not paying in the future and so he decides to make an allowance against those who are at greater risk at the end of each reporting period.

	Balance on receivables account	Balance at risk of default
	£	£
Y/e 28.2.20X6	15,200	304
Y/e 28.2.20X7	17,100	342
Y/e 28.2.20X8	21,400	214

Requirements

For each of the three reporting periods:

(a) What are the closing trade receivables and allowance for receivables balances?
(b) What charge is made to the income statement?
(c) How would receivables appear in the statement of financial position?

See **Answer** at the end of this chapter.

4 Irrecoverable debts and allowances on the ETB

Section overview

- An adjustment journal for writing off a debt debits the irrecoverable debts expense line and credits trade receivables. The debit increases the income statement expense; the credit reduces trade receivables at the end of each reporting period.

- Adjustment journal for setting up or increasing a receivables allowance: debit irrecoverable debts, credit a receivables allowance line. The debit increases the income statement expense; the credit sets up the allowance to be set against trade receivables in the statement of financial position.

So far we have looked at how irrecoverable debts and allowances are calculated then accounted for in the ledger accounts. Because decisions about irrecoverable debts and doubtful debts are usually made and accounted for after the initial trial balance has been extracted, a neater way of incorporating the relevant figures is to use the ETB.

- Calculate the amount of irrecoverable debts and the level of the allowance as usual

- Prepare the year end journals as usual

- Enter these journals in the adjustments columns of the ETB, opening new lines for irrecoverable debts expense and allowance for receivables if necessary

- Include these adjustments in the ETB cross-cast to prepare the financial statements

- Enter the journals in the ledger accounts as usual

Worked example: Irrecoverable debts and allowances on the ETB

Lorraine runs a bookshop. She has extracted the following initial trial balance as at 31 December 20X9:

	DR £	CR £
Cash at bank	4,391	
Opening capital		20,000
Loan		2,000
Non-current assets	30,000	
Trade payables		9,642
Irrecoverable debt expense	50	
Expenses	3,896	
Purchases	42,875	
Sales		96,475
Trade receivables	8,622	
Allowance for receivables		350
Drawings	38,833	
Suspense		200
Net profit (to be determined)	?	
	128,667	128,667

She needs to take account of the following matters:

(a) As at the end of the reporting period there is a debt of £695 to be written off

(b) Of the remaining receivables, Lorraine is concerned that one amount of £250 may prove difficult to recover, so wishes to make an allowance against it.

(c) During the reporting period, £200 was banked in respect of a debt which had been written off in the reporting period ended 31 December 20X8. The only entry in respect of this was in the cash at bank account.

Complete Lorraine's ETB to calculate her net profit for the reporting period.

Solution

Ledger balance	Trial balance DR £	Trial balance CR £	Adjustments DR £	Adjustments CR £	Income statement DR £	Income statement CR £	Statement of financial position DR £	Statement of financial position CR £
Cash at bank	4,391						4,391	
Opening capital		20,000						20,000
Loan		2,000						2,000
Non-current assets	30,000						30,000	
Trade payables		9,642						9,642
Irrecoverable debt expense	50		695	300	445			
Expenses	3,896				3,896			
Purchases	42,875				42,875			
Sales		96,475				96,475		
Trade receivables	8,622			695			7,927	
Allowance for receivables		350	100					250
Drawings	38,833						38,833	
Suspense		200	200					
Net profit					49,259			49,259
	128,667	128,667	995	995	96,475	96,475	81,151	81,151

The adjusting journals are as follows:

			£	£
(a)	DEBIT	Irrecoverable debt expense	695	
	CREDIT	Trade receivables		695
(b)	DEBIT	Allowance for receivables (350 – 250)	100	
	CREDIT	Irrecoverable debt expense		100
(c)	DEBIT	Suspense a/c	200	
	CREDIT	Irrecoverable debt expense		200

Summary

Irrecoverable debts

Write off:
DR   Irrecoverable debts expense (income statement)
CR   Trade receivables (statement of financial position)

Cash received re. debt written off:
DR   Cash (statement of financial position)
CR   Irrecoverable debts expense (income statement)

Doubtful debt

Set up an allowance
DR   Irrecoverable debts expense (Income statement)
CR   Allowance for receivables (statement of financial position – net off trade receivables)

ALLOWANCE FOR RECEIVABLES			
Decrease	X	Balance b/d	X
Balance c/d	X	Increase	X
	X		X

ETB

	Adj		IS		SFP	
	DR	CR	DR	CR	DR	CR
Irrecoverable debt expense						
– Write off debt	X		X			
– Increase allowance	Y		Y			
– Reduce allowance		Z		Z		
Trade receivables		X				X
Allowance for receivables	Z	Y			Z	Y

Self-test

Answer the following questions.

1 An irrecoverable debt arises in which of the following situations?

    A   A customer pays part of the account
    B   An invoice is in dispute
    C   The customer goes bankrupt
    D   A cheque received in settlement is dishonoured by the customer's bank

2 An allowance for receivables at the end of a reporting period of £4,000 is required. The allowance for receivables brought forward from the previous period is £2,000. What change is required this reporting period?

    A   Increase by £4,000
    B   Decrease by £4,000
    C   Increase by £2,000
    D   Decrease by £2,000

3 If a receivables allowance is increased, what is the effect on the income statement?

4 What is the double entry to record an irrecoverable debt written off?

5 On 1 January 20X5 Plodd had a doubtful debt allowance of £1,000. During 20X5 he wrote off debts of £600 and was paid £80 by the liquidator of a company whose debts had been written off completely in 20X4. At the end of 20X5 it was decided to adjust the doubtful debts allowance to £900.

What is the net expense for irrecoverable debts in the income statement for 20X5?

    A   £420
    B   £580
    C   £620
    D   £780

6 Smith has receivables totalling £16,000 after writing off irrecoverable debts of £500, and he has an allowance for receivables brought forward of £2,000. He wishes to carry forward an allowance of £800.

What will be the effect on profit of adjusting the allowance?

    A   £700 decrease
    B   £700 increase
    C   £1,200 decrease
    D   £1,200 increase

7 At 31 December 20X9 Folland's receivables totalled £120,000. Folland wishes to have an allowance against specific receivables of £3,600, which is 25% higher than it was before. During the year irrecoverable debts of £3,200 were written off and irrecoverable debts (written off three years previously) of £150 were recovered.

What is the net charge for irrecoverable debts for the 12 month reporting period ended 31 December 20X9?

    A   £720
    B   £900
    C   £3,770
    D   £3,950

8   During the 12 month reporting period ended 31 December 20X8 Keele decreased its receivables allowance by £600. An irrecoverable debt written off in the previous reporting period amounting to £300 was recovered in 20X8.

If the net profit of the reporting period **after** accounting for the above items is £5,000, what was it **before** accounting for them?

A   £4,100
B   £4,700
C   £5,300
D   £5,900

9   Bodkin had the following balances in its trial balance at 30 June 20X1.

	£
Trade receivables	70,000
Irrecoverable debts expense	500
Allowance for receivables at 1 July 20X0	5,000

Bodkin wishes to carry forward at 30 June 20X1 an allowance equal to 10% of trade receivables.

What is the irrecoverable debts figure in the income statement for the 12 month reporting period ended 30 June 20X1?

A   Charge of £2,450
B   Credit of £2,450
C   Charge of £2,500
D   Credit of £2,500

10 Wacko had a receivables allowance at 1 January 20X0 of £1,000. He calculates that at 31 December 20X0 a receivables allowance of £1,500 is required. In addition £2,000 of debts were written off during the reporting period, which includes £50 previously provided for.

How much should be included in Wacko's income statement in relation to irrecoverable debts for the 12 month reporting period ended 31 December 20X0?

A   £1,500
B   £2,450
C   £2,500
D   £2,550

Now, go back to the Learning Objectives in the Introduction. If you are satisfied that you have achieved these objectives, please tick them off.

Answers to Interactive questions

Answer to Interactive question 1

TRADE RECEIVABLES

	£		£
Opening balance b/fd	8,600	Cash	49,000
Sales	44,000	Irrecoverable debts expense (180 + 420)	600
		Closing balance c/d	3,000
	52,600		52,600
Opening balance b/d	3,000		

IRRECOVERABLE DEBTS

	£		£
Receivables	600	P & L	600
	600		600

Answer to Interactive question 2

The entries for the three reporting periods are shown below.

TRADE RECEIVABLES (EXTRACT)

		£		£
28.2.20X6	Balance	15,200		
28.2.20X7	Balance	17,100		
28.2.20X8	Balance	21,400		

ALLOWANCE FOR RECEIVABLES

		£			£
28.2.20X6	Balance c/d	304	28.2.20X6	P & L account	304
		304			304
28.2.20X7	Balance c/d	342	1.3.20X6	Balance b/d	304
			28.2.20X7	P & L account (bal fig)	38
		342			342
28.2.20X8	P & L account (bal fig)	128	1.3.20X7	Balance b/d	342
28.2.20X8	Balance c/d	214			
		342			342
			1.3.20X8	Balance b/d	214

PROFIT AND LOSS LEDGER ACCOUNT (EXTRACT)

		£			£
28.2.20X6	Allowance for receivables	304			
28.2.20X7	Allowance for receivables	38			
			28.2.20X8	Allowance for receivables	128

STATEMENT OF FINANCIAL POSITION: EXTRACT AS AT

	20X6	20X7	20X8
	£	£	£
Current assets			
Trade receivables	15,200	17,100	21,400
Less allowance for receivables	(304)	(342)	(214)
	14,896	16,758	21,186

1   C   When a customer becomes bankrupt there is no money with which to settle the debt, so it must be regarded as being irrecoverable. A customer settling only part of an account, an invoice being in dispute and a cheque being dishonoured by the customer's bank (ie it being returned unpaid) may all be caused by administrative problems; further analysis of the situation will need to be done before concluding that the debt is irrecoverable.

2   C   The allowance in the statement of financial position needs to be increased by £2,000 to £4,000; this will be a charge in the income statement

3   The increase in the allowance is charged as an expense in the income statement.

4   DEBIT   Irrecoverable debts account (expenses)
CREDIT Trade accounts receivable

5   A

ALLOWANCE FOR RECEIVABLES

	£		£
Irrecoverable debts	100	b/d	1,000
c/d	900		
	1,000		1,000

IRRECOVERABLE DEBTS EXPENSE

	£		£
Receivables	600	Cash	80
		Allowance for receivables	100
		Income statement	420
	600		600

6   D

ALLOWANCE FOR RECEIVABLES

	£		£
Irrecoverable debts expense	1,200	b/d	2,000
c/d	800		
	2,000		2,000

7   C

IRRECOVERABLE DEBTS EXPENSE

	£		£
Receivables	3,200	Cash	150
Allowance for receivables	720	Income statement	3,770
	3,920		3,920

ALLOWANCE FOR RECEIVABLES

	£		£
c/d	3,600	b/d (3,600 × 100/125)	2,880
		Irrecoverable debts expense	720
	3,600		3,600

8   A

	£
Profit before irrecoverable debts (balancing figure)	4,100
Add Decrease in allowance	600
Add Irrecoverable recovered	300
Profit after irrecoverable debts	5,000

9 C

ALLOWANCE FOR RECEIVABLES

	£		£
		b/d	5,000
c/d (10% × 70,000)	7,000	Irrecoverable debts expense	2,000
	7,000		7,000

IRRECOVERABLE DEBTS EXPENSE

	£		£
b/d	500	Income statement charge	2,500
Allowance for receivables	2,000		
	2,500		2,500

10 C

IRRECOVERABLE DEBTS EXPENSE

	£		£
Allowance for receivables	500	Income statement charge	2,500
Receivables	2,000		
	2,500		2,500

CHAPTER 9

Inventories

Introduction

Examination context

Topic List

Summary and Self-test

Answers to Interactive questions

Answers to Self-test

Learning objectives

- Record and account for transactions and events resulting in income, expenses, assets, liabilities and equity in accordance with the appropriate basis of accounting and the laws, regulations and accounting standards applicable to the financial statements

- Prepare an extended trial balance

- Identify the main components of a set of financial statements and specify their purpose and interrelationship

- Prepare and present a statement of financial position, income statement and statement of cash flows (or extracts therefrom) from the accounting records and trial balance in a format which satisfies the information requirements of the entity

Specific syllabus learning outcomes are: 1c, 2c, 3a, 3c

Syllabus links

The material in this chapter will be developed further in this paper, and then in the Financial Accounting and Financial Reporting papers later in the Professional stage.

Examination context

Questions on the topics in this chapter will be set as multiple choice questions, some of which may involve calculations so that the correct answer can be selected. Very often double entry questions are phrased in terms of preparing a journal.

In the exam you may be required to:

- Identify the accounting principles behind accounting for inventory

- Identify the purpose of an inventory count

- Specify what is included in the cost of inventory

- Identify the correct value for inventory using FIFO and AVCO

- Calculate net realisable values

- Use margin and mark-up to calculate closing inventory

- Identify how to account for drawings of inventory and for substantial losses of inventory

- Identify how to account for closing inventory in the ledger accounts and on the extended trial balance

- Calculate the figure in the statement of financial position for inventory

- Identify the effects of opening and closing inventory on gross and net profit in the income statement

1 Accounting for opening and closing inventories

Section overview

- In each reporting period, opening inventory is an expense in the income statement:

DEBIT	Cost of sales	£X	
CREDIT	Inventory account		£X

- Closing inventory is deducted from cost of sales in the reporting period, so it can be carried forward and matched against the revenue it earns in the next period:

DEBIT	Inventory account (statement of financial position)	£X	
CREDIT	Cost of sales		£X

In Chapter 8, we saw that in order to calculate **gross profit** it is necessary to work out the **cost of sales**. In order to calculate the cost of sales the accrual principle necessitates values for **opening inventory** (ie inventory in hand at the beginning of the reporting period) and **closing inventory** (ie inventory in hand at the end of the reporting period), so that we can carry forward the latter to the next period where it will be matched with the income it earns.

You should remember, in fact, that the income statement includes:

	£
Opening inventory	X
Plus purchases	X
Plus carriage inwards	X
Less closing inventory	(X)
Equals cost of sales	X

However, writing down this formula hides three basic problems.

- How do you manage to get a **precise count** of what inventory is held at any one time?

- Even once it has been counted, how do you **value** the inventory?

- Assuming the inventory is given a value, how does the **double entry bookkeeping** for inventory work?

The purpose of this chapter is to answer all three of these questions. In order to make the presentation a little easier to follow, we shall take the last question first.

1.1 Ledger accounting for inventories

Purchases are introduced to the profit and loss ledger account via the following double entry:

DEBIT	Profit and loss ledger account	£X	
CREDIT	Purchases account		£X

But what about opening and closing inventories? How are their values accounted for in the double entry bookkeeping system? The answer is that an inventory account must be kept, but it is **only used at the end of a reporting period**, when the business counts and values inventory, in an **inventory count**.

(a) Once an inventory count is made and the business has a value for its closing inventory, the double entry is:

DEBIT	Inventory (asset) account	£X	
CREDIT	Profit and loss ledger account		£X

Rather than showing closing inventory as a 'plus' value in the income statement (by adding it to revenue) it is shown as a 'minus' figure in arriving at **cost of sales**, as illustrated above. The debit balance on the closing inventory account represents a **current asset** in the statement of financial position.

(b) Closing inventory at the end of one period becomes opening inventory at the start of the next period. The inventory account remains unchanged, with a debit balance until the end of the next period. This value is now the opening inventory figure and is taken to the profit and loss ledger account:

DEBIT	Profit and loss ledger account	£X
CREDIT	Inventory account (opening inventory value)	£X

Worked example: Accounting for inventories

A business has opening capital of £2,000, represented entirely by inventory. During the first year's trading, when the owner took no drawings, the following transactions occurred.

	£
Purchases of goods for resale, on credit	4,300
Payments for trade payables	3,600
Sales, all on credit	8,000
Receipts from trade receivables	3,200
Non-current assets purchased for cash	1,500
Other expenses, all paid in cash	900

All 'other expenses' relate to the current year.

Closing inventory is valued at £1,800.

Requirement

Prepare the ledger accounts, including a profit and loss ledger account, for the 12 month reporting period and a statement of financial position as at the end of the reporting period.

CASH

	£		£
Trade receivables	3,200	Trade payables	3,600
Balance c/d	2,800	Non-current assets	1,500
		Other expenses	900
	6,000		6,000
		Balance b/d	2,800

CAPITAL

	£		£
Balance c/d	4,600	Inventory	2,000
		Profit and loss	2,600
	4,600		4,600
		Balance b/d	4,600

TRADE PAYABLES

	£		£
Cash	3,600	Purchases	4,300
Balance c/d	700		
	4,300		4,300
		Balance b/d	700

PURCHASES

	£		£
Trade payables	4,300	Profit and loss	4,300

NON-CURRENT ASSETS

	£		£
Cash	1,500	Balance c/d	1,500
Balance b/d	1,500		

SALES

	£		£
Profit and loss	8,000	Trade receivables	8,000

TRADE RECEIVABLES

	£		£
Sales	8,000	Cash	3,200
		Balance c/d	4,800
	8,000		8,000
Balance b/d	4,800		

OTHER EXPENSES

	£		£
Cash	900	Profit and loss	900

INVENTORY

	£		£
Capital	2,000	Profit and loss (opening inventory)	2,000
Profit and loss (closing inventory)	1,800	Balance c/d (closing inventory)	1,800
	3,800		3,800
Balance b/d	1,800		

PROFIT AND LOSS LEDGER ACCOUNT

	£		£
Opening inventory (inventory a/c)	2,000	Sales	8,000
Purchases	4,300	Closing inventory (inventory a/c)	1,800
Gross profit c/d	3,500		
	9,800		9,800
Other expenses	900	Gross profit b/d	3,500
Net profit (transferred to capital account)	2,600		
	3,500		3,500

STATEMENT OF FINANCIAL POSITION AS AT THE END OF THE PERIOD

	£	£
ASSETS		
Non-current assets		1,500
Current assets		
Inventory	1,800	
Trade receivables	4,800	
		6,600
Total assets		8,100
CAPITAL AND LIABILITIES		
Capital		
At start of period	2,000	
Profit for period	2,600	
At end of period		4,600
Current liabilities		
Bank overdraft	2,800	
Trade payables	700	
		3,500
Total capital and liabilities		8,100

The closing debit balance on the inventory account is £1,800, which appears in the statement of financial position as a current asset.

The opening inventory of £2,000 was eliminated by transferring it as a debit balance to the profit and loss ledger account, ie:

DEBIT   Profit and loss ledger account (with value of opening inventory)
CREDIT   Inventory account (with value of opening inventory)

The debit in the profit and loss ledger account then increased the cost of sales, ie opening inventory is added to purchases in calculating cost of sales.

Interactive question 1: Journals for inventory   [Difficulty level: Intermediate]

In its nominal ledger Wickham plc had a balance on its inventory account at 1 July 20X2 of £23,490. At 30 June 20X3 it had inventory of £40,285.

Prepare a journal to record the situation as at the end of the reporting period in the nominal ledger of Wickham plc, in preparation for drawing up the income statement and statement of financial position.

See **Answer** at the end of this chapter.

---

2   Inventories on the ETB

Section overview

- The closing inventory is entered into both adjustment columns of the ETB for inventory. The debit is taken across to the statement of financial position; the credit is taken to the income statement.

- Opening inventory is taken straight to the income statement as a debit.

The closing inventory figure is generally accounted for after the initial trial balance has been extracted. Therefore, only opening inventory appears on the initial trial balance. An alternative way of incorporating the relevant figures is to use the ETB.

- Calculate the value of closing inventories (see below).

- Prepare the year-end journals for opening and closing inventories as usual (see above).

- Enter the journal for **closing inventory only** in the adjustments columns of the ETB using the inventories line. (There is a debit and a credit for the same amount on this line: the debit casts across to the statement of financial position, and the credit to the income statement.)

- Include these adjustments in the ETB cross-cast to prepare the financial statements.

- Enter the journals for both opening and closing inventories in the ledger accounts.

In some ETBs there is no separate line for closing inventories, so the adjustment is made on the opening inventories line: this is the approach taken in the worked example that follows.

Worked example: Inventories on the ETB

Sam's Music Shop trial balance as at 31 December 20X5 is as follows.

Ledger balance	Trial balance Debit £	Trial balance Credit £
Cash at bank		5,123
Opening capital		10,000
Loan		12,000
Non-current assets	20,000	
Trade payables		6,800
Expenses	12,785	
Purchases	18,425	
Sales		38,745
Trade receivables	3,546	
Inventories at 1.1.X5	8,754	
Drawings	9,158	
	72,668	72,668

Closing inventories at 31 December 20X5 cost £13,855.

Requirement

Complete Sam's ETB and calculate his net profit for the year.

Solution

Step 1

To account for closing inventories on the ETB prepare the year-end journal for closing inventory:

		£	£
DEBIT	Inventory (statement of financial position)	13,855	
CREDIT	Profit and loss ledger account		13,855
	Recording closing inventory as an asset at the year end		

Step 2

Enter this journal in the debit and credit adjustment columns on the ETB on the inventory ledger account line.

Step 3

Cross-cast the ETB as follows:

- **Opening inventory** is recorded as a **debit** in the **income statement**

- The **debit** side of the **adjustment journal** is recorded as a **debit** in the **statement of financial position**

- The **credit** side of the **adjustment journal** is recorded as a **credit** in the **income statement**

Step 4

Prepare the financial statements.

Step 5

Record both journals in the ledger accounts as usual.

Sam's ETB will be as follows:

	Trial balance		Adjustments		Income statement		Statement of financial position	
Ledger balance	Debit	Credit	Debit	Credit	Debit	Credit	Debit	Credit
	£	£	£	£	£	£	£	£
Cash at bank		5,123						5,123
Opening capital		10,000						10,000
Loan		12,000						12,000
Non-current assets	20,000						20,000	
Trade payables		6,800						6,800
Expenses	12,785				12,785			
Purchases	18,425				18,425			
Sales		38,745				38,745		
Trade receivables	3,546						3,546	
Inventories	8,754		13,855	13,855	8,754	13,855	13,855	
Drawings	9,158						9,158	
Net profit					12,636			12,636
	72,668	72,668	13,855	13,855	52,600	52,600	46,559	46,559

SAM'S MUSIC SHOP – INCOME STATEMENT FOR YEAR ENDED 31 DECEMBER 20X5

	£	£
Revenue		38,745
Cost of sales		
Opening inventories	8,754	
Purchases	18,425	
Closing inventories	(13,855)	
Cost of sales		(13,324)
Gross profit		25,421
Expenses		(12,785)
Net profit		12,636

SAM'S MUSIC SHOP – STATEMENT OF FINANCIAL POSITION AS AT 31 DECEMBER 20X5

	£	£
ASSETS		
Non-current assets		20,000
Current assets		
Inventories	13,855	
Trade receivables	3,546	
		17,401
Total assets		37,401
CAPITAL AND LIABILITIES		
Opening capital		10,000
Profit for year		12,636
Drawings		(9,158)
Closing capital		13,478
Non-current liabilities		
Bank loan		12,000
Current liabilities		
Trade payables	6,800	
Bank overdraft	5,123	
		11,923
Total capital and liabilities		37,401

3 Counting inventories

Section overview

- The inventory count establishes quantities held in inventory at the end of the reporting period.

Business trading is a continuous activity, but financial statements must be drawn up at a particular date. In preparing a statement of financial position it is necessary to '**freeze**' the activity of a business so as to determine its assets, capital and liabilities at that given moment. This includes establishing the quantities of inventories held.

In simple cases, when a business holds easily counted and relatively small amounts of inventory, quantities of inventories held at the date of the statement of financial position can be determined by physically counting them in an **inventory count**.

In more complicated cases, where a business holds considerable quantities of varied inventory, an alternative approach to establishing quantities is to maintain **continuous inventory records**. This means that a record is kept for every item of inventory, showing receipts and issues from the stores, and a running total. A few inventory items are counted each day to make sure the records are correct – this is called a 'continuous' count because it is spread out over the reporting period rather than completed in one count at a designated time.

Once the quantity of inventories is determined then a policy is required for **valuing individual items**.

4 Valuing inventories

Section overview

- Inventory is valued at the lower of (historical) cost of purchase, and net realisable value (NRV).
- NRV is the expected selling price less any costs to be incurred in achieving that sale.
- Cost comprises: purchase price, carriage, duties and conversion costs to bring item to its present location and condition.

4.1 The basic valuation rule I: valuation at historical cost

There are **several methods** which, in theory, might be used for valuing items of inventory:

- At their **historical cost** (ie the cost at which they were originally bought)
- At their **expected selling price**
- At their expected selling price, less any costs still to be incurred in getting them ready for sale. This amount is referred to as inventory's **net realisable value** (NRV).
- At the amount it would cost to replace them (**replacement cost**).

The use of selling prices in inventory valuation is ruled out by the **realisation** concept because this would create a profit for the business before the inventory has been sold. **Using replacement costs** is problematic as these are very difficult to establish. The most obvious route then is to value them at **historical cost**. But what about **NRV**?

Worked example: Valuing inventory at historical cost

A trader buys two items of inventory, each costing £100. He can sell them for £140 each, but in the reporting period we shall consider, he has only sold one of them. The other is closing inventory.

Since only one item has been sold, you might think it is common sense that profit ought to be £40. But if closing inventory is valued at selling price, profit would be £80, ie profit would be taken on the closing inventory as well.

This would contradict the accounting concept of **realisation**, ie to claim a profit before the item has actually been sold.

	£	£
Revenue		140
Opening inventory	–	
Purchases (2 × £100)	200	
	200	
Less closing inventory (at selling price)	(140)	
Cost of sales		(60)
Gross profit		80

The same objection **usually** applies to the use of NRV in inventory valuation. Suppose the item purchased for £100 requires £5 of further expenditure in getting it ready for sale and then selling it (eg £5 of processing costs and distribution costs). If its expected selling price is £140, its NRV is £(140 – 5) = £135. To value it at £135 in the statement of financial position would still be to anticipate a £35 profit.

We are left with historical cost as the normal basis of inventory valuation.

4.2 The basic valuation rule II: lower of cost and NRV

The only time when (historical) cost is not used is when cost needs to be reduced to **NRV**.

Worked example: Lower of cost and NRV

Suppose that the market in the above example slumps and the expected selling price is £90. The item's NRV is then £(90 – 5) = £85 and the business will make a loss of £15 (£100 – £85) on the item. Prudence requires that assets should not be overstated, so the so loss will be recognised by valuing the item in the statement of financial position at its NRV of £85.

Inventory should be valued at the lower of cost and net realisable value.

4.3 Applying the lower of cost and NRV rule

If a business has many inventory items on hand the comparison of cost and NRV should be carried out for each item separately. It is not sufficient to compare the total cost of all inventory items with their total NRV.

Worked example: Valuing each inventory item separately

A company has four items of inventory at the end of its reporting period. Their cost and NRVs are as follows.

Inventory item	Cost £	NRV £	Lower of cost / NRV £
1	27	32	27
2	14	8	8
3	43	55	43
4	29	40	29
	113	135	107

It would be incorrect to compare total cost (£113) with total NRV (£135) and to state inventories at £113 in the statement of financial position. The company can foresee a loss of £6 on item 2 and this should be recognised immediately. If the four items are taken together in total the loss on item 2 is masked by the anticipated profits on the other items. By performing the cost/NRV comparison for each item separately the appropriate valuation of £107 can be derived. This is the value which should appear in the statement of financial position.

Interactive question 2: Inventory valuation
[Difficulty level: Exam standard]

The following figures relate to inventory held at the end of the reporting period.

	Item A	Item B	Item C
Cost	£20	£9	£14
Selling price	£30	£12	£22
Modification cost to enable sale	–	£2	£8
Marketing costs	£7	£2	£2
Units held	200	150	300

Requirement

Calculate the value of inventory for inclusion in the financial statements.

See **Answer** at the end of this chapter.

4.4 Determining the cost of inventory

Inventories may be:

- **Raw materials** or components bought from suppliers
- **Finished goods** which have been made by the business but not yet sold, or
- **Part completed items** (this type of inventory is called **work in progress** or WIP).

Definitions

Cost of inventories: All costs of purchase, of conversion (eg labour) and of other costs incurred in bringing the items to their present location and condition.

Cost of purchase: The purchase price, import duties and other non-recoverable taxes, transport, handling and other costs directly attributable to the acquisition of finished goods and materials.

4.4.1 What is included in the total cost of an item?

The total cost of an item includes all costs incurred in **bringing the item to its present location and condition.** This consists of

- The purchase cost of **raw materials**
- **Carriage**
- **Import taxes and duties**
- **Conversion costs**

Definition

Conversion costs: Any costs involved in converting raw materials into final product, including labour, expenses directly related to the product and an appropriate share of production overheads (but not sales, administrative or general overheads).

Worked example: Cost of manufactured goods

A business has the following details relating to production and sales for a reporting period:

Sales: 900 units at £600 each
1,000 units are produced with the following costs being incurred:
Opening inventory of raw materials: 200 units at £100 each
Purchases of raw materials: 1,050 units at £100 each
Closing inventory of raw materials: 250 units at £100 each

Production wages	£150,000
Production overheads	£100,000
General administration, selling and distribution costs	£100,000

The **cost of production** should include an **appropriate share of production wages and production overheads**, but not **non-production expenses**.

The income statement of this business for the reporting period is as follows:

	£	£
Sales (900 units × £600)		540,000
Cost of production (1,000 units)		
Raw materials		
Opening inventory (200 × £100)	20,000	
Purchases (1,050 × £100)	105,000	
Less: Closing inventory (250 × £100)	(25,000)	
Cost of raw materials used	100,000	
Production wages	150,000	
Production overheads	100,000	
Cost of production (1,000 units cost £350,000/1,000 = £350 each)	350,000	
Less: Closing inventory, finished goods (100 × £350)	(35,000)	
Cost of sales		(315,000)
Gross profit		225,000
General administration, selling and distribution costs		(100,000)
Net profit		125,000

The cost of production is spread over the units produced. Any unsold units are valued at a figure that reflects a share of these costs. When the inventory is eventually sold, the production overheads associated with its manufacture will be thereby properly matched with the revenues earned.

4.4.2 What is the total cost of items left in inventory?

A business may be continually adding items to finished goods inventory, or purchasing a particular component. As each consignment is received from suppliers, or each finished goods batch is added to inventory, they are stored in the appropriate place, where they will be mingled with items already there. When the storekeeper issues items to production or to despatch they will simply pull out the nearest item to hand, which may have arrived in the latest consignment/batch, in an earlier consignment/batch or in several different consignments/batches.

There are several techniques which are used in practice to attribute a cost to inventory items; remember that actual materials, components and finished goods items can be issued in any order at all irrespective of when each one entered inventory.

Definitions

FIFO (first in, first out): Items are used in the order in which they are received from suppliers, so oldest items are issued first. Inventory remaining is therefore the newer items.

LIFO (last in, first out): Items issued originally formed part of the most recent delivery, while oldest consignments remain in the bin. **This is disallowed under IASs.**

AVCO (average cost): As purchase prices can change with each new consignment received, the average value of an item is constantly changing. Each item at any moment is assumed to have been purchased at the average price of all the items together, so inventory remaining is therefore valued at the most recent average price.

Standard cost: All inventory items are valued at a pre determined cost. If this standard cost differs from prices actually paid during the period the difference is written off as a 'variance' in the income statement.

Replacement cost: The cost of an inventory unit is assumed to be the amount it would cost now to replace it. This is often (but not necessarily) the unit cost of inventories purchased in the next consignment *following* the date of the statement of financial position.

In the exam you can expect to use FIFO or AVCO for the valuation of inventory in the statement of financial position and the income statement.

Worked example: FIFO and AVCO cost

To illustrate the various pricing methods, the following transactions will be used in each case.

TRANSACTIONS DURING MAY 20X7

	Quantity Units	Unit cost £	Total cost £
Opening balance 1 May	100	2.00	200
Receipts 3 May *	400	2.10	840
Issues 4 May **	200		
Receipts 9 May	300	2.12	636
Issues 11 May	400		
Receipts 18 May	100	2.40	240
Issues 20 May	100		
Closing balance 31 May	200		
			1,916

*   Receipts mean goods are received into store.
** Issues represent the issue of goods from store.

The problem is to put a valuation on the following.

(a)   The issues of materials
(b)   The closing inventory

Requirement

How would issues and closing inventory be valued using each of the following in turn?

(a)   FIFO
(b)   AVCO

Solution

(a) **FIFO** assumes that materials are **issued out of inventory in the order in which they were delivered into inventory**, ie issues are priced at the cost of the earliest delivery remaining in inventory.

The cost of issues and the closing inventory value in the example, using FIFO, would be as follows.

Date	Quantity Units	Value issued	Cost of issues £	£
4 May	200	100 at £2.00	200	
		100 at £2.10	210	
		200		410
11 May	400	300 at £2.10	630	
		100 at £2.12	212	
		400		842
20 May	100	100 at £2.12		212
				1,464
Closing inventory value	200	100 at £2.12	212	
		100 at £2.40	240	
		200		452
				1,916

Note that the cost of materials issued plus the value of closing inventory equals the cost of purchases plus the cost of opening inventory (£1,916).

(b) **AVCO** may be used in various ways in pricing inventory issues. The most common is the **cumulative weighted average pricing** method illustrated below.

- A weighted average price for all units in inventory is calculated. Issues are priced at this average cost, and the balance of inventory remaining has the same unit valuation.

- A new weighted average price is calculated whenever a new delivery of materials into store is received.

Date	Received Units	Issued Units	Balance Units	Total inventory value £	Unit cost £	Price of issue £
Opening inventory			100	200	2.00	
3 May	400			840	2.10	
			500	1,040	2.08 *	
4 May		200		(416)	2.08 **	416
			300	624	2.08	
9 May	300			636	2.12	
			600	1,260	2.10 *	
11 May		400		(840)	2.10 **	840
			200	420	2.10	
18 May	100			240	2.40	
			300	660	2.20 *	
20 May		100		(220)	2.20 **	220
						1,476
Closing inventory value			200	440	2.20	440
						1,916

* A new unit cost of inventory is calculated whenever a new receipt of materials occurs.

** Whenever inventories are issued, the unit value of the items issued is the current weighted average cost per unit at the time of the issue.

For this method too, the cost of materials issued plus the cost of closing inventory equals the cost of purchases plus the cost of opening inventory (£1,916).

4.5 Inventory valuations and profit

FIFO and AVCO each produced different costs, both of closing inventories and also of materials issues. Since raw material costs affect the cost of production, and the cost of production works through eventually into the cost of sales, it follows that **different methods of inventory valuation will provide different profit figures.**

Worked example: Inventory valuations and profit

On 1 November 20X2 a company held 300 units of finished goods in inventory. These cost £3,600. During November 20X2 three batches of finished goods were received into store from the production department, as follows.

Date	Units received	Production cost per unit
10 November	400	£12.50
20 November	400	£14
25 November	400	£15

Finished goods sold during November were as follows.

Date	Units sold	Sale price per unit
14 November	500	£20
21 November	500	£20
28 November	100	£20
	1,100	

Identify the profit from selling inventory in November 20X2, applying the principles of:

(a) FIFO
(b) AVCO

Ignore administration, sales and distribution costs.

Solution

(a) **FIFO**

Date	Issue costs	Issue cost £	Closing inventory £
14 November	(300 units × £12) + (200 units × £12.50)	6,100	
21 November	(200 units × £12.50) + (300 units × £14)	6,700	
28 November	100 units × £14	1,400	
Closing inventory	400 units × £15		6,000
		14,200	6,000

(b) AVCO

	Units	Unit cost £	Balance in inventory £	Total cost of issues £	Closing inventory £
1 November Opening inventory	300	12.000	3,600		
10 November	400	12.500	5,000		
	700	12.286	8,600		
14 November	(500)	12.286	(6,143)	6,143	
	200	12.286	2,457		
20 November	400	14.000	5,600		
	600	13.428	8,057		
21 November	(500)	13.428	(6,714)	6,714	
	100	13.428	1,343		
25 November	400	15.000	6,000		
	500	14.686	7,343		
28 November	(100)	14.686	(1,469)	1,469	
30 November Closing inventory	400	14.686	5,874	14,326	5,874

Summary: profit

		FIFO £	AVCO £
Opening inventory		3,600	3,600
Cost of production (400 × £12.50) + (400 × £14) + (400 × £15)		16,600	16,600
Closing inventory		(6,000)	(5,874)
Cost of sales		14,200	14,326
Sales (1,100 × £20)		22,000	22,000
Profit		7,800	7,674

Different inventory valuations produce different cost of sales and profits figures. Here opening inventory values are the same, therefore the **difference in the amount of profit under each method is the same as the difference in the valuations of closing inventory.**

The profit differences are only temporary. The opening inventory in December 20X2 will be £6,000 or £5,874, depending on the inventory valuation used. Different opening inventory values will affect the cost of sales and profits in December, so that in the long run inequalities in cost of sales each month will even themselves out.

Interactive question 3: FIFO
[Difficulty level: Exam standard]

A firm has the following transactions with respect to its product R.

Year 1

Opening inventory: nil

Buys 10 units at £300 per unit
Buys 12 units at £250 per unit
Sells 8 units at £400 per unit
Buys 6 units at £200 per unit
Sells 12 units at £400 per unit

Year 2

Buys 10 units at £200 per unit
Sells 5 units at £400 per unit
Buys 12 units at £150 per unit
Sells 25 units at £400 per unit

Requirement

Using FIFO, calculate the following on an item by item basis for both year 1 and year 2.

- Closing inventory
- Sales
- Cost of sales
- Gross profit

See **Answer** at the end of this chapter.

5 Using mark-up/margin percentages to establish cost

Section overview

- Mark-up is calculated on cost.
- Margin is calculated on sales.
- Margin and mark-up can help us to establish the cost of an item of inventory.

It is common to establish standard gross profit percentages in relation to cost to set the sales price:

- Inventory that cost £120 may be sold at a **margin** of 40%, so the sales value is £120 × 100/60 = £200, and the profit is £120 × 40/60 = £80

- Inventory that cost £120 may be sold at a **mark-up** of 40% to reach a sales price of £168 (120 × 140/100)

These standard percentages can be set out as follows, using the above as an example:

	Margin on sales (sales is the 100% figure)			Mark-up on cost (cost is the 100% figure)		
	%	£		%	£	
Sales	100	200	120 × 100/60	140	168	120 × 140/100
Cost	(60)	(120)		(100)	120	
Gross profit	40	80	120 × 40/60	40	48	120 × 40/100

An exam question may ask you to use gross profit percentages in order to correct an error in recording inventory at the end of a reporting period.

Interactive question 4: Mark-up   [Difficulty level: Exam standard]

A business has valued its inventory at £1,000, being the selling price of the items.

Requirement

What is the cost of closing inventory at cost assuming the business operates:

(a) On a margin of 25%?
(b) On a mark-up of 25%?

See **Answer** at the end of this chapter.

6 Writing off inventories, and inventory drawings

Section overview

- Provided inventory actually held is valued at the lower of cost and NRV, no inventory write-off entries are needed.

- When an owner draws out inventory: debit drawings, credit purchases.

Inventory held at the end of the reporting period may be faulty in some way, so it would appear that an amount needs to be written off. How do we account for this?

In fact, if the cost: NRV valuation method is followed, it is not necessary to write anything off inventory at the end of the reporting period as all damaged inventory would have been reduced down to its NRV when computing the value of closing inventory. It follows then that **we do not need to make any year-end accounting entries at all for inventory write-offs**: we simply include the appropriate low valuation of closing inventory in our year-end journal.

Remember that **material loss of inventory during the reporting period** is accounted for by **reducing purchases** and increasing expenses in the income statement: refer back to Chapter 8 if you need to refresh your memory on this. No entries are needed in the inventory account.

6.1 Inventory drawings

If an owner takes items of inventory from the business as drawings, we do not need to adjust opening or closing inventory at all. Instead we **reduce the purchases** figure in cost of sales with the cost of items withdrawn.

DEBIT   Drawings   £X
CREDIT   Purchases   £X

Summary (1/2)

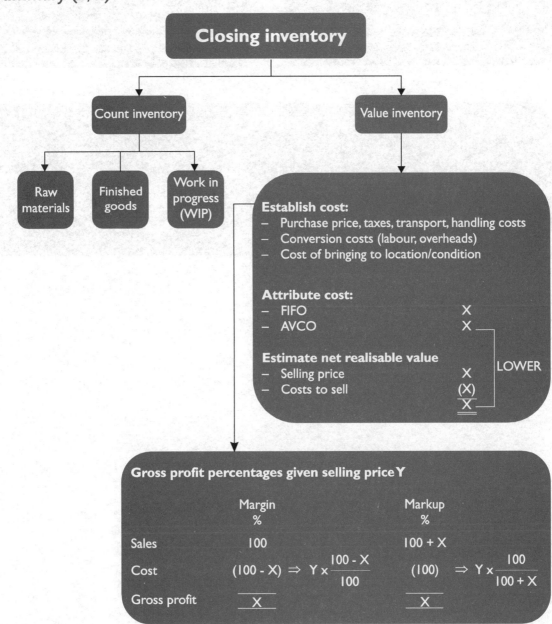

Accounting for inventories

Opening inventory:
DR   Cost of sales (income statement)
CR   Inventory account (Statement of financial position)

Closing inventory:
DR   Inventory account (statement of financial position)
CR   Cost of sales (income statement)

ETB

	TB		Adj		IS		SFP	
	DR	CR	DR	CR	DR	CR	DR	CR
Inventory								
– Opening	X							
– Closing			Y	Y			Y	
Cost of sales					X	Y		

ICAEW

Self-test

Answer the following questions.

1 Carlisle has the following inventory movements during May.

	Units	£ per unit
Opening inventory	40	9
2 May Goods in	60	10
10 May Goods out	50	
15 May Goods in	70	11
18 May Goods out	45	
24 May Goods in	80	11

Assuming that the business values inventory on a FIFO basis, what will be the value of closing inventory at the end of the month?

A   £1,615
B   £1,655
C   £1,700
D   £1,705

2 A trader used the LIFO method to value inventory at the end of July at £3,110. Sales and purchases in July were as follows.

Date	Purchases (units)	Sales (units)
3 July	100 at £20/unit	
6 July		80
10 July		40
15 July	50 at £22/unit	
22 July		20
27 July	80 at £25/unit	

The opening inventory at 1 July was 50 units valued at £15 per unit. The trader needs to adopt the FIFO method.

What is the effect of this change on the trader's profit?

A   £190 decrease
B   £420 decrease
C   £420 increase
D   £190 increase

3 The inventory records for Simmons last month were as follows.

Date	Purchases (units)	Sales (units)
2 February		500
13 February	800	
21 February		400
29 February		200

Opening inventory was 600 units valued at £12,000. Purchases in February were at £31.25 per unit.

The total cost of sales in February, using the AVCO method, is (to the nearest £):

A   £37,000
B   £28,000
C   £17,625
D   £22,000

4 What would be the effect on a business's profit of discovering that inventory with a cost of £1,250 and a net realisable value of £1,000 had been omitted from the inventory count at the end of the reporting period?

A   An increase of £1,250
B   An increase of £1,000
C   A decrease of £250
D   No effect

5 June Ltd has three lines of inventory at the end of its reporting period.

	X	Y	Z
Original purchase price (per unit)	£1.50	£6.50	£5.00
Estimated future selling price (per unit)	£4.25	£8.00	£3.50
Selling and distribution costs (per unit)	£0.75	£2.00	£0.50
Units in inventory	100	200	250

At what value should inventory appear in the financial statements at the end of the reporting period?

A £2,700
B £2,325
C £2,300
D £2,100

6 Brecon manufactures cosmetics and toiletries. It has decided to repackage its puffer talc product in new covers, and discount the selling price.

The details of puffer talc are as follows.

	Per item
Cost of manufacture	£2.50
Repackaging cost to be incurred	£0.75
Selling price	£3.00
Discount on selling price	10%

At what amount should each item of puffer talc be included in inventory?

A £3.00
B £2.70
C £2.25
D £1.95

7 During the reporting period Malcolm took items with a selling price of £280 for his own use. He trades at a 40% mark-up and had a draft profit of £15,800 before making any adjustments for this matter. His final profit is

A £15,520
B £15,800
C £15,600
D £16,000

8 Percy Pilbeam is a book wholesaler. Commission of 4% on selling price is payable by Percy for each sale.

The following information is available in respect of total inventory of three of his most popular titles at the end of his reporting period.

	Cost £	Selling price £
Henry VIII – Shakespeare	2,280	2,900
Dissuasion – Jane Armstrong-Siddeley	4,080	4,000
Pilgrim's Painful Progress – John Bunion	1,280	1,300

What is the total value of these inventories in Percy's statement of financial position?

A £7,368
B £7,400
C £7,560
D £7,640

9 Roberta Wickham decides to discount some of the slower-selling items in her music shop. These items at 31 March 20X0 are as follows.

Item	Cost	Current price	Discount to be applied (% of current price)
	£	£	%
Liszt – To Port	50	70	20
Delius – Myth	70	55	10
Offenbach – Up the Wrong Tree	150	225	10
Bax – To the Wall	30	35	50

What is the total inventory value of the above items at 31 March 20X0?

A £267.00
B £274.00
C £300.00
D £325.50

10 From the information below, calculate the value of Jock's closing inventory of foam liquid at 31 October 20X2 using each method of pricing the issue of materials to production.

Jock had 100 litres of foam liquid at 1 October 20X2, purchased at £3 per litre. During the month to 31 October 20X2 the following changes occurred.

	Date	Quantity (litres)	Cost per litre £
Purchases	7 October 20X2	200	2.50
	14 October 20X2	300	3.00
	21 October 20X2	50	4.00
	28 October 20X2	100	3.50
		650	
Issues	4 October 20X2	80	
	11 October 20X2	70	
	18 October 20X2	250	
	25 October 20X2	200	
		600	

Value of closing inventory:

FIFO basis   £ ....

AVCO basis   £ ....

Answer to Interactive question 1

			£	£
30.6.X3	DEBIT	Profit and loss ledger account	23,490	
	CREDIT	Inventory (asset)		23,490
		Clearing opening inventory to cost of sales		
30.6.X3	DEBIT	Inventory (asset)	40,285	
	CREDIT	Profit and loss ledger account		40,285
		Recording closing inventory as an asset at the end of the reporting period		

This journal could easily be amalgamated to debit the increase in inventory during the reporting period to the asset account, and to credit this to the profit and loss ledger account:

30.6.X3	DEBIT	Inventory (asset)	16,795	
	CREDIT	Profit and loss ledger account		16,795
		Recording closing inventory as an asset at the end of the reporting period, and as a deduction from the cost of sales		

Answer to Interactive question 2

Item	Cost	NRV	Lower of cost/NRV Valuation	Quantity	Total value
	£	£	£	units	£
A (NRV: 30 – 7)	20	23	20	200	4,000
B (NRV: 12 – 2 – 2)	9	8	8	150	1,200
C (NRV: 22 – 8 – 2)	14	12	12	300	3,600
					8,800

Answer to Interactive question 3

Year 1

Purchases (units)	Sales (units)	Balance (units)	Unit cost	Inventory value	Cost of sales	Sales
			£	£	£	£
10		10	300	3,000		
12		12	250	3,000		
		22		6,000		
	8	(8)	300	(2,400)	2,400	3,200
		14		3,600		
6		6	200	1,200		
		20		4,800		
	12	(12)		(3,100)*	3,100	4,800
		8		1,700	5,500	8,000

* 2 @ £300 + 10 @ £250 = £3,100

Year 2

Purchases (units)	Sales (units)	Balance (units)	Unit cost £	Inventory value £	Cost of sales £	Sales £
B/f		8		1,700		
10		10	200	2,000		
		18		3,700		
	5	(5) *		(1,100)*	1,100	2,000
		13		2,600		
12		12	150	1,800		
		25		4,400		
	25	(25) **		(4,400)**	4,400	10,000
		0		0	5,500	12,000

* 2 @ £250 + 3 @ £200 = £1,100
** (3+10) @ £200 + 12 @ £150 = £4,400

Income statement

	£	£
Year 1		
Sales		8,000
Opening inventory	0	
Purchases (3,000 + 3,000 + 1,200)	7,200	
Closing inventory	(1,700)	
Cost of sales		(5,500)
Gross profit		2,500
Year 2		
Sales		12,000
Opening inventory	1,700	
Purchases (2,000 + 1,800)	3,800	
Closing inventory	0	
Cost of sales		(5,500)
Gross profit		6,500

Answer to Interactive question 4

(a)

	%	£	
Sales	100	1,000	
COS	(75)	(750)	1,000 × 75/100
GP	25	250	

Inventory should be valued at £750 when a margin of 25% operates.

(b)

	%	£	
Sales	125	1,000	
COS	(100)	(800)	1,000 × 100/125
GP	25	200	

Inventory should be valued at £800 when a mark-up of 25% operates.

1   C   Closing inventory = 40 + 60 − 50 + 70 − 45 + 80 = <u>155 units</u>

Valued on a FIFO basis

Date of purchase	Units	£ per unit	Total cost
			£
24 May	80	11	880
15 May	70	11	770
2 May	5 (β)	10	50
	155		1,700

2   D   Closing inventory = 50 + 100 + 50 + 80 − 80 − 40 − 20 = 140 units

Closing inventory under FIFO

	£
80 @ £25 =	2,000
50 @ £22 =	1,100
10 @ £20 =	200
	3,300

So profit is (£3,110 − £3,300) = £190 more under FIFO

3   B   Closing inventory = 600 + 800 − 500 − 400 − 200 = <u>300 units</u>

Valued on an AVCO basis:

Date of purchase	Units	£ per unit	Total cost
			£
Opening inventory	600	20.00	12,000
2 Feb	(500)	20.00	(10,000)
	100		2000
13 Feb	800	31.25	25,000
	900	30.00	27,000

	£
Opening inventory	12,000
Purchases (800 × £31.25)	25,000
Closing inventory (300 x £30.00)	(9,000)
Cost of sales	28,000

4   B   It should now be included in closing inventory at £1,000 (lower of cost and NRV). This will increase profit by £1,000.

5   D

		Lower of cost and NRV
		£
X	At cost (100 × 1.50)	150
Y	At NRV (200 × (8.00 − 2.00))	1,200
Z	At NRV (250 × (3.50 − 0.50))	750
		2,100

6   D   Inventory valuation – Lower of

– Cost	£2.50
– Net realisable value (selling price less discount less repackaging cost)	£1.95

7   D

	£
Draft profit	15,800
Add back: drawings at cost £280 x 100/140	200
	16,000

8   A

	Cost	NRV SP × 0.96	Lower of cost and NRV
	£	£	£
Shakespeare	2,280	2,784	2,280
Armstrong-Siddeley	4,080	3,840	3,840
Bunion	1,280	1,248	1,248
			7,368

9   A

	Cost	NRV SP ×(100 – disc)	Lower of cost and NRV
	£	£	£
Liszt	50.00	56.00	50.00
Delius	70.00	49.50	49.50
Offenbach	150.00	202.50	150.00
Bax	30.00	17.50	17.50
			267.00

10 At 31 October 20X2 Jock has 100 + 650 – 600 = 150 litres in inventory

First in first out method (FIFO)

Quantity in inventory (litres)	Acquisition date	Cost per litre £	Closing inventory value £
100	28 October	3.50	350
50	21 October	4.00	200
150			550

Weighted average cost (AVCO)

Date	Quantity (litres)	Cost per litre	Value £	Average cost per litre £
Opening balance	100	3.00	300	3.00
4 Oct Issue	(80)	3.00	(240)	
	20		60	3.00
7 Oct Purchase	200	2.50	500	
	220		560	2.55
11 Oct Issue	(70)	2.55	(178)	
	150		382	2.55
14 Oct Purchase	300	3.00	900	
	450		1,282	2.85
18 Oct Issue	(250)	2.85	(712)	
	200		570	
21 Oct Purchase	50	4.00	200	
	250		770	3.08
25 Oct Issue	(200)	3.08	(616)	
	50		154	
28 Oct Purchase	100	3.50	350	
	150		504	3.36

Closing inventory value = 150 litres @ £3.36 = £504

CHAPTER 10

Non-current assets and depreciation

Learning objectives

- Record and account for transactions and events resulting in income, expenses, assets, liabilities and equity in accordance with the appropriate basis of accounting and the laws, regulations and accounting standards applicable to the financial statements

- Prepare an extended trial balance

- Identify the main components of a set of financial statements and specify their purpose and interrelationship

- Prepare and present a statement of financial position, income statement and statement of cash flows (or extracts therefrom) from the accounting records and trial balance in a format which satisfies the information requirements of the entity

Specific syllabus learning outcomes are: 1c, 2c, 3a, 3c

Syllabus links

The material in this chapter will be developed further in this paper, and then in the Financial Accounting and Financial Reporting papers later in the Professional stage.

Examination context

Questions on the topics in this chapter will be set as multiple choice questions, some of which may involve calculations so that the correct answer can be selected. Frequently double entry questions are expressed in terms of preparing a journal.

In the exam you may be required to:

- Identify the accounting principles behind accounting for non-current assets and depreciation

- Specify what is included in the cost of a non-current asset

- Use the straight line and reducing balance methods to calculate depreciation

- Calculate profits and losses on disposal of non-current assets, including part-exchange disposals

- Specify the effects of changing residual values, useful lives and depreciation methods on amounts in the income statement and statement of financial position

- Identify how to account for non-current assets, depreciation and disposals in ledger accounts and the extended trial balance

- Calculate the figure in the statement of financial position for non-current assets, and the figures that appear in the non-current assets note

- Calculate the depreciation charge and the figure for profits or losses on disposals in the income statement

- Identify the effects of depreciation and disposals on gross and net profit in the income statement

- Specify the uses of the asset register

- Identify the accounting treatments of intangible assets, including goodwill and development expenditure

1 Non-current assets and depreciation

Section overview

- The cost of a non-current asset includes: purchase price; delivery costs; taxes and duties; irrecoverable VAT; installation and assembly costs; professional fees; testing costs.

- Enhancement expenditure may be added to the cost subsequently.

- Part of an asset's cost may be settled by trading in an old asset in part-exchange.

- All assets except freehold land have a finite useful life.

- Many assets will have a residual value at the end of their useful lives.

- Depreciation allocates the asset's cost less its residual value over its useful life.

Where an asset has a **useful life** that extends beyond one reporting period, the accrual principle apportions the value used in a period against the income it has helped to create. These are **non-current assets**.

1.1 Cost of a non-current asset

The cost of a non-current asset includes **all amounts incurred to acquire the asset** and any amounts that can be **directly attributable** to **bringing the asset to the location and condition necessary for it to be capable of operating** in the way intended by management. With the exception of cars, where the VAT is not usually recoverable, the amount capitalised will **exclude** VAT.

Directly attributable costs include:

- Purchase price
- Delivery costs
- Stamp duty and import duties (and irrecoverable VAT on cars)
- Costs of preparing the site for installation and assembly of the asset
- Professional fees, such as legal and architects' fees
- Costs of testing whether the asset is functioning

Expenses such as general overhead costs, administration costs, training costs for staff, fuel in a vehicle on delivery and licence fees for operating the asset are **not** included as part of the total costs of the non-current asset.

The cost of **subsequent capital expenditure** on a non-current asset will be added to the cost of the asset, provided this expenditure **enhances** the benefits of the non-current asset or restores any benefits consumed. It is therefore called **enhancement expenditure**.

This means that costs of **major improvements** or a **major overhaul** may be capitalised. However, the costs of **repairs** that are carried out simply to **maintain existing performance** may **not** be capitalised: they will be treated as expenses of the reporting period in which the work is done, and charged in full as an expense in that period.

1.2 Paying for a non-current asset

A business might purchase a new non-current asset for **cash** or on **credit**, or it may hand over an old asset **in part-exchange**. This is common, for example, with motor vehicles. The supplier of the new asset agrees to take the old asset, and gives the buyer a reduction in the purchase price of the new asset. This reduction is the **part-exchange value of the old asset**.

Worked example: Part-exchange

A business purchases a new delivery van, trading in an old van in part-exchange. The cost of the new van is £25,000 and the part-exchange value of the old van is £10,000, so the business will pay the van dealer £15,000.

Because paying for a new non-current asset is rarely straightforward, non-current asset purchases are usually recorded in the **journal** as the book of original entry.

1.3 Useful life

An asset may be seen as having a **physical life** and an **economic life**.

Most non-current assets suffer physical deterioration through usage and the passage of time. Although care and maintenance may succeed in extending the **physical life** of an asset, typically it will, eventually, reach a condition where the benefits have been exhausted.

However, a business may not wish to keep an asset until the end of its physical life. There may be a point when it becomes uneconomic to continue to use the asset even though there is still some physical life left. The **economic life** of the asset will be determined by such factors as technological progress and changes in demand.

Definition

Useful life: The **estimated economic life** (rather than the potential physical life) of the non-current asset.

The only asset that is deemed to have an **unlimited useful life** is **freehold land**.

1.4 What is depreciation?

Definition

Depreciation: The systematic allocation of the cost of an asset, less its residual value, over its useful life.

In determining the expenses for a period, it is important to include an amount to represent the consumption of non-current assets during that period (that is, **depreciation**).

To calculate the depreciation charge for a reporting period, the following factors are relevant:

- Asset cost (see section 1.1 above)
- Useful life (see section 1.3 above)
- Asset residual value

1.5 Residual value

At the end of a non-current asset's useful life the business will dispose of it and any expected amounts received represent its **residual value**. For instance, an asset that is expected to be sold for £500 at the end of its useful life has a residual value of £500. If it is unlikely to be a significant amount, a residual value of zero will be assumed. The cost of a non-current asset less its residual value represents the **total amount to be depreciated** over its estimated useful life (**its depreciable amount**).

Note. For exam purposes, always assume the residual value is zero unless told otherwise.

Definition

Residual value: The estimated amount that the entity would currently obtain from disposing of the asset, after deducting estimated disposal costs.

Interactive question 1: Depreciable amount   [Difficulty level: Exam standard]

Arundel Enterprises purchased a new car for a sales representative. The invoice received contained the following information:

	£
List price of the car	18,720
Deposit paid	(6,200)
Amount due	12,520

It is estimated that the new car will have a useful life of three years and will have a residual value of £6,360.

Calculate the total amount to be depreciated in respect of the new car.

See **Answer** at the end of this chapter.

2 The objective of depreciation

Section overview

- Depreciation arises from the application of the accrual principle. The method chosen should be applied consistently.

The depreciable amount is cost less residual value, and the useful life provides the time period over which the asset should be depreciated. So how much of this depreciable amount is charged against profits in each reporting period?

2.1 Accounting concepts and depreciation

Consistency is important. The depreciation basis or method selected should be applied consistently from period to period unless altered circumstances justify a change. When the basis *is* changed, the effect on current and future periods should be quantified and disclosed, and the reason for the change should be stated.

Various methods of allocating depreciation to reporting periods are available, but whichever is chosen must be applied **consistently** (as required by IAS 1 (revised): see Chapter 1), to ensure **comparability** from period to period. A change of basis is not allowed simply because of the profitability situation of the enterprise.

The need to depreciate non-current assets arises from the **accrual principle**. If money is expended in purchasing an asset then this amount must at some time be charged against profits. If the asset is one which contributes to an entity's revenue over a number of reporting periods it would be inappropriate to charge any single period (eg the period in which the asset was acquired) with the whole of the expenditure. Instead, some method must be found of spreading the cost of the asset over its useful life.

2.2 Common depreciation misconceptions

(a) It does not **reflect the fall in value of an asset over its life**.

(b) It is not 'setting aside money' to **replace the asset at the end of its useful life**. Even if the asset was not going to be replaced, its cost should still be allocated over its useful life.

3 Calculating depreciation

Section overview

- Charge depreciation to income statement, and set up an account in the statement of financial position called accumulated depreciation. When this is offset against the asset's cost account in the statement of financial position, we have its carrying amount.

- Depreciation may be calculated on the straight line basis:

$$\frac{\text{Asset cost} - \text{residual value}}{\text{Months of useful life}} = \text{Monthly depreciation charge}$$

- Reducing balance depreciation:

    Carrying amount × % to be applied = Annual depreciation charge.

- The depreciation method used should be applied consistently. A change in method may cause an increased charge.

- When there has been enhancement expenditure, this would usually be depreciated over the remaining useful life of the whole asset.

- The carrying amount of an asset should be reviewed and if there has been an impairment this impairment loss should be accounted for immediately.

- If there is a change in the estimate of the asset's useful life or residual value, this too will cause a change in the depreciation charge.

When a non-current asset is depreciated, two things must be accounted for.

(a) The **charge for depreciation** is a cost or expense of the reporting period in the income statement.

(b) At the same time, the non-current asset is wearing out and being consumed, and so its **cost in the statement of financial position must be reduced** by the amount of depreciation charged. The value of the non-current asset in the statement of financial position will be its **carrying amount**.

Definition

Carrying amount: Cost less accumulated depreciation.

The amount of depreciation deducted from the cost of a non-current asset to arrive at its **carrying amount** will build up (or 'accumulate') over time, as more depreciation is charged in each successive reporting period. This is called **accumulated depreciation**.

Worked example: Accumulating depreciation on a non-current asset

If a non-current asset costing £40,000 has an expected useful life of four years and an estimated residual value of nil, it might be depreciated by £10,000 per annum.

	Depreciation charge for the year (income statement) (A) £	Accumulated depreciation at end of year (B) £	Cost of the asset (C) £	Carrying amount at end of year (C – B) £
At beginning of its life	–	–	40,000	40,000
Year 1	10,000	10,000	40,000	30,000
Year 2	10,000	20,000	40,000	20,000
Year 3	10,000	30,000	40,000	10,000
Year 4	10,000	40,000	40,000	0
	40,000			

At the end of year 4, the full £40,000 of depreciation charges have been made in the income statements of the four years. The carrying amount of the non-current asset is now nil.

3.1 Methods of depreciation

There are several different methods of depreciation. Of these, the ones which are relevant for *Accounting* are:

* Straight line method
* Reducing balance method

Remember that if an entity changes from one method to another this counts as a change in **accounting estimate**. There is no change in accounting policy, which remains: to **depreciate non-current assets**.

3.2 The straight line method of depreciation

Definition

Straight line depreciation: The depreciable amount (cost less residual value) is charged in **equal instalments** to each reporting period over the expected useful life of the asset. (In this way, the carrying amount of the non-current asset declines at a steady rate, or in a 'straight line' over time.)

The **annual** depreciation charge is:

$$\frac{\text{Cost of asset minus residual value}}{\text{Expected useful life of the asset in years}}$$

The **monthly** depreciation charge is:

$$\frac{\text{Cost of asset – residual value}}{\text{Useful life in years} \times 12}$$

Since straight line depreciation is charged monthly you should make the second, monthly, calculation in an exam.

Worked example: Straight line depreciation

(a) A non-current asset costing £24,000 with a useful life of 10 years and no residual value would be depreciated at the rate of:

$$\frac{£24,000}{10 \times 12} = £200 \text{ per month, or £2,400 per annum.}$$

(b) A non-current asset costing £60,000 has a useful life of five years and a residual value of £6,000. The monthly depreciation charge using the straight line method is:

$$\frac{£(60,000 - 6,000)}{5 \times 12} = £900 \text{ per month, or } £10,800 \text{ per annum}$$

The carrying amount of the non-current asset would be as follows:

	After 1 year £	After 2 years £	After 3 years £	After 4 years £	After 5 years £
Cost of the asset	60,000	60,000	60,000	60,000	60,000
Accumulated depreciation	(10,800)	(21,600)	(32,400)	(43,200)	(54,000)
Carrying amount	49,200	38,400	27,600	16,800	6,000 *

* ie its estimated residual value.

Since the straight line depreciation charge per annum is the same amount every 12 month reporting period, it is often convenient to state that depreciation is charged at the rate of x per cent per annum on the asset's depreciable amount. In the example in (a) above, the depreciation charge per annum is 10% of cost (ie 10% of £24,000 = £2,400). In (b), it is 20% of the depreciable amount (20% × (60,000 – 6,000) = £10,800)

The straight line method allocates the total depreciable amount in equal amounts between different reporting periods.

Worked example: Monthly depreciation on the straight line

A business has a reporting period from 1 January to 31 December and purchases a non-current asset on 1 April 20X1, at a cost of £24,000. The expected life of the asset is four years, and its residual value is nil. What is the depreciation charge for the reporting period to 31 December 20X1?

Solution

The monthly depreciation charge will be $\frac{£24,000}{4 \times 12} = £500$ per month

Since the asset was acquired on 1 April 20X1, the business has only benefited from the use of the asset for 9 months instead of a full 12 months. We therefore charge depreciation in 20X1 of:

9 × £500 = £4,500

3.3 The reducing balance method of depreciation

Definition

Reducing balance depreciation: The annual depreciation charge is a fixed percentage of the brought forward carrying amount of the asset.

When calculating reducing balance depreciation in an exam you will NOT be concerned with the asset's residual value nor how to calculate the percentage: just the carrying amount and the reducing balance percentage given to you.

The reducing balance method might be used to allocate a greater proportion of the total depreciable amount to the asset's earlier years and a lower proportion to its later years, as the benefits obtained by the business from using the asset decline over time.

Worked example: Reducing balance method

A business purchases a non-current asset at a cost of £10,000 on 1 January 20X1, which it plans to keep for three years to 31 December 20X3. The business wishes to use the reducing balance method to depreciate the asset, and calculates that the rate of depreciation should be 40% of the reducing balance (carrying amount) of the asset.

The depreciation charge per annum and the carrying amount of the asset as at the end of each reporting period will be as follows.

	£	Accumulated depreciation £	
Asset at cost	10,000		
Depreciation in 20X1 (40%)	(4,000)	4,000	
Carrying amount at end of 20X1	6,000		
Depreciation in 20X2 (40% of carrying amount 6,000)	(2,400)	6,400	(4,000 + 2,400)
Carrying amount at end of 20X2	3,600		
Depreciation in 20X3 (40% × 3,600)	(1,440)	7,840	(6,400 + 1,440)
Carrying amount at end of 20X3	2,160		

The annual charge for reducing balance depreciation is higher in the earlier reporting periods of the asset's life, and lower in the later reporting periods (£4,000, £2,400 and £1,440 respectively).

The balance remaining at the end of the three year useful life of £2,160 is the estimated residual value which was taken into account when calculating that 40% reducing balance was appropriate.

In an exam question, you will not have to calculate what amount of reducing balance depreciation should be charged monthly.

3.4 Applying a depreciation method consistently

A business can choose which method of depreciation to apply to its non-current assets. Once this decision has been made it should be applied **consistently from reporting period to reporting period**.

A business can depreciate different categories of non-current assets in different ways. For example, if a business owns three cars, then each car would normally be depreciated in the same way (eg by the straight line method); but another category of non-current asset, say photocopiers, might be depreciated using a different method (eg by the reducing balance method).

Interactive question 2: Depreciation [Difficulty level: Exam standard]

A lorry bought for a business cost £17,000 plus VAT at 20%. It is expected to last for five years and then to be sold for £2,000 plus VAT.

Requirement

Work out the depreciation to be charged each 12 month reporting period under:

(a) The straight line method
(b) The reducing balance method, using a rate of 35%

See **Answer** at the end of this chapter.

3.5 Depreciating enhancement expenditure

Where expenditure is incurred to **enhance** an asset after its initial purchase, this is added to the asset's cost and **depreciated over the asset's remaining useful life.**

Worked example: Depreciating enhancement expenditure

Malcolm buys a building on 1.1.X0 for £200,000. On 1.1.X2 he adds an extension that cost £50,000.

Calculate the annual depreciation charge before and after the extension is built, on the basis of straight line depreciation over 10 years, with no residual value.

Solution

Before extension: $\dfrac{£200,000}{10} = £20,000$ pa

After extension: $\dfrac{£200,000}{10} + \dfrac{£50,000}{8} = £26,250$

In the exam you will not be required to depreciate enhancement expenditure using the reducing balance basis.

3.6 Reviewing and changing the depreciation method

The depreciation method used and the carrying amount should **be reviewed annually** for appropriateness. If there are any changes in the expected pattern of use of the asset (and hence economic benefit), then the method used should be changed. The remaining carrying amount is depreciated under the new method, ie only current and future periods are affected.

Worked example: Change in method of depreciation

Jakob Co purchased an asset for £100,000 on 1.1.X1. It had an estimated useful life of 5 years and it was depreciated using the reducing balance method at a rate of 40%. On 1.1.X3 it was decided to change the depreciation method to straight line. There was no change to the useful life, and no residual value is anticipated.

Show the depreciation charge for each year (to 31 December) of the asset's life.

Solution

Year		Depreciation charge £	Accumulated depreciation £
20X1	£100,000 × 40%	40,000	40,000
20X2	£60,000 × 40%	24,000	64,000
20X3		12,000	76,000
20X4	$\dfrac{£100,000 - £64,000}{3\text{ remaining years}}$	12,000	88,000
20X5		12,000	100,000

Interactive question 3: Change in depreciation method   [Difficulty level: Exam standard]

Ford plc prepares its financial statements for the 12 month reporting period to 31 December each year. On 1 January 20X0 it bought a machine for £100,000 and depreciated it at 10% per annum on the reducing balance basis.

On 31 December 20X3, the machine will be included in Ford plc's financial statements at:

	£
Cost	100,000
Accumulated depreciation (10,000 + 9,000 + 8,100 + 7,290)	(34,390)
Carrying amount	65,610

On 1 January 20X4, the company decided to change the basis of depreciation to straight line over a total life of nine years, ie five years remaining from 1 January 20X4. There is no residual value.

Calculate the revised annual depreciation charge.

See **Answer** at the end of this chapter.

3.7 Reviewing and changing carrying amount: fall in value (impairment loss)

When the value of a non-current asset falls to less than its carrying amount and the fall in value will not be recovered from future use of the asset, it is said to have suffered an **impairment loss** and should be **written down to its new value**. The income statement charge for the impairment in the asset's value during the reporting period should be:

	£
Carrying amount at the beginning of the period	X
Less reduced value (the new carrying amount at the end of the period)	(X)
Equals the charge for impairment in the asset's value in the period (**impairment loss**)	X

Worked example: Impairment loss

A business purchased a building on 1 January 20X1 at a cost of £100,000. The building had a 20 year life. On 31 December 20X5 the business decides that since property prices have fallen sharply and future trading prospects are poor, the building is now worth only £60,000, and the value of the asset should be reduced accordingly in the financial statements of the business for the 12 month reporting period ended 31 December 20X5.

The building was being depreciated over 20 years, at the rate of 5% per annum on cost.

Before the asset is reduced in value, the annual depreciation charge is:

$$\frac{£100,000}{20 \text{ years}} = £5,000 \text{ per annum}$$

This will be charged in 20X1, 20X2, 20X3, 20X4 **and** 20X5.

As at 31 December 20X5 the accumulated depreciation is thus £25,000 and the carrying amount of the building is £75,000, which is £15,000 more than the new asset value. This £15,000 should be written off as an impairment loss in 20X5, so that the total charge in 20X5 is:

	£
'Normal' depreciation charge in 20X5	5,000
Impairment loss recognised in 20X5	15,000
Charge against profit in 20X5	20,000

An alternative method of calculation is as follows:

	£
Carrying amount of the building in 31 December 20X4 £(100,000 – 20,000)	80,000
Revised asset value at end of 20X5	(60,000)
Charge against profit in 20X5	20,000

The building has a further life of 15 years, and its value is now £60,000. From 20X6 to 20Y0, the annual charge for depreciation will be:

$$\frac{£60,000}{15 \text{ years}} = £4,000 \text{ per annum}$$

3.8 Reviewing and changing useful life or residual value

The depreciation charge on a non-current asset depends not only on the asset's cost but also on **residual value** and its **estimated useful life**. These should also be reviewed and changed if they are no longer appropriate.

Worked example: Change in useful life

A business purchased a non-current asset costing £12,000 with an estimated useful life of four years and no residual value. **If it used the straight line method of depreciation**, it would make an annual depreciation charge of 25% of £12,000 = £3,000.

The business decides after two years that the useful life of the asset has been underestimated, and it still has five more years in use to come, making its total life seven years.

For the first two years, the asset is depreciated by £3,000 per annum, so that its carrying amount after two years is £(12,000 6,000) = £6,000. If the remaining life of the asset is now revised to five more years, the remaining amount to be depreciated (£6,000) is spread over the remaining useful life, giving an annual depreciation charge for the final 5 years of:

$$\frac{\text{Carrying amount at time of change}}{\text{Revised useful life}}$$

$$= \frac{£6,000}{5 \text{ years}} = £1,200 \text{ per year}$$

Interactive question 4: Change in residual value [Difficulty level: Exam standard]

An asset had a cost of £1,000, an estimated useful life of 10 years and a residual value of £200. At the start of year 3 a review shows its remaining useful life was unchanged but the residual value was reduced to nil.

Calculate the depreciation charge for each of years 1 to 3 on the straight line basis.

See **Answer** at the end of this chapter.

When an impairment loss is recognised (see 3.7 above), the asset's remaining useful life and residual value should also be reviewed and possibly revised (if straight line depreciation is being used). The reducing balance percentage rate should be revised if relevant.

Interactive question 5: Impairment [Difficulty level: Exam standard]

On 1 January 20X1 Tiger buys a non-current asset for £120,000, with an estimated useful life of 20 years and no residual value. Tiger depreciates its non-current assets on a straight line basis. Its reporting period is the 12 months ended 31 December.

On 31 December 20X3 the asset will be included in the statement of financial position as follows:

	£
Non-current asset at cost	120,000
Accumulated depreciation (3 × (£120,000 ÷ 20))	(18,000)
Carrying amount	102,000

Requirements

Consider each of these alternatives separately.

(a) On 1 January 20X4 the remaining useful life is revised to 15 years from that date.

Calculate the revised annual depreciation charge.

(b) On 1 January 20X4 the remaining useful life is revised to 10 years from that date. An impairment review shows that the value is £95,000 as at 1 January 20X4.

Show how the impairment loss would be recorded and calculate the revised annual depreciation charge.

See **Answer** at the end of this chapter.

---

4 Accounting for depreciation

Definition

Accumulated depreciation: The total amount of the asset's depreciation amount that has been allocated to reporting periods to date.

4.1 Accounting for depreciation

There are two basic aspects of accounting for depreciation to remember.

(a) A **depreciation charge** is made in the income statement in each reporting period for every depreciable non-current asset. Nearly all non-current assets are depreciable, the most important exception being freehold land.

(b) The total **accumulated depreciation** on a non-current asset builds up as the asset gets older. The total accumulated depreciation is always getting larger, until the non-current asset is fully depreciated.

Accounting for depreciation is as follows.

* Set up an accumulated depreciation account for each separate category of non-current asset, for example plant and machinery, land and buildings, fixtures and fittings, motor vehicles.

* With the depreciation charge for the period:

    DEBIT   Depreciation expense (income statement)   £X

    CREDIT   Accumulated depreciation account (statement of financial position)   £X

* The balance on the accumulated depreciation account is the total accumulated depreciation. This is always a credit balance brought forward in the ledger account.

* **The non-current asset cost accounts are unaffected by depreciation**.

* In the statement of financial position, the balance on the **accumulated depreciation** account is set against the **non-current asset cost accounts** to derive the **carrying amount** of the non-current assets.

This is how the non-current asset cost, accumulated depreciation and depreciation charge accounts might appear in a trial balance:

		DR £	CR £
Freehold building	– cost	2,000,000	
Freehold building	– accumulated depreciation (£20,000 current reporting period)		500,000
Motor vehicles	– cost	70,000	
Motor vehicles	– accumulated depreciation (£15,000 current reporting period)		40,000
Office equipment	– cost	25,000	
Office equipment	– accumulated depreciation (£3,000 current reporting period)		15,000
Depreciation expense	(20,000 + 15,000 + 3,000)	38,000	

They would be shown at the following carrying amounts in the statement of financial position:

Non-current assets
Freehold building	1,500,000
Motor vehicles	30,000
Office equipment	10,000

In the income statement the depreciation charge would be included partly in administrative expenses and partly in distribution costs:

Administrative expenses (20,000 + 3,000)	23,000
Distribution costs	15,000
	38,000

Worked example: Accounting for depreciation I

Brian Box set up his own computer software business on 1 March 20X6. He purchased a computer system on credit from a manufacturer for £16,000. The system has an expected life of three years and a residual value of £2,500. Using the straight line method of depreciation, the non-current asset account, accumulated depreciation account and income statement (extract) and statement of financial position (extract) would be as follows, for each of the next three reporting periods ending 28 February 20X7, 20X8 and 20X9.

NON-CURRENT ASSET: COMPUTER EQUIPMENT COST

Date		£	Date		£
1.3.X6	Trade payables	16,000	28.2.X7	Balance c/d	16,000
1.3.X7	Balance b/d	16,000	28.2.X8	Balance c/d	16,000
1.3.X8	Balance b/d	16,000	28.2.X9	Balance c/d	16,000
1.3.X9	Balance b/d	16,000			

The annual depreciation charge is $\dfrac{£(16,000 - 2,500)}{3 \text{ years}}$ = £4,500 pa

ACCUMULATED DEPRECIATION

Date		£	Date		£
28.2.X7	Balance c/d	4,500	28.2.X7	Income statement	4,500
28.2.X8	Balance c/d	9,000	1.3.X7	Balance b/d	4,500
			28.2.X8	Income statement	4,500
		9,000			9,000
28.2.X9	Balance c/d	13,500	1.3.X8	Balance b/d	9,000
			28.2.X9	Income statement	4,500
		13,500			13,500
			1.3.X9	Balance b/d	13,500

At the end of three reporting periods, the asset is fully depreciated down to its residual value (£16,000 – £13,500 = £2,500). If it continues to be used by Brian Box, it will not be depreciated any further (unless its estimated residual value is reduced).

INCOME STATEMENT (EXTRACT)

Year ending:		£
28 Feb 20X7	Depreciation expense	4,500
28 Feb 20X8	Depreciation expense	4,500
28 Feb 20X9	Depreciation expense	4,500

STATEMENT OF FINANCIAL POSITION (EXTRACT) AS AT 28 FEBRUARY

	20X7	20X8	20X9
	£	£	£
Computer equipment at cost	16,000	16,000	16,000
Less accumulated depreciation	(4,500)	(9,000)	(13,500)
Carrying amount	11,500	7,000	2,500

In theory, the non-current asset is now at the end of its useful life. However, until it is sold off or scrapped, the asset will still appear in the statement of financial position at cost (less accumulated depreciation) and it should remain in the ledger accounts for computer equipment until disposal.

Worked example: Accounting for depreciation II

Brian Box prospers in his computer software business, and before long he purchases a car for himself, and later one for his chief assistant Bill Ockhead. Relevant data is as follows.

	Date of purchase	Cost	Estimated life	Estimated residual value
Brian Box car	1 June 20X6	£20,000	3 years	£2,000
Bill Ockhead car	1 June 20X7	£15,500	3 years	£2,000

The straight line method of depreciation is to be used.

Prepare the vehicles account and vehicles accumulated depreciation account for the reporting periods to 28 February 20X7 and 20X8.

Calculate the carrying amount of the vehicles as at 28 February 20X8.

Solution

(a) (i)

Brian Box car   Monthly depreciation $= \dfrac{£(20,000 - 2,000)}{3 \times 12} =$ £500 pm

Depreciation 1 June 20X6 – 28 February 20X7 (9 × £500)   £4,500
1 March 20X7 – 28 February 20X8 (12 × £500)   £6,000

(ii)

Bill Ockhead car   Monthly depreciation $= \dfrac{£(15,500 - 2,000)}{3 \times 12} =$ £375 pm

Depreciation 1 June 20X7 – 28 February 20X8 (9 × £375)   £3,375

(b)   MOTOR VEHICLES

Date		£	Date		£
1 Jun 20X6	Payables (or cash) (car purchase)	20,000	28 Feb 20X7	Balance c/d	20,000
1 Mar 20X7	Balance b/d	20,000			
1 Jun 20X7	Payables (or cash) (car purchase)	15,500	28 Feb 20X8	Balance c/d	35,500
		35,500			35,500
1 Mar 20X8	Balance b/d	35,500			

MOTOR VEHICLES – ACCUMULATED DEPRECIATION

Date		£	Date		£
28 Feb 20X7	Balance c/d	4,500	28 Feb 20X7	Income statement	4,500
			1 Mar 20X7	Balance b/d	4,500
28 Feb 20X8	Balance c/d	13,875	28 Feb 20X8	Income statement (6,000+3,375)	9,375
		13,875			13,875
			1 Mar 20X8	Balance b/d	13,875

	Brian Box car		Bill Ockhead car		Total
	£	£	£	£	£
Asset at cost		20,000		15,500	35,500
Accumulated depreciation					
Year to 28 Feb 20X7	4,500		–		
Year to 28 Feb 20X8	6,000		3,375		
		(10,500)		(3,375)	(13,875)
Carrying amount		9,500		12,125	21,625

4.2 Depreciation on the ETB

Because the final depreciation calculation is usually accounted for after the initial trial balance has been extracted, the only figure for accumulated depreciation on the initial trial balance is the one for the balance brought forward. We can incorporate the relevant figures using the ETB.

- Calculate the amount of depreciation to be charged

- Prepare the year-end journal to record depreciation expense (and impairment loss if relevant)

- Enter the journal in the adjustments columns of the ETB using the accumulated depreciation line plus a line for depreciation expense

- Include these adjustments in the ETB cross-cast to prepare the financial statements

- Enter the journals for depreciation in the ledger accounts and bring down the balance on the accumulated depreciation account.

5 Non-current asset disposals

Section overview

- A disposal account is used to calculate the profit or loss on disposal of an asset, which is the amount by which the sales proceeds of the asset differs from its carrying amount at the date of disposal.

- Accounting for disposals:

DEBIT	Disposal account with asset's carrying amount	£X	
CREDIT	Disposal account with sales proceeds		£X
DEBIT	Cash with proceeds	£X	
DEBIT	Accumulated depreciation	£X	
CREDIT	Asset cost		£X

- When an old asset has been attributed an NRV when given in part-exchange for a new one, the part-exchange value is accounted for as the old asset's disposal proceeds.

Non-current assets might be sold off at some stage during their life, either when their useful life is over or before then.

Whenever a business sells something, it will make a profit or a loss. When non-current assets are disposed of, there will be **a profit or loss on disposal**. As it is a capital item being sold, the profit or loss will be **capital income** or a **capital expense**. Profits are shown as other income, and losses are reported as administrative expenses or distribution costs in the income statement of the business, not as part of gross profit. They are commonly referred to as '**profit (or loss) on disposal of non-current assets**'.

5.1 The principles behind calculating the profit or loss on disposal

The profit or loss on the disposal of a non-current asset is the difference between:

- The **carrying amount** of the asset at the time of its sale, and
- Its **net disposal proceeds**, the value received less any costs of making the sale.

A **profit** is made when the net disposal proceeds **exceed** the carrying amount. A **loss** is made when the net disposal proceeds are **less** than the carrying amount.

Worked example: Disposal of a non-current asset I

A business purchased a non-current asset on 1 January 20X1 for £25,000. It had an estimated life of six years and an estimated residual value of £7,000 and is depreciated on the straight line basis. The asset was sold after three years on 1 January 20X4 to another trader who paid £17,500 for it.

What was the profit or loss on disposal?

Solution

$$\text{Annual depreciation} = \frac{£(25,000 - 7,000)}{6 \text{ years}} = £3,000 \text{ per annum}$$

	£
Cost of asset	25,000
Less accumulated depreciation (3 × £3,000)	(9,000)
Carrying amount at date of disposal	16,000
Disposal proceeds	17,500
Profit on disposal	1,500

This profit will be shown in the income statement as an item of **other income**, added to the gross profit to arrive at net profit.

Worked example: Disposal of a non-current asset II

A business purchased a machine on 1 July 20X1 for £39,000. The machine had an estimated residual value of £3,000 and a life of eight years. The machine was sold for £18,600 on 31 December 20X4. To make the sale, the business had to incur dismantling costs and costs of transporting the machine to the buyer's premises of £1,200.

The business uses the straight line method of depreciation. What was the profit or loss on disposal of the machine?

Solution

$$\text{Depreciation expense} \frac{£(35,000 - 3,000)}{8 \text{ years}} = £375 \text{ per month, and } £4,500 \text{ per annum}$$

In 20X1 only six months depreciation was charged, because the asset was purchased six months into the reporting period.

	£	£
Non-current asset at cost		39,000
Depreciation in 20X1 (6 × £375)	2,250	
20X2, 20X3 and 20X4 (3 × £4,500)	13,500	
Accumulated depreciation		(15,750)
Carrying amount at date of disposal		23,250
Disposal proceeds	18,600	
Costs incurred in making the sale	(1,200)	
Net disposal proceeds		(17,400)
Loss on disposal		(5,850)

This loss will be shown as part of administrative expenses in the income statement of the business. It is a capital expense, not a trading loss, and it should not therefore be part of the calculation of gross profit.

5.2 Accounting for non-current asset disposals

We record the disposal of non-current assets in a **disposals ledger account**.

(a) The following items appear in the disposals account:

(i) The value of the asset (at cost)
(ii) The accumulated depreciation up to the date of sale
(iii) The disposal proceeds, if any

(b) The profit or loss on disposal is the difference between:

(i) The disposal proceeds and
(ii) The carrying amount of the asset at the time of disposal.

(c) The ledger accounting entries are as follows.

(i) DEBIT   Disposal account   £X
      CREDIT   Non-current asset cost account   £X

with the **cost** of the asset disposed of (the cost of the asset is removed from the statement of financial position).

(ii) DEBIT   Accumulated depreciation account   £X
      CREDIT   Disposal account   £X

with the **accumulated depreciation** on the asset as at the date of sale (the accumulated depreciation on the asset is removed from the statement of financial position).

(iii) DEBIT   Cash book (or receivables)   £X
      CREDIT   Disposal account   £X

with the **disposal proceeds** of the asset.

The balance on the disposal account is the profit or loss on disposal and the corresponding double entry is recorded in the profit and loss ledger account itself, ie in the income statement.

Worked example: Accounting for the disposal of non-current assets

A business has £110,000 worth of machinery at cost. Its policy is to depreciate at 20% per annum straight line. The total accumulated depreciation now stands at £70,000. The business sells for £19,000 a machine which it purchased exactly two years ago for £30,000.

Show the relevant ledger entries.

Solution

MACHINERY – COST

	£		£
Balance b/d	110,000	Disposals	30,000
		Balance c/d	80,000
	110,000		110,000
Balance b/d	80,000		

MACHINERY – ACCUMULATED DEPRECIATION

	£		£
Disposals (20% of £30,000 for 2 years)	12,000	Balance b/d	70,000
Balance c/d	58,000		
	70,000		70,000
		Balance b/d	58,000

DISPOSAL ACCOUNT

	£		£
Machinery – cost	30,000	Machinery – accumulated depreciation	12,000
Income statement (profit on sale)	1,000	Cash	19,000
	31,000		31,000

Check:

	£
Asset at cost	30,000
Accumulated depreciation at time of sale	(12,000)
Carrying amount at time of sale	18,000
Disposal proceeds	19,000
Profit on disposal	1,000

5.3 Accounting for disposals of non-current assets given in part-exchange

Quite often a business does not receive cash for the asset, but instead get a 'part-exchange' or 'trade-in value' for it against the cost of a new asset. Instead of disposal proceeds being received in the form of cash or promised in the form of a receivable, use the **part exchange value** given to the asset by the other party as its **disposal value**.

Worked example: Accounting for part-exchange disposals I

Asset A, costing £20,000 is acquired by a business for £12,000 cash, plus its old Asset B. The part-exchange value attributed to Asset B is £20,000 – £12,000 = £8,000. This amount must be compared with Asset B's carrying amount in order to establish the profit or loss on Asset B's disposal.

Asset B cost £15,000 and has had £4,000 depreciation charged in respect of it, so its carrying amount at the date of the part-exchange disposal is £11,000. The business has made a loss of £11,000 – £8,000 = £3,000 on Asset B's disposal.

The £8,000 part-exchange value must be included in the cost of Asset A, along with the £12,000 cash handed over.

(a)

		£	£
DEBIT	Asset A cost	20,000	
CREDIT	Cash		12,000
CREDIT	Disposal account (Asset B's part-exchange value)		8,000

Being the acquisition of Asset A for cash and part-exchange of Asset B

(b)

		£	£
DEBIT	Asset B accumulated depreciation	4,000	
CREDIT	Disposal account (Asset B)		4,000
DEBIT	Disposal account (Asset B)	15,000	
CREDIT	Asset B cost account		15,000

Being the removal of Asset B from the ledger accounts

(c)

		£	£
DEBIT	Income statement	3,000	
CREDIT	Disposal account		3,000

Being the loss on disposal of Asset B (8,000 – (15,000 – 4,000))

DISPOSALS ACCOUNT

	£		£
Asset B cost (b)	15,000	Disposal proceeds (part exchange value) (a)	8,000
		Asset B accumulated depreciation (b)	4,000
		Income statement (c)	3,000
	15,000		15,000

Worked example: Accounting for part-exchange disposals II

A business trades in an asset that cost £30,000 two years ago for a new asset that costs £60,000. A cheque for £41,000 was also handed over in full settlement. Assets are depreciated on the straight line basis over five years. What are the relevant ledger account entries?

Solution

MACHINERY ACCOUNT

	£		£
Balance b/d	30,000	Disposals	30,000
Cash	41,000	Balance c/d	60,000
Disposals			
(part exchange value £ (60,000 –			
41,000))	19,000		
	90,000		90,000
Balance b/d	60,000		

The new asset is recorded in the non-current asset account at cost £(41,000 + 19,000) = £60,000.

MACHINERY ACCUMULATED DEPRECIATION

	£		£
Disposals (20% of £30,000 for 2 years)	12,000	Balance b/d	12,000

DISPOSALS

	£		£
Cost	30,000	Accumulated depreciation	12,000
Income statement (profit on sale)	1,000	Cost – part-exchange value	19,000
	31,000		31,000

Interactive question 6: Non-current asset ledger accounts

[Difficulty level: Exam standard]

A business purchased two machines on 1 January 20X5 at a cost of £15,000 each. Each had an estimated life of five years and a nil residual value. The straight line method of depreciation is used.

Owing to an unforeseen slump in market demand for its end product, the business decided to reduce its output, and switch to making other products instead. On 31 March 20X7, one machine was sold (on credit) to a buyer for £8,000.

Later in the reporting period, however, it was decided to abandon production altogether, and the second machine was sold on 1 December 20X7 for £2,500 cash.

Prepare the machinery account, accumulated depreciation of machinery account and disposal account for the 12 month reporting period to 31 December 20X7 to determine the profit or loss on disposal of each machine.

See **Answer** at the end of this chapter.

5.4 Accounting for non-current assets on the ETB

Earlier we saw how depreciation is accounted for on the ETB. We can now draw together a comprehensive example of entries on the ETB in respect of non-current assets, made after the extraction of an initial trial balance.

Worked example: Non-current assets on the ETB

Rodrigo's initial trial balance as at 31 December 20X0 is as follows.

Ledger balance	Trial balance	
	Debit £	Credit £
Current assets	87,420	
Capital at 1.1.X0		100,000
Freehold land and buildings – cost at 1.1.X0	100,000	
Freehold land and buildings – accumulated depreciation at 1.1.X0		15,000
Plant and equipment – cost at 1.1.X0	45,000	
Plant and equipment – accumulated depreciation at 1.1.X0		18,750
Motor vehicles – cost at 1.1.X0	25,000	
Motor vehicles – accumulated depreciation at 1.1.X0		14,650
Current liabilities		15,420
Expenses	5,830	
Purchases	58,740	
Sales		205,640
Drawings	47,670	
Suspense		200
	369,660	369,660

The following matters have now been discovered:

(a) On 1 January 20X0 Rodrigo disposed of an item of plant that had cost £10,000 and on which £1,250 depreciation had been charged. He received a cheque for £7,950. The only accounting entry made was to debit cash.

(b) On 1 January 20X0 he also traded in a car that had cost £8,000 and on which £4,500 depreciation had been charged for a new car costing £13,300. He handed over a cheque in addition for £7,750. The only entry with regard to this transaction was in the cash book.

(c) With regard to the assets held at 31 December 20X0, depreciation on the freehold building of £5,000, on plant and equipment of £5,290, and on motor vehicles of £6,900, is to be charged.

Requirement

Prepare Rodrigo's year-end journals as at 31 December 20X0 in respect of these matters, and complete the ETB.

Solution

(a)

		£	£
DEBIT	Suspense	7,950	
CREDIT	Disposal – plant		7,950
DEBIT	Plant and equipment – accumulated depreciation	1,250	
	Disposal – plant (carrying amount)	8,750	
CREDIT	Plant and equipment – cost		10,000

Being the correct recording of cash received on disposal of plant, and the removal of the asset's cost and accumulated depreciation

(b)

		£	£
DEBIT	Motor vehicles – cost	13,300	
CREDIT	Suspense		7,750
	Disposal – car given in part exchange (13,300 – 7,750)		5,550

Being the correct recording of purchase of a new car for £13,300

		£	£
DEBIT	Motor vehicles – accumulated depreciation	4,500	
	Disposal – car given in part exchange (carrying amount)	3,500	
CREDIT	Motor vehicles – cost		8,000

Being the removal of the cost and accumulated depreciation in relation to a car, given in part exchange for a new one

(c)

		£	£
DEBIT	Expenses (depreciation)	17,190	
CREDIT	Freehold land and buildings – accumulated depreciation		5,000
	Plant and equipment – accumulated depreciation		5,290
	Motor vehicles – accumulated depreciation		6,900

Being the depreciation charge for the reporting period

Ledger balance	Trial balance		Adjustments		Income statement		Statement of financial position	
	Debit	Credit	Debit	Credit	Debit	Credit	Debit	Credit
	£	£	£	£	£	£	£	£
Current assets	87,420						87,420	
Capital at 1.1.X0		100,000						100,000
Freehold land and buildings – cost	100,000						100,000	
Freehold land and buildings – accumulated depreciation		15,000		5,000				20,000
Plant and equipment – cost	45,000			10,000			35,000	
Plant and equipment – accumulated depreciation		18,750	1,250	5,290				22,790
Motor vehicles – cost	25,000		13,300	8,000			30,300	
Motor vehicles – accumulated depreciation		14,650	4,500	6,900				17,050
Current liabilities		15,420						15,420
Expenses	5,830		17,190		23,020			
Purchases	58,740				58,740			
Sales		205,640				205,640		
Drawings	47,670						47,670	
Suspense		200	7,950	7,750				
Disposal – plant			8,750	7,950	800			
Disposal – car			3,500	5,550		2,050		
Net profit					125,130			125,130
	369,660	369,660	56,440	56,440	207,690	207,690	300,390	300,390

6 The asset register

Section overview

- The asset register lists out all the details of each non-current asset. Its tables should reconcile to the ledger account for non-current assets in the nominal ledger.

Definition

Asset register: A listing of all non-current assets owned by the organisation, broken down by department, location or asset type, and containing non-financial information (such as chassis numbers and security codes) as well as financial information.

An asset register is maintained primarily for internal control purposes. It shows an organisation's investment in capital equipment in financial terms, and allows the business to trace from its ledger accounts for non-current assets to individual assets.

6.1 Data kept in an asset register

Details about **each non-current** asset include the following.

- The internal reference number (for physical identification purposes)
- Manufacturer's serial number (for maintenance purposes)
- Description of asset
- Location of asset
- Department which uses the asset
- Purchase date (for calculation of depreciation)
- Cost, and any enhancement expenditure
- Depreciation method and estimated useful life (for calculation of depreciation)
- Carrying amount

It is good practice to 'reconcile' or agree the net carrying amounts of all the assets on the asset register with the net carrying amount of non-current assets recorded in the nominal ledger:

	£
Assets at cost (from the non-current asset cost ledger account)	X
Accumulated depreciation (from the ledger account)	(X)
Total of carrying amounts listed in the asset register	X

Any difference should be investigated and corrected. These usually arise from computational errors or from items being taken out of the asset register with no equivalent change being made in ledger accounts, or *vice versa*, for instance because:

- Assets have been stolen, damaged or scrapped (for nil proceeds)
- Assets are obsolete
- There are new assets, not yet recorded in the register
- There have been enhancements not yet recorded in the register
- There are errors in the register

7 Intangible non-current assets

Section overview

- Purchased goodwill may appear as an asset in a company's statement of financial position. It represents the amount paid for a business in excess of what its net assets are worth.

- Some development costs are capitalised on the statement of financial position.

- Intangible non-current assets should be subject to reviews for impairment of their value.

Not all assets held for the long term can be touched; some are **intangible**.

7.1 Goodwill

If a business has **goodwill** it means that the value of the business as a going concern is greater than the book value of its assets less its liabilities.

Goodwill is created by good relationships between a business and its customers, for example:

- By building up a **reputation** (by word of mouth perhaps) for high quality products or high standards of service

- By responding promptly and helpfully to queries and complaints from **customers**

- Through the **personality** of the staff, their **attitudes** to customers and their **skills**

Although the value of goodwill to a business might be extremely significant it **is not usually valued** in the financial statements.

For example, the welcoming smiles of shop staff may contribute more to a supermarket's profits than the fact that a new electronic cash register has recently been acquired; even so, whereas the cash register will be recorded in the ledger accounts as a non-current asset, the value of staff would be ignored for accounting purposes.

- Goodwill is inherent in the business but it has not been directly paid for, so **valuation** is difficult.

- Goodwill changes from day to day. One act of bad customer relations might damage goodwill and one act of good relations might improve it. Staff with a favourable personality might retire or leave, to be replaced by staff who need time to become established. Since goodwill is continually changing in value, it cannot **reliably** be recorded in the accounts.

7.2 Purchased goodwill

The exception to the general rule that goodwill has no objective valuation arises when an existing business is purchased. The buyer has to pay for not only its non-current assets and inventories (and perhaps take over its payables and receivables too) but also for its goodwill. This is why the **purchase consideration** for most businesses is **more than the value of their net assets**.

Worked example: Goodwill

Tony Tycoon purchases Clive Dunwell's business for £30,000. Clive's business has total assets less liabilities of £25,000, all of which are taken over by Tony. Tony will be paying (£30,000 – £25,000) = £5,000 **more** for the business than its net assets are worth, because he is purchasing the **goodwill** of the business too. The statement of financial position of Tony's business when it begins operations (assuming that he does not change the value of what he has acquired) will be as follows:

TONY TYCOON
STATEMENT OF FINANCIAL POSITION AS AT THE START OF BUSINESS

	£
Intangible non-current asset: goodwill	5,000
Other net assets acquired	25,000
Net assets	30,000
Capital	30,000

Purchased goodwill is shown in this statement of financial position because it has been directly paid for. It has no tangible substance, and so it is an **intangible non-current asset**.

Definition

Purchased goodwill: The excess of the purchase consideration paid for a business over the fair value of the individual assets and liabilities acquired.

7.3 Accounting for purchased goodwill

Purchased goodwill is a premium paid for the acquisition of a business as a going concern: it is often referred to as a 'premium on acquisition'. A purchaser pays such a premium because they believe that the true value of the business includes goodwill, which has value in addition to its tangible net assets.

Goodwill continually changes. A business cannot last forever on its past reputation; it must create new goodwill as time goes on.

If the goodwill loses some or all of its value, it is deemed to have become 'impaired'. Its value in the statement of financial position is then written down by the amount of the impairment and the **impairment loss** is charged against the profit of the period.

Goodwill should be treated as an **intangible non-current asset**. It is kept at cost in the statement of financial position subject to an **annual review for impairment**. It is **not** depreciated.

7.4 How is the value of purchased goodwill decided?

The value of the goodwill is a matter for the purchaser and seller to agree upon in fixing the purchase consideration. However, two methods of valuation are worth mentioning here.

(a) The seller and buyer agree on a price without specifically quantifying the goodwill. The purchased goodwill will then be the difference between the price agreed and the value of the net assets in the books of the **new business**.

(b) The calculation of goodwill may precede fixing the purchase consideration and may become a central element of negotiation. There are many ways of arriving at a value for goodwill and most of them are related to the profit record of the business in question. For instance, they may agree to value goodwill as 2 × profit of the previous reporting period, or a similar calculation.

Goodwill shown by the purchaser in their accounts will be the difference between the purchase consideration and **their own valuation** of the tangible net assets acquired. If A values his tangible net assets at £40,000 and goodwill is agreed at £21,000 then B agrees to pay £61,000 for the business. When setting up accounts for the asset acquired, B may value the tangible net assets at only £38,000, so the goodwill in B's books will be £61,000 – £38,000 = £23,000.

We shall come back to goodwill in Chapter 13.

Interactive question 7: Goodwill [Difficulty level: Intermediate]

Toad goes into business with £10,000 capital and agrees to buy Thrush's shop for £6,500. Thrush's recent financial statements show total assets less liabilities of £3,500, which Toad values at £4,000.

Requirement

Prepare the statement of financial position of Toad's business at the following times.

(a) Before he purchases Thrush's business
(b) After the purchase

See **Answer** at the end of this chapter.

7.5 Development costs

Large companies spend significant amounts of money on development activities from which they hope to generate revenues in future periods. These amounts are credited to cash or payables and debited to an account for development expenditure. The accounting problem is **how to treat the debit balance on the development cost account** at the date of the statement of financial position.

There are two possibilities.

- The debit balance may be classified as an **expense** and transferred to the income statement. This is referred to as '**writing off**' the expenditure. The argument here is that it is an expense just like rent or wages and its accounting treatment should be the same.

- The debit balance may be classified as an **asset** and included in the statement of financial position. This is referred to as 'capitalising' or 'carrying forward' or 'deferring' the expenditure. This argument is based on the **accrual principle**. If development activity eventually leads to new or improved products which generate income, the costs should be carried forward to be matched against that income in future reporting periods.

  When development expenditure is carried forward as an asset the accounting entries are:

DEBIT	Non-current assets	£X	
CREDIT	Cash/payables		£X

The cost of this non-current asset will need to be allocated to the income statement as it is matched against the income it helps to generate. This process is essentially the same as for depreciation of tangible non-current assets, but it is called **amortisation**.

7.6 Other intangible assets

A business may have other types of intangible asset:

- **Patents** on ideas or designs that the business has developed or bought. These are used to generate income over many reporting periods. They are valued at cost and are subject to amortisation in line with the business's policy, and to regular impairment reviews, which may result in an impairment loss.

- **Investments held for the long term**. The valuation of these falls outside the scope of the *Accounting* syllabus.

8 The non-current assets note to the statement of financial position

Section overview

- The non-current assets note to the statement of financial position provides the details behind the single figure for tangible non-current assets in the statement of financial position.

There is usually a detailed note to the financial statements in respect of **property, plant and equipment**, with just the summarised figure in the statement of financial position. For each class of property, plant and equipment the note shows:

- Cost and accumulated depreciation brought forward
- Additions during the reporting period
- Disposals during the reporting period, and the related accumulated depreciation
- Depreciation charge for the reporting period
- Closing balance carried forward

Note that disposal proceeds, and gains/losses on disposal, do **not** appear in the non-current assets note.

Worked example: The non-current assets note

We prepared Rodrigo's ETB earlier in this chapter. We can now prepare his non-current assets (property, plant and equipment) note from his ETB as follows:

	Freehold land and buildings £	Plant and equipment £	Motor vehicles £	Total £
Cost				
At 1.1.X0	100,000	45,000	25,000	170,000
Additions			13,300	13,300
Disposals		(10,000)	(8,000)	(18,000)
At 31.12.X0	100,000	35,000	30,300	165,300
Accumulated depreciation				
At 1.1.X0	15,000	18,750	14,650	48,400
Charge for the reporting period	5,000	5,290	6,900	17,190
Disposals		(1,250)	(4,500)	(5,750)
At 31.12.X0	20,000	22,790	17,050	59,840
Carrying amount				
At 1.1.X0	85,000	26,250	10,350	121,600
At 31.12.X0	80,000	12,210	13,250	105,460

On Rodrigo's statement of financial position at 31 December 20X0 there will just be a single figure, for 'Property, plant and equipment', of £105,460.

Summary (1/2)

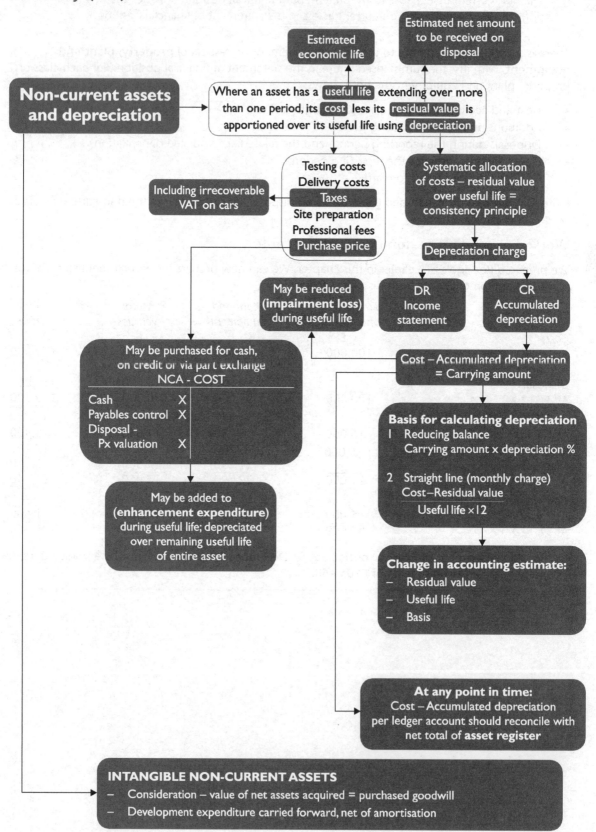

Non-current assets and depreciation

Where an asset has a useful life extending over more than one period, its cost less its residual value is apportioned over its useful life using depreciation

Estimated economic life

Estimated net amount to be received on disposal

Testing costs
Delivery costs
Taxes
Site preparation
Professional fees
Purchase price

Including irrecoverable VAT on cars

Systematic allocation of costs – residual value over useful life = consistency principle

Depreciation charge

DR
Income statement

CR
Accumulated depreciation

May be reduced (impairment loss) during useful life

Cost – Accumulated depreciation = Carrying amount

May be purchased for cash, on credit or via part exchange
NCA - COST

Cash	X	
Payables control	X	
Disposal -		
Px valuation	X	

May be added to (enhancement expenditure) during useful life; depreciated over remaining useful life of entire asset

Basis for calculating depreciation
1 Reducing balance
   Carrying amount x depreciation %

2 Straight line (monthly charge)
   $\dfrac{Cost - Residual\ value}{Useful\ life} \times 12$

Change in accounting estimate:
– Residual value
– Useful life
– Basis

At any point in time:
Cost – Accumulated depreciation per ledger account should reconcile with net total of **asset register**

INTANGIBLE NON-CURRENT ASSETS
– Consideration – value of net assets acquired = purchased goodwill
– Development expenditure carried forward, net of amortisation

Summary (2/2)

Accounting for non-current assets

1 Acquire asset

DR	Cost	X	
CR	Cash/payables/disposal		X

2 Depreciate asset

DR	Depreciation charge	X	
CR	Accumulated depreciation		X

3 Dispose of asset

DISPOSAL

Cost	X	Accumulated depreciation	X
		Cash/payables/ Px valuation	X
IS (profit)	X	IS (loss)	X
	X		X

NON-CURRENT ASSETS (PPE) NOTE TO STATEMENT OF FINANCIAL POSITION

	Land and buildings £	Plant and equipment £	Motor vehicles £	Total £
Cost				
B/d	X	X	X	X
Additions	X	X	X	X
Disposals	(X)	(X)	(X)	(X)
C/d	X	X	X	X
Accumulated depreciation				
B/d	X	X	X	X
Charge for year	X	X	X	X
Disposals	(X)	(X)	(X)	(X)
C/d	X	X	X	X
Carrying amount				
B/d	X	X	X	X
C/d	X	X	X	X

Self-test

Answer the following questions.

1   Materials purchased and used by P & Co for repairs to office buildings have been included in the draft financial statements as purchases.

The necessary amendment will

A   Increase gross profit with no effect on net profit
B   Increase gross profit and reduce net profit
C   Have no effect on either gross profit or net profit
D   Reduce gross profit and increase net profit

2   Marcellus acquired new premises at a cost of £250,000 on 1 January 20X1. Marcellus paid the following further costs during the year ended 31 December 20X1.

	£
Costs of initial adaptation	13,900
Legal costs relating to purchase	1,200
Monthly cleaning contract	9,600
Office furniture	6,500

What amount should appear as the cost of premises in the company's statement of financial position at 31 December 20X1?

A   £250,000
B   £263,900
C   £265,100
D   £271,600

3   Why is depreciation provided on non-current assets?

A   To ensure that sufficient funds are available to replace the assets
B   To show the assets at replacement cost on the statement of financial position
C   To spread the cost of the assets over their useful lives
D   To show the fall in market value of the assets in the income statement

4   ABC, whose reporting period is the 12 months ended 31 December, has provided depreciation monthly at the rate of 10% per annum on cost on a piece of plant bought on 1 September 20X0 costing £15,000. The depreciation method was changed from straight line to 10% reducing balance at the end of 20X3.

The depreciation charge on this asset for 20X5 was

A   £1,500
B   £945
C   £900
D   £889

5   A business with a reporting period of the 12 months ended 30 June buys a non-current asset on 1 July 20X3 for £200,000. Depreciation is charged at 15% per annum on the reducing balance basis. On 30 June 20X5 the asset was sold for £54,800.

What was the loss on sale of the asset?

A   £89,700
B   £85,200
C   £68,025
D   £55,200

6   In the year ended 31 December 20X7 B traded in for £6,860 a vehicle costing £12,000 on 1
     November 20X5 against the cost (£9,600) of a replacement vehicle. The balance due for the new
     vehicle has been paid in cash and debited to the cost of vehicles account, no other entries relating
     to the transaction having been made.

     What net adjustment is required to the company's cost of vehicles account as a result of this
     transaction?

     A   £9,600 DR
     B   £12,000 CR
     C   £6,800 DR
     D   £5,140 CR

7   A business acquired a car on 1 October 20X5 for £117,000 and has depreciated it on a reducing
     balance basis at 20% per annum. On 30 September 20X7 the car was sold for £58,000.

     What is the loss on disposal of the car in the financial statements for the 12 month reporting period
     to 30 September 20X7?

     A   £14,560
     B   £14,800
     C   £16,880
     D   £29,360

8   A business buys a machine on 1 January 20X1 for £10,000 and depreciates it at 10% per annum
     straight line. At the end of 20X2 the machine's remaining useful life is reassessed at six years
     remaining and it is now believed that the machine has a residual value of £500.

     What is the depreciation charge for the third year of the machine's use?

     A   £950
     B   £1,250
     C   £1,267
     D   £1,350

9   The following information relates to the disposal of two machines by Paddock.

     | | Machine 1 | Machine 2 |
	£	£
Cost	120,000	140,000
Disposal proceeds	90,000	80,000
Profit/(loss) on disposal	30,000	(40,000)

     What was the total carrying amount of both machines sold at the date of disposal?

     A   £100,000
     B   £160,000
     C   £180,000
     D   £240,000

10   On 1 June 20X1 Quandry bought a non-current asset for £50,000 which had an estimated useful
     life of 10 years and a residual value of £2,000. Quandry depreciates its non-current assets on a
     straight line basis. Quandry's reporting period is the 12 months ended 31 December.

     On 1 January 20X4 the asset's remaining useful life is revised to eight years from that date with no
     residual value. An impairment review at that date shows that the recoverable amount of the asset is
     considered to be only £25,000.

     What is the total depreciation and impairment loss charge for this asset in 20X4?

     A   £3,125
     B   £12,400
     C   £15,725
     D   £18,000

     Now, go back to the Learning Objectives in the Introduction. If you are satisfied that you have achieved
     these objectives, please tick them off.

Answer to Interactive question 1

	£
Cost	18,720
Less Estimated residual value	(6,360)
Total amount to be depreciated	12,360

The deposit represents part of the payment for the new vehicle and is not relevant in calculating the depreciable amount of the new car.

Answer to Interactive question 2

(a) Under the straight line method, depreciation for each of the five years is:

$$\text{Annual depreciation} = \frac{£(17,000 - 2,000)}{5} = £3,000$$

Remember that VAT on lorries is recoverable; it is only in respect of cars that it is irrecoverable.

(b) Under the reducing balance method, depreciation for each of the five years is as follows:

Year	Depreciation		£
1	35% × £17,000	=	5,950
2	35% × (£17,000 – £5,950) = 35% × £11,050	=	3,868
3	35% × (£11,050 – £3,868) = 35% × £7,182	=	2,514
4	35% × (£7,182 – £2,514) = 35% × £4,668	=	1,634
5	35% × (£4,668 – £1,634) = 35% × £3,034	=	1,062

Answer to Interactive question 3

$$\text{New annual charge from 20X4} = \frac{£65,610}{5 \text{ years}} = £13,122 \text{ per annum}$$

Answer to Interactive question 4

	Year 1 £	Year 2 £	Year 3 £
Cost	1,000	1,000	1,000
Accumulated depreciation	(80)	(160)	(265)
Carrying amount	920	840	735
Charge for the year (W)	80	80	105

WORKING

	Year 1	Year 2	Year 3
	$\dfrac{1,000 - 200}{10}$	$\dfrac{1,000 - 200}{10}$	$\dfrac{840}{8}$

Answer to Interactive question 5

(a) Revised annual depreciation charge

Revised annual charge $= \dfrac{\text{Carrying amount at revision} - \text{Residual value}}{\text{Revised remaining life}}$

$= \dfrac{£102,000}{15}$

$= \underline{£6,800}$ per annum

(b) Impairment loss and revised annual depreciation charge

		£
31 December 20X4		
Impairment loss (102,000 – 95,000)		7,000
Annual charge $\dfrac{£95,000}{10}$		9,500
Total income statement charge in 20X4	$=$	16,500

Answer to Interactive question 6

MACHINERY ACCOUNT

		£			£
20X7			*20X7*		
1 Jan	Balance b/d (2 × £15,000)	30,000	31 Mar	Disposal of machinery account	15,000
			1 Dec	Disposal of machinery account	15,000
		30,000			30,000

MACHINERY – ACCUMULATED DEPRECIATION

		£			£
20X7			*20X7*		
31 Mar	Disposal account (W1)	6,750			
			1 Jan	Balance b/d (24 × $\dfrac{30,000}{5 \times 12}$)	12,000
1 Dec	Disposal account (W2)	8,750	31 Mar	Charge to disposal $\dfrac{15,000}{60} \times 3$	750
			1 Dec	Charge to disposal $\dfrac{15,000}{60} \times 11$	2,750
		15,500			15,500

WORKING

1 Depreciation at date of disposal = (15,000/60) × 27 = £6,750
2 Depreciation at date of disposal = (15,000/60) × 35 = £8,750

DISPOSAL ACCOUNT

		£			£
20X7			*20X7*		
31 Mar	Machinery	15,000	31 Mar	Receivables (proceeds)	8,000
			31 Mar	Accumulated depreciation	6,750
			31 Mar	Loss on disposal	250
1 Dec	Machinery	15,000	1 Dec	Cash (proceeds)	2,500
			1 Dec	Accumulated depreciation	8,750
			31 Dec	Loss on disposal	3,750
		30,000			30,000

Answer to Interactive question 7

(a) Toad's statement of financial position before the purchase is:

	£
Cash	10,000
Capital	10,000

(b) Thrush's valuation of the assets to be acquired is irrelevant to Toad, who sees the situation thus:

	£
Consideration (cash to be paid)	6,500
Less total assets less liabilities acquired (at Toad's valuation)	(4,000)
Difference (purchased goodwill)	2,500

Toad must put through the following journal on acquisition, opening up a goodwill ledger account.

		£	£
DEBIT	Assets/liabilities (shop)	4,000	
DEBIT	Goodwill	2,500	
CREDIT	Cash		6,500

Toad's statement of financial position immediately after the purchase is therefore:

	£
Goodwill	2,500
Assets/liabilities acquired in shop	4,000
Cash (£10,000 – £6,500)	3,500
	10,000
Capital	10,000

(Normally one would have more detail as to the breakdown of the assets and liabilities, but this is not relevant here. The main point is that the assets/liabilities acquired are tangible whereas the goodwill is not.)

This question highlights the difference between 'internally generated' goodwill, which (as in Thrush's case above) is not shown in the books and 'purchased' goodwill, which is. The purchased goodwill in this case is simply Thrush's internally generated goodwill, which has changed hands, bought by Toad at the consideration shown in Toad's accounts.

1   A   To correct reduce purchases (increase to GP and NP), increase repairs (decrease NP, no effect on GP).

         The decrease and increase to NP cancel out. Overall effect on GP is an increase.

2   C

	£
Purchase price	250,000
Adaptation	13,900
Legal costs	1,200
	265,100

3   C   Depreciation spreads (cost – residual value) over useful life

4   C

	£
Cost	15,000
Accumulated depreciation to 31 December 20X3 ($\frac{15,000}{120} \times 40$)	(5,000)
Carrying amount at date of change	10,000
Depreciation for 20X4 (10,000 × 10%)	(1,000)
	9,000
Depreciation for 20X5 @ 10%	900

5   A

	£
Cost 1 July 20X3	200,000
Depreciation to 30 June 20X4	(30,000)
	170,000
Depreciation to 30 June 20X5	(25,500)
	144,500
Less Proceeds	(54,800)
Loss on sale	89,700

6   D

	£	
Debit with trade in allowance (to get to total cost of new vehicle of £9,600)	6,860	DR
Credit with cost of old vehicle (to remove cost of old vehicle)	(12,000)	CR
Net adjustment	(5,140)	CR

7   C

	£
Cost 1 October 20X5	117,000
Depreciation to 30 September 20X6	(23,400)
	93,600
Depreciation to 30 September 20X7	(18,720)
	74,880
Loss on sale (58,000 – 74,880)	16,880

8 B

		£
Cost		10,000
Depreciation	20X1 (10% × 10,000)	(1,000)
		9,000
	20X2 (10% × 10,000)	(1,000)
Carrying amount at end 20X2		8,000
Depreciation charge for 20X3 ($\frac{8,000 - 500}{6}$)		1,250

9 C

	Machine 1 £	Machine 2 £	Total £
Disposal proceeds	90,000	80,000	
Carrying amount (β)	(60,000)	(120,000)	(180,000)
Profit/(loss) on disposal	30,000	(40,000)	

10 C

	£
Cost	50,000
Accumulated depreciation to 31 December 20X3 $\frac{50,000 - 2,000}{120} \times 31$	(12,400)
Carrying amount at 31 December 20X3	37,600
Impairment loss (37,600 – 25,000)	12,600
Annual charge (25,000 ÷ 8)	3,125
	15,725

CHAPTER 11

Company financial statements

Introduction

Examination context

Topic List

1   The nature of a limited company

2   Equity: share capital

3   Equity: retained earnings and other reserves

4   Rights issues and bonus issues of shares

5   Non-current liabilities (debt capital)

6   Provisions

7   Tax

8   The regulatory framework for company financial statements

9   The income statement (IAS 1 (revised))

10 The statement of financial position (IAS 1 (revised))

11 Applying the IAS 1 (revised) formats

Summary and Self-test

Technical reference

Answers to Interactive questions

Answers to Self-test

Learning objectives

Tick off

- Record and account for transactions and events resulting in income, expenses, assets, liabilities and equity in accordance with the appropriate basis of accounting and the laws, regulations and accounting standards applicable to the financial statements

☐

- Record and account for changes in the ownership structure and ownership interests in an entity

☐

- Prepare an extended trial balance

☐

- Identify the main components of a set of financial statements and specify their purpose and interrelationship

☐

- Prepare and present a statement of financial position, income statement and statement of cash flows (or extracts therefrom) from the accounting records and trial balance in a format which satisfies the information requirements of the entity

☐

Specific syllabus learning outcomes are: 1c, d, 2c, 3a, c

Syllabus links

The material in this chapter will be developed further in this paper, and then in the Financial Accounting and Financial Reporting papers later in the Professional stage.

Examination context

Questions on the topics in this chapter will be multiple choice questions, which may involve calculations so that the correct answer can be selected. Very often double entry questions are phrased in terms of preparing a journal.

In the exam you may be required to:

- Specify the unique features of company financial statements: equity (share capital and reserves), provisions and tax

- Specify the distinctions between equity shares, and redeemable and irredeemable preference shares

- Identify how to account for issues of shares

- Identify how loans should be split into their current and non-current liability categories for the statement of financial position

- Identify how to account for tax, including under-provisions and over-provisions

- Identify how expenses should be categorised into cost of sales, administrative expenses, distribution costs and finance costs

- Specify the requirements of IAS 1 (revised) in relation to company financial statements

1 The nature of a limited company

Section overview

- Companies are legally separate from their owners, so the presentation of owners' capital is particularly important.

- A company's initial capital is divided into shares which have a par or 'nominal' value, and an issue value that can exceed that amount.

- A private company may not issue securities (shares and loan stock) to the public at large. A public company may do so, either through a public listing or otherwise.

- Particular features of company accounting relate to: owners' capital (equity); debt capital; provisions; tax.

Limited companies are the most common form of private sector business organisation. Businesses that are not limited companies tend to be small in size, or provide specialised professional services, such as firms of accountants or solicitors.

A company has a **separate legal existence**, independent of its owner(s). It can enter contracts in its own name, it can sue or be sued, and it is liable to the tax authorities for tax on the profits that it earns. The profits available to the owners of a company are profits **after** deducting taxation.

Because a company has this legal identity, separate from its owners, the way it raises capital from its owners, and is accountable to its owners for the capital that it holds, is more formalised than for sole traders or partnerships.

1.1 Share capital and shareholders

A company's **initial capital** is divided into units of equal size, known as **shares**, issued to individuals or companies, called **shareholders**. The total capital raised is referred to as **equity share capital**.

Ownership of a share entitles the shareholder to receive payment of a share of profit, or **dividend**.

By law, shares must have a **par value** (the Companies Act 2006 calls this the 'nominal value'), which can be any amount, for example 1p, 5p, 10p, 25p, 50p, £1 and so on. However, all shares of the same type ('class') have the same par value. For example, £100,000 par value of share capital might be represented by 100,000 shares of £1 each, or 200,000 shares of 50p each, or 1,000,000 shares of 10p each, and so on. It is possible to have differing classes of share which carry different rights for their owners.

The par value of shares will rarely bear any relationship to either:

- The **issue price** at which the share was originally issued by the company, to raise capital; or

- The **current market value** of the share if the shares of the company are traded on a stock market.

The original **issue price of a share matters to a company** because it is the amount of cash raised for each share issued. A company will often issue shares at above ('at a premium to') par value. For example, a company with shares of £1 might issue shares at £1.50 per share when the company is first incorporated, then make a further issue of shares some years later at, say, £2 each, and then a further issue some time after that at, say, £3.50 each.

The **current market value of a share** has no bearing on company financial statements at all, because this is the price at which an existing shareholding is sold by one person (not the company) to another person (not the company). Such transactions do not give rise to anything that has to be recorded in the company's accounting records.

1.2 Public and private companies

Companies are either public or private companies.

- A **public company** has 'plc' in its name. A public company may offer its securities (shares and loan stock such as bonds) for sale to persons who are unrelated to the company ('the public'), but is subject to stricter regulation than private companies. In particular, a public company must have issued capital of at least £50,000. Before it can trade, at least £12,500 plus the whole of any premium on issue must have been received as cash. Effectively this means that a public limited company must have net assets (assets less liabilities) of at least £12,500. Note that all companies whose shares are traded on a stock market must be 'plcs', but not all plcs have their shares traded on a stock market.

- A **private company** ends its name with 'Limited' or 'Ltd'. A private company is any company that is not a public company. Private companies cannot offer their securities for sale to the public at large. There is no minimum level of net assets.

1.3 Accounting for companies

Companies have distinctive characteristics to be accounted for. The following are examinable in *Accounting*:

- Equity (owners' capital comprising share capital, retained earnings and other reserves), rights issues and bonus issues

- Forms of debt capital (non-current liabilities)

- Provisions

- Tax on profits

Note that accounting for dividends is no longer examinable in *Accounting*.

2 Equity: share capital

Section overview

- Share capital can be split into:
  - Equity shares (no entitlement to a set amount of dividend)
  - Irredeemable preference shares (set entitlement to dividends)

- Redeemable preference shares are entitled to a set amount of dividend but are treated as non-current liabilities (debt capital).

- The figure for called-up share capital at par value appears on the statement of financial position. This may be less than the figure for issued share capital. If an amount of called-up capital is unpaid, this is treated as an 'other receivable'.

- Of the issue price, any excess or 'premium' received over par value is credited to share premium (a reserve or 'other component of equity').

2.1 Equity shares and preference shares

Companies often have just one class of share, ordinary shares, which are referred to in the Companies Act 2006 as '**equity share capital**' because each share represents an equal interest in the ownership of the company. (Occasionally, a company might have two classes of equity or ordinary share, usually known as 'A ordinary' and 'B ordinary' shares. Most public companies in the UK, however, have just one class of equity share.)

A company might also issue **preference shares**, which entitle their holders to a dividend out of profits (preference dividend) **before** equity shareholders are entitled to any equity dividend.

Once the preference dividend has been paid, the remaining profit 'belongs' to the equity shareholders. However, the directors will usually decide to retain some profits (**retained earnings**) within the company, and the equity dividend will be an amount declared by the directors as being appropriate and affordable.

Accounting for dividends of any kind is outside the scope of the *Accounting* syllabus.

2.2 Issued and called-up share capital

The **issued share capital** of a company (also known as its **allotted share capital**) is the par value of the shares that have actually been issued to shareholders.

If a company issues shares but 'calls up' the issue amounts in instalments, instead of raising cash immediately, it then has **called-up share capital** that is less than its issued share capital.

Worked example: Called-up share capital

A company issues 100,000 shares of £1 at par value, but only calls up 75p per share as a first instalment. The issued share capital is £100,000, but the called-up share capital is only £75,000. The figure in the statement of financial position will be £75,000.

In a company's statement of financial position, the figure for share capital is the called-up share capital.

On the face of the company's statement of financial position, or in a note, called-up equity share capital and irredeemable preference share capital at par value are shown separately.

STATEMENT OF FINANCIAL POSITION (EXTRACT)

	£'000
Equity	
Share capital: equity shares of 50p each (81.5m shares)	40,750
Share capital: 6% irredeemable preference shares of £1 (9m shares)	9,000
	49,750

If a company has called-up share capital, but is waiting for payment from some shareholders, it has **paid up capital** of less than its called-up capital.

Worked example: Paid up capital

A company issues one million shares of £1 at par, and asks for payment in full on issue, but it is still owed £5,000 by shareholders who have yet to pay what they owe. The called-up share capital is £1,000,000, but the paid up share capital is only £995,000. In the statement of financial position, the **share capital** (a credit balance) is the called-up share capital of £1,000,000, and the unpaid capital of £5,000 is shown as an '**other receivable**' (a debit balance).

2.3 Irredeemable and redeemable preference shares

- Only preference shares which the company is not entitled to buy back or redeem at some stage in the future, known as **irredeemable preference shares**, are treated as **share capital**.

- Preference shares which the company is entitled to buy back from its shareholders or 'redeem' at some future time are called **redeemable preference shares**, treated as **non-current liabilities (debt capital)**.

In an exam question it will be specified whether preference shares are redeemable or irredeemable.

2.4 Accounting for share capital

- When shares are issued at their **par value** and they are **fully paid**:

		£	£
DEBIT	Cash	X	
CREDIT	Share capital (par value)		X

- When shares are issued at a **premium to their par value**, and the full amount is paid:

		£	£
DEBIT	Cash	X	
CREDIT	Share capital (par value)		X
	Share premium (excess over par value)		X

- When shares are issued at their par value but an amount remains **uncalled** by the company

		£	£
DEBIT	Cash	X	
CREDIT	Share capital (called-up amount of issued shares)		X

- When shares are issued and called-up at their par value but an amount remains **unpaid**:

		£	£
DEBIT	Cash	X	
	Other receivables (unpaid capital)	X	
CREDIT	Share capital (par value)		X

3 Equity: retained earnings and other reserves

Section overview

- Retained earnings: built up with each reporting period's profits, depleted by dividends and losses. Amounts may also be transferred to or from other reserves, or reclassified as share capital in a bonus issue.

- Share premium: set up with premium over par value of issued share capital (equity and irredeemable preference shares). The account may be reduced by a bonus issue.

- General reserve: created by a transfer from retained earnings.

Share capital is shown in the statement of financial position at its called-up value. Any other amounts attributable to owners (equity shareholders) are shown separately as **reserves** (referred to in IAS 1 (revised) as either 'retained earnings' or 'other components of equity').

A company might have a number of different reserves, each set up for a different purpose, including the following which are examinable in *Accounting*:

- Retained earnings
- Share premium
- General reserve

3.1 Retained earnings

Definition

Retained earnings: A reserve used to accumulate the company's retained earnings.

Retained earnings comprise the income (profits and gains less losses) that the company retains within the business, ie income that has not been paid out as dividends or transferred to any other reserve.

The retained earnings ledger account would look like this (note that if there was a loss this would be debited to the ledger account):

RETAINED EARNINGS

	£		£
Dividends of the period	X	Balance b/d (opening statement of financial position)	X
Transfers to general reserve	X	Profit for the reporting period (from income statement)	X
Balance c/d (closing statement of financial position)	X		
	X		X

Dividends are shown here for information only; accounting for dividends is outside the scope of the *Accounting* syllabus.

We shall look at the transfer to general reserve shortly.

The balance carried down on the retained earnings ledger account represents the company's **accumulated profits and losses over time** out of which it may, if it wishes, pay dividends to its shareholders in the future.

3.2 Share premium

The Companies Act 2006 prohibits shares from being issued at a price below ('at a discount to') their par value. Commonly they are issued at a **price above par value**. When this happens, the excess of the issue price above the par value is added to a share premium reserve.

Worked example: Share premium

A company issues 1 million 50p equity shares at a price of £4.20 per share for cash.

The shares are issued at a premium of £3.70 (£4.20 – £0.50) above their par value, and the share issue should be recorded in the ledger accounts as follows.

		£	£
DEBIT:	Cash	4,200,000	
CREDIT:	Share capital: equity shares of 50p		500,000
	Share premium		3,700,000

There are tight legal restrictions on the use of the share premium reserve. **Dividends** cannot be paid out from it, but it may be reclassified as share capital via a **bonus issue**, as we shall see shortly.

3.3 General reserve

A company might hold retained earnings that it has no intention of distributing to owners as a dividend at any time in the future in a **general reserve** rather than in retained earnings. This is a decision that the company makes in line with its constitution. Unless there is a specific rule in the constitution, general reserves remain distributable as dividends.

A company might have other reserves in its financial statements. It is sufficient for you to know at this stage that such reserves might exist, without needing to know why and how they are used.

4 Rights issues and bonus issues of shares

Section overview

- A rights issue of shares is made to existing owners in proportion to their shareholdings.

- Amounts from retained earnings and share premium may be reclassified as share capital in a bonus issue:

		£	£
DR	Share premium	X	
	Retained earnings	X	
CR	Share capital		X

4.1 Rights issues of shares

Large share issues to raise new cash are often in the form of a rights issue.

Definition

Rights issue: New shares are offered to existing owners in proportion to their existing shareholding, usually at a discount to the current market price.

For example, a company with 20 million shares in issue decides to raise more cash by issuing 5 million new shares. It can offer the new shares to existing owners in a '1 for 4' rights issue: each existing owner is offered one new share for every four currently held (20 million/5 million = 4).

Interactive question 1: Rights issue   [Difficulty level: Exam standard]

The statement of financial position of Omnibus plc contains the following information.

ASSETS	£'000
Non-current assets	18,600
Current assets	2,900
Total assets	21,500

EQUITY AND LIABILITIES	
Equity	
Share capital: equity shares of 20p each	6,000
Share premium	5,700
Retained earnings	7,000
Total equity	18,700
Total liabilities	2,800
Total equity and liabilities	21,500

The company decides to make a 1 for 3 rights issue for cash, fully paid, at a price of £1.80 per share.

Requirement

What are the balances for (a) current assets, (b) share capital and (c) share premium after the rights issue?

See **Answer** at the end of this chapter.

4.2 Bonus issues of shares

Definition

Bonus issue (or **capitalisation issue** or **scrip issue**): An issue of fully paid shares to existing owners, free of charge, in proportion to their existing shareholdings.

A bonus issue does not involve any cash inflow for the company. The company converts some of its reserves (share premium **or** retained earnings **or** both) into new fully-paid share capital issued at its par value. The double entry for the **par value** of the bonus shares issued is:

DEBIT   Share premium OR retained earnings (OR both)
CREDIT   Share capital

The balance on share premium cannot (by law) be paid to owners as dividends. There are only a few transactions that can ever reduce share premium. One of these is a **bonus issue** of shares.

In an exam you should assume that a company uses the share premium account as fully as it can before using retained earnings, unless told otherwise.

Worked example: Bonus issue

A company has the following statement of financial position.

	£'000
ASSETS	30,000
EQUITY AND LIABILITIES	
Equity	
Share capital: equity shares of £1 each	5,000
Share premium	1,300
Retained earnings	9,700
Total equity	16,000
Total liabilities	14,000
Total equity and liabilities	30,000

The company decides to make a 2 for 5 bonus issue of shares.

The company is issuing (£5m/5 × 2) = 2,000,000 new shares of £1 each to its owners, in proportion to their existing shareholdings. It will:

		£	£
DEBIT	Share premium (total balance of the share premium reserve)	1,300,000	
DEBIT	Retained earnings (remainder)	700,000	
CREDIT	Share capital		2,000,000

The statement of financial position after the issue shows no change in assets or liabilities, but equity has changed, as follows.

	£'000
ASSETS	30,000
EQUITY AND LIABILITIES	
Equity	
Share capital: equity shares of £1 each (£5m + £2m)	7,000
Share premium (£1.3m – £1.3m)	0
Retained earnings (£9.7m – £0.7m)	9,000
Total equity	16,000
Total liabilities	14,000
Total equity and liabilities	30,000

Interactive question 2: Bonus issue   [Difficulty level: Intermediate]

The statement of financial position of Canvat plc at 31 December 20X1 is as follows:

	£'000
ASSETS	2,000
EQUITY AND LIABILITIES	
Equity	
Share capital: 800,000 50p equity shares	400
Share premium	500
Retained earnings	300
Total equity	1,200
Total liabilities	800
Total equity and liabilities	2,000

The directors decide to make a 1 for 5 bonus issue, followed by a 1 for 3 rights issue at £1.60 per share.

Show the revised statement of financial position of Canvat plc after both share issues have taken place.

See **Answer** at the end of this chapter.

5 Non-current liabilities (debt capital)

Section overview

- Non-current liabilities comprise debt securities (debentures, loan stock and bonds), plus bank loans and redeemable preference shares.

- Interest on non-current liabilities is a contractual obligation and must be accrued for in the calculation of profit before tax.

- Any amounts that are repayable in less than 12 months must be classified as current liabilities. The balance is treated as non-current liabilities: long-term borrowings.

A company is a legal person so when it borrows it is solely liable for the debt (a sole trader and partners are personally liable for loans to their businesses).

A company may borrow directly from a bank or it may borrow in the form of **debt securities** (loan stock, debenture loans or bonds). These securities are normally issued as certificates, each with a par value, in return for cash (the loan principal). The certificate's owner is legally entitled to interest on its par value, and is entitled to repayment of the principal 'at maturity', ie when the loan period reaches its end at a specifiable future date. This is known as redemption. It is a contractual obligation to pay interest on debt securities.

Debt securities are similar in concept to any other type of loan. Unless they are due to reach maturity within 12 months, they are included in **non-current liabilities** in the statement of financial position. Any amount due for redemption within 12 months is shown under **current liabilities**. Interest is part of **finance costs** in the income statement; unpaid interest at the statement of financial position date is shown as **other payables**.

5.1 Accounting for non-current liabilities

On issue of debt:

DEBIT	Cash	£X	
CREDIT	Non-current liabilities		£X

On repayment of debt:

DEBIT	Non-current liabilities	£X	
CREDIT	Cash		£X

Remember that:

- any **redeemable preference shares** in issue will also be treated as liabilities (either current or non-current) rather than equity

- any debt that is due for repayment in less than 12 months after the statement of financial position date is reclassified from non-current to **current liabilities**.

6 Provisions

Section overview

- Provisions are liabilities that can only be measured using estimation, so they are disclosed separately from other liabilities.

Provisions are liabilities of a company that are shown separately from other liabilities because the amount of a provision can be measured only by using a substantial degree of estimation. An example is a **provision for claims under warranty**, where a manufacturer agrees to make good any deficiencies in a product becoming apparent within, say, 12 months of the date of sale. It is known that warranty claims will arise but the precise number, value and timing are unknown. So judgement has to be used in deciding how much the **warranty provision** should be for.

Provisions may be included as current or non-current liabilities, depending on the circumstances.

Note that a provision differs from an actual accrual for, say, gas supplies, where it is known that there will be one gas bill, to be paid X weeks after the end of the reporting period for roughly £Y.

7 Tax

Section overview

- Any tax due on profits is the company's liability and therefore must be shown:

    - As a deduction in the income statement
    - As a payable in the statement of financial position.

- Any over-provision or under-provision in previous reporting periods is credited/debited in the current reporting period's income statement.

A company as a separate legal entity is liable to pay tax on its profits to HMRC itself: the liability is not that of its owners'. Tax is therefore treated as a **deduction from profit**. Any outstanding liability for unpaid tax is shown as a **liability** on the statement of financial position (**tax payable**), either current or non-current depending on the circumstances.

7.1 Accounting for tax

Different methods of accounting for tax (excluding VAT) can be used, but in this Study Manual a single tax payable ledger account is used for both the expense in the income statement and the liability in the statement of financial position.

When a tax liability arises and is identified, the double entry to record it is:

DEBIT	Tax expense (income statement)	£X	
CREDIT	Tax payable account		£X

When a tax payment is made:

DEBIT	Tax payable account	£X	
CREDIT	Cash		£X

At the end of the reporting period, any balance on the tax payable account is carried down. Usually this is a credit balance and is shown as 'Tax payable' under current liabilities on the statement of financial position.

Worked example: Tax I

Hardwork plc has estimated that £90,000 is payable in tax on the profits earned in the year ended 31 December 20X1. None of this tax has been paid by the date of the statement of financial position.

The tax will be accounted for as follows:

TAX PAYABLE ACCOUNT

20X1	£	20X1	£
Balance c/d	90,000	Tax expense (income statement)	90,000
	90,000		90,000
		20X2	
		Balance b/d	90,000

Since a company's income statement is usually prepared before the tax due is finally agreed with HMRC, the expense in the income statement is an estimate. It nearly always proves to be too high (**over-provision**) or too low (**under-provision**). Instead of going back to the financial statements for the reporting period and changing them:

- Any **over-provision** from the previous reporting period **reduces the tax expense for the subsequent reporting period**

- Any **under-provision** from the previous reporting period **increases the tax expense for the subsequent reporting period**

Worked example: Tax II

In the year to 31 December 20X2, Hardwork plc has a credit balance brought down on its tax payable account of £90,000 (1). It agrees with HMRC that the tax due on 20X1's profits is £87,000, which it pays in February 20X2 (2). Its over-provision for 20X1 is therefore £3,000 (3). It estimates that its tax due on 20X2's profits should be £100,000 (4).

Hardwork plc's net tax expense in the income statement for the year to 31 December 20X2 will be £100,000 (4) less the over-provision of £3,000 (1) in the previous reporting period, ie £97,000. Its statement of financial position current liability is £100,000 (5).

The ledger account is as follows.

TAX PAYABLE ACCOUNT

20X2	£	20X2	£
Cash (2)	87,000	Balance b/d (1)	90,000
Income statement: over-provision		Income statement: charge for	
20X1 (3)	3,000	20X2 (4)	100,000
Balance c/d (5)	100,000		
	190,000		190,000
		20X3	
		Balance b/d: Tax payable	100,000

Note that any balance owed to HMRC in respect of VAT or PAYE/NIC is disclosed as **other payables**, not as **tax payable**.

8 The regulatory framework for company financial statements

Section overview

- Extensive regulation covers the content and format of company financial statements, and the methods used to prepare some, if not all, of the figures.

- Prescribed formats enable users to find information and to make comparisons more easily.

- Income statements should usually cover a reporting period of 12 months. Both the income statement and the statement of financial position must be clearly named and dated.

Company financial statements prepared for **external** publication are extensively regulated to protect investors who use information to make economic decisions, especially when comparing different companies. **Published financial statements** are therefore prepared on the same basis by all companies so investors can make meaningful comparisons. Rules and regulations are applied to:

- **Content**: what information the financial statements should contain, and what supporting information should go with them

- **Accounting concepts:** how figures should be prepared

- **Presentation:** how the financial statements should be presented.

The main sources of accounting regulations for companies are:

- Accounting standards (IASs and IFRSs); and
- Legislation, in particular the Companies Act 2006.

In this Study Manual we have already covered most of what you need to know at this stage of your studies regarding the content, concepts and presentation of financial statements prepared under IASs. We now need to draw it all together into the **IAS 1 (revised) formats** for the income statement and statement of financial position.

8.1 Why does IAS 1 (revised) include formats?

The purpose of setting out formats for an income statement and statement of financial position is to make it easier for the users of financial statements:

- To **find the items they are particularly interested in:** companies are prevented from using complex layouts and formats that make the financial statements more difficult to understand

- To **make comparisons of the results of different companies**, or between the results of the same company from one reporting period to the next.

It is for this second reason that IAS 1 (revised) requires **comparative figures for the previous reporting period to be shown**, as well as the figures for the reporting period being reported. In some cases a statement of financial position from an even earlier reporting period may be required as well.

8.2 Structure and content of financial statements

- On each statement of financial position and income statement, the following information needs to be prominently displayed:

  - **Name** of the company

  - **Date of the statement of financial position/reporting period covered** – financial statements should not normally cover reporting periods longer than 12 months

- The statement of financial position must distinguish between **current and non-current assets** and **current and non-current liabilities**. Current items are to be settled within 12 months of the date of the statement of financial position

- In the **accounting policies note** to the financial statements the entity must disclose the **measurement basis** used in their preparation (historical cost or net realisable value, for instance), and the other **accounting policies** used that are relevant to an understanding of the financial statements.

9 The income statement (IAS 1 (revised))

Section overview

- The income statement must show balances as set out in the IAS 1 (revised) format, including gross profit, profit before tax and (post-tax) profit for the reporting period.

The IAS 1 (revised) **income statement functional format** to be learned is shown in the example below (Ducat plc). This includes the minimum disclosure requirements of IAS 1 (revised). The main requirement is that **all items of income and expense recognised in a period shall be included in profit or loss**.

Note that the income statement stops at profit (or loss) for the reporting period.

The presentation of the final retained earnings figure for the reporting period, as seen in the statement of financial position, is beyond the scope of *Accounting*, **as it is presented in a separate statement which is not examinable, called the statement of changes in equity (SCE).**

Worked example: Income statement

Ducat plc's income statement is presented below.

DUCAT PLC
INCOME STATEMENT FOR THE YEAR ENDED 31 DECEMBER 20X3

	£
Revenue	623,000
Cost of sales	(414,000)
Gross profit	209,000
Other income	26,000
Distribution costs	(73,000)
Administrative expenses	(32,000)
Finance costs	(15,000)
Profit before tax	115,000
Tax expense	(35,000)
Profit for the period	80,000

9.1 Revenue

This includes both credit and cash sales, net of trade discount, refunds and VAT. Cash discounts allowed to customers are **not** deducted when arriving at the revenue figure (these are normally shown as administrative expenses).

9.2 Cost of sales, distribution costs and administrative expenses

The allocation of expenses to each of these three headings calls for judgement. In practice the rules are not rigid. IAS 1 (revised) states that an entity shall present an analysis of expenses using a classification based on either the nature of expenses or their functions within the entity, whichever provides information that is reliable and more relevant. The format and classification used here is the **functional** one. Additional disclosures on the nature of expenses, including depreciation and amortisation, are required.

For the *Accounting* exam you should expect to make the following classifications.

Cost of sales	Distribution costs	Administrative expenses
Purchases plus carriage inwards adjusted for opening and closing inventory, and any substantial losses of inventory. In a manufacturing company wages of production staff, and maintenance and depreciation expenses of production non-current assets, plus losses on their disposal, are also included.	Wages etc of marketing and distribution staff. Sales commission Distribution expenses such as vehicle running costs and carriage outwards. Depreciation of motor vehicles used for distribution, and marketing costs such as advertising and promotion, and any loss on disposal of such assets. Depreciation of other non-current assets used by distribution operations and any loss on disposal of such assets. The cost of advertising and selling activities, since these are a part of distributing goods and services to customers.	Wages of administrative staff. Depreciation of non-current assets used by non-production and non-distribution operations, and any loss on disposal of such assets. Amortisation of intangible assets. Cash discount allowed to customers. Expense of substantial loss of inventory Irrecoverable debts expense

9.3 Other income

Income other than income classified as revenue should be shown separately. Examples of other income include:

- Dividends received on investments
- Interest received on savings
- Rent received from property
- Discounts received from suppliers
- Insurance claim proceeds
- Profits on disposal of non-current assets.

9.4 Finance costs

- Interest payable on bank loans and overdrafts
- Interest on debt securities

10 The statement of financial position (IAS 1 (revised))

Section overview

- The statement of financial position is split between total assets and total equity plus liabilities.
- Both assets and liabilities must show the current/non-current split.

The IAS 1 (revised) statement of financial position format is as follows.

DUCAT PLC
STATEMENT OF FINANCIAL POSITION AS AT 31 DECEMBER 20X3

	£	£
ASSETS		
Non-current assets		
Property, plant and equipment		427,000
Goodwill		15,000
Other intangible assets		110,000
		552,000
Current assets		
Inventories	51,000	
Trade and other receivables	102,000	
Other current assets (eg prepayments)	20,000	
Cash and cash equivalents	33,000	
		206,000
Total assets		758,000
EQUITY AND LIABILITIES		
Equity		
Share capital: £1 equity shares		150,000
Share capital: 10% £1 irredeemable preference shares		20,000
Reserves: share premium		125,000
Reserves: retained earnings		161,000
Reserves: general		65,000
Total equity		521,000
Non-current liabilities		
Long-term borrowings		158,000
Current liabilities		
Trade and other payables (including accruals)	36,000	
Short-term borrowings	22,000	
Provisions	10,000	
Current tax payable	11,000	
		79,000
Total equity and liabilities		758,000

Points to note

- All tangible assets (including land and buildings) are combined under the heading 'property, plant and equipment'. The user would refer to the non-current assets note, as covered in Chapter 10, for detail.

- Trade receivables and any other receivables (including VAT due) are combined as 'trade and other receivables'; prepayments are included in the heading 'other current assets'. The allowance for receivables is set off here.

- Cash in hand and at bank are combined as 'cash and cash equivalents'.

- Any long-term liabilities such as bank loans or debt securities that are not repayable within 12 months are combined as 'long-term borrowings' under 'non-current liabilities'. Redeemable preference shares would be included here.

- There are detailed disclosure requirements for share capital in IAS 1 (revised), in particular of the issued, fully paid and partly paid share capital, and of the par value. The figure included in the statement of financial position is the called-up share capital, both paid and unpaid.

- Bank overdrafts, which are technically repayable on demand, are called 'short-term borrowings'. They are not offset against any cash and cash equivalent asset balances.

- Trade payables and other payables (including VAT, PAYE/NIC and sales commission owed, interest payable and accruals) are combined as 'trade and other payables'.

- Current amounts of tax payable are each shown as a separate item under current liabilities.

11 Applying the IAS 1 (revised) formats

Section overview

- To apply the IAS 1 (revised) formats:
    - Extract a trial balance
    - Draw up adjustment journals
    - Complete the ETB
    - Gather the ledger accounts together appropriately regarding the income statement cost of sales, administrative expenses and distribution cost headings
    - Complete the formats for income statement and statement of financial position

The formats we use here are adapted from IAS 1 (revised). The Standard sets out a minimum requirement for what should appear on the face of the statement of financial position, although additional items are allowed to make the information more relevant. No set order of items is presented in IAS 1 (revised); entities are encouraged to adapt the order and the descriptions to enhance **relevance**, though in practice **comparability** encourages similar entities to adopt similar presentations.

Where a single figure or 'line item' appears in the statement of financial position, the company must disclose further sub-classifications in the notes in a manner that is appropriate to its operations.

Worked example: Preparing IAS 1 (revised) format financial statements

To draw together everything we have covered so far we shall work through a full example of how to use the ETB to prepare an IAS 1 (revised) format income statement and statement of financial position.

The chief accountant of Format plc has extracted the following trial balance from the ledger as at 31 December 20X2.

FORMAT PLC
TRIAL BALANCE AS AT 31 DECEMBER 20X2

	£'000	£'000
Issued equity shares of £1		800
10% irredeemable preference shares of £1 each		200
Trade receivables and trade payables	1,820	1,866
Bank	80	
Inventory at 1.1.X2	1,950	
6% debentures		1,000
Sales		9,500
Rental income		200
Debenture interest (six months to 30.6.X2)	30	
Administration and general expenses, excluding salaries	650	
Administration salaries	275	
Distribution expenses	616	
Purchases	5,125	
Salaries associated with manufacture of goods	300	
Carriage inwards	100	
Property costs	300	
Retained earnings		1,100
Freehold land, at cost	2,120	
Fixtures and fittings, at cost	2,000	
Accumulated depreciation, fixtures and fittings		900
Allowance for irrecoverable debts		100
Goodwill	300	
	15,666	15,666

The following items have yet to be dealt with.

1. An inventory count has revealed the closing inventory figure to be £2,020,000.

2. The company depreciates fixtures and fittings at 20% straight line cost.

3. An impairment review has shown that 10% should be written off goodwill. The charge should be to administrative expenses.

4. The credit controller has said that a debt of £15,000 should be written off as irrecoverable, and the allowance for receivables should be increased to £200,000.

5. The tax due on profits for the year is estimated at £750,000.

6. The allocation of expenditure between cost of sales, distribution costs and administrative expenses should be as follows.

	Distribution	Administrative
	%	%
Property costs	25	75
Depreciation	50	50

7. The debentures are repayable in full in ten years time. Interest is paid in two equal instalments per annum.

Requirement

Prepare year-end journals and an ETB for Format plc, and present an income statement for Format plc for the year ended 31 December 20X2 and a statement of financial position as at that date.

Solution

The year-end journals to be put through in the adjustments column are as follows:

			£'000	£'000
1				
DEBIT	Closing inventory (statement of financial position)		2,020	
CREDIT	Closing inventory (income statement)			2,020
2 and 6				
DEBIT	Administrative expenses		200	
	Distribution costs		200	
CREDIT	Fixtures and fittings – accumulated depreciation (2,000 × 20%)			400
3				
DEBIT	Administrative expenses		30	
CREDIT	Goodwill (300 × 10%)			30
4				
DEBIT	Administrative expenses		115	
CREDIT	Trade receivables			15
	Allowance for irrecoverable debts (200 – 100)			100
5				
DEBIT	Tax expense (income statement)		750	
CREDIT	Tax payable (statement of financial position)			750
6				
DEBIT	Administrative expenses (300 × 0.75)		225	
	Distribution costs (300 × 0.25)		75	
CREDIT	Property costs			300
7				
DEBIT	Debenture interest		30	
CREDIT	Trade and other payables			30

The extended trial balance is as follows:

	Trial balance		Adjustments		Income statement		Statement of financial position	
	Debit	Credit	Debit	Credit	Debit	Credit	Debit	Credit
	£'000	£'000	£'000	£'000	£'000	£'000	£'000	£'000
£1 equity shares		800						800
10% £1 irredeemable preference shares		200						200
Trade receivables	1,820			15			1,805	
Trade payables		1,866		30				1,896
Bank	80						80	
Inventory	1,950		2,020	2,020	1,950	2,020	2,020	
6% debentures		1,000						1,000
Sales		9,500				9,500		
Rental income		200				200		
Debenture interest	30		30		60			
Administrative expenses	650		570*		1,220			
Administration salaries	275				275			
Distribution expenses	616		275**		891			
Purchases	5,125				5,125			
Manufacturing salaries	300				300			
Carriage inwards	100				100			
Property costs	300			300				
Retained earnings		1,100						1,100
Freehold land – cost	2,120						2,120	
Fixtures and fittings – cost	2,000						2,000	
F&F – accumulated depreciation		900		400				1,300
Allowance for irrecoverable debts		100		100				200
Goodwill	300			30			270	
Tax			750	750	750			750
Profit					1,049			1,049
	15,666	15,666	3,645	3,645	11,720	11,720	8,295	8,295

* 200 (Jnl 2) + 30 (Jnl 3) + 115 (Jnl 4) + 225 (Jnl 6) = 570
** 200 (Jnl 2) + 75 (Jnl 6) = 275

FORMAT PLC
INCOME STATEMENT FOR THE YEAR ENDED 31 DECEMBER 20X2

	£'000
Revenue	9,500
Cost of sales (W1)	(5,455)
Gross profit	4,045
Other income	200
Administrative expenses (W1)	(1,495)
Distribution costs (W1)	(891)
Finance costs	(60)
Profit before tax	1,799
Tax expense	(750)
Profit for the period	1,049

FORMAT PLC
STATEMENT OF FINANCIAL POSITION AS AT 31 DECEMBER 20X2

	£'000	£'000
ASSETS		
Non-current assets		
Property, plant and equipment (W3)		2,820
Goodwill		270
		3,090
Current assets		
Inventories	2,020	
Trade and other receivables (1,805 – 200 allowance)	1,605	
Cash and cash equivalents	80	
		3,705
Total assets		6,795
EQUITY AND LIABILITIES		
Equity		
Equity share capital: £1 equity shares		800
Preference share capital: 10% £1 shares		200
Retained earnings (W2)		2,149
Total equity		3,149
Non-current liabilities		
Long-term borrowings: 6% debentures		1,000
Current liabilities		
Trade and other payables	1,896	
Tax payable	750	
		2,646
Total equity and liabilities		6,795

WORKINGS

(1) Analysis of expenses

	Cost of sales £'000	Distribution costs £'000	Admin expenses £'000
Opening inventory	1,950		
Administrative expenses			1,220
Salaries	300		275
Distribution costs		891	
Purchases	5,125		
Carriage inwards	100		
Closing inventory	(2,020)		
	5,455	891	1,495

(2) RETAINED EARNINGS

	£'000		£'000
		Balance b/d	1,100
		Profit for the period (income statement)	1,049
Balance c/d	2,149		
	2,149		2,149

(3) Property, plant and equipment note

	Freehold land £'000	Fixtures and fittings £'000	Total £'000
Cost			
At 1.1.X2	2,120	2,000	4,120
Additions			
Disposals			
At 31.12.X2	2,120	2,000	4,120
Accumulated depreciation			
At 1.1.X2		900	900
Charge for the year (£2,000 × 20%)		400	400
Disposals			
At 31.12.X2		1,300	1,300
Carrying amount			
At 1.1.X2	2,120	1,100	3,220
At 31.12.X2	2,120	700	2,820

Summary and Self-test

Summary (1/2)

Statement of financial position
Accounting implications

Limited companies

Income statement
Accounting implications

Tax liability

Separate legal entity
Equity and reserves
- Equity (ordinary) shares
- Irredeemable preference shares
- Share premium
- Retained earnings
- General and other reserves

Tax charge + over/under
provision in the IS

Called up share capital (NV)
Share premium (premium)
Other receivables (unpaid shares)

Bonus issue
DR   Share premium   X
CR   Equity shares   X

B/d	X
Profit	X
Loss	(X)
Reserve transfers	X/(X)
Dividends	(X)
C/d	X

Debt capital (non-current liabilities)
- Loan stock
- Redeemable preference shares
- Long-term bank loans
Provisions (current liabilities)
- Warranty provisions

Interest/dividends
= Finance costs in IS

IAS 1 (revised) formats

Satisfy qualitative characteristics of
- Comparability (comparative year's figures required)
- Understandability

IAS 1 formats

Income statement for the reporting period

	£'000
Revenue	623,000
Cost of sales	(414,000)
Gross profit	209,000
Other income	26,000
Distribution costs	(73,000)
Administrative expenses	(32,000)
Finance costs	(15,000)
Profit before tax	115,000
Tax expense	(35,000)
Profit for period	80,000

Statement of financial position at the reporting period end

	£	£
ASSETS		
Non-current assets		
Property, plant and equipment		427,000
Goodwill		15,000
Intangible assets		110,000
		552,000
Current assets		
Inventories	51,000	
Trade and other receivables	102,000	
Prepayments	20,000	
Cash and cash equivalents	33,000	
		206,000
Total assets		758,000
EQUITY AND LIABILITIES		
Equity		
Equity share capital: £1 equity shares		150,000
Preference share capital: 10% £1 irredeemable preference shares		90,000
Share premium		55,000
General reserve		65,000
Retained earnings		161,000
Total equity		521,000
Non-current liabilities		
Long-term borrowings		158,000
Current liabilities		
Trade and other payables	29,000	
Short-term borrowings	22,000	
Accruals	5,000	
Provisions	10,000	
Tax payable	13,000	
		79,000
Total equity and liabilities		758,000

Satisfy qualitative characteristics of
- Comparability
- Relevance and verifiability

Accounting powers
- Relevant IASs are mandatory
- Where no relevant IAS, apply judgement in line with Conceptual Framework
- Applied consistently

Self-test

Answer the following questions.

1   A company's assets and liabilities at the beginning and end of a reporting period were as follows.

	Beginning £	End £
Non-current assets (carrying amount)	85,000	150,000
Current assets	120,000	110,000
Equity shares of £1	100,000	125,000
Share premium	5,000	10,000
Retained earnings	50,000	67,000
Trade and other payables	30,000	40,000
Tax payable	20,000	18,000

During the reporting period the company issued a further 25,000 shares at £1.20 each. £22,000 for tax expense was shown in the income statement.

The company's profit before tax for the reporting period was

A   £17,000
B   £20,000
C   £27,000
D   £39,000

2   You are supplied with the following extract from Niton plc's statements of financial position at 31 January 20X9 and 20X8.

	31 January 20X9 £m	31 January 20X8 £m
Equity shares of £1 each	120	100
Share premium	260	220

Notes

(1)   On 1 July 20X8 there was a 1 for 10 bonus issue.
(2)   On 30 September 20X8 there was a rights issue.
(3)   There are no other reserve balances.

What was the total amount received from the issue of shares for the year ended 31 January 20X9?

A   £10m
B   £20m
C   £50m
D   £60m

3   The figure for equity in the IAS 1 (revised) statement of financial position is represented by

A   Called-up share capital plus share premium
B   Total assets less current liabilities
C   Paid share capital plus retained earnings
D   Total assets less total liabilities

4   Which of the following would cause a company's profit for the period to increase?

A   Issue of 100,000 £1 equity shares at £1.02

B   Discount allowed of £255

C   Disposal for £8,500 of a fork-lift truck which originally cost £15,000 and has a carrying amount of £9,250

D   Receipt of £25 in respect of a receivable previously written off as irrecoverable

5 Which **two** of the following transactions could affect a company's retained earnings for the reporting period?

    A   Rights issue of shares
    B   Transfer to the general reserve
    C   Purchase of land
    D   Repayment of debentures at their par value
    E   Increase of tax due

6 The following information is available in relation to the tax figures to be included in the financial statements of Godshill plc.

	31 December 20X7 £	31 December 20X6 £
Tax payable	271,500	237,600
Income statement tax expense	269,700	219,800

What is the total tax paid during the year ended 31 December 20X7?

    A   £185,900
    B   £235,800
    C   £237,600
    D   £269,700

7 If tax is under-provided in the income statement for 20X7, in the following year's income statement the effect will be:

    A   A reduction in profit for the reporting period
    B   An increase in profit for the reporting period
    C   A reduction in gross profit
    D   An increase in gross profit

8 Raymond plc issues 135,000 equity shares with a par value of £3 each at a price of £5 each for cash.

Which of the following sets of entries would be made to record this transaction?

    A   Credit Bank £675,000, Debit Share capital £405,000, Debit Share premium £270,000
    B   Debit Bank £675,000, Credit Share capital £135,000, Credit Share premium £540,000
    C   Debit Bank £675,000, Credit Share capital £405,000, Credit Share premium £270,000
    D   Credit Bank £675,000, Debit Share capital £135,000, Debit Share premium £540,000

9 Mince plc is preparing its financial statements for the year ended 30 September 20X6, having prepared an initial trial balance. The initial trial balance shows the following balances:

	£
Administrative expenses paid (including rent)	32,874
Discounts allowed (to be included in administrative expenses)	1,085
Prepayment of rent at 1 October 20X5	2,894

On 31 August 20X6 Mince plc paid its quarterly rent in advance of £5,400. In Mince plc's income statement the figure for administrative expenses will be:

    A   £31,453
    B   £32,495
    C   £32,874
    D   £33,253

Now, go back to the Learning Objectives in the Introduction. If you are satisfied that you have achieved these objectives, please tick them off.

1 Structure and content of company financial statements

- Comparative figures for the previous reporting period must be shown

  IAS 1 (revised)
  para 38

- Name of the company, and the date of the statement of financial position or the reporting period covered, must be prominently displayed

  IAS 1 (revised)
  para 51

- Financial statements should not normally cover reporting periods longer than one year

  IAS 1 (revised)
  para 36

- The statement of financial position must distinguish between current and non-current assets and current and non-current liabilities. Current items are to be settled within 12 months of the date of the statement of financial position

  IAS 1 (revised)
  paras 60 and 61

- Share capital and reserves disclosures

  IAS 1 (revised)
  para 79

- Minimum requirements and adaptation of format of statement of financial position; additional disclosures

  IAS 1 (revised)
  paras 54, 55, 57, 77

- All items of income and expense recognised in a reporting period shall be included in profit or loss; minimum disclosure requirements are set out

  IAS 1 (revised)
  paras 81, 82 and 88

- An entity shall present an analysis of expenses using a classification based on either the nature of expenses or their function within the entity, which provides information which is more reliable and relevant. Additional disclosures on the nature of expenses, including depreciation and amortisation, are required

  IAS 1 (revised)
  paras 99, 103 and 104

- A note must disclose the measurement bases used in preparing the financial statements, and other accounting policies that are relevant to an understanding of them

  IAS 1 (revised)
  para 117

2 Format of income statement and statement of financial position

- Formats, including income statement in functional format

  IAS 1 (revised)
  IG6

3 Additional comparative information

  IAS 1 (revised)
  para 39

- When an entity applies an accounting policy retrospectively, makes a retrospective restatement of items in its financial statements or reclassifies items in its financial statements, an additional statement of financial position as at the beginning of the earliest comparative period must be presented.

Answer to Interactive question 1

There are 30 million shares of 20p in issue (£6 million/20p per share). A 1 for 3 rights issue involves an issue of 30 million/3 = 10 million shares at £1.80, to raise cash of £18 million. The issued share capital goes up by 10 million shares at 20p each, £2m. The share premium on the issue is £1.80 - 20p = £1.60 per share, or £16 million in total.

	£'000
ASSETS	
Non-current assets	18,600
Current assets (2.9m+18m) (a)	20,900
Total assets	39,500
EQUITY AND LIABILITIES	
Equity	
Share capital: equity shares of 20p each ((6m/3) + 6m) (b)	8,000
Share premium ((6m/(0.2 × 3)) × £1.60) + 5.7m) (c)	21,700
Retained earnings	7,000
Total equity	36,700
Total liabilities	2,800
Total equity and liabilities	39,500

Answer to Interactive question 2

Canvat plc: statement of financial position at 31 December 20X1

	£'000
TOTAL ASSETS (2m + (320,000 × 1.60))	2,512
EQUITY AND LIABILITIES	
Equity	
Share capital (400 + 80 + 160)	640
Share premium (500 + 352 – 80)	772
Retained earnings	300
Total equity	1,712
Total liabilities	800
Total equity and liabilities	2,512

The bonus issue is of 800,000/5 = 160,000 50p shares:

DEBIT	Share premium	£80,000	
CREDIT	Share capital		£80,000

The rights issue is of (800,000 + 160,000)/3 = 320,000 50p shares at £1.60 each, ie £512,000:

		£	£
DEBIT	Cash	512,000	
CREDIT	Share capital (320,000 × 50p)		160,000
	Share premium (320,000 × (1.60 – 0.50))		352,000

The ledger accounts are as follows:

SHARE CAPITAL

	Number	£		Number	£
Balance c/d	1,280,000	640,000	Balance b/d	800,000	400,000
			1 for 5 bonus issue	160,000	80,000
			1 for 3 rights issue	320,000	160,000
	1,280,000	640,000		1,280,000	640,000

SHARE PREMIUM

	£		£
Bonus issue	80,000	Balance b/d	500,000
Balance c/d	772,000	Rights issue: cash	352,000
	852,000		852,000

RETAINED EARNINGS

	£		£
Balance c/d	300,000	Balance b/d	300,000

1 D

	£
Opening net assets (85,000 + 120,000 – 30,000 – 20,000) or (100 + 5 + 50)	155,000
Closing net assets (150,000 + 110,000 – 40,000 – 18,000)	202,000
Increase in net assets	47,000
Less: Proceeds of share issue (25,000 × £1.20)	(30,000)
Retained profit for reporting period (67,000 – 50,000)	17,000
Add: Tax charged	22,000
Profit before tax	39,000

2 D

SHARE CAPITAL

	£m		£m
		b/d	100
		Bonus issue (100 ÷10)	10
c/d	120	Rights issue (β)	10
	120		120

SHARE PREMIUM

	£m		£m
Bonus issue	10	b/d	220
c/d	260	Rights issue (β)	50
	270		270

Therefore, the rights issue was of 10,000,000 shares at a premium of £5 per share. Total raised was £60,000,000.

3 D Total equity = share capital and reserves = net assets (assets less liabilities).

4 D The premium on the issue of shares must be credited to share premium. Discount allowed to suppliers is an expense that decreases profits. The disposal of the truck results in a loss which reduces profit. Reduction in irrecoverable debts expense increases profits.

5 B and E

A	DR	Cash	CR	Share capital/share premium
B	DR	Retained earnings	CR	General reserve
C	DR	Non-current assets	CR	Cash
D	DR	Debentures	CR	Cash
E	DR	Income statement (tax expense)	CR	Tax payable

6 B **TAX PAYABLE**

	£		£
Paid (β)	235,800	b/d	237,600
c/d	271,500	Income statement	269,700
	507,300		507,300

7 A A previous reporting period's under-provision means an additional expense in the current reporting period's income statement. This has no effect on gross profit; it is profit for this reporting period that is reduced.

8 C Cash raised is 135,000 × £5 = £675,000, which is debited to cash at bank. The credit to share capital is 135,000 × £3 par value = £405,000, while the credit to share premium is 135,000 × £2 = £270,000

9 D The opening prepayment of rent of £2,894 needs to be debited to administrative expenses, and the closing prepayment of £5,400 × 2/3 = £3,600 needs to be credited. Total administrative expenses will therefore be £32,874 + £1,085 + £2,894 – £3,600 = £33,253

CHAPTER 12

Company financial statements under UK GAAP

Introduction

Examination context

Topic List

Summary and Self-test

Answers to Interactive questions

Answers to Self-test

Introduction

Learning objectives

- Record and account for transactions and events resulting in income, expenses, assets, liabilities and equity in accordance with the appropriate basis of accounting and the laws, regulations and accounting standards applicable to the financial statements

- Prepare an extended trial balance

- Identify the main components of a set of financial statements and specify their purpose and interrelationship

- Prepare and present balance sheet, profit and loss account and cash flow statement (or extracts therefrom) from the accounting records and trial balance in a format that satisfies the information requirements of the entity

Specific syllabus learning outcomes are: 1c; 2c; 3a, c

Syllabus links

The material in this chapter will be developed further in this paper, and referred to as well in the Financial Accounting and Financial Reporting papers later in the Professional stage.

Examination context

Questions on the topics in this chapter will be set as multiple choice questions, some of which may involve calculations so that the correct answer can be selected. Very often double entry questions are phrased in terms of preparing a journal.

In the exam you may be required to:

- Identify what comprises UK GAAP

- Specify the key differences between UK GAAP and IAS formats of financial statements, especially in terms of the net assets UK GAAP balance sheet

- Use UK GAAP when identifying balances in preparing the profit and loss account and balance sheet of a company

1 What is UK GAAP?

Section overview

- Financial statements are prepared under UK GAAP for most private, unlisted companies, partnerships and sole traders.

In this Study Manual so far we have looked at how financial transactions are recorded in books of original entry and in ledgers, and at the techniques that are then used (such as the profit and loss ledger account and/or the extended trial balance) to summarise those ledgers and produce statements

- Of the business's **financial performance** over a period of time (which we have called its **income statement**), and

- Of the business's **financial position** at the end of that time period (which we have called its **statement of financial position**)

These techniques are universal, arising out of the key accounting principles of:

- Accruals
- Going concern, and
- Double entry bookkeeping

However, there are quite a number of issues in relation to which accounting practice around the world is diverse, in particular:

- Terminology, and
- The formats used to present financial statements.

We have so far adopted an approach to these issues based on international accounting and financial reporting standards (specifically IAS 1 (revised)) and on the *Conceptual Framework.* You need to be aware however that this 'international standards' approach currently only applies in the UK to a limited number of companies; the remainder still produce their financial statements under what has come to be called UK generally accepted accounting practice, or UK GAAP.

Definition

UK GAAP: The rules, from whatever source, that govern accounting and financial reporting in the UK.

1.1 The constituents of UK GAAP

In the UK generally accepted accounting practice is a combination of:

- Company law (the Companies Act 2006)

- UK accounting standards

- The effects of stock exchange listing requirements (which apply directly to listed companies but which are influential more widely) and

- The effects of international accounting and financial reporting standards

UK accounting standards have more impact than IASs in UK GAAP, but UK standards are increasingly being 'converged' with international ones, so the differences between them are disappearing.

GAAP is in fact a dynamic concept: it changes constantly as circumstances alter through new legislation, standards and practice. This idea that GAAP is constantly changing is recognised by the UK's ASB in its *Statement of Aims,* where it states that it expects to issue new standards and amend old ones in response to 'evolving business practices, new economic developments and deficiencies identified in current practice.'

The problem of what is 'generally accepted' is not easy to settle, because new practices are obviously not generally adopted yet. The criteria for a practice being 'generally accepted' depend on factors such as whether the practice is addressed by UK accounting standards or legislation, or their international equivalents, and whether other companies have adopted the practice. Most importantly perhaps, the question should be whether the practice is consistent with the needs of users and the objectives of financial statements, and whether it is consistent with the 'true and fair' concept (see below).

To understand better the importance of UK GAAP we need to look briefly at why and how companies in the UK are required to publish annual financial statements, or 'published accounts'.

2 Published accounts

Section overview

- UK companies are required by law to publish financial statements annually and file them with the Registrar of Companies ('published accounts').

- Such accounts must show a true and fair view.

- Listed companies are required by the Listing Rules to apply IASs in preparing and presenting their published accounts. Unlisted companies may choose to use UK standards, which are converging with IASs.

2.1 Publishing annual accounts

Under the Companies Act 2006 UK limited companies must produce accounts (financial statements) annually, and large companies must appoint an independent person to audit and report on them. Once prepared, a copy of the accounts must be sent to the Registrar of Companies, who maintains a separate file for every company. The Registrar's files may be inspected for a nominal fee, by any member of the public. This is why the 'statutory accounts' are often referred to as **published accounts**.

Definition

Statutory accounts: Financial statements which limited companies are obliged by law to publish in a particular form.

The company's directors must publish accounts which show a **true and fair view** (a phrase used in s393 Companies Act 2006) of the company's assets, liabilities, financial position and profit or loss (profit and loss account and balance sheet) for a financial year. The board evidences its approval of the accounts by the signature of one director on the balance sheet. Once this has been done, and the auditors have completed their report, the accounts are sent to shareholders and, in the case of a public company, are presented to the body of shareholders at a general meeting. When the shareholders have adopted the accounts they are sent to the Registrar for filing.

2.2 True and fair view

The Companies Act 2006 requirement that the accounts show a **true and fair view** is paramount. A company's accounts can show a true and fair view when prepared using *either* Companies Act (UK GAAP) formats *or* IAS formats.

Although the Companies Act 2006 lays down numerous rules on the information to be included in published accounts and the format of its presentation, any such rule may be **overridden** if compliance with it would prevent the accounts from showing a **true and fair view**.

When prepared under UK GAAP the accounts must include:

- A profit and loss account (equivalent to an income statement)

- A balance sheet as at the date to which the profit and loss account is made up (equivalent to a statement of financial position)

- A directors' report, and a directors' remuneration report in the case of a quoted company

- An auditors' report addressed to the members (not to the directors) of the company

All we are concerned with in the *Accounting* syllabus is the **profit and loss account** and **balance sheet**.

2.3 Published accounts of listed and unlisted companies

Listed companies must comply with the Listing Rules set out by the UK Listing Authority (part of the Financial Services Authority). These require that listed companies should prepare their published accounts under international accounting standards. This is permitted by the Companies Act 2006, as we have seen above.

The **terminology and formats** of international financial statements are different from the ones set out in the Companies Act 2006 and UK GAAP, however. In the UK therefore there is currently the situation whereby:

- **Listed companies** produce an income statement and statement of financial position following international terminology and formats.

- **Non-listed companies** can choose between UK GAAP or international terminology and formats for their published accounts.

3 UK GAAP terminology and formats

Section overview

- UK terminology and IAS terminology vary in a number of areas

- UK formats set down in the Companies Act 2006 apply a net assets approach to the balance sheet: total assets – total liabilities = total equity.

So far in this Study Manual we have exclusively used the international terminology and formats: we need now to introduce the UK GAAP versions.

3.1 UK GAAP terminology

UK GAAP uses different terminology in many important respects regarding financial statements, as follows:

International term	UK GAAP term
Income statement	Profit and loss account
Statement of financial position	Balance sheet
Non-current asset	Fixed asset
Carrying amount	Net book value
Inventories	Stock
Receivables	Debtors
Irrecoverable debt	Bad debt
Irrecoverable debt expense	Bad and doubtful debts expense
Allowance for irrecoverable debts	Allowance for doubtful debts

International term	UK GAAP term
Retained earnings	Retained profits (reserve)
Payables	Creditors
Non-current liabilities	Creditors: amounts falling due after more than one year
Current liabilities	Creditors: amounts falling due in less than one year
Revenue	Turnover
Finance costs	Interest payable

3.2 UK formats

The format of the balance sheet and profit and loss account of a limited company under the Companies Act 2006 is shown below, with some simplifications (it is derived from the formats set down by the Companies Act 1985, which are adopted by the 2006 Act). Note in particular that the UK GAAP balance sheet presents **net assets,** with current liabilities deducted from current assets, and long-term liabilities deducted to arrive at net assets. The lower half of the balance sheet comprises the owners' interests only.

TYPICAL LIMITED COMPANY
BALANCE SHEET AS AT...

		£	£	£
Fixed assets				
Intangible assets	Development costs		X	
	Concessions, patents, licences, trademarks		X	
	Goodwill		X	
				X
Tangible assets	Land and buildings		X	
	Plant and machinery		X	
	Fixtures, fittings, tools and equipment		X	
	Motor vehicles		X	
				X
				X
Current assets	Stocks		X	
	Debtors and prepayments		X	
	Cash at bank and in hand		X	
			X	
Creditors: amounts falling due within one year				
	Debenture loans (nearing their redemption date)	X		
	Bank overdraft and loans	X		
	Trade creditors	X		
	Provisions	X		
	Taxation	X		
	Accruals	X		
			(X)	
Net current assets				X
Total assets less current liabilities				X
Creditors: amounts falling due after more than one year				
	Debentures			(X)
Net assets				X
Capital and reserves				
	Equity shares			X
	Preference shares			X
	Share premium account			X
	Other reserves			X
	Retained profits			X
				X

The UK GAAP profit and loss account is as follows.

TYPICAL LIMITED COMPANY
PROFIT AND LOSS ACCOUNT FOR THE YEAR ENDED...

	£
Turnover*	X
Cost of sales	(X)
Gross profit	X
Distribution costs	(X)
Administrative expenses	(X)
	X
Other operating income	X
Operating profit	X
Interest payable and similar charges	(X)
Profit before taxation	X
Taxation	(X)
Profit after taxation	X

* Note that the turnover figure is net of trade discount, refunds and VAT, as the revenue figure is under IASs.

3.3 Fixed assets

3.3.1 Intangible fixed assets

Intangible fixed assets represent amounts of money paid by a business to acquire benefits of a long term nature. **Goodwill** and **deferred development expenditure** are two intangible assets; these were discussed in detail in Chapter 10 and the same principles apply under UK GAAP.

If a company purchases some **patent rights**, or a concession from another business, or the right to use a trademark, the cost of the purchase can be accounted for as an intangible fixed asset. These assets are subject to **amortisation** over their useful lives (called '**economic life**' under UK GAAP).

3.3.2 Tangible fixed assets

Tangible fixed assets are shown in the balance sheet at their net book value (ie at cost less accumulated depreciation).

Under UK GAAP a fixed asset note is normally needed to give the required detail. Alternatively on the face of the balance sheet we can present each item as follows:

	Cost	Accumulated depreciation	Net book value
	£	£	£
Land and buildings	X	(X)	X
Plant and machinery	X	(X)	X
Fixtures and fittings	X	(X)	X
Motor vehicles	X	(X)	X
	X	(X)	X

3.4 Current and long-term liabilities

The term '**creditors: amounts falling due within one year**' is used in the Companies Act 2006 to mean '**current liabilities**'.

Similarly, the term '**creditors: amounts falling due after more than one year**' is the Companies Act 2006 term for **non-current liabilities**.

Worked example: Company financial statements

To see how UK GAAP is used when preparing financial statements, we shall work through a full practical example.

The accountant of Hartpeace Ltd has prepared the following trial balance as at 31 December 20X7.

	£'000
50p equity shares (fully paid)	350
7% £1 irredeemable preference shares (fully paid)	100
10% debentures	200
Retained profit 1.1.X7	242
General reserve 1.1.X7	171
Freehold land and buildings 1.1.X7 (cost)	430
Plant and machinery 1.1.X7 (cost)	830
Accumulated depreciation:	
Freehold buildings 1.1.X7	20
Plant and machinery 1.1.X7	222
Stock 1.1.X7	190
Sales	2,695
Purchases	2,152
Debenture interest paid	10
Wages and salaries	254
Light and heat	31
Sundry expenses	113
Suspense account	420
Debtors	464
Creditors	195
Cash at bank	141

Notes

(a) Sundry expenses include £9,000 paid in respect of insurance for the year ending 1 September 20X8. Light and heat does not include an invoice of £3,000 for electricity for the three months ending 1 January 20X8, which was paid in February 20X8. Light and heat includes £20,000 relating to sales commission payable to employees.

(b) The suspense account is in respect of the following items:

	£'000
Proceeds from the issue of 100,000 equity shares	120
Proceeds from the disposal of plant on 1.1.X7	300
	420

(c) The freehold property was acquired 10 years ago, the buildings element being £100,000. Their estimated economic life was 50 years at the time of purchase.

(d) The plant disposed of on 1.1.X7 cost £350,000 and had a net book value of £274,000. £36,000 depreciation is to be charged on plant and machinery for 20X7.

(e) The debentures are not redeemable for some years.

(f) The directors wish to provide for:

   (i)   Debenture interest due
   (ii) A transfer to general reserve of £16,000
   (iii) Audit fees of £4,000

(g) Stock as at 31 December 20X7 was valued at cost of £220,000.

(h) Taxation is to be ignored.

Requirement

Prepare journals and an ETB for Hartpeace Ltd, plus a draft profit and loss account and balance sheet.

Solution

WORKING for adjustment (f)

	£'000
Charge needed in profit and loss account for debenture interest (10% × £200,000)	20
Amount paid so far, as shown in trial balance	(10)
Accrual – presumably six months' interest now payable	10

		£'000	£'000
(a)	DEBIT Prepayment (9,000 × 8/12)	6	
	CREDIT Sundry expenses		6
	DEBIT Light and heat	3	
	CREDIT Accrual		3
	Accrual of electricity and prepayment of insurance		
	DEBIT Wages and salaries	20	
	CREDIT Light and heat		20
	Correction of misposting of sales commission		
(b)	DEBIT Suspense	120	
	CREDIT Share capital (100,000 × 0.5)		50
	Share premium		70
	Being correct treatment of proceeds of share issue		
	DEBIT Suspense	300	
	CREDIT Disposals		300
	Being correct treatment of sales proceeds re plant		
(c)	DEBIT Disposals	274	
	Accumulated depreciation – Plant and machinery (350 – 274)	76	
	CREDIT Plant and machinery: cost		350
	Being disposal of plant on 1.1.X7		
	DEBIT Depreciation expense	38	
	CREDIT Freehold property: accumulated depreciation (£100,000/50)		2
	CREDIT Plant and machinery: accumulated depreciation		36
	Being depreciation for 20X7		
(d)	DEBIT Debenture interest	10	
	Audit fee	4	
	CREDIT Accruals		14
	Being accruals of debenture interest and audit fee for 20X7		
	DEBIT Retained profit	16	
	CREDIT General reserve		16
	Being transfer to general reserve		
(e)	DEBIT Stock (balance sheet)	220	
	CREDIT Stock (profit and loss account)		220
	Being closing stock at 31.12.X7		

Here is Hartpeace Ltd's ETB from which we can prepare its profit and loss account and balance sheet:

	Trial balance Debit £'000	Trial balance Credit £'000	Adjustments Debit £'000	Adjustments Credit £'000	P&L account Debit £'000	P&L account Credit £'000	Statement of financial position Debit £'000	Statement of financial position Credit £'000
Issued ordinary shares of 50p		350						400
7% £1 irredeemable preference shares of £1 each		100						100
10% debentures		200						200
Retained profits		242						226
General reserve		171	16	16				187
Freehold land and buildings	430						430	
Freehold land and buildings – accumulated depreciation		20		5				25
Plant and machinery – cost	830			350			480	
Plant and machinery – accumulated depreciation		222	76	36				182
Stock	190		220	220	190	220	220	
Sales		2,695				2,695		
Purchases	2,152				2,152			
Debenture interest	10		10		20			
Wages and salaries	254		20		274			
Light and heat	31		3	20	14			
Sundry expenses	113			6	107			
Suspense account		420	420					
Debtors	464						464	
Creditors		195						195
Cash at bank	141						141	
Accruals				17*				17
Prepayments			6				6	
Audit fee			4		4			
Depreciation expense			41		41			
Disposal			274	300		26		
Share premium				70				70
Net profit					139			139
	4,615	4,615	1,090	1,090	2,941	2,941	1,741	1,741

* Accruals = 3 (a) + 14 (f)

ICAEW

Here is Hartpeace Ltd's draft profit and loss account and balance sheet, taken direct from the ETB before being 'tidied up' for publication.

HARTPEACE LTD
PROFIT AND LOSS ACCOUNT
FOR THE YEAR ENDED 31 DECEMBER 20X7

	£'000	£'000
Sales		2,695
Less cost of sales		
Opening stock	190	
Purchases	2,152	
Less closing stock	(220)	
		(2,122)
Gross profit		573
Profit on disposal of plant		26
		599
Less expenses		
Wages and salaries	274	
Sundry expenses	107	
Light and heat	14	
Depreciation expense: freehold property and plant	38	
Audit fees	4	
Debenture interest	20	
		(457)
Net profit		142

HARTPEACE LTD
BALANCE SHEET AS AT 31 DECEMBER 20X7

	Cost/val'n £'000	Dep'n £'000	£'000
Fixed assets			
Tangible assets			
Freehold property	430	(22)	408
Plant and machinery	480	(182)	298
	910	(204)	706
Current assets			
Stock		220	
Debtors		464	
Prepayments		6	
Cash		141	
		831	
Creditors: amounts falling due within one year			
Creditors	195		
Accrued expenses	17		
		(212)	
Net current assets			619
Total assets less current liabilities			1,325
Creditors: amounts falling due after more than one year			
10% debentures			(200)
			1,125
Capital and reserves			
Called up share capital			
50p equity shares		400	
7% £1 preference shares		100	
			500
Reserves			
Share premium		70	
General reserve		187	
Retained profits (226 + 142)		368	
			625
			1,125

C
H
A
P
T
E
R

12

3.5 Company financial statements for publication

Hartpeace Ltd's financial statements would appear as follows if presented for **external** purposes using the full standard Companies Act 2006 formats.

HARTPEACE LTD
PROFIT AND LOSS ACCOUNT FOR THE YEAR ENDED 31 DECEMBER 20X7

	£'000
Turnover	2,695
Cost of sales	(2,122)
Gross profit	573
Administrative expenses (274 + 107 + 14 + 38 + 4)	(437)
Operating profit	136
Other operating income	26
Interest payable and similar charges	(20)
Profit before taxation	142
Taxation	0
Profit after taxation	142

HARTPEACE LTD
BALANCE SHEET AS AT 31 DECEMBER 20X7

	£'000	£'000
Fixed assets		
Tangible assets		706
Current assets		
Stocks	220	
Debtors	464	
Prepayments	6	
Cash at bank and in hand	141	
	831	
Creditors: amounts falling due within one year	(212)	
Net current assets		619
Total assets less current liabilities		1,325
Creditors: amounts falling due after more than one year		(200)
		1,125
Capital and reserves		
Called up share capital		500
Share premium account		70
Other reserves		187
Retained profits		368
		1,125

Note that under UK GAAP in financial statements for publication there is less detail on the face of the balance sheet; the detail that we saw earlier in the Companies Act 2006 format is normally shown in notes to the financial statements.

Interactive question 1: UK GAAP financial statements I   [Difficulty level: Exam standard]

The following is an extract from the trial balance of Tafford Ltd, at 30 September 20X1:

	£'000	£'000
Machinery:		
Cost:	3,000	
Accumulated depreciation at 1 October 20X0		1,700
Motor vehicles:		
Cost	1,180	
Accumulated depreciation at 1 October 20X0		500
Stock at 1 October 20X0	13,000	
Sales		41,600
Purchases	22,600	
Distribution costs	6,000	
Administrative expenses	5,000	
Allowance for doubtful debts, 1 October 20X0		1,300
Bad debts written off	600	
10% Debentures (issued 20W9)		10,000
Interest paid on debentures	500	
Suspense account		100

Notes

(1) Closing stock at 30 September 20X1 was £15,600,000.

(2) Bad debts written off and the movement on the allowance for doubtful debts are to be included in administrative expenses. The allowance for doubtful debts is to be reduced to £500,000.

(3) The balance on the suspense account is the disposal proceeds of motor vehicles, entered to the suspense account pending correct treatment in the records.

The vehicles were sold on 1 October 20X0. They had cost £180,000 and at 1 October 20X0 their net book value was £60,000. The vehicles sold were all used in distributing the company's goods. Any profit or loss is to be included in distribution costs.

(4) Depreciation is to be provided for on the straight line basis as follows:

Machinery   10%

Motor vehicles   25%

Depreciation of motor vehicles is to be divided equally between distribution costs and administrative expenses, and depreciation of machinery is to be charged wholly to distribution costs.

(5) Prepayments and accruals at 30 September 20X1 were as follows:

	Prepayments £'000	Accruals £'000
Distribution costs	200	100
Administrative expenses	100	60

(6) The estimated tax charge for the year is £3,000,000.

Requirement

For Tafford Ltd's profit and loss account for the year ended 30 September 20X1 calculate the figures to be included for (a) cost of sales, (b) distribution costs, (c) administrative expenses and (d) interest payable.

See **Answer** at the end of this chapter.

Interactive question 2: UK GAAP financial statements II   [Difficulty level: Exam standard]

The following information is available about the balances and transactions of Alpaca Ltd:

BALANCES AT 30 APRIL 20X1	£'000
Fixed assets – cost	1,000
– accumulated depreciation	230
Stocks	410
Debtors	380
Cash at bank	87
Creditors	219
Issued share capital – equity shares of £1 each	400
Retained profits	818
10% Debentures	200
Debenture interest owing	10

TRANSACTIONS DURING YEAR ENDED 30 APRIL 20X2	£'000
Sales	4,006
Purchases	2,120
Expenses	1,640
Interest on debentures paid during year	20
Issue of 100,000 £1 equity shares at a premium of 50p per share	

There were no purchases or disposals of fixed assets during the year.

ADJUSTMENTS AT 30 APRIL 20X2

(1)   Depreciation of £100,000 is to be charged.
(2)   Bad debts of £20,000 are to be written off.

BALANCES AT 30 APRIL 20X2

	£'000
Stocks	450
Debtors (before writing off bad debts shown above)	690
Cash at bank	114
Creditors	180

Requirement

Prepare Alpaca Ltd's balance sheet as at 30 April 20X2 under UK GAAP as far as the information available allows, including a working showing how the retained profits figure in the balance sheet is calculated.

See **Answer** at the end of this chapter.

Summary

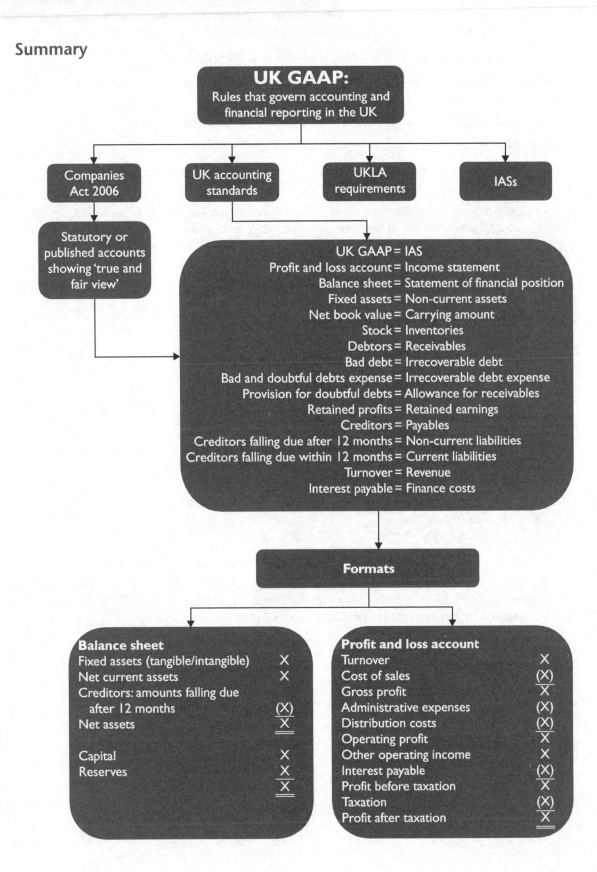

UK GAAP:
Rules that govern accounting and financial reporting in the UK

- Companies Act 2006
- UK accounting standards
- UKLA requirements
- IASs

Statutory or published accounts showing 'true and fair view'

UK GAAP	=	IAS
Profit and loss account	=	Income statement
Balance sheet	=	Statement of financial position
Fixed assets	=	Non-current assets
Net book value	=	Carrying amount
Stock	=	Inventories
Debtors	=	Receivables
Bad debt	=	Irrecoverable debt
Bad and doubtful debts expense	=	Irrecoverable debt expense
Provision for doubtful debts	=	Allowance for receivables
Retained profits	=	Retained earnings
Creditors	=	Payables
Creditors falling due after 12 months	=	Non-current liabilities
Creditors falling due within 12 months	=	Current liabilities
Turnover	=	Revenue
Interest payable	=	Finance costs

Formats

Balance sheet

Fixed assets (tangible/intangible)	X
Net current assets	X
Creditors: amounts falling due after 12 months	(X)
Net assets	X
Capital	X
Reserves	X
	X

Profit and loss account

Turnover	X
Cost of sales	(X)
Gross profit	X
Administrative expenses	(X)
Distribution costs	(X)
Operating profit	X
Other operating income	X
Interest payable	(X)
Profit before taxation	X
Taxation	(X)
Profit after taxation	X

Self-test

Answer the following questions.

1   Y Ltd purchased some plant on 1 January 20X0 for £38,000. The payment for the plant was correctly entered in the cash book but was entered on the debit side of plant repairs account.

Y Ltd charges depreciation on the straight line basis at 20% per annum.

How will Y's profit for the year ended 31 March 20X0 be affected by the error?

A   Understated by £30,400   C   Understated by £38,000
B   Understated by £36,100   D   Overstated by £1,900

2   The closing stock of X Ltd was £116,400 *excluding* the following two stock lines:

- 400 items which cost £4 each, but which were expected to sell for £3 each, with selling expenses of £200 in total.

- 200 different items which had cost £30 each, but which are defective. Rectification work will cost £1,200, after which they can be sold for £35 each, with selling expenses totalling £300.

What will appear on X Ltd's balance sheet for stock?

A   £122,300   C   £122,900
B   £121,900   D   £123,300

3   At 1 January 20X0 the capital structure of Q Limited was as follows:

	£
Issued share capital 1,000,000 equity shares of 50p each	500,000
Share premium account	300,000

On 1 April 20X0 the company made an issue of 200,000 50p shares at £1.30 each, and on 1 July the company made a 1 for 4 bonus issue.

Which of the following correctly states the company's share capital and share premium account at 31 December 20X0?

	Share capital	Share premium account
A	£750,000	£230,000
B	£875,000	£285,000
C	£750,000	£310,000
D	£750,000	£610,000

4   W Ltd bought a new printing machine at a cost of £80,000. The installation costs were £5,000 and the employees received training on how to use printing machines at a cost of £2,000. A regulatory test to ensure the machine functioned safely cost £1,000.

What is the cost of the machine in the company's balance sheet?

A   £80,000   C   £86,000
B   £85,000   D   £88,000

5   The electricity account for the year ended 30 June 20X1 was as follows.

	£
Opening balance for electricity accrued at 1 July 20X0	300
Payments made during the year	
1 August 20X0 for three months to 31 July 20X0	600
1 November 20X0 for three months to 31 October 20X0	720
1 February 20X1 for three months to 31 January 20X1	900
30 June 20X1 for three months to 30 April 20X1	840

Which of the following is the appropriate entry for electricity?

	Accrued at 30 June 20X1	Charge to profit and loss account year ended 30 June 20X1
A	£Nil	£3,060
B	£460	£3,320
C	£560	£3,320
D	£560	£3,420

6   The year end of M Ltd is 30 November 20X1. The company pays for its gas by a standing order of £600 per month. On 1 December 20X0 the statement from the gas supplier showed that M Ltd had overpaid by £200. M Ltd received gas bills for the four quarters commencing on 1 December 20X0 and ending on 30 November 20X1 for £1,300, £1,400, £2,100 and £2,000 respectively.

Which of the following is the correct charge for gas in M Ltd's profit and loss account for the year ended 30 November 20X1?

A   £6,800
B   £7,000
C   £7,200
D   £7,400

7   Teasdale Ltd, whose year end is 31 December, bought a car on 1 January 20X0 for:

	£
Cost	10,000
Road tax	150
Total	10,150

The car was depreciated at 25% per annum reducing balance then traded in for a replacement vehicle on 1 January 20X3 at an agreed value of £5,000.

What was the profit on disposal of the car?

A   £718
B   £781
C   £1,788
D   £1,836

8   Which of the following items does NOT appear under the heading 'reserves' on a company balance sheet?

A   Share premium account
B   Retained profits
C   Debentures
D   General reserve

9   Which of the following statements regarding a company profit and loss account is correct?

A   The Companies Act 2006 defines the expenses which are reported under 'cost of sales'

B   'Depreciation' appears as a separate heading in the profit and loss account

C   Interest payable is deducted from profit after taxation

D   Bad debts are included under one of the statutory expense headings (usually administrative expenses)

10   At the end of its first year of trading on 30 June 20X7 Lindman Ltd's net assets are £324,854. It has equity 25p share capital of £100,000 issued at 50p each, and a retained profits reserve of £59,854.

In relation to Lindman Ltd's balance sheet which of the following statements could be true?

A   It has share premium of £115,000
B   It has a general reserve of £65,000
C   It has share capital of £200,000
D   It has a general reserve of £115,000

Now, go back to the Learning Objectives in the Introduction. If you are satisfied that you have achieved these objectives, please tick them off.

Answer to Interactive question 1

TAFFORD LIMITED
PROFIT AND LOSS ACCOUNT FOR THE YEAR ENDED 30 SEPTEMBER 20X1

		£'000
	Turnover	41,600
(a)	Cost of sales (W1)	**(20,000)**
	Gross profit	21,600
(b)	Distribution costs (W2)	**(6,285)**
(c)	Administrative expenses (W3)	**(4,885)**
	Operating profit	10,430
(d)	Interest payable (10% × £10,000,000)	**(1,000)**
	Profit before taxation	9,430
	Taxation	(3,000)
	Profit after taxation	6,430

WORKINGS

(1) *Cost of sales*

	£'000
Opening stock	13,000
Purchases	22,600
	35,600
Less closing stock	(15,600)
	20,000

(2) *Distribution costs*

	£'000
Distribution costs (6,000 – 200 + 100)	5,900
Depreciation: machinery (10% × £3,000)	300
motor vehicles (25% × ½ × £(1,180 – 180))	125
Profit on sale of vehicles (100 – 60)	(40)
	6,285

(3) *Administrative expenses*

	£'000
Administrative expenses (5,000 – 100 + 60)	4,960
Bad debts	600
Reduction in allowance for doubtful debts	(800)
Depreciation: motor vehicles (25% × ½ × £(1,180 – 180))	125
	4,885

Answer to Interactive question 2

ALPACA LIMITED
BALANCE SHEET AS AT 30 APRIL 20X2

	£'000	£'000	£'000
Fixed assets			
Cost/ Accumulated depreciation (230 + 100)	1,000	(330)	670
Current assets			
Stock		450	
Debtors (690 – 20)		670	
Bank		114	
		1,234	
Less Creditors: amounts falling due in less than one year			
Creditors	180		
Accruals (W1)	10		
		(190)	
Net current assets			1,044
			1,714
Less Creditors: amounts falling due after more than one year			
10% Debentures			(200)
			1,514
Capital and reserves			
Share capital (400 + 100)			500
Share premium (100 × 50p)			50
Retained profits (W2)			964
			1,514

WORKINGS

(1)   *Accruals*

DEBENTURE INTEREST

	£'000		£'000
Bank	20	Bal b/d	10
Bal c/d (bal fig)	10	P+L	20
	30		30

(2)   *Retained profits*

	£'000	£'000	£'000
Bal b/f			818
Sales		4,006	
Opening stock	410		
Purchases	2,120		
Closing stock	(450)		
		(2,080)	
Gross profit		1,926	
Expenses	1,640		
Depreciation	100		
Bad debts written off	20		
Debenture interest payable (W1)	20		
		(1,780)	
Net profit for year			146
Balance c/f			964

1	B	DEBIT	Fixed assets	£38,000	
		CREDIT	Plant repairs		£38,000
		DEBIT	Dep'n expense (3/12 × 20% × £38,000)	£1,900	
		CREDIT	Accumulated dep'n		£1,900

Profit is understated by £38,000 – £1,900 = £36,100

2　C

	£
Draft figure	116,400
Line 1: (400 × £3) – £200	1,000
Line 2: (200 × £35) – £300 – £1,200	5,500
Final valuation	122,900

3　C

	£
Share capital @ 1.1.20X0	500,000
Issue on 1.4.20X0 (200,000 @ 50p)	100,000
Bonus issue (1.2m ÷ 4) @ 50p	150,000
Share capital as at 31.12.20X0	750,000

	£
Share premium @ 1.1.20X0	300,000
1.4.20X0 200,000 shares @ (130p – 50p)	160,000
Bonus issue (as above)	(150,000)
	310,000

4　C

	£
Cost of machine	80,000
Installation	5,000
Testing	1,000
	86,000

The employee training was general and not specifically related to bringing the asset into use, so its cost cannot be included.

5　C

ELECTRICITY ACCOUNT

			£			£
				Balance b/fwd		300
20X0:						
1 August	Paid bank		600			
1 November	Paid bank		720			
20X1:						
1 February	Paid bank		900			
30 June	Paid bank		840			
30 June	Accrual £840 × $^2/_3$		560	Profit and loss a/c		3,320
			3,620			3,620

6   A

GAS SUPPLIER ACCOUNT

	£			£
Balance b/fwd	200			
Bank £600 x 12	7,200	28 February	invoice	1,300
		31 May	invoice	1,400
		31 August	invoice	2,100
		30 November	invoice	2,000
		30 November	bal. c/d	600
	7,400			7,400

GAS ACCOUNT

		£			£
28 February	invoice	1,300			
31 May	invoice	1,400			
31 August	invoice	2,100			
30 November	invoice	2,000	30 November	Profit and loss a/c	6,800
		6,800			6,800

7   B

	£
Cost	10,000
20X0 Depreciation 25%	(2,500)
	7,500
20X1 Depreciation 25%	(1,875)
	5,625
20X2 Depreciation 25%	(1,406)
	4,219
20X3 Part exchange value	(5,000)
Profit on disposal	781

8   C   This is correct because debentures are accounted for as liabilities in the financial statements.

A and B are statutory reserves, while the general reserve can be created by the company if its constitution allows.

9   D   Correct, company will usually include this under distribution costs or administrative expenses.

A   Incorrect, the expenses in cost of sales are not defined by statute.

B   Incorrect, depreciation is included under the relevant statutory expense heading (eg office equipment depreciation goes into administrative expenses).

C   Incorrect, profit after taxation is calculated after interest has been deducted.

10   B

	£
Share capital	100,000
Share premium $\left(\dfrac{100,000}{25p} \times 25p \right)$	100,000
Retained profits reserve	59,854
Balancing figure	65,000
Net assets	324,854

This figure could be a general reserve of £65,000.

CHAPTER 13

Sole trader and partnership financial statements under UK GAAP

Introduction

Examination context

Topic List

Learning objectives

Tick off

- Record and account for transactions and events resulting in income, expenses, assets, liabilities and equity in accordance with the appropriate basis of accounting and the laws, regulations and accounting standards applicable to the financial statements ☐

- Record and account for changes in the ownership structure and ownership interests in an entity ☐

- Prepare an extended trial balance ☐

- Identify the main components of a set of financial statements and specify their purpose and interrelationship ☐

- Prepare and present a balance sheet, profit and loss account and cash flow statement from the accounting records and trial balance in a format which satisfies the information requirements of the entity ☐

Specific syllabus learning outcomes are: 1c, d; 2c; 3a, c

Syllabus links

You will encounter the accounting principles related to changes in ownership structure later in your Professional studies; legal and commercial issues related to partnerships are seen in Law and Business and Finance at the Professional stage as well.

Examination context

Questions on the topics in this chapter will be set as multiple choice questions, some of which may involve calculations so that the correct answer can be selected. Very often double entry questions are phrased in terms of preparing a journal.

In the exam you may be required to:

- Manipulate opening and closing balance sheets for sole traders to identify profit for the year using the accounting equation

- Use UK GAAP terminology when identifying figures in the profit and loss account and balance sheet of a sole trader or partnership

- Identify the unique features of accounting for general partnerships, especially capital and current accounts, drawings, profit sharing ratios, interest on capital and drawings, salaries, the profit appropriation statement, guaranteed shares, and loans from partners

- Identify figures when accounting for changes in partnership structure, including goodwill

- Prepare extracts from a cash flow statement

- Calculate the cash flow from operating activities

1 Sole trader financial statements

Section overview

- Sole trader financial statements are similar in terminology and format to those of companies prepared under UK GAAP, but there are important differences.

- Tax is not included in sole trader accounts.

- There are no formal requirements as to headings in the profit and loss account.

- The ownership interest half of the balance sheet shows opening capital, plus capital introduced, less drawings, plus profits, less losses to arrive at the closing net assets figure at the balance sheet date.

In terminology sole trader financial statements are very similar to a profit and loss account and balance sheet prepared under UK GAAP for a limited company. Where they differ is in relation to:

- **Tax**: a business operated by a sole trader has no legal identity separate from its owner, so the liability to pay tax on profits is the owner's and not the business's. This means that there is no tax expense in the profit and loss account, and no tax creditor in the balance sheet

- The **format** of the profit and loss account: there is no need to aggregate expenses under set headings

- The **ownership interest half of the balance sheet**: sole traders do not have share capital or reserves. Instead they show the following (this should look similar to the capital part of the accounting equation):

	£
Opening capital = net assets at start of period	X
Capital introduced in the period	X
Net profit/net loss of the period	X/(X)
Drawings (of cash, or of inventory at cost)	(X)
Closing capital = net assets at end of period	X

Worked example: Sole trader financial statements

Wasto had the following trial balance as at 31 December 20X4:

	£'000	£'000
Owner's capital at 1.1.X4		450
Bank loan		613
Freehold land and buildings	430	
Freehold land and buildings – accumulated depreciation		20
Plant and machinery – cost	830	
Plant and machinery – accumulated depreciation		222
Stock	190	
Sales		2,695
Purchases	2,152	
Loan interest	10	
Wages and salaries	254	
Drawings	31	
Sundry expenses	113	
Suspense account		420
Debtors	464	
Creditors		195
Cash	141	
	4,615	4,615

The following matters have now been discovered:

(a) On 1 January 20X4 Wasto injected a further £190,000 into the business. The only entry made was to debit cash.

(b) On 1 January 20X4 an item of plant that had cost £350,000 and on which depreciation of £74,000 had been charged was disposed of for £230,000. The only entry made was to debit cash.

(c) Depreciation of £36,000 needs to be charged on the remaining plant and machinery, and £5,000 on the land and buildings.

(d) Loan interest of £10,000 should be accrued at 31 December 20X4.

(e) Stock on hand at 31 December 20X4 cost £220,000.

Requirement

Prepare Wasto's ETB, his profit and loss account for the year ended 31 December 20X4 and his balance sheet at that date.

Solution

Wasto's ETB is as follows:

	Trial balance Debit £'000	Trial balance Credit £'000	Adjustments Debit £'000	Adjustments Credit £'000	P&L account Debit £'000	P&L account Credit £'000	Balance sheet Debit £'000	Balance sheet Credit £'000
Owner's capital at 1.1.X4		450						450
Bank loan		613						613
Freehold land and buildings	430						430	
Freehold land and buildings – accumulated depreciation		20		5				25
Plant and machinery – cost	830			350			480	
Plant and machinery – accumulated depreciation		222	74	36				184
Stock	190		220	220	190	220	220	
Sales		2,695				2,695		
Purchases	2,152				2,152			
Loan interest	10		10		20			
Wages and salaries	254				254			
Drawings	31						31	
Sundry expenses	113				113			
Suspense account		420	420					
Debtors	464						464	
Creditors		195						195
Cash	141						141	
Capital introduced				190				190
Disposals			276	230	46			
Depreciation expense			41		41			
Accruals				10				10
					2,816	2,915		
Net profit					99			99
	4,615	4,615	1,041	1,041	2,915	2,915	1,766	1,766

WASTO: PROFIT AND LOSS ACCOUNT FOR YEAR ENDED 31 DECEMBER 20X4

	£'000	£'000
Sales		2,695
Cost of sales		
Opening stock	190	
Purchases	2,152	
Closing stock	(220)	
		(2,122)
Gross profit		573
Expenses		
Loan interest	20	
Wages and salaries	254	
Sundry expenses	113	
Loss on disposal	46	
Depreciation expense	41	
		(474)
Net profit		99

WASTO: BALANCE SHEET AS AT 31 DECEMBER 20X4

	Cost £'000	Acc. depn. £'000	£'000
Fixed assets			
Freehold land and buildings	430	25	405
Plant and machinery	480	184	296
	910	209	701
Current assets			
Stock		220	
Debtors		464	
Cash		141	
		825	
Current liabilities			
Accruals		10	
Creditors		195	
		205	
Net current assets			620
Non-current liabilities			
Bank loan			(613)
			708
Ownership interest			
Opening capital			450
Capital introduced			190
Profit for year			99
Drawings			(31)
Closing capital			708

Interactive question 1: Sole trader financial statements   [Difficulty level: Exam standard]

In 20X5 Wasto takes drawings of £40,000 and ends 20X5 with net assets of £850,000. He did not introduce any capital in the year.

What was Wasto's net profit in 20X5?

See **Answer** at the end of this chapter.

2 Partnerships

Section overview

- A partnership is a business run by two or more people together; unless it is a limited liability partnership (LLP) it is not a separate legal entity so tax does not appear in the accounts.

- Parties agree how to appropriate the profits made by the business each year. Sometimes there are salaries, and there is always a profit sharing ratio (PSR).

A general **partnership** is an arrangement between two or more individuals in which they share the risks and rewards of a joint business operation, as if they were joint sole traders.

Definition

Partnership: The relationship which exists between persons carrying on a business in common with a view of profit.

Usually a general partnership is established formally with a written **partnership agreement**. However, if individuals act as though they are in partnership even if no written agreement exists, then it is presumed that a partnership does exist and that its terms are as laid down in the Partnership Act 1890.

2.1 The partnership agreement

A partnership agreement contains the terms of the partnership, in particular the financial arrangements between partners and how profit/loss should be appropriated. It should cover the following issues.

- **Capital**. Each partner puts in a share of the capital. Any minimum fixed amount should be stated.

- **Interest on capital**. Partners can pay themselves interest at an agreed rate on the capital they put into the business. **Interest on capital is treated as a profit appropriation**.

- **Partners' salaries**. Partners can pay themselves salaries. These are **not** salaries in the same way that an employee of the business is paid a wage or salary; **partners' salaries are an appropriation of profit, and not a profit and loss account expense**. Paying salaries gives each partner an income before the **residual profits** are shared out in PSR.

- **Profit-sharing ratio (PSR)**. Partners can agree to share **residual profits and losses after interest and salaries** in any profit-sharing ratio they choose. For example, three partners might agree to share profits equally, but if one partner does a greater share of the work, or has more experience and ability, or puts in more capital, the ratio of profit sharing might be different.

- **Guaranteed minimum profit shares**. Partners can agree that one or more partners should get a guaranteed minimum profit share, even if the partnership makes a smaller than expected profit, or a loss. If the amount allocated by using **interest on capital, salaries** and the **profit-sharing ratio** (PSR) is lower than this, the partner receives the guaranteed minimum profit share and the remaining profits are shared between the other partners in the profit-sharing ratio. Occasionally, **one partner will guarantee another partner's minimum profit share**. That partner will alone make up the difference.

- **Drawings**. Partners can withdraw profits from the business just like sole traders. They can agree to put a limit on how much they should draw out in any period, and they can be charged interest on their drawings during the year. **Interest on drawings is treated as a negative appropriation of profit**.

2.2 Appropriating partnership profit

The partnership's net profit is calculated in the same way as for a sole trader using a profit and loss ledger account, or the ETB. We then prepare an **appropriation statement**, which

- **Allocates** interest on capital, interest on drawings, and salaries to each partner, then
- **Shares** out the **residual profit** in the PSR

Worked example: Appropriating partnership profits

Bill and Ben are partners sharing profits in the PSR 2:1, after they each take a salary of £10,000 per year. Net profit **before** deducting salaries is £26,000.

How much profit is appropriated to each partner?

Solution

First, the two salaries are deducted from profit, leaving £6,000 (£26,000 – £20,000).

This £6,000 has to be distributed between Bill and Ben in the ratio 2:1, so Bill will receive twice as much as Ben. (£4,000:£2,000)

Profit appropriation statement

Ratio	2 :	1	
	Bill	Ben	Total
	£	£	£
Salary	10,000	10,000	20,000
Share of residual profits (£6,000 in ratio 2:1)	4,000	2,000	6,000
Total profit share	14,000	12,000	26,000

Interactive question 2: Profit share [Difficulty level: Exam standard]

Tom, Dick and Harry want to share out net profit of £170,000, in the ratio 7:3:5. Dick gets a salary of £20,000 pa. How much would each partner get?

See **Answer** at the end of this chapter.

2.3 Guaranteed minimum profit share

Partners can agree that one or more partners will receive a **minimum appropriation of profit,** even if the business makes a loss, or one partner is appropriated a loss while the others take all the profit.

Worked example: Guaranteed minimum profit share

Sita, Nisha and Zelda share profits in the ratio of 2:2:1 but Zelda has a guaranteed minimum profit of £18,000. The net profit for the year is £75,000.

The sum of the ratio 'parts' is 2 + 2 + 1 = 5. Each part is worth £15,000 so if we just used the PSR the profits would be allocated as follows:

Ratio	2 :	2 :	1	
	Sita	Nisha	Zelda	Total
	£	£	£	£
Initial profit share	30,000	30,000	15,000	75,000

However, this leaves Zelda with less than her guaranteed minimum, so a further reallocation of profits is made from the other two partners equally, because they share 2:2, to give her the minimum amount.

Ratio	2	:	2	:	1	
	Sita		Nisha		Zelda	Total
	£		£		£	£
PSR	30,000		30,000		15,000	75,000
Reallocation (2:2)	(1,500)		(1,500)		3,000	0
Total profit share	28,500		28,500		18,000	75,000

Interactive question 3: Profit appropriation   [Difficulty level: Exam standard]

Anna, Brian and Clare have a profit-sharing ratio of 3:2:1, with Clare due a salary of £8,000. Brian has a minimum profit share of £16,000 guaranteed by Anna. The partnership made a profit of £26,000 in the year.

How much profit will be appropriated to each partner?

See **Answer** at the end of this chapter.

3 Preparing partnership accounts

Section overview

- Each partner's interest in the partnership is shown in a capital account and a current account.

- If a partner has made a loan to the partnership, this is treated the same as a third party loan, with interest deducted before arriving at net profit. Interest may be credited to the partner's current account rather than being paid in cash.

- A profit appropriation statement is used as a working to appropriate salaries, interest on capital, interest on drawings and residual profit share to each partner.

3.1 How does accounting for partnerships differ from accounting for sole traders?

Partnership accounts are **identical** in many respects to the accounts of sole traders.

(a) Assets and liabilities are like the **net assets** of any other business, and are accounted for in the same way. Even where a **loan to a partnership** comes from a partner, this is accounted for as if it were a third party loan, in the top half of the balance sheet.

(b) **Net profit** is calculated in the same way as the net profit of a sole trader. If a partner makes a loan to the business (as distinct from a capital contribution) then interest on the loan is an expense in the profit and loss account, in the same way as interest on any other loan from a third party.

(c) Just like a sole trader **tax** does not appear in partnership accounts.

There are two respects in which partnership accounts are **different**, however.

(a) The **ownership interest** of each partner must be shown.
(b) The net profit must be **appropriated** between the partners and shown in the accounts.

Definition

Appropriation of profit: Sharing out profits in accordance with the partnership agreement.

3.2 Accounting for each partner's ownership interest

- Initial capital contributions are recorded in **capital accounts** for each partner. (Since each partner is ultimately entitled to repayment of capital it is clearly vital to keep a record of how much is owed to whom.)

- Profits and losses appropriated over time, less drawings, are shown in a **current account** for each partner.

Definition

Current account: A record of the **profits retained in the business** by the partner.

A current account increases when the partnership makes profits, and decreases when the partner makes drawings, or when the partnership makes a loss.

Differences between capital and current accounts are as follows.

- The balance on the **capital account** remains **static** from year to year (with one or two exceptions).

- The balance on the **current account** is continually **fluctuating** up and down, as the partnership makes profits and losses which are shared out between the partners, and as each partner takes out drawings.

If the partnership agreement provides for interest on capital, partners receive **interest on the balance in their capital account, but not on the balance on their current account.**

If the amount of a partner's **drawings** exceeds the balance on his/her current account, the current account will show **a debit balance** brought forward at the beginning of the next period.

The **ownership interest** side of the partnership balance sheet will therefore consist of:

- Capital accounts for each partner.
- Current accounts for each partner.

3.3 Accounting for loans by partners

A partner making a loan to the partnership becomes its creditor. On the balance sheet the loan is shown separately as a long term liability (unless repayable within twelve months, in which case it is a current liability). **Interest on the loan is a deduction from profit to arrive at net profit, not an appropriation of profit.** Interest is payable at 5%.

Interest on partners' loans is usually credited to the partner's current account as this is administratively more convenient, especially when the partner does not particularly want to be paid the loan interest in cash immediately it becomes due.

3.4 Accounting for appropriation of net profit/loss

The net profit of a partnership is shared out in the PSR in an **appropriation account**, which follows on from the profit and loss ledger account itself.

The accounting entries for an individual share of profits for each partner are:

(a) DEBIT   P & L ledger account with net profit c/d
      CREDIT   P & L appropriation account with net profit b/d

(b) DEBIT   P & L appropriation account
      CREDIT   The current accounts of each partner

The steps to take are as follows.

Step 1
Establish the net profit, after deducting interest on loans from partners.

Step 2
Appropriate interest on capital and salaries first. These items are appropriations of profit and do not appear in the P & L account.

Step 3
Charge partners interest on their drawings where relevant.

Step 4
Residual profits are shared out between partners in the PSR.

Step 5
Each partner's share of profits is credited to his/her current account.

The calculations involved in steps 2 to 4 are made in a **profit appropriation statement**.

In practice each partner's capital account will be a separate ledger account, as will their current account, but the examples which follow use a columnar form to show how it works.

Worked example: Partnership accounts

Locke, Niece and Munster are in partnership and share profits in the ratio 3:2:1. They also agree that:

(a)   All three should receive interest at 12% on capital.

(b)   Munster should receive a salary of £6,000 per annum.

(c)   Interest will be charged on drawings at the rate of 3% (a full year charged on any drawings in the year).

(d)   The interest rate on the £6,000 loan from Locke is 5%.

Their capital and current accounts as at 1 January 20X5 are as follows:

	£	£
Capital accounts as at 1.1.X5		
Locke	20,000	
Niece	8,000	
Munster	6,000	
		34,000
Current accounts as at 1.1.X5		
Locke	9,500	
Niece	3,300	
Munster	8,800	
		21,600

Drawings made during the year to 31 December 20X5 were:

	£	£
Drawings in 20X5		
Locke	(6,000)	
Niece	(4,000)	
Munster	(7,000)	
		(17,000)
		38,600

The net profit for the year to 31 December 20X5 was £24,870 **before** deducting loan interest.

Requirement

Prepare a profit and loss appropriation statement for the year to 31 December 20X5, and the partners' capital accounts and current accounts at that date.

Solution

The interest payable to Locke on his loan is:

5% of £6,000 = £300

This is **debited** to net profit in the profit and loss account and **credited** to Locke's current account. As a result, the profit to be appropriated is:

	£
Draft net profit	24,870
Interest	(300)
	24,570

The interest payable by each partner on their drawings during the year is:

		£
Locke	3% of £6,000	180
Niece	3% of £4,000	120
Munster	3% of £7,000	210
		510

LOCKE, NIECE AND MUNSTER: PROFIT APPROPRIATION STATEMENT

Ratio	3: Locke £	2: Niece £	1 Munster £	Total £
Interest charged on drawings	(180)	(120)	(210)	(510)
Salary			6,000	6,000
Interest on capital				
12% × £20,000	2,400			
12% × £8,000		960		
12% × £6,000			720	4,080
Share of residual profit: (24,570 + 510 – 6,000 – 4,080) = £15,000 in 3:2:1 ratio	7,500	5,000	2,500	15,000
Total profit share	9,720	5,840	9,010	24,570

PARTNERS' CURRENT ACCOUNTS

	Locke £	Niece £	Munster £		Locke £	Niece £	Munster £
Drawings	6,000	4,000	7,000	Bal b/d	9,500	3,300	8,800
				Interest	300		
Bal c/d	13,520	5,140	10,810	Profit share	9,720	5,840	9,010
	19,520	9,140	17,810		19,520	9,140	17,810

PARTNERS' CAPITAL ACCOUNTS

		Locke £	Niece £	Munster £
	Balance b/d	20,000	8,000	6,000

3.5 Partnership accounts on the ETB

The ETB can be used to help prepare partnership accounts. The differences to sole trader ETBs are as follows:

- **Accrued interest on a partner's loan** is accounted for in the adjustments column and included in the cross-casts, so the net profit figure in the debit column of the profit and loss account is then the amount to be appropriated

DEBIT	Interest expense	£X	
CREDIT	Current account		£X

- Each partner's drawings are transferred in the adjustments columns from the drawings accounts to the current account

DEBIT	Current accounts	£X
CREDIT	Drawings accounts	£X

- The profit appropriation statement is prepared as a separate working, then each partner's total profit share is accounted for as follows

DEBIT	Profit and loss account	£X
CREDIT	Current accounts (balance sheet)	£X

Worked example: Partnership accounts on the ETB

Frank and Myra are in partnership sharing profits 2:1. Each partner has an annual salary of £6,750. Frank's loan to the partnership attracts interest at 5% per annum. Their trial balance at 30 June 20X4 is as follows

	Debit £	Credit £
Loan from Frank		20,000
Fixed assets – NBV	100,000	
Stock at 1 July 20X3	15,000	
Debtors	18,000	
Creditors		14,000
Sales		85,000
Purchases	52,000	
Loan interest		
Expenses	12,500	
Drawings		
Frank	14,000	
Myra	15,000	
Cash	6,300	
Capital accounts		
Frank		20,000
Myra		20,000
Current accounts at 1 July 20X3		
Frank		38,400
Myra		35,400
	232,800	232,800

You are told that closing stock cost £16,500.

Requirement

Prepare Frank and Myra's extended trial balance at 30 June 20X4.

Solution

We process the adjustment for interest and the transfer of drawings as above, then make the adjustment for closing stock. Next we extend the ETB to calculate the net profit for appropriation:

	Trial balance Debit £	Trial balance Credit £	Adjustments Debit £	Adjustments Credit £	P&L account Debit £	P&L account Credit £	Balance sheet Debit £	Balance sheet Credit £
Loan from Frank		20,000						20,000
Fixed assets – NBV	100,000						100,000	
Stock	15,000		16,500	16,500	15,000	16,500	16,500	
Debtors	18,000						18,000	
Creditors		14,000						14,000
Sales		85,000				85,000		
Purchases	52,000				52,000			
Loan interest			1,000		1,000			
Expenses	12,500				12,500			
Drawings								
Frank	14,000			14,000				
Myra	15,000			15,000				
Cash	6,300						6,300	
Capital accounts								
Frank		20,000						20,000
Myra		20,000						20,000
Current accounts								
Frank		38,400	14,000	1,000				
Myra		35,400	15,000					
Net profit for appropriation					21,000			
	232,800	232,800	46,500	46,500	101,500	101,500		

PROFIT APPROPRIATION STATEMENT

Ratio	2 Frank £	1 Myra £	Total £
Salaries	6,750	6,750	13,500
PSR (2:1)	5,000	2,500	7,500
Total profit share	11,750	9,250	21,000

The final ETB is as follows:

	Trial balance Debit £	Trial balance Credit £	Adjustments Debit £	Adjustments Credit £	P&L account Debit £	P&L account Credit £	Balance sheet Debit £	Balance sheet Credit £
Loan from Frank		20,000						20,000
Fixed assets – NBV	100,000						100,000	
Stock	15,000		16,500	16,500	15,000	16,500	16,500	
Debtors	18,000						18,000	
Creditors		14,000						14,000
Sales		85,000				85,000		
Purchases	52,000				52,000			
Loan interest			1,000		1,000			
Expenses	12,500				12,500			
Drawings								
Frank	14,000			14,000				
Myra	15,000			15,000				
Cash	6,300						6,300	
Capital accounts								
Frank		20,000						20,000
Myra		20,000						20,000
Current accounts								
Frank*		38,400	14,000	1,000				37,150
Myra**		35,400	15,000					29,650
Appropriated net profit								
Frank					11,750			
Myra					9,250			
	232,800	232,800	46,500	46,500	101,500	101,500	140,800	140,800

** Myra's current account balance is 35,400 – 15,000 + 9,250 = 29,650

The profit and loss account for the partnership will be presented as for sole traders. The balance sheet is as follows:

FRANK AND MYRA
BALANCE SHEET AS AT 30 JUNE 20X4

	£	£
Fixed assets		100,000
Current assets		
Stock	16,500	
Debtors	18,000	
Cash	6,300	
	40,800	
Current liabilities		
Creditors	(14,000)	
Net current assets		26,800
Non-current liabilities		
Loan from Frank		(20,000)
		106,800
Capital accounts		
Frank		20,000
Myra		20,000
Current accounts		
Frank		37,150
Myra		29,650
		106,800

4 Accounting for changes in partnership structure

Section overview

- When a partner dies or retires, the remaining parties normally carry on the business, buying out the departing partner's share of the net assets, including goodwill.

4.1 Retirement or death of a partner

Any changes in a partnership require a new agreement. Unless the agreement specifically states otherwise, legally the old partnership is dissolved and a new partnership is created. However, from an accounting viewpoint, it is more realistic to treat the partnership as **continuing** but with a change in the partners and the PSR.

On the retirement or death of a partner, we need to:

- Calculate the profits up to the **date of change** and appropriate them according to the **old PSR**.
- Appropriate the profits **after** the date of change according to the **new PSR**.

Worked example: Retirement

Returning to the example of Locke, Niece and Munster, assume that Locke retired on 30 September 20X5 and Niece and Munster decided to continue the partnership on the same terms as before, but with a PSR of 1:1. Locke's drawings of £6,000 were taken in the period to 30 September 20X5 and Locke's loan remained with the partnership after his retirement.

Requirement

Prepare the relevant profit appropriation statements for the year to 31 December 20X5.

Solution

We need to treat the accounting year as being in two sections:

(a)   Period to 30 September 20X5 (9 months), with partners Locke, Niece and Munster.
(b)   Period from 1 October to 31 December 20X5 (3 months), with partners Niece and Munster.

Up to the date of retirement the profit to be appropriated net of interest is £24,570 x 9/12 = £18,427, since the loan was not repaid at retirement and we can assume that interest accrues evenly over the year.

Locke, Niece and Munster: Profit appropriation statement

Ratio to 30 September 20X5	3: Locke £	2: Niece £	1 Munster £	Total £
Interest charged on drawings (9/12 for N&M)	(180)	(90)	(158)	(428)
Salary 9/12			4,500	4,500
Interest on capital				
12% × £20,000 × 9/12	1,800			
12% × £8,000 × 9/12		720		
12% × £6,000 × 9/12			540	3,060
Share of residual profit: (18,427+ 428 –				
4,500 – 3,060) = £11,295 in 3:2:1 ratio	5,648	3,765	1,882	11,295
Total profit share	7,268	4,395	6,764	18,427

From Locke's retirement the profit to be appropriated net of interest is £24,570 × 3/12 = £6,143.

Ratio from 30 September 20X5	1: Niece £	1 Munster £	Total £
Interest charged on drawings (3/12)	(30)	(52)	(82)
Salary 3/12		1,500	1,500
Interest on capital			
12% × £8,000 × 3/12	240		
12% × £6,000 × 3/12		180	420
Share of residual profit: (6,143 + 82 – 1,500 – 420)			
= £4,305 in 1:1 ratio	2,152	2,153	4,305
Total profit share	2,362	3,781	6,143

4.2   Goodwill in the partnership accounts

Usually on a partner's retirement or death a **valuation of the partnership's net assets** is carried out, or the partners simply agree that as well as a share of the profits to the date of retirement the retiring partner should also take a **share in the partnership's goodwill,** in the form of **a settlement in cash or other assets** from the other partners. Once the partner has gone the goodwill is then removed from the accounts.

The principles behind how we account for retirement or death of a partner when there is a settlement which includes recognition of the value of the partnership's goodwill are the same as we used when converting and selling a sole trader's business.

In the example that follows we combine each partner's capital and current accounts for ease of explanation.

Worked example: Death of a partner

George, Amanda and Henry have been in partnership for many years, sharing profits equally and preparing accounts to 31 December each year. As at 1 January 20X2 each partner's combined capital and current accounts were as follows:

	£
George	138,540
Amanda	95,400
Henry	125,950
	359,890

During 20X2 the partnership made profits of £584,580 and each partner took drawings of £50,000.

On 31 December 20X2 Henry died. The remaining partners value goodwill at £300,000 at that date, but do not wish this valuation to remain in the accounts. George and Amanda will continue in partnership, sharing profits equally.

Solution

Henry's estate is entitled to receive payment for his ownership of a share in the partnership. When Henry dies there are two options:

- Break up the partnership by selling all the assets and sharing out the net proceeds among George, Amanda and Henry's estate.

- A 'buy out' of Henry's share of the partnership by George and Amanda

The parties have agreed on the second option, but need to determine how much Henry's share is worth, and therefore how much his estate should be paid as consideration.

It is possible to determine how much the remaining partners will need to pay simply by using the capital/current accounts.

(a) Appropriate profits (£584,580/3 = £194,860 each)
(b) Share out the goodwill in old PSR: £300,000/3 = £100,000 each
(c) Calculate the amount Henry's estate will be paid in cash, being the balancing figure on the account
(d) Remove the goodwill in the new PSR: £300,000/2 = £150,000 each
(e) Carry down the balances on the remaining two partners' accounts

PARTNERS' CAPITAL AND CURRENT ACCOUNTS

	George £	Amanda £	Henry £		George £	Amanda £	Henry £
Drawings	50,000	50,000	50,000	Bal b/d	138,540	95,400	125,950
Cash (bal fig) (c)			370,810	Profit share (a)	194,860	194,860	194,860
Goodwill (d)	150,000	150,000		Goodwill (b)	100,000	100,000	100,000
Bal c/d (e)	233,400	190,260					
	433,400	390,260	420,810		433,400	390,260	420,810

To prove these calculations are correct we can reconstruct the balance sheet after the payment has been made:

	£
Opening net assets = total of the three capital/current accounts at 1.1.X2	359,890
Add net profit for the year	584,580
Less drawings (3 × £50,000)	(150,000)
Closing net assets at 31.12.X2	794,470
Less cash paid to Henry's estate	(370,810)
	423,660
George's capital/current account	233,400
Amanda's capital/current account	190,260
	423,660

4.3 Admission of a partner

When a new partner is admitted, a new agreement is needed to cover the appropriation of profits.

If the new partner introduces **additional capital** into the partnership, the total amount they bring in must be **credited** to their capital account.

The existing partners' share of the partnership's goodwill at the date of admission is credited to them in the old PSR and then (assuming they do not wish to retain goodwill in the accounts) debited in the new PSR. The result is that the new partner will be shown to have purchased a share of the goodwill by introducing cash.

Worked example: Admission of a partner

Oil and Grease, equal partners in a vehicle repair business, agree to Detergent becoming a partner on 1 January 20X1. At that date Oil and Grease value the business's goodwill at £5,000 and their capitals are Oil – £12,000; Grease – £9,000. Detergent agrees to introduce £2,000 capital. The partners agree to share profits in the ratio – Oil 2: Grease 2: Detergent 1, and not to retain goodwill in the accounts.

The partners' capital accounts are as follows, showing that £1,000 of Detergent's cash introduced has actually been paid in equal shares to Oil and Grease in respect of their shares of the business's goodwill:

CAPITAL ACCOUNTS

Ratio	2:	2:	1		1:	1	
	Oil	Grease	Detergent		Oil	Grease	Detergent
	£	£	£		£	£	£
				Balances b/d	12,000	9,000	
Goodwill in new PSR	2,000	2,000	1,000	Goodwill in old PSR	2,500	2,500	
Balances c/d	12,500	9,500	1,000	Cash introduced			2,000
	14,500	11,500	2,000		14,500	11,500	2,000

5 Cash flow statements

Section overview

- Cash flow statements are a useful addition to the financial statements because accounting profit is not the only indicator of performance. Cash flow statements concentrate on the sources and uses of cash and are a useful indicator of liquidity and solvency.

It has been argued that 'profit' does not always give a useful or meaningful picture of a company's operations. Readers of a company's financial statements might even be misled by a reported profit figure.

(a) Shareholders might believe that if a company makes a profit after tax, of say, £100,000 then this is the amount which it could afford to pay as a dividend. Unless the company has sufficient cash available to stay in business and also to pay a dividend, the shareholders' expectations would be wrong.

(b) Employees might believe that if a company makes profits, it can afford to pay higher wages next year. This opinion may not be correct: the ability to pay wages depends on the availability of cash.

(c) Cash is the lifeblood of the business. Survival of a business entity depends not so much on profits as on its ability to pay its debts when they fall due. Such payments might include 'profit and loss' items such as material purchases, wages, interest and taxation etc, but also capital payments for new fixed assets and the repayment of loan capital when this falls due (for example on the redemption of debentures).

From these examples, it may be apparent that a company's performance and prospects depend not so much on the 'profits' earned in a period, but more realistically on liquidity or cash flows.

The great advantage of a cash flow statement is that it is unambiguous and provides information which is additional to that provided in the rest of the accounts. It also describes the cash flows of an organisation by activity and not by balance sheet classification.

5.1 Basic cash flow statement

A very basic cash flow statement follows.

	£
Net cash flow from operating activities	X
Returns on investment and servicing of finance	X
Taxation	X
Capital expenditure	X
Equity dividends paid	X
Management of liquid resources	X
Financing	X
Increase/(decrease) in cash	X/(X)

5.2 Net cash flow from operating activities

One way of arriving at net cash flow from operating activities is to start from operating profit and adjust for non-cash items, such as depreciation, debtors etc. This is known as the indirect method. A proforma calculation is given below.

	£
Operating profit (P&L)	X
Add depreciation	X
Loss (profit) on sale of fixed assets	X
(Increase)/decrease in stocks	(X)/X
(Increase)/decrease in debtors	(X)/X
Increase/(decrease) in creditors	X/(X)
Net cash flow from operating activities	X

It is important to understand why certain items are added and others subtracted. Note the following points.

(a) Depreciation is not a cash expense, but is deducted in arriving at the profit figure in the profit and loss account. It makes sense, therefore, to eliminate it by adding it back.

(b) By the same logic, a loss on a disposal of a fixed asset (arising through underprovision of depreciation) needs to be added back and a profit deducted.

(c) An increase in stocks means less cash – you have spent cash on buying stock.

(d) An increase in debtors means debtors have not paid as much, therefore less cash.

(e) If we pay off creditors, causing the figure to decrease, again we have less cash.

You will probably need to use the **indirect method** in examination questions based around FRS 1 (see below).

The **direct method** pro-forma is shown below.

	£
Cash received from customers	X
Cash payments to suppliers	X
Cash payments to and on behalf of employees	X
Net cash flow from operating activities	X

Worked example: Net cash from operating activities

Quest Ltd has operating profit for the year to 31 December 20X6 of £850, after charging £650 for depreciation and making a profit on sale of a car of £120.

The balance sheet for the year shows the following entries:

	20X6	20X5
Stock	586	763
Trade debtors	1,021	589
Trade creditors	443	1,431

Requirement

Calculate the net cash from operating activities

Solution

	£
Operating profit	850
Add depreciation	650
Deduct profit on disposal	(120)
Add decrease in stocks	177
Deduct increase in debtors	(432)
Deduct decrease in creditors	(988)
Net cash from operating activities	137

5.3 Returns on investments and servicing of finance

Cash flows from investing activities and servicing of finance are calculated separately in the cash flow statement.

The pro-forma for return on investments

Interest paid	(X)
Interest received	X
Dividends received	X
Cash flow from investing activities and servicing of finance	X

Worked example: Cash flows

Pearl Ltd acquired a new factory in the year to 30 June 20X6 for a cost of £805,000. They sold their old factory for £425,000. They also received interest on surplus funds of £350,000. Calculate cash flows arising from investing activities.

Solution

	£
Interest received	350,000
Return on investments	350,000

Note. The movements on fixed assets will be part of the capital expenditure calculation.

C
H
A
P
T
E
R

13

5.4 Cash flows from financing activities

The pro-forma to learn for this part of the cash flow statement is:

Proceeds from issue of share capital	X
Proceeds from long-term borrowing	X
Cash flow from financing activities	X

Worked example: Cash flows from financing activities

Spear Ltd issued 87,500 £1 shares at par during the year to 31 December 20X6. Loans taken out increased from £18,000 at the beginning of the year to £30,000 at the end of the year. The company declared a dividend of 10p per share. Calculate the cash flows from financing activities.

	£
Proceeds from issue of shares	87,500
Increase in loans	12,000
Cash flows from financing activities	99,500

Please note that only dividends paid (as opposed to declared) in the period represent cash flows. Interest paid on the loans will be shown under 'Returns on investments and servicing of finance'.

5.5 FRS 1 Cash flow statements (revised)

FRS 1 sets out the structure of a cash flow statement and it also sets the minimum level of disclosure. In the exam you will be asked to calculate an element of the cash flow statement (such as cash flows from activities).

5.6 Objective

The FRS begins with the following statement.

'The objective of this FRS is to ensure that reporting entities falling within its scope:

(a) Report their cash generation and cash absorption for a period by highlighting the significant components of cash flow in a way that facilitates comparison of the cash flow performance of different businesses.

(b) Provide information that assists in the assessment of their liquidity, solvency and financial adaptability.'

5.7 Scope

The FRS applies to all financial statements intended to give a true and fair view of the financial position and profit or loss (or income and expenditure), except those of various exempt bodies in group accounts situations or where the content of the financial statement is governed by other statutes or regulatory regimes. In addition, small entities are excluded as defined by companies legislation.

5.8 Format of the cash flow statement

An example is given of the format of a cash flow statement for a single company and this is reproduced in Section 5.12.

A cash flow statement should list its cash flows for the period classified under the following **standard headings**:

(a) **Operating activities** (using either the direct or indirect method)
(b) **Returns on investments and servicing of finance**
(c) **Taxation**
(d) **Capital expenditure** and financial investment
(e) **Acquisitions and disposals**
(f) **Equity dividends paid**
(g) **Management of liquid resources**
(h) **Financing**

The last two headings can be shown in a single section provided a subtotal is given for each heading. Acquisitions and disposals **are not on your syllabus**; the heading is included here for completeness.

Individual categories of inflows and outflows under the standard headings should be disclosed separately either in the cash flow statements or in a note to it unless they are allowed to be shown net. Cash inflows and outflows may be shown net if they relate to the management of liquid resources or financing and the inflows and outflows:

(a) Relate in substance to a single financing transaction (unlikely to be a concern here).

(b) Or are due to short maturities and high turnover occurring from rollover or reissue (for example, short-term deposits).

The requirement to show cash inflows and outflows separately does not apply to cash flows relating to operating activities.

Each cash flow should be classified according to the substance of the transaction giving rise to it.

5.9 Links to other primary statements

Because the information given by a cash flow statement is best appreciated in the context of the information given by the other primary statements, the FRS requires two reconciliations, between:

(a) Operating profit and the net cash flow from operating activities
(b) The movement in cash in the period and the movement in net debt.

Neither reconciliation forms part of the cash flow statement but each may be given either adjoining the statement or in a separate note.

The reconciliation in point (a) above has already been given in the formula to learn in Section 5.2.

The **movement in net debt** should identify the following components and reconcile these to the opening and closing balance sheet amount:

(a) The cash flows of the entity
(b) Other non-cash changes
(c) The recognition of changes in market value and exchange rate movements

5.10 Definitions

The FRS includes the following important definitions (only those of direct concern to your syllabus are included here). Note particularly the definitions of cash and liquid resources.

(a) An **active market** is a market of sufficient depth to absorb the investment held without a significant effect on the price. (This definition affects the definition of liquid resources below.)

(b) **Cash** is cash in hand and deposits repayable on demand with any qualifying financial institution, less overdrafts from any qualifying financial institution repayable on demand. Deposits are repayable on demand if they can be withdrawn at any time without notice and without penalty or if a maturity or period of notice of not more than 24 hours or one working day has been agreed. Cash includes cash in hand and deposit denominated in foreign currencies.

(c) **Cash flow** is an increase or decrease in an amount of cash.

(d) Liquid resources are current asset investments held as readily disposable stores of value. A readily disposable investment is one that:

   (i)   Is disposable by the reporting entity without curtailing or disrupting its business
   (ii) Is either:

         (1)   Readily convertible into known amounts of cash at or close to its carrying amount, or
         (2)   Traded in an active market.

(e) Net debt is the borrowings of the reporting entity less cash and liquid resources. Where cash and liquid resources exceed the borrowings of the entity reference should be to 'net funds' rather than to 'net debt'.

(f) Overdraft is a borrowing facility repayable on demand that is used by drawing on a current account with a qualifying financial institution.

5.11 Classification of cash flows by standard heading

The FRS looks at each of the cash flow categories in turn.

5.11.1 Operating activities

Cash flows from operating activities are in general the cash effects of transactions and other events relating to operating or trading activities, normally shown in the profit and loss account in arriving at operating profit. They include cash flows in respect of operating items relating to provisions, whether or not the provision was included in operating profit.

A reconciliation between the **operating profit** reported in the profit and loss account and the **net cash flow from operating activities** should be given either adjoining the cash flow statement or as a note. The reconciliation is not part of the cash flow statement: if adjoining the cash flow statement, it should be clearly labelled and kept separate. The reconciliation should disclose separately the movements in stocks, debtors and creditors related to operating activities and other differences between cash flows and profits.

You must know the **reconciliation** and **format** of the cash flow statement.

5.11.2 Returns on investments and servicing of finance

These are receipts resulting from the ownership of an investment and payments to providers of finance and non-equity shareholders (eg the holders of preference shares).

Cash inflows from returns on investments and servicing of finance include:

(a) Interest received, including any related tax recovered

(b) Dividends received, net of any tax credits

Cash outflows from returns on investments and servicing of finance include:

(a) Interest paid (even if capitalised), including any tax deducted and paid to the relevant tax authority.

(b) Cash flows that are treated as finance costs (this will include issue costs on debt and non-equity share capital).

(c) The interest element of finance lease rental payments.

(d) Dividends paid on non-equity shares of the entity.

5.11.3 Taxation

These are cash flows to or from taxation authorities in respect of the reporting entity's profits and gains. VAT and other sales taxes are discussed below.

(a) Taxation cash inflows include cash receipts from the relevant tax authority of tax rebates, claims or returns of overpayments.

(b) Taxation cash outflows include cash payments to the relevant tax authority of tax.

5.11.4 Capital expenditure and financial investment

These cash flows are those related to the acquisition or disposal of any fixed asset other than one required to be classified under 'acquisitions and disposals' (discussed below), and any current asset investment not included in liquid resources (also dealt with below). If no cash flows relating to financial investment fall to be included under this heading the caption may be reduced to 'capital expenditure'.

The cash inflows here include:

(a)   Receipts from sales or disposals of property, plant or equipment.
(b)   Receipts from the repayment of the reporting entity's loans to other entities.

Cash outflows in this category include:

(a)   Payments to acquire property, plant or equipment
(b)   Loans made by the reporting entity

5.11.5 Acquisitions and disposals

These cash flows are related to the acquisition or disposal of any trade or business, or of an investment in an entity that is either an associate, a joint venture, or a subsidiary undertaking (these group matters are beyond the scope of your syllabus).

(a)   Cash inflows here include receipts from sales of trades or businesses.
(b)   Cash outflows here include payments to acquire trades or businesses.

5.11.6 Equity dividends paid

The cash outflows are dividends paid on the reporting entity's equity shares.

5.11.7 Management of liquid resources

This section should include cash flows in respect of liquid resources as defined above. Each entity should explain what it includes as liquid resources and any changes in its policy. The cash flows in this section can be shown in a single section with those under 'financing' provided that separate subtotals for each are given.

Cash inflows include:

(a)   Withdrawals from short-term deposits not qualifying as cash
(b)   Inflows from disposal or redemption of any other investments held as liquid resources

Cash outflows include:

(a)   Payments into short-term deposits not qualifying as cash
(b)   Outflows to acquire any other investments held as liquid resources

5.11.8 Financing

Financing cash flows comprise receipts or repayments of principal from or to external providers of finance. The cash flows in this section can be shown in a single section with those under 'management of liquid resources' provided that separate subtotals for each are given.

Financing cash inflows include:

(a)   Receipts from issuing shares or other equity instruments

(b)   Receipts from issuing debentures, loans and from other long-term and short-term borrowings (other than overdrafts)

Financing cash outflows include:

(a)   Repayments of amounts borrowed (other than overdrafts)
(b)   The capital element of finance lease rental payments
(c)   Payments to reacquire or redeem the entity's shares
(d)   Payments of expenses or commission on any issue of equity shares

5.12 Example: Single company

The following example is provided by the standard for a single company.

XYZ LIMITED
Cash flow statement for the year ended 31 December 1996

Reconciliation of operating profit to net cash inflow from operating activities

	£'000
Operating profit	6,022
Depreciation charges	899
Increase in stocks	(194)
Increase in debtors	(72)
Increase in creditors	234
Net cash inflow from operating activities	6,899

Cash flow statement

	£'000
Net cash inflow from operating activities	6,889
Returns on investments and servicing of finance (note 1)	2,999
Taxation	(2,922)
Capital expenditure (note 1)	(1,525)
	5,441
Equity dividends paid	(2,417)
	3,024
Management of liquid resources (note 1)	(450)
Financing (note 1)	57
Increase in cash	2,631

Reconciliation of net cash flow to movement in net debt (note 2)

	£'000	£'000
Increase in cash in the period	2,631	
Cash to repurchase debenture	149	
Cash used to increase liquid resources	450	
Change in net debt*		3,230
Net debt at 1.1.96		(2,903)
Net funds at 31.12.96		327

* In this example all changes in net debt are cash flows.

The reconciliation of operating profit to net cash flows from operating activities can be shown in a note.

Notes to the cash flow statement

1   **Gross cash flows**

	£'000	£'000
Returns on investments and servicing of finance		
Interest received	3,011	
Interest paid	(12)	
		2,999
Capital expenditure		
Payments to acquire intangible fixed assets	(71)	
Payments to acquire tangible fixed assets	(1,496)	
Receipts from sales of tangible fixed assets	42	
		(1,525)
Management of liquid resources		
Purchase of treasury bills	(650)	
Sale of treasury bills	200	
		(450)
Financing		
Issue of ordinary share capital	211	
Repurchase of debenture loan	(149)	
Expenses paid in connection with share issues	(5)	
		57

Note. These gross cash flows can be shown on the face of the cash flow statement, but it may sometimes be neater to show them as a note like this.

2   Analysis of changes in net debt

	As at 1 Jan 1996 £'000	Cash flows £'000	Other changes £'000	At 31 Dec 1996 £'000
Cash in hand, at bank	42	847		889
Overdrafts	(1,784)	1,784		
		2,631		
Debt due within 1 year	(149)	149	(230)	(230)
Debt due after 1 year	(1,262)		230	(1,032)
Current asset investments	250	450		700
Total	(2,903)	3,230	–	327

6 Preparing a cash flow statement

Section overview

- In essence, preparing a cash flow statement is very straightforward. You should therefore simply learn the format and apply the steps noted in the example below.

Note that the following items are treated in a way that might seem confusing, but the treatment is logical if you think in terms of cash.

(a) Increase in stock is treated as negative (in brackets). This is because it represents a cash outflow; cash is being spent on stock.

(b) An increase in debtors would be treated as negative for the same reasons; more debtors means less cash.

(c) By contrast an increase in creditors is positive because cash is being retained and not used to pay off creditors. There is therefore more of it.

Worked example: Preparation of a cash flow statement

Kane Ltd's profit and loss account for the year ended 31 December 20X2 and balance sheets at 31 December 20X1 and 31 December 20X2 were as follows.

KANE LIMITED
PROFIT AND LOSS ACCOUNT FOR THE YEAR ENDED 31 DECEMBER 20X2

	£'000	£'000
Sales		720
Raw materials consumed	70	
Staff costs	94	
Depreciation	118	
Loss on disposal	18	
		300
Operating profit		420
Interest payable		28
Profit before tax		392
Taxation		124
Profit after tax		268

KANE LIMITED
BALANCE SHEETS AS AT 31 DECEMBER

	20X2		20X1	
	£'000	£'000	£'000	£'000
Fixed assets				
Cost		1,596		1,560
Depreciation		318		224
		1,278		1,336
Current assets				
Stock	24		20	
Trade debtors	66		50	
Recoverable corporation tax	10		8	
Bank	48		56	
	148		134	
Current liabilities				
Trade creditors	12		6	
Taxation	102		86	
	114		92	
Net current assets		34		42
		1,312		1,378
Long-term liabilities				
Long-term loans		200		500
		1,112		878
Share capital		360		340
Share premium		36		24
Profit and loss		716		514
		1,112		878

Dividends totalling £66,000 were paid during the year.

During the year, the company paid £90,000 for a new piece of machinery.

Requirement

Prepare a cash flow statement for Kane Ltd for the year ended 31 December 20X2 in accordance with the requirements of FRS 1 (revised).

Solution

Step 1.

Set out the proforma cash flow statement with all the headings required by FRS 1 (revised). You should leave plenty of space. Ideally, use three or more sheets of paper, one for the main statement, one for the notes (particularly if you have a separate note for the gross cash flows) and one for your workings. It is obviously essential to know the formats very well.

Step 2.

Complete the reconciliation of operating profit to net cash inflow as far as possible. When preparing the statement from balance sheets, you will usually have to calculate such items as depreciation, loss on sale of fixed assets and profit for the year (see Step 4).

Step 3.

Calculate the figures for tax paid, purchase or sale of fixed assets, issue of shares and repayment of loans if these are not already given to you (as they may be). Note that you may not be given the tax charge in the profit and loss account. You will then have to assume that the tax paid in the year is last year's year-end provision and calculate the charge as the balancing figure.

Step 4.

If you are not given the profit figure, open up a working for the profit and loss account. Using the opening and closing balances, the taxation charge and dividends paid you will be able to calculate profit for the year as the balancing figure to put in the statement.

Step 5.

Complete Note 1, the gross cash flows, if asked for it. Alternatively, the information may go straight into the statement.

Step 6.

You will now be able to complete the statement by slotting in the figures given or calculated.

Step 7.

Complete Note 2, the analysis of changes in net debt, if asked.

KANE LIMITED
CASH FLOW STATEMENT FOR THE YEAR ENDED 31 DECEMBER 20X2

Reconciliation of operating profit to net cash inflow

	£'000
Operating profit	420
Depreciation charges	118
Loss on sale of tangible fixed assets	18
Increase in stocks	(4)
Increase in debtors	(16)
Increase in creditors	6
Net cash inflow from operating activities	542

CASH FLOW STATEMENT

	£'000	£'000
Net cash flows from operating activities		542
Returns on investment and servicing of finance		
Interest paid		(28)
Taxation		
Corporation tax paid (W1)		(110)
Capital expenditure		
Payments to acquire tangible fixed assets	(90)	
Receipts from sales of tangible fixed assets	12	
Net cash outflow from capital expenditure		(78)
		326
Equity dividends paid		(66)
		260
Financing		
Issues of share capital (360 + 36 – 340 – 24)	32	
Long-term loans repaid (500 – 200)	(300)	
Net cash outflow from financing		(268)
Decrease in cash		(8)

NOTES TO THE CASH FLOW STATEMENT

Analysis of changes in net debt

	At 1 Jan 20X2	Cash flows	At 31 Dec 20X2
	£'000	£'000	£'000
Cash in hand, at bank	56	(8)	48
Debt due after 1 year	(500)	300	(200)
Total	(444)	292	(152)

WORKINGS

1 **Corporation tax paid**

	£'000
Opening CT payable (86 – 8)	78
Charge for year	124
Net CT payable at 31.12.X2 (102 – 10)	(92)
Paid	110

2 **Fixed asset disposals**

COST

	£'000		£'000
At 1.1.X2	1,560	At 31.12.X2	1,596
Purchases	90	Disposals	54
	1,650		1,650

ACCUMULATED DEPRECIATION

	£'000		£'000
At 31.1.X2	318	At 1.1.X2	224
Depreciation on disposals	24	Charge for year	118
	342		342

	£'000
NBV of disposals	30
Net loss reported	(18)
Proceeds of disposals	12

Summary (1/2)

Sole trader financial statements

- Less regulated, so can show expenses separately in profit and loss account
- Tax does not appear
- Ownership interest:

Opening capital/net assets	X
Capital introduced	X
Net profit/(loss)	X/(X)
Drawings	(X)
Closing capital/net assets	X

Partnerships

- Business run by two or more people together
- Tax does not appear
- Partners agree:
  - Capital contributions
  - Whether interest on capital and/or drawings is paid
  - Whether salaries are to be paid
  - Profit-sharing ratio (PSR), including any guaranteed minimum
  - Loans from partners accounted for as if from third parties
- Financial statements:
  - Profit and loss account + net assets balance sheet like sole trader's
  - Ownership interest:

	A	B	Total
Capital account	X	X	X
Current account	X	X	X
	X	X	X

CHAPTER

13

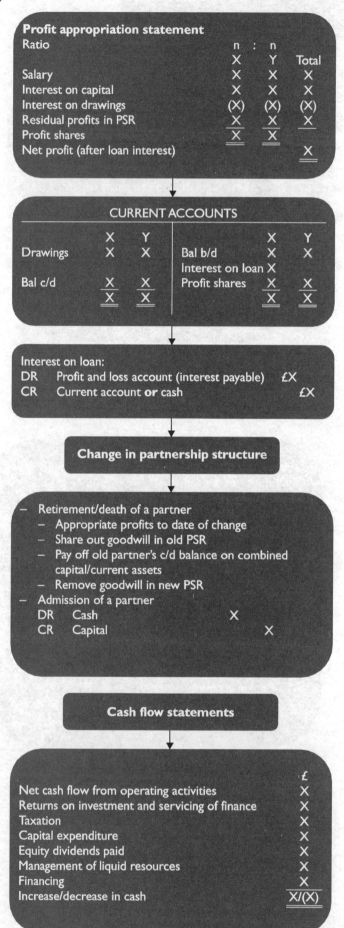

Profit appropriation statement

Ratio	n	:	n	
	X		Y	Total
Salary	X		X	X
Interest on capital	X		X	X
Interest on drawings	(X)		(X)	(X)
Residual profits in PSR	X		X	X
Profit shares	X		X	
Net profit (after loan interest)				X

CURRENT ACCOUNTS

	X	Y		X	Y
Drawings	X	X	Bal b/d	X	X
			Interest on loan	X	
Bal c/d	X	X	Profit shares	X	X
	X	X		X	X

Interest on loan:

DR	Profit and loss account (interest payable)	£X	
CR	Current account **or** cash		£X

Change in partnership structure

- Retirement/death of a partner
  - Appropriate profits to date of change
  - Share out goodwill in old PSR
  - Pay off old partner's c/d balance on combined capital/current assets
  - Remove goodwill in new PSR
- Admission of a partner

DR	Cash	X	
CR	Capital		X

Cash flow statements

	£
Net cash flow from operating activities	X
Returns on investment and servicing of finance	X
Taxation	X
Capital expenditure	X
Equity dividends paid	X
Management of liquid resources	X
Financing	X
Increase/decrease in cash	X/(X)

Self-test

Answer the following questions.

1   A, B and C are in partnership with a profit sharing ratio of 3:2:1. For the year ended 31.12.X9, the partnership profits are £18,000. What is B's share of the profits?

    A   £3,000
    B   £6,000
    C   £9,000
    D   £18,000

2   Madro had net assets of £35,000 at 1 January 20X8, and these grew by £22,500 in the year. He took drawings of £14,000 and made a net profit of £23,900. How much capital did Madro inject in the year?

    A   £9,900
    B   £12,600
    C   £67,400
    D   £102,400

3   Serko commenced trading as a sole trader in 20X6 and made a profit of £20,000 in that year. He made a net profit of £50,000 in 20X7. He has calculated that tax at 25% is due on the 20X7 profit. Serko took drawings of £40,000 in 20X7. What is the tax charge in Serko's profit and loss account for 20X7?

    A   £0
    B   £10,000
    C   £12,500
    D   £17,500

4   Pam's capital account is £10,000 at the end of 20X3, and her partner Mike's is £20,000. Their current accounts are £27,820 and £16,910 respectively. In 20X3 the partnership made a net profit of £42,300. What are its net assets at the end of 20X3?

    A   £30,000
    B   £44,730
    C   £74,730
    D   £117,030

5   Rene, Hughie and Paul are partners sharing profit 4:3:1. Paul gets a salary of £12,000. Hughie retires 3 months into 20X4. In 20X4 a profit of £67,040 is made. How much profit is appropriated to Hughie when he retires?

    A   £5,160
    B   £6,285
    C   £6,880
    D   £20,640

6   Sarah has a minimum profit share of £10,000 guaranteed by Richard. On initial appropriation Sarah is allocated £8,000 and Richard is allocated £16,000. What is Richard's final appropriation of profit?

    A   £10,000
    B   £14,000
    C   £16,000
    D   £18,000

7   Which of the following headings is not a classification of cash flows in FRS 1?

    A   Operating activities
    B   Capital expenditure and financial investment
    C   Administration
    D   Financing

8. A company has the following information about its fixed assets.

	20X7 £'000	20X6 £'000
Cost	750	600
Accumulated depreciation	250	150
Net book value	500	450

Plant with a net book value of £75,000 (original cost £90,000) was sold for £30,000 during the year.

What is the cash flow from capital expenditure for the year?

A £95,000 inflow
B £210,000 inflow
C £210,000 outflow
D £95,000 outflow

9. A company has the following extract from a balance sheet.

	20X7 £'000	20X6 £'000
Share capital	2,000	1,000
Share premium	500	–
Debenture	750	1,000

What is the cash flow from financing for the year?

A £1,250 inflow
B £1,750 inflow
C £1,750 outflow
D £1,250 outflow

10. When adjusting the profit before tax to arrive at cash generated from operating activities, a decrease in debtors is added to operating profit. Is this statement

A True
B False

Now, go back to the Learning Objectives in the Introduction. If you are satisfied that you have achieved these objectives, please tick them off.

Answers to Interactive questions

Answer to Interactive question 1

	£'000
Opening capital	708
Capital introduced in the period	0
Net profit of the period (balancing figure)	182
Drawings	(40)
Closing capital = net assets	850

Answer to Interactive question 2

Tom, Dick and Harry: Profit appropriation statement

Ratio	7: Tom £	3: Dick £	5 Harry £	Total £
Salary	0	20,000	0	20,000
Share of residual profit ((£170,000 – £20,000) in 7:3:5 PSR)	70,000	30,000	50,000	150,000
Total profit share	70,000	50,000	50,000	170,000

Answer to Interactive question 3

Anna, Brian and Clare: Profit appropriation statement

Ratio	3: Anna £	2: Brian £	1 Clare £	Total £
Salary	0	0	8,000	8,000
Share of residual profit (£26,000 – £8,000) in 3:2:1	9,000	6,000	3,000	18,000
Initial profit share	9,000	6,000	11,000	26,000
Reallocation from Anna to Brian	(10,000)	10,000	0	0
Total profit share	(1,000)	16,000	11,000	26,000

1   B   Each 'share' is worth $\dfrac{£18,000}{6}$ = £3,000. B's share is, therefore, £6,000.

2   B   35,000 + 23,900 – 14,000 – (35,000 + 22,500)

3   A   As the business is a sole tradership, no tax charge or tax liability will appear in the financial statements

4   C   (10,000 + 20,000 + 27,820 + 16,910) = £74,730. We ignore the net profit figure as we have been given the year-end capital and current account figures, after appropriation.

5   A $\dfrac{(67,040 - 12,000)/4}{(4 + 3 + 1)} \times 3 = £5,160$

6   B   16,000 – (10,000 – 8,000) = £14,000

7   C   Administration costs are a classification in the profit and loss account, not the cash flow statement.

8   C

FIXED ASSETS AT COST

	£'000		£'000
Opening balance	600	Disposals	90
Purchases (bal fig)	240	Closing balance	750
	840		840

	£'000
Purchase of fixed assets	240,000
Proceeds of sale of fixed assets	(30,000)
Net cash outflow	210,000

9   A

	£'000
Issue of share capital (2,000 + 500 – 1,000)	1,500
Repayment of debentures (1,000 – 750)	(250)
Net cash inflow	1,250

10   A   True

Index

REVIEW FORM – ACCOUNTING STUDY MANUAL

Your ratings, comments and suggestions would be appreciated on the following areas of this Study Manual.

	Very useful	Useful	Not useful
Chapter Introductions	☐	☐	☐
Examination context	☐	☐	☐
Worked examples	☐	☐	☐
Interactive questions	☐	☐	☐
Quality of explanations	☐	☐	☐
Technical references (where relevant)	☐	☐	☐
Self-test questions	☐	☐	☐
Self-test answers	☐	☐	☐
Index	☐	☐	☐

	Excellent	Good	Adequate	Poor
Overall opinion of this Study Manual	☐	☐	☐	☐

Please add further comments below:

Please return to:

The Learning Team
Learning and Professional Department
ICAEW
Metropolitan House
321 Avebury Boulevard
Milton Keynes
MK9 2FZ
ACAFeedback@icaew.com
www.icaew.com